CIVILIZATION
BEFORE
GREECE AND ROME

pian

●Tepe Hissar

●Sialk

I R A N

AFGHANISTAN

Badakhshan

Hindu Kush

●Shahdad ●Shahr-i-Sokhta

●Tepe Yahya

Indus

P A K I S T A N

I N D U S   V A L L E Y   C U L T U R E

Harappa●

Mohenjo-
daro●

M

s i a
f

TILMUN

OMAN

Lothal●

Arabian   Sea

I
A

MODERN STATES
ANCIENT PEOPLES, COUNTRIES
Archaeological Sites
Rivers, Seas, Regions

0 50 100 150 200 250 miles

CIVILIZATION
BEFORE
GREECE AND ROME

H. W. F. SAGGS

Yale University Press
New Haven and London

Published in the United Kingdom 1989 by B. T. Batsford, Ltd.
Published in the United States 1989 by Yale University Press

Printed in the United States of America

Library of Congress catalog card number: 88-50828
International standard book number: 0-300-05031-3

10   9   8

Contents

The Illustrations

Authors' Note

Square brackets in the text indicate either restorations in broken texts or explanatory comment. Round brackets indicate words necessary for English idiom or clarity but not present verbatim in the original.

Chronological Chart

Date	CRETE	EGYPT	HITTITES	SYRIA and PALESTINE	MESOPOTAMIA South	MESOPOTAMIA North	INDUS	Date
3500					The first cities			3500
3400		Local groups coalesce into two kingdoms						3400
3300								3300
3200								3200
3100		Unification The first hieroglyphics Dynasties I–II			Invention of writing			3100
3000				Trade links with Egypt and Mesopotamia			Pre-Harappan cultures	3000
2900					Early dynasties in Sumer			2900
2800								2800
2700		Old Kingdom; Dynasties III–V						2700
2600		Pyramid building						2600
2500				Rise of Ebla as mercantile centre			Trading contacts with Sumer	2500
2400					Sargon of Agade (2371–2316); first Empire; expansion to Syria (and Anatolia?)			2400
2300				Ebla destroyed by Agade	Gutian invasion	First Assyrian kingdom	Mature Indus civilization; Indus script	2300
2200		Disintegration						2200
2100			Migration into Anatolia		Third Dynasty of Ur Amorite invasion			2100
2000	Pictographic script (early form)	Middle Kingdom; Dynasties XI–XII			Amorite Dynasties; First Dynasty of Babylon (1894–1595)	Kingdom of Shamshi-Adad I	Decline of Indus civilization	2000
1900	Pictographic script (later form)							1900
1800			Old Kingdom					1800

Date	CRETE	EGYPT	HITTITES	SYRIA and PALESTINE	MESOPOTAMIA		INDUS	Date
					South	North		
1700	Linear A	Hyksos domination					Extinction	1700
1600				Alphabetic writing begins	Kassite Dynasty			1600
1500	Greek element present	New Kingdom Dynasties XVIII–XX				Mittanni dominant		1500
1400	Linear B (alternative dates)	Wars in Syria. El Armarna correspondence	Empire			Revival of Assyria		1400
1300				Ugaritic script				1300
1200			Fall of Hittite empire		Native Babylonian Dynasty			1200
1100			Neo-Hittite kingdoms in Anatolia and north Syria		Aramaeans from middle Euphrates overrun Babylonia and Assyria			1100
1000				Aramaeans settle into kingdoms				1000
900		Rule by foreign dynasties; of Libyan origin		Increasing Assyrian control	Native kings subject to Assyria	Assyrian imperial expansion; to Syria (c. 870)		900
800		Ethiopian (751–)				to Palestine (c. 740)		800
700		Assyrian (675–651)				to Egypt (675). Fall of Nineveh (612)		700
600				Babylonian rule	New Babylonian Empire (605–539); Nebuchadnezzar (605–562)			600
500		Persian (525–)			Persian Empire (539–331)			500

Absolute datings usually depend upon the interpretation of a combination of archaeological and textual data and radiocarbon determinations, with the assistance in some instances of ancient records of astronomical phenomena. In consequence, authorities differ on exact datings.

Chronologies for Egypt and Mesopotamia are disputable by up to a century at the beginning of the third millennium, reducing to about a decade by the late second millennium; there are corresponding doubts on Cretan and Hittite chronology.

Dates offered for the beginning of Harappan civilization have a spread of 500 years. The dates adopted here are those of D. P. Agrawal, *The Archaeology of India* (Curzon Press, 1982).

1

Pushing back the Frontiers

'The grand object of travelling', pronounced Doctor Samuel Johnson in the eighteenth century, 'is to see the shores of the Mediterranean. On those shores were the four great Empires of the world; the Assyrian, the Persian, the Grecian, and the Roman. All our religion, almost all our law, almost all our arts, almost all that sets us above savages, has come to us from the shores of the Mediterranean.'

The good Doctor's geography has stood the test of subsequent discovery better than his history. The beginnings of civilization are indeed linked with the shores of the Mediterranean, since those shores were the bounds of all the peoples who contributed to it; but the peoples he credits with these achievements all came late in the rise from savagery which we call civilization.

Samuel Johnson is not to be blamed because he short-circuited history. Almost all the discoveries which have revealed high civilizations before those he named came after his time. A late eighteenth-century work called *A View of Universal History from the Creation to the Present Time* pessimistically remarks:

> *What remains of [the] annals of [the Babylonians and Assyrians] resembles an inscription upon a tomb; we feel that mighty nations have fallen, but find, at the same time, the impossibility of attaining the knowledge of their history.*

Yet there was a source to hand which, rightly read, could have given some hints on the earliest stages of civilization. That source is the Bible. Within its earliest chapters are several references to man's very early cultural history. The story of the expulsion from the Garden of Eden is a case in point. Whatever religious interpretation one puts upon it, on the cultural level it is a folk-memory of the beginnings of agriculture. With that stage, mankind no longer dwelt idyllically in parkland, feeding on wild fruits; man had begun toilsome tillage for the cultivation of cereals:

I

Cursed is the ground for thy sake;
in sorrow shalt thou eat of it all the days of thy life;
Thorns also and thistles shall it bring forth to thee; . . .
In the sweat of thy face shalt thou eat bread (Genesis 3:17–18)

A little later there is mention of the beginning of metallurgy, in the account of Tubal-Cain, 'an instructer of every artificer in brass [properly, bronze] and iron' (Genesis 4:22), whilst the origin of musical instruments is touched upon in the reference to Jubal, who was 'the father of all such as handle the harp' (Genesis 4:21). Genesis 11:2–3 correctly links the invention of baked bricks with south Iraq ('a plain in the land of Shinar'), and whatever one makes of the story of Noah's Ark in Genesis 6–7, it certainly transmits a memory of advanced shipbuilding at a period long before the Hebrew settlement in Palestine at about 1200 BC. Memory of the beginning of vine-culture is also linked to Noah (Genesis 9:20).

But in the eighteenth century the Bible in its earliest parts was thought of simply as religious teaching about God's plan for man: it was to be believed as absolute truth in its own right, not treated as a source for a wider understanding of the development of ancient civilization. Advances in the knowledge of human development outside the religious area had to come by other channels.

During the eighteenth century France and Great Britain were competing for control of India. By 1764 the British had finally won. Then came the French Revolution and with it Napoleon. Napoleon began to dream of an oriental empire, and as the first step towards his final goal, India, he saw it necessary to gain control of Egypt. His ambitions went beyond mere military conquest: he intended to win for the glory of France not only new economic resources but also the treasures of oriental history and culture. It was because of this latter objective that, when he sailed to Egypt with his army in May 1798, he took with him 175 men of learning and the arts—astronomers, chemists, minerologists, orientalists, painters and poets.

Napoleon's dreams of an oriental empire were shattered when Nelson destroyed his fleet in Aboukir Bay, and in August 1799 he had to withdraw. But the work of Napoleon's savants in Egypt had more lasting consequences than his military adventure; in that brief time they had taken the first steps towards the re-discovery of ancient Egyptian civilization.

Ancient Egypt

Knowledge of ancient Egypt had never been entirely lost. Greek and

Latin authors recorded traditions, ranging from reliable to incredible, about Egyptian history and institutions, and, of course, the Bible mentioned it, particularly in the stories of Joseph and Moses. Travellers had brought back tales of strange buildings and tombs, and of three vast mysterious stone pyramids which stood in the desert at Giza as mute witness to a former great civilization. But no one had a clear picture of what that civilization was like.

It was Napoleon's savants who began to rescue Egyptian civilization from oblivion. Of first importance was Baron Dominique-Vivant de Denon, a many-sided aristocrat and former diplomat, whom Napoleon took to Egypt as an artist. Denon, then aged fifty-one, marched with Napoleon's army throughout the length of Egypt, sketching the ruins of the lost Egyptian civilization. On his return to France he brought ancient Egypt with him, in the form of two volumes of his researches with 141 impressive plates,[1] and these introduced the monuments of the lost civilization into the consciousness of the educated European public.

But ancient Egypt was a literate civilization, and no one can enter into the heritage of a literate civilization until its documents can be read. The French researches had found great quantities of writing everywhere—on temples, tombs, statues, coffins and fragments of papyri; the keen-eyed Denon had recognized that the writing took three different forms, which we now call hieroglyphic (the earliest, with pictorial signs), hieratic (a simplification of this), and demotic (a late cursive script).

Amongst the finds of the French expedition was a basalt slab, now known as the Rosetta Stone, inscribed in hieroglyphic and cursive Egyptian and in Greek: we now know that it was a decree by the Egyptian priesthood in honour of King Ptolemy V in 196 BC. The Greek could of course easily be read. The first steps towards solving the cursive Egyptian script were taken by a Swedish scholar as early as 1802. By correctly assuming that it would have the same proper names as the Greek text, he worked out the value of about half the cursive signs and showed that the language was Coptic, the latest form of ancient Egyptian, which still survived as the liturgical language of the Coptic Church in Egypt. In 1814–15 an Englishman, Thomas Young, made another advance. The hieroglyphic inscription on the Rosetta Stone contained certain groups of signs enclosed in an oval frame, which we now call a cartouche, and Young deduced that these must be royal names. By correctly guessing some of the names, he was able to work out the values of some of the hieroglyphic signs.

The final breakthrough was due to a young Frenchman, Jean François Champollion, who had a passion for oriental languages. He set himself the ambition of deciphering Egyptian, and to this end learned Coptic and studied every hieroglyphic inscription which became available. He worked to such good effect that in 1822 he was able to send to the Secretary of the Academy of Inscriptions in Paris a letter announcing substantial success, and in 1824 he published a definitive account of his decipherment of the hieroglyphic system. Before he died in 1832, at the age of forty-one, he could make out the sense of most Egyptian historical inscriptions.

The interest in Egypt led to a rush to collect relics for European museums. This was hardly yet archaeology, for, with some exceptions such as that of Denon, the earliest work there was little more than plundering for loot. Scientific archaeology began to take over from the middle of the century. Ancient Egyptian history was not totally unknown. A certain Manetho, an Egyptian priest of the third century BC, had left a list in Greek of all the Egyptian kings arranged in thirty dynasties,[2] with their lengths of reigns, and this could now be combined with the new information from excavation and the reading of inscriptions. Together they established that Egyptian civilization began at around 3000 BC, and that its manifestation can be divided into three main periods. We now know these as the Old, Middle and New Kingdoms, and date them respectively at about 2635–2155 BC, 2060–1700 BC, and 1554–1080 BC.[3]

Ancient Mesopotamia

International political ambitions played their part in the recovery of yet another ancient civilization. Over to the east of Egypt sprawled the ramshackle Turkish empire. This was of particular interest to both England and France, in that it controlled a large part of the land route to India. There, in the region we now know as Iraq, formerly called Mesopotamia, were a number of great mounds, representing the ruins of ancient cities. Two of the biggest of these mounds were traditionally recognized as Babylon and Nineveh, ancient capitals famous both in the Bible and in classical authors. Both sites had for centuries been places of pilgrimage for adventurous European travellers. For example, the witty seventeenth-century gossip writer Aubrey says of Colonel Charles Cavendish, second son of the earl of Devonshire, that he 'was so extremely delighted in travelling, that he went into Greece, all over; and that would not serve his turne but he would goe to Babylon, and then his Governour would not adventure to goe any further with him; but to see Babylon he was to march in the Turks armie.' One or two of the travellers had brought home relics which included examples of a curious writing found on these sites and others in southwest Iran, composed of wedge-shaped signs. The East India Company, which until the Indian Mutiny in 1857 looked after all British concerns related to India, had since about 1725 had a British Resident to protect their interests in Mesopotamia, originally based at Basra, later at Baghdad. In 1808 a new British Resident was installed, an extremely able young man named C. J. Rich. Rich upheld British interests with great pomp, but there were other sides to him. In addition to his political and mercantile work, he was interested in archaeology, and this led him to make a visit to Babylon, where he undertook a short period of excavation. He gave his results in two memoirs, published in Europe in 1813 and 1818. This caused quite a stir, which is reflected in a poem by Byron, who wrote of

> . . . *some infidels, who don't*
> *Because they can't, find out the very spot*
> *Of that same Babel, or because they won't*
> *(Though Claudius Rich, Esquire, some bricks has got,*
> *And written lately two memoirs upon't).*

Rich also undertook some investigations at the traditional site of Nineveh. He died in Persia at the early age of thirty-five, from cholera caught in bravely nursing victims of an epidemic, when the local prince and his family and all the nobles and higher classes had fled. His collection of antiquities passed to the British Museum.

Other travellers followed Rich to Babylon and Nineveh, publishing travel books which, if they did not much advance knowledge, did serve to keep alive within the educated world an interest in Mesopotamian ruins. The big advance came in the 1840s. In 1842 the French Government established a consulate at Mosul, the main city in north Iraq, just across the Tigris from Kuyunjik, the site of ancient Nineveh, and appointed to it Paul Emile Botta. Botta was an experienced consular official, with the added qualification, from his Government's point of view, of having a good record of opposing British interests. However, he was also interested in antiquities, and the Asiatic Society of Paris, impressed by the collection made by Rich, promised him full support for any archaeological work he might undertake. He made his first attempts at Kuyunjik, but did not dig deep enough to obtain any useful results. But when in March 1843 he shifted operations to a different site, Khorsabad, some ten miles to the north-northeast, he met immediate success, revealing walls of stone slabs covered with vivid scenes in bas-relief. When news of this reached Paris, the French Government made ample funds available to Botta to continue the work.

It was now the turn of England to play a part. A footloose young Englishman, Henry Austen Layard, a newly qualified solicitor on his way overland to Ceylon to practise law there, was bitten by the romance of the Middle East and got no further than western Persia (Iran). After undertaking some unofficial intelligence work for the British Ambassador in Constantinople (Istanbul), he won his backing for a period of excavation in north Mesopotamia (Iraq), where he chose a huge mound called Nimrud, twenty miles south of Mosul.

When Layard began his work, the situation was, as he put it, that 'a case [in the British Museum] scarcely three feet square enclosed all that remained, not only of the great city, Nineveh, but of Babylon itself!' He rapidly altered this: his results were spectacular, with the finding of stone slabs bearing a splendid series of reliefs of what we now know was Assyrian warfare, great limestone winged bulls fourteen feet high, and many examples of the wedge-shaped inscriptions on stone. These finds, together with those of Botta, created a sensation in Europe, so that Layard's account of his researches, published in 1849, became an immediate bestseller.[4]

The decipherment of the wedge-headed inscriptions set the learned world a challenge. There had been scholars working on it since the late eighteenth century. A Dane, Carsten Niebuhr, who travelled in Arabia and Persia in the 1770s, had noticed that at Persepolis in Persia there were inscriptions on stone with three different forms of wedge-headed (or, as it later came to be called, cuneiform) script. Now writing can use one sign for a whole word (as & for 'and'), or one sign for each syllable, or one sign for each significant sound. Obviously, if the language uses whole-word signs, the number of signs it needs may run into thousands, whereas an alphabetic system will certainly not reach fifty different signs; writing by means of syllables will fall somewhere between. Neibuhr observed that one of the forms of writing at Persepolis contained well under fifty different signs, and correctly deduced that it must be alphabetic. A young German scholar, G. F. Grotefend, worked on this script, and by 1802 produced a paper correctly identifying about a third of the characters. The language was the earliest form of Persian.

There was no significant advance upon Grotefend's partial decipherment until the 1840s, when a breakthrough was effected by another East India Company officer. This was Henry Creswicke Rawlinson, a linguist in the intelligence branch who was serving as a military adviser in Persia. He spent his spare time copying inscriptions, the most important being a very long one, in the three different scripts already mentioned, on a high cliff known as Bisitun not far from Kermanshah, only reached at some risk to life and limb. This much longer inscription gave Rawlinson an advantage over Grotefend, and in 1846 he was able to publish a paper giving a complete decipherment of the Old Persian alphabetic cuneiform.

6

Controversy has rumbled on ever since as to whether the credit should go to Grotefend or Rawlinson, pointlessly, since both were great men.

But the two other scripts still remained to be solved. Rawlinson recognized that one of these was obviously used for the language of Babylon, since the same system was found on bricks from that city. We now call that language, which is of the Semitic group and related to Hebrew and Arabic, Akkadian; Babylonian was one main dialect of it and Assyrian another. Rawlinson took up the challenge. In the long trilingual inscription, his decipherment of the old Persian version gave him the general sense and a number of proper names. Using this, and new inscriptions which Layard made available to him, Rawlinson had taken major steps towards the decipherment of Akkadian cuneiform by 1849. Other scholars were also working on the script, and it quickly became possible to make out the sense of long texts and to begin to recover the details of the ancient history of the two main kingdoms of the area in the first and second millennia BC, Babylonia and Assyria. There proved to be a good deal which linked up with the Old Testament, and in the religious climate of the time this heightened public interest in Mesopotamian archaeology.

Layard himself gave up archaeology for politics after 1851, but others continued his work; and the biblical implications of Mesopotamian archaeology ensured considerable public interest in England, France, Germany and America. As early as 1852 a major library of clay tablets inscribed in cuneiform was found at Nineveh, and when scholars became able to read these documents, and other collections found later, it began to be possible to understand ancient Mesopotamian civilization in depth. It soon became clear that some of the texts were written in a tongue which was not the Semitic language Akkadian. Eventually it was recognized that this was the language which we now call Sumerian. This was an important breakthrough, as Sumerian proved to be the language of the people who first set ancient Mesopotamian civilization under way at the beginning of the third millennium BC. It was not until well into the twentieth century that Sumerian could be read with any depth of understanding, but once that stage was reached it began to be possible to reconstruct the picture of ancient Mesopotamian civilization and society right back to 3000 BC. Meanwhile archaeology had been revealing the prehistoric background against which Sumerian civilization arose. The eventual picture obtained was, with severe simplification, as follows.

No civilization can develop until there is an assured food supply. The civilizations of Greece and Rome faced no problem here, since they grew up on the basis of agriculture which had long before reached a high degree of efficiency further East. But in the Near East, we see the earliest civilizations in direct succession to the stage in which man had been learning to control his food supply. The details of early man's achievement of assured food supply still affect us today. Our primary cereal crops—wheat and barley—are the plants domesticated by neolithic man in the Near East. A similar situation holds for the main food animals, with the sheep domesticated in the Near East and the cow in southeast Europe.

Northern Mesopotamia was settled from 6000 BC, but southern Mesopotamia not until round about 5000 BC. Physical conditions in the south meant that the earliest settlers there had learnt to control water courses, so that an irrigation economy developed. The large-scale cooperation this called for resulted in the creation, before 3000 BC, of the first cities, mainly along branches of the lower Euphrates. Just before 3000 BC these people invented what was originally a picture writing to assist in keeping records of their economic and administrative operations. This developed over the next few centuries, and by the time we can read the writing the language in use was Sumerian: quite probably it was Sumerian from the beginning. Semitic Akkadian began to be written soon afterwards, as the language of the second population element of southern Mesopotamia. City-states developed, which came to be ruled by hereditary dynasties, so that we call the period from about 2900–2400 BC the Early Dynastic period. Soon after the middle of the third millennium came the first attempts at empire, the earliest major success being that of Sargon of Agade (2371–2316 BC), who subjugated all the city-states of south Mesopotamia and used military force to extend a measure of control as far as Syria and Anatolia. The empire he founded crumbled after about a century, to be followed eventually by a very bureaucratically organized empire, that of the Third Dynasty of Ur; the latter collapsed under the pressure of further Semitic (Amorite) immigration from the desert just before 2000 BC.

The early second millennium saw the rise across Mesopotamia and Syria of new petty kingdoms under rulers of Amorite descent, of whom the best known in south Mesopotamia was Hammurabi, who united the country and made his city, Babylon, its permanent capital. Assyria further north also became a powerful state at this time, and by the end of the second millennium had supplanted Babylonia as the main military power in Mesopotamia, although Babylonia always remained the cultural centre. In the early first millennium Assyria created the New Assyrian Empire, which eventually controlled all the Near East from Eygpt to western Iran. Assyria collapsed just before 600 BC, Babylonia succeeding to much of its empire until 539 BC, when the whole fell to the Persian ruler, Cyrus the Great. Two centuries later the whole of the Near and Middle East passed from the Persians to Alexander the Great and so into the mainstream of western origins.

Egypt and Mesopotamia were the two major formative elements for all subsequent civilization. But there were other ancient civilizations which, although all to some extent derivative from these two, had significant features of their own and played important roles in the transmission of early civilization to Greece. The first of these to be recovered was that of Crete.

Ancient Crete

The story of the recovery of this civilization begins with a German merchant, Heinrich Schliemann, who, after making a fortune in the indigo trade, gave up business in his forties and in 1868 set off to Greece and Asia Minor to trace and examine Homeric sites. After correctly identifying Troy just east of the Dardanelles and digging there with successful but highly controversial results, he excavated Mycenae in mainland Greece. In early Greek tradition Mycenae was amongst the most celebrated of cities: in Homer's *Iliad*, its king, Agamemnon, was the paramount Greek ruler. Schliemann's discoveries justified the fame of Mycenae, for he found a considerable treasure of gold, silver, bronze and ivory, which was evidently from a major civilization long preceding that of classical Greece. Greek literary sources led some scholars to link the origins of the Mycenaean civilization to Crete, a conclusion reinforced when objects obviously related to Mycenaean civilization were found at Knossos in Crete in 1878. Schliemann accordingly visited Knossos in 1886 with a view to the archaeological possibilities. He recognized a palace related to the material from Mycenae, but apart from a small trial excavation pit was disappointed in his aspirations, as he was unable to reach agreement with the owner of the site. The Oxford scholar Arthur Evans (later Sir Arthur) was more fortunate and was able to buy part of the site, where he began excavation in 1899, continuing until 1914 and then from 1920 to 1932.

Sir Arthur Evans' results were striking. He revealed a hitherto unknown civilization of the second millennium which was the equal of contemporary Egypt and Mesopotamia. It had seagoing ships, splendid two-floored palaces with efficient arrangements for sewage disposal, a vigorous art, thriving trade, bronze foundries and a social structure in which women had unusual freedom, to judge by the way in which they are frequently represented as mixing unveiled and décolleté with men, and even taking part in men's sports. Crete also had its own writing system – indeed, four different writing systems, the latest of them, best attested from just before or after 1400 BC, used to represent Greek, an indication of

9

Greek immigration some time earlier. Evans named this civilization Minoan, after the legendary king Minos of Crete, and his discoveries showed Mycenaean civilization to be a late form of the Minoan.

The Hittites

There was another Near Eastern civilization yet to be revealed. From the eighteenth century onwards there had been spasmodic reports of strange stone monuments in north Syria, inscribed with a picture-writing which was not Egyptian hieroglyphics. Egyptian documents mentioned a major international power in north Syria called Kheta, and the cuneiform inscriptions knew of a land of Hatti linked to Carchemish on the Euphrates in north Syria. Hatti and Kheta were evidently the same name as that behind the 'children of Heth' and 'Hittites'' in the Bible. In 1876 the brilliant but sometimes erratic British orientalist Archibald Sayce raised the question: were the unidentified monuments and script of north Syria relics of the Hittites?

In 1887 a collection of clay tablets inscribed in cuneiform was found at El Amarna in middle Egypt; it proved to be the correspondence of Amenophis III and his son Akhenaten between about 1370 and 1349 BC.[5] They were mainly letters from Palestinian and Syrian vassals, written in Akkadian, and some of them mentioned the king of Hatti. But there was also a letter from the king of Hatti himself, sending Akhenaten good wishes on his accession. In addition there were two letters in an unknown language, one of them addressed to the king of a country Arzawa; it was possible to read the name even though the language was unknown, because this writing used the same syllabic signs as Akkadian cuneiform. A Norwegian, Knudtzon, set to work on the unknown language, which was provisionally called Arzawan, and in 1902 was able to conclude that it was of the Indo-European family.

Meanwhile, archaeological work had started in north Syria: the British began excavations at Carchemish in 1878, and ten years later Germans started work at another north Syrian site, Zinjirli. But although both sites produced monuments and inscriptions of the expected kind, neither gave evidence of being the centre of a major civilization. Where then was the Hittite capital? Sayce pointed out that monuments and inscriptions similar to those of north Syria had been found over a much wider area, extending well north into Asia Minor and Anatolia. As early as 1834 ruins of an ancient city with such remains had been reported from Boghazkoi, east of Ankara. French archaeologists examined that site in 1862, and Germans twenty years later, but it was not until 1906 that the German

Oriental Society began excavations there. They proved very productive. About 10,000 clay tablets inscribed in cuneiform were found, some of them in Akkadian, easily read, but most of them in the language formerly called Arzawan and still at that time largely unintelligible. The Akkadian tablets established that Boghazkoi was indeed the Hittite capital, and that its ancient name was Hattusha. The unknown language formerly called Arzawan was thus obviously the language of the Hittites. It was gradually deciphered, and in 1915 a Czech scholar, Hrozny, published a grammar showing that Knudtzon had been correct in treating Arzawan, that is, Hittite, as belonging to the Indo-European family: it was in fact closely related to Greek and Latin. During the next two decades scholars penetrated further into the language, so that the texts are now an important source for the culture of the second millennium BC, and we have a considerable knowledge of the history and way of life of the Hittites.

The hieroglyphic texts of the Hittites remained a problem much longer. It was not possible to read them to any extent until after the second World War; American, Italian, German, Swiss, Czech, French and British scholars all contributed to major advances in their understanding, and the decipherment was finally clinched by the finding of a text written bilingually in Phoenician and a late form of hieroglyphic Hittite. It proved that there were two main periods in which the Hittite hieroglyphic writing was used. It was employed by later kings of the Hittite empire during the second millennium, and was used again in the states which developed in north Syria after that empire collapsed at about 1200 BC. The language of the hieroglyphic texts, although related to the form of Hittite written in cuneiform, was not identical with it. It was actually derived from the dialect of a cognate people known as Luwians, who had been the predominant element in the south and west of Asia Minor before the Hittites proper spread out from their original settlement area in the north. In addition to its use in the hieroglyphic script, Luwian might also be written in cuneiform, and is sometimes found in documents from Hattusha; Hittite was never written except in cuneiform. The hiero-glyphic texts of the two periods have added some historical information but nothing of basic importance for our understanding of ancient culture.

The major importance of the Hittite area in the history of civilization was in the transmission of Mesopotamian ideas (received via the Hurrians; see below) to Asia Minor, from where they eventually reached Greece. There was, however, one development of the highest consequence there; this was the beginning of iron technology in the second millennium, which ushered in the Iron Age (p. 204).

The Hurrians

The Hurrians were a people whose prehistoric homeland was probably somewhere in Armenia or further north, whence they migrated into Mesopotamia and Syria during the third millennium. By the second millennium they formed a strong element from north Mesopotamia to Syria, and by the middle of the millennium there had developed a powerful Hurrian kingdom, Mittanni. This was centred on the Habur valley but at its widest controlled the whole region from Lake Van and the Zagros to the Mediterranean coast, and politically and militarily was the equal of Egypt and the Hittites.

The Haran district, which the Old Testament links with the Patriarchs Abraham, Isaac and Jacob, lay within the central Hurrian area, and some scholars argue that Hurrian institutions, particularly legal practices, underlay a number of Israelite traditions.

The other main cultural significance of the Hurrians was that they constituted a channel through which Mesopotamian ideas and elements of Mesopotamian culture were transmitted to the Hittites, whence in some provable instances those influences reached western Asia Minor and Greece.

The Indus Valley Civilization

One further ancient culture remains to be mentioned. The classical geographer Strabo reports that

> *Aristobulus . . . says that when he was sent upon a certain mission [in India] he saw a country of more than a thousand cities, together with villages, that had been deserted because the Indus had abandoned its proper bed.[6]*

What Aristobulus must have seen was the remains of an Indus civilization which flourished in the third millennium BC and came to an end before the middle of the second, not to be known again for some 3500 years.

In 1826 a traveller in northwest India noted, and later wrote about, impressive ruins of a dead city at a site named Harappa, near a tributary of the Indus. Thirty years later, when a railway was under construction in that region, the engineers in charge used bricks from these ruins for track ballast. A British archaeologist, A. Cunningham, visited Harappa at this time and obtained various antiquities, including some stamp seals bearing writing in an unknown script. But nothing more of archaeological consequence happened until 1920, when excavation began at Harappa. Two years later work was undertaken at another site of a ruined city,

Mohenjo-daro, on the Indus about 370 miles to the southwest. During the following decade and a half, other associated sites were recognized and some dug. It became clear that Harappa and Mohenjo-daro had been major cities of an urban civilization which flourished between about 2500 and 1600 BC, with links with Mesopotamia in the earlier stages. Many other sites have been recognized subsequently, showing that this civilization (now usually called Harappan) spread over an area about the size of France. There is a good deal of similarity between major cities, but not complete uniformity, and probably there were several culturally associated groups rather than a single large political complex. Earlier conclusions about rigorously geometrical town planning have had to be modified (p. 116), but certainly the grouping of buildings showed that these complexes had not developed haphazard. One striking feature in some of the cities was an exceptionally efficient sewage system, in which household drains led into main sewers of baked brick fitted with inspection holes. Another feature of this civilization was a pictographic writing system, distinct from that used in Mesopotamia; it is still undeciphered despite many attempts.

Harappan civilization thrived by a combination of agriculture and trade. The Sumerians traded by sea with a place they called Meluhha, which was probably this region. The importance of Harappan sea trade is highlighted if those archaeologists are correct who see a structure at one of its sites, Lothal, as a dock for ships: the structure in question measures 710 by 120 feet, with walls of baked brick.[7] Some of the Harappan sites certainly cultivated rice, making it probable that this culture was responsible for the introduction of rice to the world's regular food supply.

Gradual decline brought this civilization to an end by about 1600 BC. The reason for its final collapse is a fruitful source of speculation. Some scholars suggest invasion by Aryan tribes, others floods, and others climatic change. Or the Harappans themselves may have ruined their land resources either by deforestation which brought erosion, or by making the fields saline by over-irrigation without adequate drainage. Or Harappan society could even have destroyed itself, without the interposition of war or natural disasters. This could have happened if succeeding generations rejected the traditional customs and social values established by their forebears, and abandoned administrative practices and modes of behaviour essential to the running of an advanced civilization.

Minor centres of civilization

There were other ancient Near Eastern peoples who, without founding major civilizations, made contributions to human advance before the rise of Greece. Most of these peoples have long been known from either the Bible or classical sources, but in some cases archaeology has significantly increased our knowledge of them.

Best known amongst such minor ethnic groups are the Israelites. Because of their major contribution to subsequent western religious thought, it is difficult to make an impartial assessment of their cultural importance within the ancient Near East. Their own folk-history carries their origin as an identifiable ethnic group back to Abraham, near the beginning of the second millennium, but most of their institutions are linked to the period of Moses, at about 1300 BC. According to their traditions, before their settlement in Palestine soon after 1200 BC they were a group of nomadic tribes, united by the worship of their deity Yahweh as the focus of their tribal confederacy. It was not until shortly before 1000 BC that they adopted kingship.

Palestine was always commercially significant because it stood astride two major trade routes—that linking Egypt and Asia and that running north from Arabia to Syria. Once the Israelites had accepted kingship aɪ.d been welded by Saul and David into a united kingdom, their pivotal position gave them a period of international commercial importance, reflected in the Bible in such narratives as the visit of the Queen of Sheba, Solomon's navy on the Red Sea, and his international trading activities in horses and chariots. The subsequent fracture of the Israelites into two kingdoms, frequently in rivalry, reduced their ability to benefit fully from their strategic position, although they were not without further periods of economic prosperity. This importance of Palestine ensured that the Israelites were never wholly isolated from events amongst the major powers, a situation reflected in the Old Testament prophets and the Books of Kings.

Thus, quite apart from any special intervention there may have been from God—and here one asks for forbearance both from those who assert and from those who deny—their history gave the Israelites a unique background. The tribal nomadism of their traditions, when they were landless and at one period virtually slaves, contrasted strongly with their later situation as citizens of a settled prosperous kingdom. The circumstances of their settlement in Palestine were highly formative. There they found themselves amidst peoples with a long background of agriculturalism, some features of which aroused their hostility whilst others encouraged assimilation; this forced the Israelites into critical examination of their old institutions alongside those of their new environment, and they had to make conscious decisions either to accept or to reject. Self-examination was not a general feature of ancient Near Eastern societies; in most places, although changes did occur, they came by gradual modification, with the new coexisting with the old, and the old slowly falling into desuetude, seldom overtly challenged. For example, in Mesopotamia, there came a time when ancient polytheistic religion no longer satisfied, but this did not result—as it did in Israel—in a stark assertion of monotheism; rather there was a gradual bland drift towards the idea that all gods were but aspects of the One. This difference meant that Israel stood out in the ancient Near East as the one society in which venerable ancient concepts could be violently challenged. It also became (for good or bad) the least tolerant of ancient Near Eastern societies, and the most self-critical.

There was another factor which reinforced this. In various parts of western Asia there were persons who went into a kind of trance (religious ecstasy), and in that state delivered messages which they claimed, and which their contemporaries generally believed, came from a god. It was of obvious advantage to a ruler to have at his disposal such channels of communication with the divine powers, and in consequence ecstatics of this kind tended to be absorbed into the state religion. In such a context, they would be under pressure to adjust their messages to what they knew the royal court would like to hear. There undoubtedly were some prophets in Israel who accommodated themselves to the court in this way, as the Bible makes clear, but there were others who did not: 1 Kings 22:6–28, which records a dispute between the leader of 400 court prophets, and the independent prophet Micaiah who refused to be bullied into giving a prophecy favourable to the king, is a case in point. Prophets like Micaiah had another and higher loyalty, and resisted royal pressure. This religious independence had vital social consequences.

We have seen that kingship was one of the latest of Israelite institutions to develop, and the idea of absolute royal power was never generally accepted: we see its rejection in the northern kingdom in the story of Naboth's vineyard (1 Kings 21:1–25), where it was only the Phoenician princess Jezebel who thought that the Israelite king should be free to do as he wished. Outside the capitals, Samaria and Jerusalem, there were many other ancient sanctuaries of Yahweh, some linked in tradition with Patriarchs, and the many people who worshipped at such sanctuaries directed their loyalties primarily to the traditions of Moses and the tribal confederacy under Yahweh rather than to the institution of kingship.

Ecstatic prophets of the calibre of those whose messages are preserved in the Bible were not necessarily outside the religious establishment, but they refused to be absorbed into the royal state religion at Jerusalem or Samaria, and retained the freedom to pass judgement upon national policy and upon the conduct of the king himself. The first major figure to do this consistently was Elijah, but earlier Nathan—although actually one of the Jerusalem establishment—had dared to rebuke king David for injustice (2 Samuel 12:1–10). Kings and their ministers might make threats in reply, but they could take no effective counter-action, because the person of the ecstatic prophet was held sacrosanct, inasmuch as he was a messenger from God.

There was no parallel to this situation anywhere else in the ancient Near East. Thinking men in other ancient civilizations were no less capable of recognizing social evils, and they sometimes expressed condemnation of them, but they condemned evils only in the abstract, not particular evils done by particular powerful men. The charismatic prophet in Israel was unparalleled in the forceful context in which he could denounce particular cases of social evils, holding up any individual, however powerful, to public condemnation.

This ability to challenge ancient institutions and ideas, and publicly to condemn abuses, marked off Israel from other ancient societies. Israelites and Judaeans were in touch with other peoples of the ancient Near East, and one would expect that the ideas they transmitted would have acted as a leaven. It must be said that there is no indisputable proof that this actually happened, but there are some pointers. Merodach-baladan, a Chaldaean chief who was a thorn in the side of Assyria at the end of the eighth century, sent an embassy to Hezekiah of Judah (2 Kings 20:12), who (unsuccessfully) joined him in an anti-imperialist rebellion. There were opportunities there for discussion of religious judgements upon political actions. Nabonidus, the principal successor of Nebuchadnezzar, attempted religious reforms away from the old Babylonian polytheism, so strenuously that they brought down upon him the full opposition of the Babylonian religious establishment; and since there were high-ranking Jewish captives in Babylon at the time and in touch with the royal court, it is not unreasonable to guess that Jewish religious ideas were available to him and perhaps influenced him.

The fall of Jerusalem in 586 BC, with the flight of some Jews to Egypt and the deportation of others to Babylonia, began the Jewish diaspora. By the time of the world conquests of Alexander the Great in the late fourth century BC, there were many Jewish communities outside Palestine from Egypt to Persia. There resulted a vigorous and widespread interaction between Jewish ideas and Hellenism, providing one of the channels of transmission of ideas from the ancient Near East to the western world.

Canaanites and Phoenicians

A second minor ethnic group, who played a subsidiary part in the

16

development of ancient Near Eastern civilization, were the people we know as Canaanites. According to Israelite tradition, supported by archaeology, they were the original inhabitants of Palestine and part of Syria. A major source of information about these people was a city which, although not wholly Canaanite ethnically, showed considerable Canaanite cultural influence: this was Ugarit, near the Syrian coast opposite Cyprus, which excavations show to have been occupied from before 3500 BC down to its destruction by the 'Sea Peoples' (p. 46) at about 1200 BC. It became wealthy as a major international trading centre, from its position as a terminal of trade routes from Mesopotamia up the Euphrates, and from metal-producing regions of Anatolia. There were also vigorous trading contacts with Egypt, and, towards the end of its life as a major city, with Mycenaean Greece. It reached the height of its prosperity at about 1400 BC, and that time saw an important experiment there: the devising of an alphabet.

The former way of writing at Ugarit, which continued in use for lawsuits and diplomatic correspondence, was in the Akkadian language, using a mixture of word-signs (technically, ideograms or logograms) and syllable-signs (syllograms) written with combinations of wedges impressed on tablets of clay. The new form of writing invented at Ugarit continued to employ groups of wedges impressed on clay tablets, but the signs used were now limited to thirty, each of which denoted one letter of an alphabet, not a word or a syllable as in the older writing.

A group of texts written in this alphabet was excavated in the years following 1939, and proved very important as preserving many of the myths of the Canaanites, of which we previously had no more than hints from the Old Testament. Myths were not the only texts: there were others, important for the information they give on trade and administrative practices, as for example a kind of passport which gave a man and his son permission to trade by sea with Cyprus, free of customs duties.

The Phoenicians were the descendants of the Canaanites, as we meet them from about 1100 BC inwards. By that time, as a consequence of various movements of peoples, they had become restricted to the coastal fringes from Tyre northwards. The Phoenicians played a major part in spreading aspects of Near Eastern civilization to the western Mediterranean (p. 153), and they were instrumental in the transmission of the alphabet to the Greeks (pp. 84–9).

Aramaeans

Two other peoples, important as traders, need to be mentioned. One group was the Aramaeans, a Semitic-speaking people who emerged from the Syrian desert in the second half of the second millennium, to maraud and eventually settle in Syria and along the Euphrates. In the former area they developed into petty kingdoms and in the latter introduced into Assyria and Babylonia a strong and in places predominant Aramaean ethnic element. Their nomadic origins and ethnic continuum, which made it easy for them to pass on goods from settlement to settlement, produced a background from which they became the principal traders across the whole area from the Persian Gulf to the Mediterranean. The wealth their trade brought them is reflected in the 'very much bronze' taken by king David when he defeated Zobah (2 Samuel 8:8), the earliest Aramaean state to crystallize in Syria, and by the huge quantities of booty—silver, gold, tin, bronze, linen garments, chariots—taken by an Assyrian king in the first half of the ninth centuries when he brought Aramaean settlements along the Habur and the Euphrates under his control.[8]

The trading activities of the Aramaeans spread their language over much of the Near East, so that by the time of the Persian Empire (from 539 BC) it had become the international language of diplomacy. Indeed, it was already beginning to take on that role more than two centuries earlier, for when the Assyrians were besieging Jerusalem in 701 BC, the Judaean authorities requested that the Assyrian general should conduct negotiations in Aramaic, which they as diplomatists understood although the mass of the population of Jerusalem spoke only Hebrew (2 Kings 18:26). A century after the Babylonian Exile, many Jews were losing their Hebrew (Nehemiah 13:23–24), leaving Aramaic as the only language common to them all. Aramaic in its various dialects became the general language of much of the region from Palestine to Mesopotamia from the second half of the first millennium BC, and had the same importance as a cultural unifying force that was later enjoyed in the same region by Arabic, which displaced it after the Islamic conquest in the seventh century AD.

Aramaic-speaking groups circulated in the Roman empire as merchants, soldiers and slaves, and played a part in the spread of various oriental religions, not least Judaism and Christianity: at Pompeii there is a Christian graffito from the first century, written in Aramaic. Aramaic was used for major parts of two of the later books of the Old Testament, Daniel and Ezra; and in another dialect it was the language of the Targums, translations of the Old Testament used in synagogues when Hebrew was no longer understood. Aramaic in various dialects was also the mother tongue of Jesus and his disciples; the language of the whole eastern early Christian church and of the first translations of the gospels from Greek, made at Edessa; and the language of that vast Jewish commentary on the Bible, and repository of ancient wisdom, called the Talmud. Dialects of Aramaic remain spoken even today in a few villages of Syria, Turkey and Iraq.

The Arabs

The southernmost part of western Asia is the Arab peninsula, a region which, except for its luxuriant southwest, is arid and inhospitable. The term 'Arabs' should properly be restricted to those who spoke Arabic, the language of the north of the peninsula, and whose way of life was associated with the desert. In the fertile south-west there was another population group, often loosely but inaccurately called Arabs, who lived a very different way of life based on agriculture and trade. Their languages, collectively called South Arabian, were related to Arabic but distinct from it.

The best-known native mammal of the arid regions of the Arabian peninsula is the single-humped camel, uniquely adapted to desert terrain. This was domesticated at some time before 1200 BC by proto-Arabs, who thereby gave the human race a valuable new means of transport, which opened up areas and routes which were not available by any other means.

In the fertile and luxuriant southwestern corner of the Arabian peninsula there developed in the first millennium BC four kingdoms, of which Saba (Sheba of the Bible) was the oldest and most important. Its people created a great dam at Marib, which made a considerable contribution to agricultural prosperity. The dam finally burst catastrophically in the sixth century AD, an event referred to in the Koran.

But the main importance of the kingdoms of southwest Arabia in the ancient world was not their agriculture but their trade. Amongst the native flora of the area are species of trees which produce two luxury products, frankincense and myrrh. The only other source is in the same geographical region, in Somalia on the other side of the Red Sea, whence the Egyptians obtained these valued substances from as early as the third millennium. From Egypt the demand for these materials spread to other civilizations of the Fertile Crescent and the Mediterranean regions, and the peoples of south Arabia developed a lucrative export trade to fill this need, using the camel-riding Arabs of north Arabia as their intermediaries. By this means there developed important trade routes parallel with the Red Sea, with one branch running to Egypt and another skirting the Dead Sea. Classical authors from Theophrastus to Strabo speak of the wealth deriving from the incense and spice trade. The South Arabians did what they could to preserve their monopoly, by spreading stories of the terrifying flying serpents and bats which guarded the sources of these products.[9]

There were other peoples of the pre-classical Near East, all mentioned in the Bible, who had some political importance in their day. Three of them deserve a brief comment. Ararat of Genesis 8:4 was the kingdom of Urartu in the mountainous territory of eastern Turkey; in the early first millennium it was briefly a rival to Assyria, but its main cultural importance was its fine metal-work. Elam of Genesis 10:22 was a kingdom in southwest Iran from the third to the first millennium, ethnically distinct from south Mesopotamia but culturally largely derivative and frequently playing a part in political developments there. Madai of Genesis 10:2 represented one of the best-known latecomers to the Near East. They were the Medes, people who entered northwest Iran in the late second millennium and, after coming heavily under the cultural influence of Assyria, played a major part in its overthrow; through the contacts of their congeners the Persians with the Egyptians and Greeks, they formed part of the chain of the westward spread of Mesopotamian culture.

2

City-States and Kingdoms

Of all changes in the pattern of human life, the most radical came with the beginnings of agriculture and the domestication of animals. This, often called the Neolithic Revolution, had its origins in the Near East, in the foothills from Palestine to the Taurus and the Zagros: it began soon after the end of the last Ice Age, and was well under way by 8000 BC, with north Iraq as one of its first centres. Neolithic farmers gradually spread southwards into the plains, and first settled south Mesopotamia at about 5000 BC. If there were hunting-and-gathering groups there earlier, as there may have been, they left no detectable remains.

There were no permanent agricultural settlements anywhere in Egypt much before 5000 BC, although it had had a human population several thousand years before that. This lag behind the most advanced parts of the Near East was not a mark of backwardness. Humans, left a free choice, prefer to remain hunters and gatherers and do not settle permanently to the toil of farming until it is forced upon them. Herodotus tells us, on the authority of Egyptian tradition, that before the beginning of Egyptian civilization, most of Egypt, except a stretch in the neighbourhood of Thebes, was still untamed. This is credible: the natural vegetation alongside a flooding river in a hot climate is lush marsh and jungle, and the uncontrolled annual inundation of the Nile would have left pools and swamps, with vast reed thickets of papyrus, full of fish, wild fowl, wild pigs, hippopotamuses and crocodiles. The wadis would support trees as a kind of parkland. Archaeology shows that down to the fourth millennium Egypt was still the home of a rich fauna, including the elephant, rhinoceros, giraffe, baboon, antelope, gazelle, ostriches and lions. It was probably because the environment was so favourable for a hunting-and-gathering economy, that the Egyptians saw no advantage in changing their way of life until population increase compelled it. Even when agriculture was adopted, it did not immediately supplant older sources of food, and catching water birds and hunting wild animals, including hippopotamus in the Nile, remained important well after 3000 BC: wall reliefs of the Fifth and Sixth Dynasties (2450 BC onwards) still show people hunting in jungle marshes, and tomb painting of the second millennium depict high officials relaxing by boating in the swamps, where, as accompanying texts describe, they amused themselves spearing fish.

Early Egyptians were interested in their wild animals, and not only as hunters. They were keenly experimental. After taking over the animals already domesticated elsewhere, they tried to domesticate others, achieving permanent success with some, such as geese and ducks, but finding problems with such species as gazelle, ibex and hyena. They tamed the mongoose, a useful animal for catching snakes, but at about 2000 BC gave it up in favour of the cat, which did it even better. Yet unwittingly they brought about the disappearance from north Egypt of several large mammals during the first half of the third millennium. This came not from over-hunting, but from disturbing the ecological balance, particularly by setting under way increasing dessication away from the Nile. On much of the land annually inundated by the Nile there had been permanent plant cover; to meet the needs of agriculture, man destroyed this, thereby robbing wild beasts of areas which had earlier been their haunts. Man further upset the balance as he sought new pastures for his domesticated animals, driving out animals from regions where they could have survived. Amongst jungle and savannah mammals so lost were the elephant, rhinoceros and giraffe. In wetter places man drained swamps to make more land available—and thus brought further ecological changes by destruction of the papyrus beds and associated wild life.

Such ecological changes were not limited to Egypt. The past 10,000 years have seen occasional small variations in rainfall and temperatures in Egypt and the Near East, but the effects of these upon the environment have been slight compared with the changes man himself has wrought. Humans have felled and burned vast forests in Anatolia, north Syria, Lebanon, Palestine, Cyprus and the Zagros. In Iraq, the network of natural water channels from the Tigris and Euphrates originally supported forests of date-palms and other trees, which in the natural state grew in dense impenetrable thickets. These have long gone. Destruction of trees allows a more violent fluctuation in temperatures, which changes the pattern of wind circulation and precipitation. Precipitation which does occur is more violent, and, falling on the denuded soil, results in flooding, with rapid run-off and consequent erosion, finally leaving bare rock or barren desert.

All the great civilizations began in alluvial plains, and, at least in Egypt and Mesopotamia (information is less complete for the Indus valley), the behaviour of the rivers was a major factor in the form they took.[1]

Egypt depended upon the Nile, south Mesopotamia upon the Euphrates and the Tigris. But there were significant differences between the different river systems. The Nile floods in a very regular, predictable and predominantly benign pattern, between late summer and autumn, when one harvest is in and all is ready for the next sowing. This did not preclude the need for hard work, but it did mean that the ancient Egyptians could be sure that their hard work would usually be well rewarded. Small differences of level divide the land along the Nile into a large number of flood basins, which constitute natural territorial units.

The hydrology of the Euphrates and Tigris fits less well than does the Nile with the agricultural year, and demands more control if it is to be used to advantage. Both the Euphrates and Tigris are normally at their lowest in early autumn, and then begin their rise. The Tigris is usually highest in March or April, and the Euphrates a month later: these are times when, if the rivers burst their banks, they are likely to wreak havoc upon the ripening crops.

Although the Euphrates and Tigris water the same plain, and their ancient courses in south Mesopotamia were nowhere as much as a hundred miles apart, one was much more important for early settlement than the other. The Tigris is lower in its bed than the Euphrates, faster flowing, carries almost twice the amount of water and at maximum flow has almost twice the rise, making it particularly difficult to use for irrigation. This discouraged early settlement, except along its tributary, the Diyala, a less formidable stream. Consequently, most early major settlements in south Mesopotamia were concentrated along channels of the Euphrates.

In Egypt, some of the settlements which grew up along the Nile from 5000 BC onwards had by the fourth millennium grown into towns, each controlling a strip of territory based on a flood basin. The excellent communications along the Nile, and the narrowness of the habitable area, with no viable hinterland into which dissidents could withdraw, made it easy for a determined ruler enjoying the support of his immediate territory to bring large stretches of the Nile under his control. In consequence, before 3000 BC Egypt had coalesced into two kingdoms, Upper Egypt, from about Aswan to Memphis south of Cairo, and Lower Egypt, comprising the Delta region from Memphis northwards. Scenes of warfare on the earliest Egyptian monuments (plate 8) reflect strife between the two kingdoms, as does the myth of Osiris, the god of the dead (p. 275). In the myth, Osiris, the god who ruled the Delta, was defeated by Seth of Upper Egypt, and behind the myth there may lay a real prehistoric king of Lower Egypt, killed after a struggle with his rival.

The unification of Egypt

Now the pace of advance accelerated. Some earlier scholars wished to credit this to the arrival of a hypothetical Dynastic Race, presumably innately more able, but evidence to support this view is flimsy if not entirely lacking. Most of the supposed differences between the hypothetical Dynastic Race and earlier Egyptians may be no more than differences between those who had incorporated agriculture into their way of life, and those who had not. The only physical evidence of a Dynastic Race, for what it is worth, is the claim that skeletons from this time differ so markedly from those of the earlier population that the later people could not have derived from the earlier groups. But knowledge of the physical anthropology of Neolithic Egyptians is limited to a very few sites, and Neolithic Egypt may well have nurtured a wider variety of human types than we know of.

Some scholars have attempted to link the striking Egyptian cultural advance at the beginning of the third millennium to contacts with south Mesopotamia. It is probable that there were contacts of some kind, particularly in connection with the invention of writing, where Mesopotamia seems to have had priority (p. 72). Parallels in art motifs also point to some kind of link. But such features could have resulted from contacts by a few alert long-distance traders of the Marco Polo type; they do not require us to imagine major migrations from south Mesopotamia to Egypt.

The crucial political change in early Egypt came at about 3100 or 3000 BC; different scholars use different chronologies. Then, according to tradition, Menes, the king of Upper Egypt, conquered Lower Egypt and made the two kingdoms into one. But history shows that a stable major state does not come about suddenly as the result of a single incident of conquest. The innovation which we call the unification of Egypt must have been the final stage of a long period of convergence. Yet even if not as sudden as tradition represents it, it did mark a major step in deliberate social organization; by it, Menes made all Egypt into a single political and economic unit—a good half millennium before any comparable development in Mesopotamia. Admittedly there were those in ancient Egypt who might have denied that Menes made the whole into one kingdom, since to the end the Pharaohs preserved the pretence of the duality of the system, not only in their title 'King of Upper and Lower Egypt', but also in wearing a composite crown which incorporated separate crowns for the original two kingdoms; but in practical terms the country was undoubtedly one. To emphasize the essential unity, Menes created a new capital, Memphis, at the point where the two former kingdoms met.

24

Tradition, recorded by Herodotus but not otherwise proved, recounts that Menes built a dyke to change the course of the Nile, and founded Memphis on the land so reclaimed.[2] Even if this tradition was not literally true, it at least implied a very early explicit recognition that life in Egypt depended upon regulation of the flood waters.

'There's a divinity doth hedge a king.' Rule by one man depends upon the existence of sanctions so powerful that the rest of the population are willing to accept his direction unquestioningly. In ancient Egypt the sanctions were religious and had prehistoric origins. In many primitive societies, the central figure is a magician who is believed to be so intimately linked with the supernatural world that he can control rain or fertility and other aspects of life. So long as his magic proves effective, his power is absolute, but when his powers fail he is sent back to the supernatural world by being put to death. The ancient collection of rituals and myths called the Pyramid Texts, from about 2400 BC in their extant form but incorporating beliefs from prehistoric times, shows behind the Egyptian king of historical times a magician of this category. That this person was originally put to death when his powers failed is hinted at by traces of cannibalism and human sacrifice in the Pyramid Texts, but the clearest indication is in a ceremony called the Sed festival. This was a ceremony to rejuvenate the king's failing powers after thirty years of rule. It began with the ritual burial of the king, which surely indicates that originally, when the powers of the king or his magician predecessor failed, he was put to death and there was a real burial.

From the beginning, these prehistoric antecedents invested the living king in Egypt with the aura of a divine being. Because the king was an incarnate god, with Egypt's welfare in his care, it was in everyone's interest to conform to his will. His religious sanction was everywhere evident, for he was nominally the chief priest in every temple. The very circumstances of the unification of Egypt may have served to reinforce belief in the divine nature of the pharaoh. If Menes did indeed divert the sacred life-giving Nile and drain a huge area to build a great capital where formerly there had been swamps, his divine powers could not be doubted. Also, since he controlled the whole Nile valley, he unquestionably had power over the water-supply to every part of the land, an aspect of royalty graphically illustrated in one of the earliest representations of a pharaoh, which shows him cutting the dyke of an irrigation canal with a hoe. From very early times the king of united Egypt had measurements taken of the height of the Nile as it was rising in the south, so that he could accurately predict the area which could be irrigated further north. All these factors meant that, from the point of view of an ancient Egyptian, the king was, quite literally, a fertility giver and controller of the Nile and all the life of the land; from the Egyptians' point of view he was, without question, a god upon whom the life of the land depended. Moreover, because of the ease of navigation from one end of the country to the other by means of the gentle Nile, it was relatively easy to produce a unified system of government (even if administered in duplicate for north and south separately). We shall see that the situation was markedly different in south Mesopotamia.

The definiteness of the tradition makes it likely that Menes was a real king, but which? The name does not occur in native Egyptian records. Three kings, known to egyptologists as Scorpion, Narmer, and Hor-aha, have left monuments from about the time attributed to Menes. If one of these kings has to be picked as Menes, the most probable seems to be Narmer, but quite possibly more than one of them contributed to the tradition. This would accord with the probability that the unification was not an innovation abruptly introduced after conquest, but came about gradually over several reigns.

With Menes we enter the Dynastic Period. This terminology derives from an Egyptian priest, Manetho, who at about 300 BC compiled in Greek a list of all Egyptian kings from the beginning, divided into thirty dynasties (later extended to thirty-one), with, of course, Menes as the first king of the First Dynasty. Apart from the name and length of reigns of each ruler, Manetho gives us little snippets of information, such as that Menes 'was taken by a hippopotamus and died', or that his successor 'built the palace at Memphis; his writings on anatomy remain, for he was a doctor', or of the third in succession to him that in his time 'a severe famine gripped Egypt'. Particularly notable, from the records of the Third Dynasty ruler Zoser, is the mention of 'Imuthes, regarded by the Egyptians as Asclepios for his skill in medicine, the inventer of building in hewn stone'; this was the celebrated Imhotep, architect of the Step Pyramid (pp. 50f).

There are more theories than evidence about the running of the early Egyptian state. There are virtually no administrative records, and the text called the Palermo Stone provides less than it seems to promise, for whilst it gives us a record of one or more outstanding events for each year down to the Fifth Dynasty, these are mainly about festivals, divine statues, building works or expeditions abroad, with few details directly bearing on administration.

There is one type of evidence which is plentiful in this area: the titles of officials. Some scholars have used these in an attempt to build up a picture of the administrative network. Ancient Egyptians who could afford it delighted in arranging for their autobiographies to be written on their tombs, and Klaus Baer has analysed tomb inscriptions of over 600 notables, who between them recorded nearly 2000 titles in use during the Old Kingdom.[3] But in fact this mass of titles—legal, scribal, fiscal, religious, organizational, linked to the king or the royal court, or purely honorific—tells us less about the details of the administrative system than we might expect. Some titles which obviously began as marks of function quickly became at first markers of rank within a hierarchy and then merely honorific. The excessive number of titles borne by some officials points this up: when we find, as we do, that a particular notable had a string of well over 200 titles, we can be certain that, unless the man was an administrative genius, only a small portion of these can have related to functions he personally performed or carried responsibility for during his working life.

Baer was unable to make any significant links between the 2000 titles and the pattern of administration, but he did show that a large number of the titles could be placed in ranking order, in a way strangely similar to the British Order of Precedence. What this mass of titles gives us, therefore, is not an outline of the administrative system but a picture of a society obsessed with considerations of rank. Paradoxically, this non-functional use of titles performed a useful function. An evolving society creates new offices and ceases to need old ones. But without a mechanism for sweeping away obsolete offices, there grows up an enormous amount of unproductive dead wood. Conversion of old functional offices, no longer required, into honorific titles discharged this burden.

Although official titles do not give us an adequate picture of how the early Egyptian state was run, the material does enable us to extract information about a few of the greatest offices in the state, sufficient to give us a rough sketch of the administrative framework, mainly in the time of the Fifth Dynasty. At that period all senior functions in the state were shared amongst six classes of official; these bore the titles, the Overseer of the Great Mansions, the Overseer of the Scribes of the Royal Records, the Overseer of Works, the Overseer of Granaries, the Overseer of the Treasuries, and what we usually translate as the Vizier.

The 'Great Mansions' of the first title were the courts of justice. There are indications that there were originally six such courts, but their location is unknown.

The 'Overseer of the Scribes of the Royal Records' was the head of the scribal administration, responsible for the preparation and filing of all state documents. There was at least one occasion during the Fifth Dynasty when two persons held this title simultaneously; since one of the two was the vizier, the greatest officer of state, he presumably had overall control, leaving the other holder of the title to supervise details.

The Overseer of Works was responsible for organizing work-forces for such operations as building, agriculture, expeditions to distant places to obtain materials, and probably (although there is no specific Old Kingdom evidence) digging and maintaining canals. Several holders may have shared this title, each responsible for a particular sector of public works.

The general area of the duties of the 'Overseer of the Granaries' is obvious, but the details are not clear. Sometimes there were simultaneous holders of the title. Little is known of the location of state granaries, but these officials presumably used them to stockpile corn against future shortages as Joseph is said to have done in Genesis 41:48–9; since the state could not survive unless it kept its peasantry fed, this was a vital need. There were also granaries on private estates, where the Overseers of Granaries may have been responsible for assessment for taxation. This would explain their close connection with the Overseer of the Treasuries.

A major part of the duties of Overseer of Treasuries in the Old Kingdom was recording and collecting dues from private estates. Mention of a 'treasury of the residence' in the late Fifth and early Sixth Dynasties suggests there was a central treasury at the capital Memphis, for which this official would have been responsible. There were apparently also provincial treasuries. Later the collection of taxes came into the orbit of the vizier.

The most important officer in the state administrative system was undoubtedly the vizier. His office must already have existed by the beginning of the Third Dynasty, since the title occurs on stone vessels found beneath the Step Pyramid, built by the first king of that Dynasty. The earliest viziers were all royal princes, a relic from the original situation in which the king kept all authority within the circle of his kinsmen. The people nearest to the pharaoh in life were also those nearest in death, and the grouping of tombs associated with pyramids in Sakkara and Giza indicates that down to the Fourth Dynasty his immediate executives were mainly his close male relatives—sons, uncles, cousins, nephews. In the Fifth Dynasty this ceased to be the case, and high officials, including viziers, were no longer necessarily princes by birth. But even when no longer royal by birth, the men appointed as viziers, and sometimes other officials, were given the rank of prince by the honorific title King's Son.

The vizier needed to be a man of considerable ability, since his task was to oversee the whole administration, judiciary and economy of the country: second only to the king in status, in some circumstances he was of greater importance in practice. By the time of the Middle Kingdoms, this office had become divided into two, with separate viziers for Upper and Lower Egypt; there is the possibility that this division went back to the Old Kingdom.

The third millennium provides no detailed account of the duties of a vizier, but texts and reliefs from the tomb of Rekhmire^c, who held that office in the fifteenth century, tell us what they had become.[4]

Rekhmire^c ranked second only to the king, and all the royal courtiers did obeisance to him. The king, who was ultimately responsible for justice, appointed Rekhmire^c to act on his behalf, with no one able to override his decision. Rekhmire^c prided himself on his administration of justice. He claimed to be 'smiter of the smiter', to judge rich and poor impartially, to rescue the weak from the strong, to defend the widow and relieve the aged, to establish a son in his paternal inheritance, to give food and drink to the hungry and thirsty and clothing to the destitute. He gave judgement daily in his audience hall, seated upon a cushion on a chair, with a rug on the floor and a cushion beneath his feet. His scribes and other staff were ranged near him and petitioners queued to be heard in strict order. In the first instance they had to present their petitions in writing, but this must have been followed by oral examination, for Rehkmire^c specifically says that he took no offence if litigants gave way to their passions.

At some point every day Rekhmire^c conferred with the king. He also received reports from the chief treasurer, from the officers responsible for military security, and from all other senior officials, since all functions of the state—judiciary, treasury, army and navy, police, and agriculture— were under the supervision of the vizier. To communicate with various departments, the vizier had a staff of messengers, who had the right of immediate admission to any official. Wills had to be brought before the vizier to be sealed.

Reliefs in his tomb show Rekhmire^c accepting tribute from foreigners, and receiving the taxes from representatives of various cities. Much of the latter was in gold or silver, but it also included commodities in such forms as hides, bows, cedar wood, apes, cloth, oxen, corn, honey.

The various high offices of the Old Kingdom, little as we know in detail about their functions, show that already by the middle of the third millennium there was considerable departmentalization in the running of the Egyptian state. The directives of the great officers of state at the top were implemented by lower ranking officials, in a departmental system which probably went back in origin to the organization of servants in the royal household.

The administrators had the efficient running of Egypt in their hands, and good government was threatened if those administrators sank to the level of bureaucrats. It could happen. Instead of concentrating upon getting necessary work done, officials might act as though what mattered was to adhere at all costs to established procedures, whether or not it was the most efficient way of performing the task in hand. A letter found at Saqqara shows a case of bureaucratic palsy as early as 2200 BC. The writer was an officer in charge of quarry workers, and obviously a man who took a pride in doing his job well. He expostulated at having been ordered to take his men across the river to government headquarters to receive their clothing, an unwarranted interruption in his duties. In the past, he pointed out, this procedure had wasted up to six days, as a result of delays at the issuing office. Why, he asked, should not the clothes be sent to him by barge, when the whole business could be settled within a single day?

The king himself was not a mere figurehead. Since the earliest viziers were royal princes, there is the possibility that some of those who succeeded as kings may earlier have served in that role. Certainly kings undertook specific functions in the administration of the kingdom. From very early in the Dynastic Period, the king made periodic tours by river to inspect the whole land, and from the reign of the Fourth Dynasty ruler Sneferu, this became a census of all the cattle, normally biennially, occasionally in successive years. This was in effect a periodic assessment of wealth, and must imply the beginning of a national system of taxation. It was this that brought the king the economic power which eventually made possible such huge public works as the building of the Giza pyramids.

From prehistoric times the hydrology of the Nile had sub-divided Egypt into a number of flood basins. These may have been the basis of the territorial divisions called nomes (totalling about forty, with variations from time to time), which formed the later units of provincial administration. They were already assuming that function by the Third Dynasty, and from soon after that time the administrators in charge of the nomes began to acquire a degree of independence of the capital. In addition, local officials received grants of land for their maintenance, which, in consequence of customarily being regranted to heirs, gradually became treated as private property; with their own estates, such officials became less subject to control from the capital. All this contributed to a weakening of centralized control. The culmination of these trends, combined with other factors which may have included a series of famines resulting from exceptionally low Nile floods, brought a gradual disintegration of the central power, and finally the collapse of the Old Kingdom at the end of the Sixth Dynasty (2155 BC).

Mesopotamia

The rise of a centralized power came much later in Mesopotamia than in

Egypt, and by a very different course. But in some other respects, Mesopotamia had priority.

The earliest settlements known in south Mesopotamia date from 5000 BC or a little before. Archaeologists name this stage *Ubaid*, after the site in south Iraq, near Ur of the Chaldees, at which evidence for it was first found. So successful was the *Ubaid* economy that it spread throughout all Mesopotamia and into neighbouring lands, although it remained essentially a peasant economy based on villages.

Rainfall in south Iraq is well below the minimum necessary to bring crops to maturity, and some form of irrigation is essential. Unlimited water was, of course, available from two of the world's great rivers, the Euphrates and the Tigris, but means had to be devised of using it. For thousands of years before human occupation of Mesopotamia, the Euphrates had periodically changed its course by bursting its banks and finding a new lower level after raising its old bed by silt deposits. In consequence, by the time of the *Ubaid* settlements there was an extensive network of seepages and old channels, which might carry water ranging from a trickle to a major flow. Early settlers could have utilized natural irrigation by seeding the banks of such water-courses as were perennial streams, but the chances of success would depend upon a critical balance between waterlogging and drying out. To be certain of a crop it was necessary to have land high enough above the water table to provide drainage, and a flow of water which could be fed on to the land as needed. The greatest significance of the *Ubaid* people was that they solved this technical problem and developed irrigation to increase the area of land available for grain and vegetable production. It is likely that they began by digging out old silted-up channels for use as canals, fed from the main river. This called for a substantial well-organized labour force, and this need constituted a factor which was eventually to have a fundamental effect upon the way society developed, since the larger the group and the better organized it was, the more land could be irrigated and the more prosperous the whole community would be. In the *Ubaid* context the limiting factor was the traditional size of the village, but it needed only one group to grow beyond village size to provide a model for widespread change.

From the middle of the fourth millennium, there were developments in south Mesopotamia of the highest consequence. The most striking features in this were the rise of the first cities, the beginning of monumental architecture, the more widespread use of metals, and above all the invention of writing. The last is discussed in chapter 4. Archaeologically this new stage is known as the *Uruk* culture, from the ancient name of the site (Erech in the biblical form) which is the most

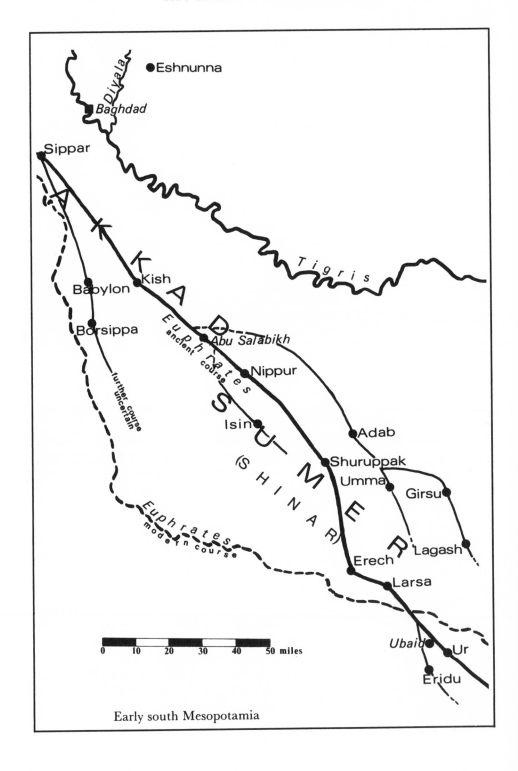

Early south Mesopotamia

important source for it. These radical developments lead some scholars to postulate the entry of a new stratum of population which they identify as the Sumerians. This view is not to be rejected out of hand, but the changes can be explained otherwise.

Human conservatism often has the result that even where there are forces pointing the way towards change, it does not occur until pressure becomes irresistible. We may reasonably assume that pressure for change did develop during the *Ubaid* period: the value of communal effort in irrigation was evident to all, and as command of irrigation technology advanced, larger-scale works could be attempted, but these would require populations larger than a single village. If several villages combined into a larger social structure for such a purpose, other economic and political advantages would appear, such as increased opportunities for specialization, and greater bargaining power with other groups; and the advantages inherent in growth in community size would become evident, generating pressure towards development of cities.

Social changes would follow. Families descended from the earliest settlers would have taken possession of all the land best placed for irrigation, and as successful settlements sucked in the populations of less favoured villages, the newcomers would extend the irrigation systems to provide land for themselves. But there are limits to the area of land which can be watered from a particular network of canals, and a time would come when further extension was impracticable. Later immigrants, if they wished to settle, would have to work for the original landowners, either as labourers or as tenants paying their rent in the form of a share of their crops. A consequence of this would be the beginning of social stratification, in which it was only members of the old landowning families who enjoyed full citizen rights.

The best archaeological evidence for the development of cities comes from Erech. We have postulated the growth of the first cities from the combination of several earlier smaller settlements, and Erech did demonstrably develop on that basis. By 3000 BC it was a rapidly expanding city, with a population estimated at 50,000. As it expanded, old *Ubaid* settlements in the surrounding area became deserted, implying that their populations were being attracted into the developing city. Early in the third millennium a great enclosing defensive wall was built round Erech; this must surely indicate rivalry with other groups, most probably other developing cities, giving the threat of war. By this time the predominant language spoken in south Mesopotamia was certainly Sumerian, and it is proper to speak of the people as Sumerians, provided we do not import into that term any assumptions about racial origins.[5]

Although the city may have grown out of a group of villages, it was something more than a mere overgrown village: it developed into a completely new social institution. Certainly a large proportion of its citizens continued to be concerned with work on the land, but the larger social structure made possible a degree of specialization which had no place in a village. It also served as a market, a centre for trade, and a regional shrine. The citizens, whether concerned with land, manufacturing, religion, or trade, all had their dwelling-places within the city walls, and all developed a sense of identity with the city, which created a powerful social force. The city was more than an urban complex: it was the centre of what it is now usual to call a city-state.

City-states

The term city-state was originally used in connection with Greece; Aristotle paid considerable attention to the concept. There the city-state was a region usually smaller than an English county, centred on an urban centre, with a population typically of between ten and twenty thousand, who governed themselves by an assembly of all citizens. It was to this form of political institution that the Greeks applied the term *demokratia*, democracy. Is it proper to apply the same terms to the institutions of early Sumer? The geographical structure was undoubtedly analogous. As to the form of early Sumerian society, we learn something of it from myths and epics, which originated in this period and presumably reflected human society at the time they arose. These indicate that originally government within Sumerian cities was by the assembly of all citizens, with particular influence resting with heads of families. This certainly conforms to Aristotle's definition of a city-state, and the form of government in the earliest stage of the Sumerian city-states leads some scholars to speak of it as primitive democracy.[6]

In view of these parallels, it is legitimate to ask, was there any historical connection between the early Sumerian and the Greek political institutions? A distinguished Greek historian has hinted at possible oriental influences upon the political form of the Greek city-states, by the tentative suggestion that they may have been modelled on, or at least coloured by, the system found in early first-millennium Phoenicia.[7]

But it is questionable whether there were any Phoenician city-states in the Greek sense. Certainly they met the geographical criteria, but their political systems were very different from those we associate with a city-state. We see this in the biblical account of Queen Jezebel of Israel. The story of Naboth's vineyard (1 Kings 21:1–16) puts it beyond doubt that Jezebel, a princess from one of the Phoenician royal houses in the ninth century, had no concept of citizens' rights: she considered it intolerable that the ruler should not have absolute power over all the land of the state—a negation of one of the basic concepts of the city-state as known in both earliest Sumer and first-millennium Greece. Furthermore, we have inscriptions of Phoenician kings, which show them to have been hereditary and absolute, ruling as representatives of the gods; their political relations were with other kings, not with their own citizens. But even were it proper to speak of Phoenician city-states, they could not have originated under Sumerian influence, since down to late in the second millennium the main external political force in the region which afterwards became Phoenicia was always Egypt, not Mesopotamia. By the time Mesopotamia, in the form of Assyria, asserted its dominance there, the concept it brought was empire, not the city-state. There was, therefore, no possibility of dissemination of the political concept of the city-state from third-millennium Sumer to first-millennium Greece via Phoenicia. Similarities were the result only of parallel development under similar demographic and geographical conditions.

The rise of kingship

In earliest Sumer, although decision-making was a matter for the citizens as a whole, it was sometimes necessary to grant executive powers to one man. Typical instances were the need for someone to take the leading part at the city's rites for the New Year, to organize and direct communal canal-digging, or to lead the city's forces against an aggressor. Although appointments to such offices would in the first instance be on a temporary basis, they could soon take on a permanent nature. Military leaders have opportunities for establishing personal authority through the physical power they control, and leaders in the cult can do so by virtue of their ability to manipulate divine approval. Kingship in Sumer grew out of this, but kings did not immediately become absolute. One of the earliest kings was Gilgamesh, ruler of Erech at about 2700 BC, and the subject of several epics. One of these is particularly instructive about the balance of power in a city-state.[8] It tells how envoys came to Erech from the powerful city of Kish further north, demanding submission. Before making a decision, Gilgamesh, king though he was, had to consult the citizens. He first went to the city elders, and proposed resistance to the demands of Kish by force of arms. The elders, however, disagreed and timorously decided upon submission. Gilgamesh was unwilling to accept this, but it appears that he had no authority to overrule the elders on his own initiative, and he therefore put the case for resistance before the assembly of all the men of the city of fighting age. This full assembly overruled the elders and backed Gilgamesh in his war plans. Here we see a situation in which, although there was a king as war leader, the normal forum for decisions was a council of elders, with the final decision reverting to the citizens as a whole in matters of the highest consequence.

The development of permanent kingship in Mesopotamian city-states eroded the earlier system of primitive democracy, but this did not bring conflict: there were both social and religious forces to ensure to the ruler the support of the citizens. Even after the citizens ceased to be the primary decision-makers, they continued to have rights in their city-state—land, access to water for irrigation, protection from violence against the person and economic exploitation, justice in disputes with other citizens, protection from external attack—and it was a primary function of the ruler to defend those rights. So long as he did so, he received the support of the citizenry, in courses of action which might involve war or trade missions outside the city-state territory. The ruler's role as a defence against aggression was particularly a source of support, for the people of the third millennium city-states felt a deep emotional attachment to their cities. When Ur was devastated at the end of the third millennium, a poet expressed the current feeling in a lamentation: in it he enumerated and mourned over the different parts of the city—its encircling wall, its great gate, its roads and avenues, its houses, the places where the citizenry were wont to take part in games and festivals, its temples—and showed that every feature was dear to him.[9]

But the strongest force making for acceptance of kingship was religion. Mesopotamian kingship, unlike Egyptian, was not essentially divine, but it had a religious dimension. In consequence, once it was fully developed, Mesopotamian theology incorporated it into the pattern of religious thought, so that it became established doctrine that kingship was one of the basic institutions of human life devised by the gods for mankind. This view was well represented by a work called the *Sumerian King List*.[10] This composition, originally compiled just before 2100 BC, purported to list all the kings of all dynasties ruling all Sumer from the beginning. Its opening words read

When the kingship was lowered from heaven, the kingship was in Eridu

and it then goes on to name two kings in Eridu who between them reigned 64,800 years. The kernel of truth behind this was that Eridu was indeed, as archaeology confirms, perhaps the most ancient of settlements inhabited continuously into Sumerian times, and in that sense it was the oldest centre of Sumerian civilization. But the supposed kings were as much a fantasy as the preposterously overlong reigns attributed to them:

they were an invention of priestly scribes, who believed that kingship was of divine origin and had existed since civilization began, and who could not imagine a prestigious city-state without a king. The actual names of the supposed kings could derive from ancient tribal leaders of the *Ubaid* period, vaguely remembered in oral tradition, but this is a guess. Apart from the absurd lengths of reign, historically there was no king who succeeded in extending his rule beyond his own city-state until the second quarter of the third millennium, and there were certainly no kings of Eridu who ruled all Sumer.

With due respect to the *Sumerian King List*, which is a document of unrivalled value for some aspects of early Sumerian history and civilization, historically kingship did not develop until well after 3000 BC, in what is referred to as the Early Dynastic period. The first kings in the list whose traditions can be linked to identifiable human beings are those of the cities of Kish and Erech at about 2700 BC. But these were still not comparable in the extent of their territory and power to the rulers of Egypt, where kingship over the whole country had already existed for 300–400 years. These earliest major Mesopotamian rulers made attempts at expanding their power, but with limited success. An epic already touched upon narrates how Akka, king of Kish, the strongest city in the north of south Mesopotamia, sought to obtain the submission of Erech in the south, where Gilgamesh reigned—and failed. Kish did, however, at this time achieve a measure of expansion, so that a king of Kish not long afterwards made himself the head of a federation of other city-states and was able to guarantee and enforce treaties between them. The rulers of less important states in such a confederation did not use the term *Lugal*, king, as their title, but called themselves *Ensi*, usually translated city-governor; there was a difference in status, but theologically an *Ensi* was, equally with a king, a ruler who acted on behalf of the gods.

Compared with Egypt, kingship in Mesopotamia came late. This was a matter partly of geography and partly of social structure. All settlements in Egypt were adjacent to the Nile and linked by it, a situation which enabled a central authority to exercise control equally everywhere. In southern Mesopotamia, although most settlements were associated with the Euphrates, the situation was geographically more complex. The Euphrates had at least six major channels, some of them further sub-divided, and some flowing into lakes or disappearing into marshes, so that it was impossible to establish the royal power throughout the country by a single progress along the Euphrates, as it was (except in the Delta) along the Nile. There was also a considerable hinterland of thickets of poplar, willow and date palm, as well as great areas of marsh, into which disaffected peoples could withdraw. Not until the second half of the third millennium was a king first able to conquer all the city-states of south Mesopotamia and make them into the nucleus of an empire, and even then the unification was precarious. This meant that no early king in south Mesopotamia could tax the whole land on a regular basis as the pharaoh did in Egypt, and in consequence the economic resources controlled by Early Dynastic rulers were in no way comparable to those of contemporary Egyptian kings. Even the most powerful Mesopotamian ruler down to well after the middle of the third millennium would have been quite unable to attempt any such vast public work as the building of a major pyramid. Another factor in the lesser power of a Mesopotamian king was that he lacked the supreme sanction of being a god; a deficiency which, however, in due course some rulers attempted to remedy.

The Early Dynastic period

As city-states developed during the Early Dynastic period (roughly 2900–2400 BC) specialization increased, with many categories of craftsmen represented—potters, metalworkers, jewellers, makers of cylinder seals, leatherworkers, masons, manufacturers of textiles—and trade links were forged with other cities and regions abroad. But irrigation-based agriculture remained central to the economy, and ownership of land played a vital part in the social, economic and administrative structure.

The old basic social unit, going back to before the rise of the city, was the extended family. The earliest communities were made up of groups of such families, all of which, in the early settlements, had a share in the community land. Every member of an extended family had rights in the use of the family land, but the land was not divided up into individually owned plots. Women as well as men could enjoy land rights.

There were factors which eventually eroded the original social and economic equalities of families in the community. The layout of irrigation canals could make land in some parts of a developing city-state considerably more productive than that elsewhere, and families so favoured in their land would become exceptionally prosperous and be in a position to wield particular influence through their economic strength. When community leaders were needed, they would be likely to be chosen from such families. This would be the social setting of the first kings, and of the persons whom they appointed as their lieutenants and courtiers.

Other families might be so disadvantageously placed that ultimately they would be driven to give up their land. Family land could be sold, but only with the consent of all persons with rights in it; such sales were usually negotiated by senior representatives of the family, with other members acting as witnesses. To sell family land involved a major break with tradition and a loss of status, and would only happen under severe economic pressure. By buying out the land of families in distressed circumstances, members of the wealthier groups could build up large personal holdings. Later in the Early Dynastic period, we find that members of the ruling circle typically owned private estates running to several hundred acres. Thus there came to be a wealthy nobility and a class of landless citizens alongside the original landowning families.

There also developed temple estates. At the earliest stage of settlement, the priest responsible for the community's religious rituals would receive a plot from the community land, which, in view of his vital specialist duties, other members of the community worked for him. But the divine sanctions he wielded would ensure further donations of land and manpower to the shrine, so that its lands would gradually grow into a considerable estate. Since there may originally have been more than one primitive shrine within the territory which grew into the city, several temple estates could develop within one city-state. In one city-state for which approximate figures are available later in the Early Dynastic period, it is calculated that more than a quarter of all the land belonged to temple estates.[11]

Once kingship had developed, there also came to be royal estates. The nucleus of these would be the private landholdings of the early kings, but as the king's powers moved in the direction of despotism, he became in a position to extend the royal estates. We find cases of family land being sold to the king at so low a price (the equivalent of two years' crops or less) that it must have been a forced sale.

Thus we see the origin of a tripartite system, with landholding families, royal estates and temple estates. But there were also landless citizens. Their nucleus comprised later immigrants to the city-state, who did not share the rights in communal land enjoyed by older families, and their numbers were eventually swelled by members of former landowning families who had sold their land under economic pressure. There were various ways in which such people might maintain themselves: they might use a skill in some craft, or become hired workers or sharecroppers with landowning families, or take service in temple estates or in the royal administration. Members of landholding families as well as landless citizens could serve as administrators for the temples or the king.

The king would normally reward those who served him with a grant of land; legally the ownership of such land remained with the king, but it could become de facto an hereditary holding if the grantee had a son able to succeed to his duties. Royal administrators might include the collection of taxes amongst their duties, and in view of the opportunities that gave for extortion, they could become wealthy men, able to buy up plots of land to form their own private estates.

The various groups in the city-state should not be thought of as rival blocks. Certainly clashes of interest could arise, in which family landholdings were the most vulnerable, but serious conflict was held in check by mutual inter-dependence. The temple authorities knew that their agriculture and trade depended upon a ruler able to give stable government and protect the state from aggression; citizens needed the king to enforce just laws and the gods to give fertility; and the king depended upon the approval of the gods and loyal support from the citizens.

Imperialism

A major change came with the beginning of imperialism. Even during the Early Dynastic period, some ambitious rulers had attempted to subdue other city-states by military conquest, but with only limited and transitory success. The first to succeed was a ruler known as Sargon, in the twenty-fourth century.

Although we speak of the civilization of the Early Dynastic period as Sumerian civilization, there were people of language groups other than Sumerian who contributed to it: in the northern half of south Mesopotamia there were many people whose mother tongue was the Semitic language Akkadian. Throughout history, Semitic-speakers have entered from the Syrian desert to settle in Mesopotamia; Semitic loanwords in the earliest Sumerian texts show that some Semitic-speakers had already settled there in the fourth millennium. Some historians have seen Semites and Sumerians as two distinct ethnic or racial groups in competition for south Mesopotamia, but this would have left evidence of inter-racial conflict, and there is none. Quite a number of Early Dynastic 'Sumerian' kings bore Semitic names, and so did many scribes who wrote in Sumerian. The fact is that what for convenience we call Sumerian civilization was a joint creation of peoples who had met and mixed in south Mesopotamia, and who, after centuries or millennia in the same geographical background, differed in little other than their mother tongue.

Sargon (2371–2316 BC) was one of the Semitic-speaking group. He had been a high official of a king of Kish, under whom he founded his own city, Agade, not far from where Babylon later rose to supremacy. After the formerly powerful Kish had been eclipsed by an expansionist king of Erech, Sargon overthrew the latter. He now made a clever use of religion to obtain formal recognition of himself as the overlord of the whole country. He did this by displaying the conquered king in a neck-stock before the great Sumerian god Enlil in the central city of Nippur and claiming that it was Enlil who had given him the victory, a claim in which the Nippur priesthood concurred. He then proceeded to use a combination of religious propaganda and military conquest to gain control of all city-states in south Mesopotamia.

Sargon was the first ruler to have a permanent professional army, and spoke of 5400 soldiers who daily took their meals in his presence. As he conquered other city-states he destroyed their walls to deprive potential rebels of strongholds. Where the *Ensi* (city-governor) was willing to transfer his allegiance, he left the old administration in office; in other cities, he filled governorships with his own townsmen. By these means he began the breakdown of the autonomy of the old city-state system, and started a move towards centralized government. These measures left Sargon with a much stronger economic and military base than any of his predecessors, and gave him the resources to make possible expansion outside south Mesopotamia. He and his successors conquered the principal cities in a region stretching from 'the cedar forest and the Silver mountains', that is, the Amanus in north Syria and the Taurus in Asia Minor beyond, to well down the Persian Gulf, and into southwest Iran. This was a commercial rather than a political empire. It was primarily directed towards trade, but, to serve that end, the Sargonic rulers were ready and able to attack and destroy cities whose competition as major trading centres injured the interests of Agade. They also set up garrisoned fortresses at strategic points to protect trade routes. Sargon's interest in trade is reflected in the fact that he made his capital Agade the principal port on the Euphrates, and boasted of ships berthed there from Tilmun, Magan and Meluhha, probably respectively Bahrein with some of the Arabian coast, Oman or the Iranian coast opposite, and the Indus valley (on these contacts see pp. 139–42). Such activities made Agade a city of great wealth, and Sargon's grandson, Naram-Sin, felt sufficiently exalted in status to write his name in a way which implied that he was a god.

The empire founded by Sargon lasted just over a century. Its final collapse was triggered by invasion by a people from the Zagros, who dislocated trade and ruined the irrigation system, but essentially was due to its inherent instability: both Sargon and his successors had to put down revolts. When, near the end of the third millennium, a new power structure developed, known as the Third Dynasty of Ur, its territory was more limited, but it benefited by a more efficient infrastructure, in the form of a highly bureaucratic royal administration, of which we have the records in cuneiform tablets running to hundreds of thousands.

Class and race in ancient society

Economic stratification in the early states put members of one class into a position to exploit and oppress those of another. But in both Egypt and Mesopotamia a social conscience developed to condemn such oppression. Very early it was accepted that it was a major responsibility of the king to protect the economically weak against the powerful. Perhaps the springs of this concern were not without an element of self-interest. To leave a major population element subject to intolerable hardship brought the risk of disorder and instability; to allow one social stratum to ride roughshod over another could end in a challenge to the royal power itself. But however it came about, kings and great princes accepted the defence of the weak as a primary duty. In Mesopotamia this principle was incorporated into written law, and may have been a major factor in its origin (p. 162). It was no less important in Egypt, where it became incorporated into religious thought, and as a principle in the administration of justice. Some rulers boasted of their concern for their people. A prince under the Eighteenth Dynasty says: 'No one was hungry in my time. In famine years I ploughed the fields in my nome, . . . to keep its people alive. . . . I gave to the widow and the married woman alike.'

The most depressed class was the slaves. Slavery was an internal development within ancient societies and not an essential element in their origin. None of the pre-classical societies were economically dependent upon slave labour, although most increasingly came to use slaves, as military conquests brought in more and more prisoners-of-war. The earliest slaves in Mesopotamia were men or women captured in raids on the mountains, so that the ideograms for 'slave' and 'slave-girl' were compounds from the signs for 'man' or 'woman' plus the sign for 'mountain'. As states developed their potential for aggression against their neighbours, the numbers enslaved increased. The Agade king Rimush, just before 2300 BC, attacked his eastern neighbours, slaughtering (so he proudly claimed) 17,000 men and taking 4000 prisoner. Of the captives, he dedicated six slaves to the god Enlil, retaining the rest as forced labour for the state. Two centuries later, Shu-Sin of Ur organized his war-captives in labour camps.

The story was similar in Egypt. From early in the third millennium there are references in texts, or reflections in art, of royal raids into Palestine for cattle and human booty, and under the Sixth Dynasty we find a royal officer boasting of the multitude of captives he brought back from a major expedition there. In the middle of the second millennium Tuthmosis III listed war prisoners from Palestine, taken to Memphis as state labour, totalling, with their families, 89,600.[12]

But despite the increasing number of prisoners-of-war as slaves, most state work in the third millennium, in both Mesopotamia and Egypt, including the building of the pyramids, was undertaken by free men, who had an obligation for corvée service. Corvée service doubtless at times produced hardship, but free men could, and did, strike if conditions became too harsh. A Babylonian myth tells of junior gods going on strike and burning their tools because their irrigation work was too hard, and in Egypt during the reign of Ramesses III (1193–1162 BC) workmen went on strike when their rations fell into arrears.

In Mesopotamia later in the third millennium, the practice developed of reducing citizens to slavery for debt, and such slavery was well institutionalized by the eighteenth century, since five of Hammurabi's laws controlled aspects of it. Later, children were often made over to temples to save their lives in times of famine, and an economically important class of temple slaves grew up from this source in first-millennium Babylonia. Such slaves might come to hold important positions within the temple administration.

Slavery as an institution, apart from state slaves captured abroad, began in Egypt only in the Middle Kingdom. By about 1750 BC, we hear of wealthy people owning slave establishments of the order of forty or fifty men, women and children, whom they used to run their households and estates. But in both Mesopotamia and Egypt, state and temple slave labour always remained more prominent than domestic slaves.

Other regions give a similar picture of the relative unimportance of domestic slaves as a social and economic factor. Although the Hittite laws reveal a social stratification, the less privileged group were hardly slaves as we understand the term, since they could own property and received compensation for injury. For this reason, where I have had occasion to mention such people I have used the term 'unfree' rather than 'slave'. They seemed to correspond quite closely to the *mushkenum* class in Hammurabi's laws (p. 44). In Crete of the late second millennium, Linear B tablets show the presence of domestic slaves, but give no suggestion that the economy was dependent upon slave labour. The Israelites had slaves and legislated about them, but the institution was socially so insignificant that it rarely surfaces in the biblical narratives. Enslavement of an Israelite sold for debt was limited to six years and when such a slave was released he had to be set up with livestock and food (Deuteronomy 15:12–14). This provision had a parallel in Mesopotamia, where kings in the Old Babylonian period sometimes issued an edict of *mesharum*, literally 'righteousness' or 'justice', which was an economic measure which included the release of citizens who had had to sell themselves into slavery for debt.

Despite their stratification, ancient societies were not rigid caste systems, and always retained a degree of social mobility. The possibility of rising within society is specifically mentioned in Egyptian texts from the Old Kingdom period; the *Instruction of the Vizier Ptahhotep* counsels a man who has become rich after being poor not to pride himself upon his wealth, and a man who serves an official who rose from humble circumstances not to be presumptuous towards him on that account.

Social mobility could extend even to the top, for in both Mesopotamia and Egypt it from time to time happened that a man not of royal birth became king. Any problems to which this gave rise were not social but religious; the main difficulty was that the king was a god in Egypt, and in Mesopotamia the chief earthly representative of the god, but the priests had means of soothing these problems away. It happened with Sargon of Agade. In tradition his father was unknown, indicating not bastardy but rather that he was of humble birth. But there were ways of giving a man of humble origin the necessary link with the divine: in Sargon's case, the establishment created the legend that he was the son of a High Priestess, who, because she should not have yielded herself to a man, bore him secretly. Such a mother's son was worthy to be a king, for a High Priestess was often of royal blood and always the wife of a god. Near the end of ancient Egypt's history, Alexander the Great received priestly promotion when he conquered the country in 332 BC. Foreigner though he was, with no claim of divinity and no shadow of former link with Egypt, he became recognized as the legitimate god-king of the country by a visit to the oracle of the god Amun in the oasis of Siwa, where the god decreed that Alexander was his own son and thus himself a god.

Nor were other social distinctions fixed and final: the man who began landless could become a landowner, the slave could be granted his freedom, and the free man could be reduced to slavery for debt. There were several paths to land ownership. Kings needed administrators, and rewarded them with grants of land. A merchant who became wealthy by trade was able to buy plots of land and consolidate them into an estate; even in regions where customary law forbade the sale of ancestral land, wealthy merchants could get round the prohibition by the legal fiction of being adopted by the seller and receiving the land by inheritance.

At one stage in the early second millennium, there was briefly a more formal class division in Mesopotamia. Hammurabi's laws recognized three social classes and graded penalties for offences according to whether the victim was a gentleman (*awilum*, a member of one of the old landowning families), a landless free citizen (*mushkenum*), or a slave (*wardum*). But the distinction at law between *awilum* and *mushkenum* disappeared after the Old Babylonian period.

Ethnic divisions played little part in major ancient Near Eastern societies. This is very clear for Mesopotamia. The third millennium knew no split on racial lines between the speakers of different languages, and no such split developed later. The cultural pressure of Mesopotamian society ensured that although many diverse ethnic groups entered Mesopotamia, all were eventually assimilated, and none permanently stood apart.

We see a good example of this in the Amorites, nomads from the Syrian desert. When they started to enter Mesopotamia in the late third millennium, the established population mocked them as savages, barbarians unacquainted with corn and with no proper burial rites. But once the Amorites had settled and adopted Mesopotamian institutions, this attitude disappeared. Hammurabi, of Amorite origin, did not think of himself as a foreigner imposing a new system on Mesopotamia; he saw himself as part of the old society, and in the prologue to his laws (p. 158) he attributed his success to his call by the old Sumerian gods. And although in his laws Hammurabi recognizes the social division between gentleman, free man, and slave, he nowhere makes any distinctions between his subjects on the grounds of their ethnic origin.

The Cassite Dynasty which followed the First Dynasty of Babylon was another case. Undoubtedly of foreign origin and of a different ethnic group, after a century they were just Babylonians in almost every respect. The only relics of their foreign origin was that they had introduced a new type of boundary-stone to mark land grants, and some of their kings (but not all) still bore names of Cassite origin. Within a hundred years their religion, their language, their buildings, their economy, and their social institutions had all become Babylonian.

In Assyria, the Hurrian annexation of the country in the fifteenth century left a strong Hurrian ethnic element, reflected in Hurrian names and ancestries of Assyrian officials of later times. But yet there is nowhere the slightest evidence of discrimination against anyone on the grounds that he was of Hurrian descent.

It was the same too with the Aramaeans, nomads who entered Mesopotamia from about 1200 BC. Some of them did remain outside the main stream of the life of Assyria and Babylonia for several centuries. But this was not because of rejection by the older populations on ethnic grounds; it was a matter of their own tribal social structure. Those Aramaeans who chose to settle were so rapidly assimilated that before 1050 BC an Aramaean had made himself king of Babylonia, and was so readily accepted that, usurper though he was, the king of Assyria married his daughter. More than that, the union was consciously recognized as making for harmony amongst peoples: by it, the marriage agreement said, 'the people of Assyria and Karduniash [Babylonia] were mingled together'.

The case for ethnic tolerance in Egypt is less easy to establish. Indeed, the Bible could be taken to show that it did not exist, since Genesis 43:32 makes the statement that 'The Egyptians might not eat bread with the Hebrews, for that is an abomination unto the Egyptians'. But this is an editor's comment from the first millennium, and may reflect Israelite rather than Egyptian attitudes.

Egypt's borders provided strong natural defences against major invasions, so that the large-scale immigration of foreign ethnic groups was far less common than in Mesopotamia. Nonetheless from earliest times small-scale infiltration took place from Sinai, Libya and Nubia. Provided this was not too massive, it was frequently tolerated, so that we have, for example, records of nomadic tribesmen being allowed to enter Egypt from Sinai to pasture their cattle, just as Genesis 47:1–6 tells us of the Israelites.

There was only one successful major invasion of Egypt before the first millennium. This was the entry from Palestine of the people known as the Hyksos. Beginning as infiltration in the late eighteenth century, by the early seventeenth it had become an invasion, by which Hyksos rulers imposed themselves on the Delta area. Eventually their control of Egypt extended southwards to somewhere short of Thebes, where a native Egyptian king continued to rule. They were finally expelled by the middle of the sixteenth century BC. The Hyksos were never fully assimilated and in later Egypt they were always thought of as barbarous foreigners.

But the basis of the Egyptian attitude to the Hyksos was not racialist. The earliest immigrant phase of the Hyksos entry was not opposed; the subsequent Egyptian objection to them was because they were no longer immigrants sharing the Egyptian way of life, but conquerors seeking to impose alien institutions and subjugate native Egyptians.

Later attempted invasions brought a similar reaction—vigorous opposition founded not on racial hostility but on determination to defend the Egyptian way of life. In the thirteenth century groups known as the Sea peoples attempted to settle along the coasts of Palestine and Egypt. Some, such as the Pelestu (Philistines), succeeded. But they were finally beaten off from Egypt, in a major sea battle in about 1186 BC. But the Egyptians, much as they disliked the Sea Peoples as invaders, had no objection to them as an ethnic group, since some of the earliest wave, called Sherden, who later gave their name to Sardinia, were taken into Ramesses II's bodyguard and later received grants of land.

3

Pyramids and Ziggurats

In the second century BC, the philosopher Antipater of Sidon compiled a list of the seven wonders of the world. At the head stood the pyramids of Egypt.

There are about 35 major pyramids and many smaller ones, but those Antipater had in mind were the three giant ones at Giza. These, all from the Fourth Dynasty (mid-third millennium BC), comprise the Great Pyramid, built by Cheops (Khufu), that of Chephren (Kha^{c}pre^c), and the somewhat smaller pyramid of Mycerinus (Menkaure^c). They well merited Antipater's admiration. The Great Pyramid, with a base area of some 13 acres, is the largest all-stone building the world has ever known, and, reaching 481 feet into the sky, is overtopped by only one stone structure, the twin spire of Cologne cathedral. The accuracy of its layout is equally remarkable: its sides are orientated almost exactly east to west and north to south, and the whole formed an almost perfect square, with sides of about 756 feet and a variation between the longest and shortest of less than eight inches.

The pyramid, vast as it was, was only one part of the royal funerary monument. The first of the other components was a chapel on the edge of the desert, sited near to cultivation to ensure that it would be accessible by boat during the inundation. From this there was a causeway to the funerary temple proper, which was immediately east of the pyramid. A false door from the pyramid to the funerary temple magically allowed the dead king to emerge from his tomb to partake of the offering provided in the temple. Finally, there were full-sized wooden boats inside a special roofed trench near the pyramid, in some cases on more than one side of the pyramid. Archaeologists excavated such a boat associated with Cheops: it proved to be 143 feet long, with a cabin just aft of midships, oars for rowing and steering oars. A canopy spread over the cabin to seal a layer of air gave insulation from the heat and served as primitive air conditioning.

In the case of Chephren there was a further monument: this was the

Sphinx, a giant human-headed stone lion, which was probably, as to the head, a portrait of the king (plate 19). The sphinx symbol later spread to other parts of the Near East and finally Greece, and the cherubim of the Old Testament were probably forms of it.

When Herodotus visited the pyramids in the fifth century BC, he was understandably curious to know how such vast projects could ever have been achieved. The priests he questioned obliged with details. It was done, they said, by a tyrant king reducing all his subjects to slavery and using them as a vast labour force; Herodotus was given to understand that they worked in three-month shifts of a hundred thousand men.

Herodotus and his priestly informants had grasped the problem of their construction but not the heart of the solution. To create such a vast structure as the Great Pyramid, with nearly six million tons of stone blocks up to 50 tons in weight built into a form of perfect symmetry, required more than brute force: a structure of that magnitude was not created merely by laying on the lash to a hundred thousand toiling men.

Vision, planning and organizational skill of an exceptional order were required. First, someone's imagination was fired with the concept of a structure in solid stone far vaster than anyone had ever built before. The project agreed upon, someone had to calculate exact details of shape, size, angles and quantities, and that with no long tradition of arithmetic and geometry. Internal passages required detailed planning, to integrate corridors and chambers with the main solid structure. The exact orientation of the pyramid had to be worked out by astronomical observation and the corner points set out. There was then the problem of levelling the site on which the structure was to stand: this was achieved with incredible accuracy, with the whole perimeter of the thirteen-acre site, around a central rocky outcrop, levelled to an accuracy of half an inch. Then there was the quarrying. It was not a mere matter of breaking out stone at random. Over two million stone blocks had to be marked out in the quarry, cut to the required shape, and extracted. Then came the question of transport. The greater part of the stone was limestone from west of the Nile, near where the pyramid was to be built, but, although the distance it had to be moved was quite short, a causeway was first levelled to facilitate the task. The finer facing blocks came from further afield, east of the Nile, and there roads had to be levelled for their passage to the river, and at the river bank shipping had to be ready to carry the blocks across. For columns, lintels, jambs and roof-slabs for chambers within the pyramid, granite was needed, and this was quarried at Aswan nearly 500 miles to the south and brought down by ship. At all the different quarries, gangs had to be organized, some to extract the stone, others to drag, and others to provide a continuous stream of rollers for the blocks to run on.

At the pyramid site, there had to be some means of raising the stone blocks from one level to another: Herodotus was informed that cranes were used for this, but archaeologists have found evidence suggesting that it was done by means of giant ramps, set against the faces of the growing pyramid. Housing had to be organized: archaeologists found a group of buildings nearby with accommodation for 4000 men, probably the masons who would be working there from year's end to year's end. These were a small minority amongst the tens of thousands of unskilled labourers employed seasonally for hauling the stone from the quarries, when the Nile was in flood and they had no work to do on their fields. Rations had to be issued, surgeons had to be available for the inevitable accidents, and scribes were needed to record details of every stage of the work. And there had to be a chain of command from the architect at the top through officers responsible for particular aspects of the operation down to the foremen of individual labour-gangs. And the operations as a whole had to fit between harvest and seed time, so that vital tillage of the fields was not impeded.

The first pyramid builder

There is no reason to think that Cheops in person planned and executed his pyramid, and we do not know his architect. But we do know the name of the man who, a little earlier, was credited with being the first to devise and build a pyramid in stone. To see how he came to create this new architectural form, we need to look at the Egyptian attitude to death, and early Egyptian burial customs.

Archaeology shows that the practice in Upper Egypt in predynastic times, before the unification of the country, had been to bury the dead in the sandy desert away from settlements, with the grave marked by a mound of sand. In the hot dry sand of Egypt a body rapidly dessicates and so, if not disturbed, remains indefinitely as a recognizable dried-up corpse without rotting. This encouraged the idea that an essential element in the afterlife was preservation of the physical body. So long as the physical body was there, the Egyptians concluded, the dead person could continue to enjoy in the afterlife the kind of life he had enjoyed in this. And so southern predynastic graves were pits in the sand, where the dead were laid with their treasured possessions and food and drink for the next life. But the Egyptians learned from experience that a body so buried could become exposed and destroyed, either by a storm blowing the loose sand away or by prowling animals digging it up; to deal with this, some Upper Egyptian graves came to be lined with bricks and given a roof.

49

When, at about 3000 BC, Egypt was unified by the conquest of the north by the south, the rulers from Upper Egypt brought their burial practices to the Memphis area with them. But they made some changes, possibly under the influence of the different practices of the northerners, who had been accustomed to bury their dead inside settlements, sometimes under the floor of a house. It was now felt that the dead person had the same need for a house as a living person, and to satisfy this need a box-like superstructure of mud brick was erected over the subterranean tomb. The structure that resulted is usually referred to as a mastaba, from its shape resembling a mud-brick bench, which is what the word means in Egyptian Arabic.

The earliest mastabas had the subterranean burial pit divided into several compartments, one containing the body, and the others the dead person's treasured possessions. Inside the larger brick super-structure above ground, there were compartments for food, drink and other necessities. Around the mastaba were brick walls, and, some way off, a wooden boat was buried for the use of the dead person in the afterworld.

But the people from Upper Egypt also had the custom, going back to prehistoric times, of raising a mound of sand above the grave. In the course of time this feature, originally purely practical, had become invested with a magical significance, and consequently was considered indispensable. To fulfil this requirement, in the earliest mastabas a mound of sand and rubble, cased in bricks, was placed inside at ground level immediately above the pit containing the body. But as this did not give a very firm support for the mastaba, the central mound soon evolved into sloping embankments cased with layers of bricks arranged in stepped form.

Mastabas gradually became more elaborate, but the details of this are not relevant to our present purpose. One change was, however, important—the beginning, in the Third Dynasty, of the use of stone instead of brick.

The Third-Dynasty king Zoser (some scholars transcribe this name Djoser) had as his general factotum a man named Imhotep, and in his capacity of chief architect he was responsible for Zoser's tomb. Imhotep began the tomb as a mastaba, with an elaborate network of shafts, tunnels, ramps, corridors and chambers in its substructure, with a central chamber intended for the king's body, and provision for the burial of other members of the royal family. But then Imhotep introduced a novel feature. He extended the already large mastaba and made it the lowest of four stages with sides of successively lesser length. Subsequently two further layers were added, continuing the same pattern, and the whole was faced with fine dressed limestone. The final result was a spectacular six-stage stepped pyramid, on a base of 411 by 358 feet, rising to a height of 204 feet (plate 3). Around the pyramid was a complex of other buildings to serve the needs of the king in his afterlife, and the whole complex was enclosed by a wall of over a mile in circumference and 33 feet high.

Why did the form of the king's tomb change from that of a mastaba to a pyramid? The answer turns on the mound of sand anciently heaped over predynastic graves in Upper Egypt, which had come to be felt to have a magico-religious function. The Egyptians well knew that, as the annual inundation gradually subsided and high points of land became visible as hillocks amidst the falling waters, new life emerged. By analogy from this, their mythology in very early times developed the idea that creation arose from the god Atum sitting on a primeval hill. The mound of sand over a grave came to be thought of as magically equated with this primeval hill, and to have the same life-giving power, and it was for this reason that it was felt essential to incorporate it in the tomb. What Imhotep did was to transform the old mound of sand, encased in a stepped arrangement of bricks, into a massive structure which covered and enclosed the complete tomb. The pyramid was therefore, to the Egyptians, a representation, or commemoration, of the primeval hill. This explanation does not depend upon theoretical deduction: the connection between the pyramid and the god Atum on the primeval hill is explicitly made in a text carved on a pyramid; by this identification the pyramid was linked to the origins and maintenance of all life, and to the continuation of life beyond physical death.

The gods controlled all that made for a good life—the rising of the Nile which brought fertility to the land, national prosperity, human and animal fecundity, freedom from disease, victory in war—and the closer the Egyptians could bring themselves to their gods the better for them. There is reason to suppose that the Egyptian king developed out of a prehistoric magician who could control fertility—possibly as a rain-giver if the earliest Egyptians had migrated from somewhere where rainfall was important. It was the magician-king who was the primary link with the supernatural world. With the unification of Egypt and the development of centralized control, the king became in very fact the ultimate power over all aspects of life. This, superimposed upon his magical status, reinforced the concept that the king was himself divine, an incarnation of a god. There was, of course, the problem inherent in any theology of incarnation, that the incarnate god has a human body which suffers disease and pain and eventually dies. The Egyptians well knew that their king would eventually die: probably his magician predecessor of prehistoric times had been ceremonially put to death (sent back to the supernatural world from which he came) when his powers began to fail. They explained the king's death as the god taking a new incarnation (the next ruler), whilst the dead king passed to another divine form after death. But the dead king was still a god, although now hidden from them, and the power the old king-god had mediated to Egypt from the divine world could remain for ever if an appropriate link existed. And what could serve that function better than the departed divine king's tomb in the form of a primeval hill?

Zoser's Third Dynasty successors followed him in building further step pyramids, although some of them were never completed. At Meidum there was built a pyramid which was originally of seven steps, subsequently enlarged to eight. At some still later stage, the steps themselves were filled with a stone packing, and the whole structure was faced with limestone, producing the first structure with the true pyramid shape. The precise date of this pyramid is uncertain, but one possibility is that it was at the end of the Third Dynasty that it was built in its forms with first seven and then eight steps, and that the final modification to the true pyramid shape was due to the first Fourth Dynasty king, Sneferu. Sneferu was also probably responsible for two great pyramids at Dahshur, built in stone but with the blocks not in flat courses as in later pyramids.

This was the situation when Cheops, the successor of Sneferu, began the Great Pyramid. Unlike the Meidum pyramid, from the beginning it was planned (at least as to its external appearance) in its final form, showing the remarkable skill of the architect. Internally there were changes in the course of building, but these were not because of any failure to foresee technical building problems. Rather, they must have reflected developing views about the theology of the king's tomb, since the main change was abandonment of a burial place originally planned in the substructure in the solid rock beneath the pyramid, in favour of a new burial place well up almost in the centre of the pyramid itself.

Manpower in pyramid building

The greatest wonder in the Great Pyramid is not its mere size, but the fact that people soon after 2600 BC could organize the resources of manpower and building and quarrying and engineering and masonry skills to create this monument and the other two major Giza pyramids. How long, and how many men, did the building of the Great Pyramid take? This is a question easier to speculate upon than to answer. Herodotus spoke of a labour force of 100,000 at a time for twenty years (wrongly thought of as slaves), but this was more than 2000 years after the event, and we have no means of knowing how far his Egyptian informants were speaking from accurate tradition and how far from guesswork.

It is possible, however, to attempt a crude calculation of the manpower needed, by estimating the total physical effort involved, and relating this to the work an average man can do in one day. The three major operations involved were the quarrying, the skilled work of the masons, and the labour of moving the stone blocks from the quarries to their final place in the pyramid. The two former tasks could have continued on a year-long basis, but the needs of agriculture limited the period of the main working force, the stone-heavers, to about three months in the year. Obviously the workers operated in gangs, but the maximum pull a man can exert is the same whether he is working on his own or in a gang, so that it is valid to make calculations on the basis of a single man dealing with stone blocks of the maximum size he could move. As we have noted, there were various sources for the stone, but the bulk of it came from quarries quite near to the pyramids. What had to be done was to drag stone blocks from the quarry to the final position in the pyramid. The completed Great Pyramid was 481 feet high, but because of its shape it can be calculated mathematically that the average height to which stone had to be raised was about 140 feet, or more if the base of the pyramid was above quarry level. For an average man, the maximum weight he can drag up a gentle slope indefinitely is certainly not more than a quarter of a ton, and this would take him a full working day if, as seems likely, the average distance from quarry or river bank to the pyramid was at least a mile. There were about six million tons of stone to be moved, which on these assumptions would take a minimum of 24 million man-days. Since this work was largely limited to the flood season, say, about 90 days per year, it would require about 270,000 man-years. If the 100,000 shifts quoted by Herodotus has any historical basis, this would mean that the minimum time for the work could have been as little as just under three years, and even if we accept the possibility of errors of 100% in the assumptions, it needs not have been more than six years. Quarrymen and masons would of course have been additional to the postulated 100,000 stone-heavers.

There is in fact some archaeological evidence indicating a figure consistent with these calculations for the time it took to build a major pyramid. A pyramid at Dahshur contains two dated blocks, one in the base and the other half-way up, with the latter a year later than the former. This implies a rate of progress which would have had the pyramid (a little earlier than the Great Pyramid and with a base area of just under twelve acres) completed within three years.

Large-scale works of this kind were only possible because there existed a power structure able to command all the human and other resources of

Egypt. This had its seeds in geography, in prehistoric and predynastic times.

The natural levels of the Nile divided the alluvial plain into naturally irrigated flood basins of upwards from a few square miles in size. From about 5000 BC, each year as the floods receded, Neolithic groups sowed their seed in fields which had sufficient stored moisture and a high enough water table to bring crops to maturity. There were, however, year-to-year fluctuations in flood level, and once the population had reached the maximum supportable by natural irrigation, years of low flood would be a stimulus to artificial irrigation to increase crop acreage. In the first instance, this would be done by breaching natural levees to flood those natural basins which the inundation had been too low to reach. Where necessary, control of the flood basins would be facilitated by raising new artificial dykes to subdivide them. Work of this kind required a large cooperating labour force, and this dictated the direction in which the social structure developed, since it would require organization based on a particular flood basin or group of flood basins. The grouping of a number of flood basins gave rise to the territorial unit later called by the Greek word 'nome', which became the basic regional administrative unit of Egypt.[1] Since all the flood basins had direct access to the Nile, they were not—in contrast to the situation in parts of Mesopotamia—in competition for water for irrigation, and this encouraged a high degree of cooperation between nomes, which, still in prehistoric times, came together into two kingdoms. One was Lower Egypt, from the Delta to about forty miles south of Cairo, and the other was Upper Egypt, along some 400 miles of the Nile further south. A war monument of a predynastic king of Upper Egypt, named Scorpion, depicts symbols which later represented the nomes, each with its hereditary governor or nomarch, and this suggests that the power of the predynastic southern kingdom derived from a federation of rulers of smaller territories under an overlord, a system well suited for the hierarchical exercise of power from top to bottom. The importance of irrigation within this power structure is reflected in another scene on king Scorpion's monument, which shows him wielding a hoe to breach a dyke at the beginning of the flood season.[2]

It may have been Scorpion's immediate successor Narmer (whom many Egyptologists identify with the Menes whom Manetho names as founder of the First Dynasty) who conquered Lower Egypt, thereby bringing a single royal control over the whole of Egypt.

The absolute power of the Egyptian king was further reinforced by religious considerations: his prehistoric antecedents (p. 25) made him a god, upon whom the prosperity of the land and all aspects of life depended, and it was therefore in the interests of each Egyptian individually to conform to the will of the supreme ruler. It was this situation which put kings of the Old Kingdom into the position of being able to muster all the resources of Egypt for such major works as the building of pyramids. But those huge structures did not rise out of the exploitation of the masses to the glory of a single individual, the ruler. They arose as an eternal expression of the will of the whole community, who felt that their life and well-being depended on the god-king. Like all great building works, they were an assertion of the values of the society which created them.

Ziggurats

No monuments remain from ancient Mesopotamia comparable with the pyramids, but the Bible speaks of a giant Tower of Babel, and classical sources tell us of a remarkable structure called the Hanging Gardens of Babylon, which Antipater of Sidon placed second only to the pyramids as a world wonder.

What were these Hanging Gardens? Diodorus Siculus, of the first century BC, says that they were built to please a Persian concubine of one of the Babylonian kings. Other sources amplify this to tell us that the king was Nebuchadnezzar and the lady his queen from Media: the lady was homesick for the mountain meadows of her native land, and the gardens were devised as an artificial hill planted with trees. According to the account of Diodorus, it took the form of a series of superimposed terraces of reducing size, rising to a height of 75 feet. The whole was equipped with concealed machines for raising water from the Euphrates. Other classical authors give supplementary details. Strabo, at the end of the first century BC, makes it much bigger than Diodorus, reporting the base of the Hanging Gardens to be a square with sides of about 400 feet.[3]

Excavation at Babylon revealed, within part of Nebuchadnezzar's palace, a subterranean complex consisting of a narrow passage with, leading off from it on each side, a row of seven narrow vaulted chambers with massive walls; these walls could have supported a considerable superstructure. Associated with this system of vaults was a well with three shafts. Some archaeologists interpreted this structure as the base of the Hanging Gardens, with the well supplying irrigation by means of a winch and an endless chain of buckets. But wells have been found in other ancient palaces in Mesopotamia, where there was no question of irrigation of Hanging Gardens; and, so far as classical tradition may be relevant, Strabo says that the irrigation water came from the Euphrates. As to the form of the building, one wonders why, if the primary requirement was to bear the weight of a raised garden, the putative builder, Nebuchadnezzar, should have used vaulted chambers, however massive, rather than a solid base. One may also note that if one calculates from the measurements of the vaulted chambers (shortest side about 70 feet), and assumes an artificial hill built on it with sides sloping at 65 degrees from the horizontal (surely the maximum possible for stability), one finds that the height of the garden would not have exceeded 70 feet, hardly meriting a reputation of a world wonder second only to the pyramids, at up to 481 feet.

For these reasons we reject that explanation of the Hanging Gardens of Babylon, and see them as a Greek's interpretation of a gigantic ziggurat covered with verdure.

It is also relevant that Herodotus, who visited Babylon during the fifth century BC, and described it in some detail and showed himself impressed by many of its architectural features, says nothing about Hanging Gardens. It may be objected that neither does he say anything about trees on Babylon's ziggurat. But this does not prove the absence of trees on the ziggurat. Herodotus makes no mention of trees at all when he is describing Babylon, although elsewhere he comments in passing that date-palms grew everywhere. Clearly, trees were so common in Babylon that he took them for granted and saw no need to catalogue them in any particular place. A corresponding explanation would not cover the absence of mention of the Hanging Gardens, had they been a remarkable structure distinct from the ziggurat.

It was a ziggurat which was the basis of the biblical tradition of the Tower of Babel. Since the Lord had allegedly scattered the builders 'from there over the face of all the earth', so that 'they left off building the city' (Genesis 11:8), the story presumably originated in connection with a ruined ziggurat in some deserted Mesopotamian city.

Ziggurats existed long before Babylon became a city of importance. They had their origin in Sumer, in the *Uruk* period, just before 3000 BC. The earliest form, attested at Erech and one or two other sites, consisted of a high terrace of trodden clay and mudbrick, covering about an acre and serving as the base for a temple, reached by a stairway or ramp. In later developments, further terraces of reducing size were added, giving a stepped structure of at first four and finally seven stages.

Architecturally ziggurats were less complex than the pyramids of Giza, and did not house, as the latter did, a complex of corridors and rooms. They were also considerably smaller. The base of the largest, the ziggurat of Babylon, was only about 300 feet square, so that it covered just over two acres, as against the thirteen acres of the Great Pyramid. Whereas the whole of the three major pyramids was of stone, the core of the ziggurat of

Babylon (like other ziggurats) was of trodden clay and mudbrick, although with a thick cladding of baked brick. Between the successive stages of a ziggurat there were damp courses of reeds and bitumen, and the platforms were fitted with drainage holes. These were necessary because although total rainfall in south Mesopotamia is low, such as there is comes in a few very heavy storms. But the damp courses and drainage only limited the penetration of the wet and did not stop it altogether. The mudbrick at the core of the structure would soften and under the weight of the higher stages the ziggurat would start to bulge and would quickly become misshapen. This is not speculation: the ancient texts are full of references to it. Kings often had to rebuild ziggurats, and in their dedication texts after doing so they usually included a reference to 'when this ziggurat falls into ruins'. (The same rapid deterioration happened for the same reason to temples and palaces, which generally had to be rebuilt after not more than a century, and often much sooner; the bulging of walls was such a familiar sight in the ancient Near East that Isaiah used it in his imagery, Isaiah 30:13). The few ziggurats which remain recognizable as such today are no more than stumps of the original structures (plate 20), in stark contrast to the stone-built pyramids, which have stood unchanged (except by the ravages of Arabs despoiling them for building material) for four and a half thousand years.

The total height of the seven stages of the ziggurat of Babylon was claimed in a Babylonian text (we have no means of checking it archaeologically) as about 300 feet; this contrasts with the 481 feet of the Great Pyramid. Third millennium ziggurats typically had a base area of about an acre. The difference in size between third millennium ziggurats and the principal pyramids was an index of the difference between the human and economic resources at the disposal of Sumerian city-state rulers on the one hand and the Egyptian king on the other.

Despite a degree of superficial resemblance, ziggurats were wholly distinct from pyramids in their purpose. They were not tombs but structures to bring mankind into relation to the gods; the one in Sippar actually bore a name meaning 'The Staircase to Holy Heaven'. The manner in which they linked the human and the divine was to provide a means for the gods to descend from heaven. Normally a ziggurat had two temples associated with it; at its crown there was a 'high temple' for the god when he was still up in the sky, and there was a 'low temple' at its foot to receive the god when he came down to earth.

Although not comparable with the major pyramids in their dimensions, ziggurats must none the less have been spectacular structures, dominating their cities, above all when seen from a distance across the flat and featureless south Mesopotamian landscape.

Both pyramids and ziggurats were elements in a larger complex. Both had associated temples, but the temples had quite different functions. In the pyramid complex the temple was primarily a mortuary chapel where priests carried out funerary rites and presented offering for the dead king, although it also included the cult of the chief deity of that area. But the temple at the foot of a ziggurat was the main temple of the city, upon which were centred all the chief festivals of the city, and in the case of Babylon of the state also. The Egyptian temples which corresponded to the latter were situated not on the edge of the desert with the pyramids but inside the cities.

Survivals

The rites in the temples are touched upon elsewhere (pp. 276, 284). Here we are concerned only with survivals. Because the Egyptians built in stone, and the Mesopotamians to a large extent in brick, there are abundant visible remains of Egyptian temples, mainly from the New Kingdom and later, whereas in Mesopotamia there is nothing to see except what is excavated from the ground. But despite the lack of visible relics above ground in Mesopotamia, there has in some places been a remarkable continuity. The temple area in the city of Nineveh remains unexcavated and inviolable, because it is still considered to be sacred: a Christian church was built on the site in very early times, and after the Muslim conquest this was converted to a mosque. In the mosque, called Nebi Yunus ('the prophet Jonah') hangs something which purports to be the skeleton of the fish which swallowed Jonah, but in reality this fish connection is a survival from something much more ancient than Jonah: the fish symbol was connected with Nineveh from as early as the third millennium, as part of the ideogram with which the name of Nineveh was written in cuneiform.

There are many other mosques and ancient churches in Iraq which are built on archaeological mounds, and quite probably on sites of pre-classical temples. A good example of the same kind of continuity in Egypt may be seen at Luxor, where there is a mosque inside the ruins of a church which in turn is inside the ruins of an Egyptian temple (plate 2).

Neither pyramids nor ziggurats left any major influence upon later architectural forms. The only place the ziggurat occurred outside Mesopotamia proper was in Elam (southwestern Iran), which was in many respects a peripheral area of Mesopotamian culture. The ziggurat was incomprehensible to other cultures; the Bible shows this in the story of the Tower of Babel, where a ruined ziggurat was interpreted as a frustrated attempt to make a ladder up to heaven. Iraq contains one later building, a very early Islamic minaret at Samarra, of which, according to some authorities on Islamic architecture, the form may have been influenced by the ziggurat. The typical minaret is a slender pinnacle with an internal stairway by which the muezzin may ascend to call the faithful to prayer, but the one at Samarra is a great solid round tower, decreasing in diameter towards the top, with an external spiral stairway.

The pyramids are not even mentioned in the Bible, despite the many generations supposedly spent in Egypt by the descendants of Joseph's brothers. They were, however, later given a bogus biblical significance, even in the face of an accurate tradition of their purpose. The mediaeval traveller Sir John Maundeville, who set out from St Albans in Hertfordshire in 1322 to visit the East, wrote:

> I will speak of another thing that is . . . between Africa and Egypt; that is, of the granaries of Joseph, that he caused to be made, to keep the grains against the dear years. They are made of stone, well made by masons' craft; two of them are marvellously great and high, the others are not so great. And each granary has a gate to enter within, a little above the earth. . . . Within they are all full of serpents; and above the granaries without are many writings in divers languages. And some men say that they are sepulchres of great lords that were formerly; but that is not true, for all the common rumour and speech of the people there, both far and near, is that they are the granaries of Joseph. . . . If they were sepulchres, they would not be empty within; for you may well know, that tombs and sepulchres are not made of such magnitude or elevation; wherefore it is not credible that they are tombs or sepulchres.[4]

There are other prominent Egyptian monuments which have seized the imagination of non-Egyptians since ancient times. These are the great obelisks popularly known as Cleopatra's Needles.[5] They go back ultimately to Egyptian Creation mythology. Different Egyptian cities had different Creation myths, but the dominant mythology was that of Heliopolis. This held that at the Creation a primeval hill arose from the waters, and the Sun-god, Re^c-Atum, the Creator, sat on that hill. A symbolic representation of this primordial hill stood inside the main sanctuary at Heliopolis, and on it was a sacred stone, perhaps of meteoric origin, called the *benben*; the derivation of that term is obscure. Out of the *benben* stone, on its substructure representing the primeval hill, developed the religious symbol which we know as the obelisk. There were already small examples of this in some third millennium tombs, and by the first century of the second millennium very large ones were being carved out of granite. With one exception they were always made in pairs. The first two major ones of which we know, 66 feet high, were erected at Heliopolis by

Sesostris I (twentieth century BC). The largest of all were two pairs set up by Hatshepsut, the royal lady who made herself ruler (c 1490–1470 BC) when regent for the young Tuthmosis III. We have texts in which her treasurer refers to the work on one of the pairs. It was a formidable task. Huge blocks of granite ninety-seven feet long and weighting over three hundred and twenty tons had to be cut out in the granite quarries in Aswan in south Egypt, extracted, moved to the river, put on barges, taken downstream, moved to their final site, erected and carved. Reliefs in Hatshepsut's mortuary temple commemorate this feat, and one of Hatshepsut's obelisks still stands.

The first foreigner to take a fancy to removing Egyptian obelisks as souvenirs was Ashurbanipal, when he invaded Egypt for the second time in 663 BC. He stated that he took away 'two great obelisks cast in electrum [an alloy of gold and silver]'. He does not state the height, but he gives the weight as 2500 talents, which is about 74 tons: transporting them a thousand miles overland to Assyria must have presented his engineers with a considerable task. Either the word we translate as 'cast' (Akkadian *pitiq*) has a less precise sense than we give it, or Ashurbanipal's scribes were mistaken, for we know that these great obelisks were always carved from solid stone, usually granite. However, some of them were, as Egyptian texts tell us, overlaid with electrum, and this must have been the basis for Ashurbanipal's description.

The Romans in their turn were very much taken with Egyptian obelisks. Caesar Augustus moved a pair of them from Heliopolis and set them up in Alexandria, and later emperors took some to Rome and Constantinople (Byzantium, now Istanbul). Altogether forty-eight are recorded as having been transported to Rome, of which six giant ones and seven smaller still stand there, mainly in public squares. Of those taken to Constantinople, one remains standing in front of a mosque, and there are fragments of another. The two obelisks which Caesar Augustus removed to Alexandria had further journeys in the nineteenth century, when one of them came to London, to stand on the Embankment as Cleopatra's Needle, and the other went to New York. A number of other obelisks, or fragments of them, are scattered across cities of Europe, Great Britain and America.

Other Egyptian monuments, famous in classical times and still extant, are the colossi, giant seated statues of Pharaohs. The first pair, erected at Thebes as part of a temple complex in honour of Amenophis III (1405–1367 BC), were of quartz from a quarry northeast of Cairo, which had to be transported by river over 400 miles upstream. Each stands 68 feet high (plate 21). The Greeks knew them as the colossi of Memnon, and recorded that the more northerly of the pair emitted a sound at sunrise. Samuel

Butler used this as the basis of the giant seated statues standing guard on the borders of Erewhon: 'The inhuman beings into whose hearts the Evil One had put it to conceive these statues, had made their heads into a sort of organ-pipe, so that their mouths should catch the wind and sound with its blowing.' Another colossus, 56 feet high and weighing 1000 tons, cut out of granite from Aswan in the far south, was set up by Ramesses II (1290–1224 BC) in the courtyard of the mortuary temple called the Ramasseum at Thebes: the Greeks took this colossus as representing Ozymandias, and Shelley enshrined it in verse:

> *I met a traveller from an antique land*
> *Who said: 'Two vast and trunkless legs of stone*
> *Stand in the desert. . . . ,*
> *And on the pedestal these words appear:*
> *"My name is Ozymandias, king of kings:*
> *Look on my works, ye Mighty, and despair!"'.'*

4

Writing

No invention has been more important for human progress than writing. Like so many other aspects of civilization, this has a biblical link. The link in this case is through a place which Genesis 10:10 identifies as one of the first cities—Erech in the land of Shinar. Shinar, a variant of the name 'Sumer', denoted south Mesopotamia, the southern part of what is now Iraq, and Erech was one of its oldest and greatest cities, known in the language of Sumer as Uruk. It was at Uruk (today represented by a great ruin mound called Warka) that the earliest writing was found, dated to between 3500 and 3000 BC. This writing takes the form of signs drawn with a pointed instrument (probably a sharpened reed or stick) on cushion-shaped lumps of clay of a size to fit into the palm of the hand. Slightly later examples of writing systems using similar although not identical signs have been found at other sites from Syria to Iran.

The form of the signs in the earliest system should tell us something about the origin of writing. The following are some typical examples:

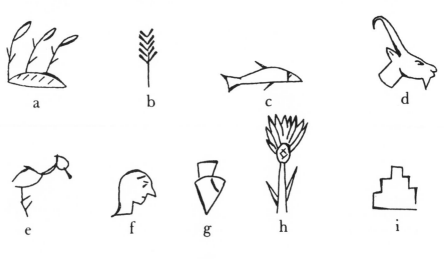

The pictorial element in these signs is obvious; we can at once see that they represent (a) a group of reeds, (b) an ear of corn, (c) a fish, (d) a goat, (e) a bird, (f) a human head, (g) some kind of pot, (h) a palm tree, and (i) a building of the kind we call a temple-tower or ziggurat. Clearly, the early Uruk writing system was at least in part of pictographic origin.

But the matter is complicated by the presence of other signs with no obvious pictographic connection, for example:

How did signs of this type originate? One possibility is that these signs also began as pictures, which by the time we meet them had become so much modified that their pictographic origin is no longer recognizable. But, if this is the explanation, how long did this take? Writing habits once acquired are retained with only minor changes throughout life. No one at the time writing was invented would go on altering the forms of his own signs until his original pictographs had become unrecognizable; modifications of that extent would take several lifespans. If these apparently non-pictographic signs did develop out of pictographs, the tablets from Uruk on which they occur—the earliest we have—must be separated from the original invention of writing by at least a century. But why, in that case, have we no evidence for the earlier stage? There are two possible answers. Either, the invention of writing took place not in southern Mesopotamia but in some other place not yet excavated; or else, the earliest writing material was not clay but something perishable and now lost, such as palm leaves, and the system was only later adapted to clay tablets.

A scholar in Texas, Professor Denise Schmandt-Besserat, has proposed an ingenious alternative theory to explain the presence of non-pictographic signs in the earliest writing.[1] At sites spread across the Near East from Egypt to Iran, and datable from the ninth millennium onwards, archaeologists have found groups of tokens, mostly of clay, typically about the size of a small marble. These come in various shapes, mainly based on spheres, discs, cones and rods; some of them bear incised lines or punch holes. At some of the later sites (fourth millennium), tokens of this kind were found inside hollow clay balls (usually referred to by the Latin term *bullae*, plural of *bulla*), up to the size of a tennis ball. What was their purpose? A much later find suggests one possible answer. The find in question, from about 1500 BC, was a clay *bulla* containing 48 small tokens; on its outer surface it bore an inscription reading:

Stones: 21 breeding ewes, 6 she-lambs, 8 rams, 4 he-lambs, 6 breeding nanny-goats, 1 billy-goat, 2 she-kids. Seal of Ziqarru.

Despite the inscription, the tokens inside were not stones, but balls of clay. Obviously 'stones' had become a technical term, going back to when the counters used really were pebbles. The inscription proves that in this example from 1500 BC, the 'stones' were a means of keeping reckoning of a flock. This cannot be taken as proof that all—or, indeed, any—of the prehistoric tokens were used for the same sort of purpose, but it suggests the possibility. Professor Schmandt-Besserat and other scholars therefore use this to explain certain features of the origin of writing. They argue that, by the time writing was invented, tokens had for millennia been employed in a system using particular shapes to represent particular commodities. To take a specific case, they say that there must have been a token to represent a sheep. Then, when the inventors of writing needed to represent a sheep, they found it convenient to take over a two-dimensional form of the 'sheep' token, rather than draw an actual picture of the animal.

Now, one of the more common prehistoric tokens was a sphere incised with two intersecting circles. Looked at symmetrically, the two-dimensional representation of this would have been ⊗ (a circle enclosing a cross), and a sign in this form occurs in the early Uruk writing. In subsequent stages, we can trace how the sign which began from this shape developed into a form which denoted 'sheep'. But this argument is not conclusive. Firstly, there is no independent evidence that the prehistoric token in question meant 'sheep'; this is only deduced from the fact that the Uruk sign which resembles it had that meaning, so that the argument linking the Uruk sign to the prehistoric token is circular. Secondly, a circle with an enclosed cross is a very simple symbol, and it could well have arisen without having to be the two-dimensional representation of something else. Thus, a link between the prehistoric token system and the earliest writing is not proved, even for the supposed 'sheep' token. Moreover, even if this particular instance happens to be valid, it stands almost alone: the keenest advocates of this hypothesis can suggest no more than a handful of signs in the early Uruk writing which bear any credible comparison with prehistoric tokens, and all of these could equally well be explained as pictographs simplified beyond recognition. We therefore take the view that writing was wholly, or almost wholly, of pictographic origin, and that prehistoric tokens had little or no direct effect upon its development.

But what about the inscribed *bulla* from 1500 BC? This need have been no more than two unrelated recording systems—writing, and an ancient pre-writing device—used together. As to the prehistoric tokens, even if some of them were used in a recording system, this would not make them precursors of writing: the credit for the invention of writing still rests either with southern Mesopotamia or with some unidentified area closely linked to it.

Contents of the earliest inscribed tablets

Scholars cannot with any confidence read the early Uruk writing, although some make a bold attempt. We are not even certain what language was spoken by its users, but we guess it was Sumerian, because that was the predominant language there a century or two later. It is not impossible that the earliest inscribed tablets from Syria, south Iraq and Iran all represented different languages, despite sharing a common writing system, since a simple writing system which involves nothing more than signs for complete words is not restricted to a particular language. For example,

$$8 \div 4 = 2$$

can be read either as English 'eight divided by four makes (or "equals") two', or as French 'huit divisé par quatre fait deux'. But these uncertainties do not wholly shut us off from knowing what the earliest writing was about.

If we examine the early Uruk tablets, we find that most of them contain groups of impressions of a shape which one might describe as a truncated oval or a D-shape, deep at the straight end and reducing to nothing at the oval end; their shape makes it obvious that these impressions were formed by punching some cylindrical object, such as a round reed, into the clay at an oblique angle. For convenience we shall refer to these as 'D-shapes', even though they are sometimes much more elongated than a normal D. These marks occur in groups ranging from one to nine; this grouping makes it reasonable to conclude that they represent numerals in a decimal system. In some of the tablets, these D-shapes are accompanied by circular punchholes, evidently formed by pushing the end of a cylindrical reed (or whatever the instrument was) into the clay, not obliquely this time, but at right angles. We shall call these impressions 'round-marks'. If the D-shapes represent units, then it is a reasonable inference that the round-marks represent tens.

Assyriologists use the term 'obverse' for the first side of a clay tablet to be inscribed, and 'reverse' for the other. Many of the Uruk tablets have the obverse divided into boxes by means of vertical and horizontal lines.

Typically these boxes contain groups of D-shapes, sometimes with a round-mark in addition, plus one or more incised writing signs. The reverse typically contains a single group of round-marks and D-shapes and perhaps an incised sign or two. A simple but clear example of this is shown in the following drawing, from an Uruk tablet:

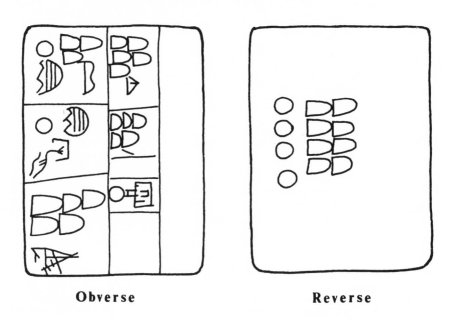

Obverse   **Reverse**

Here the obverse is divided into six boxes, which together contain punched marks adding up to three rounds and eighteen truncated ovals (D-shapes). The reverse contains nothing but a group of four round-marks and eight D-shapes, which it is reasonable to take as representing the total of all the punch marks on the obverse. We therefore arrive at the following equation: four round-marks plus eight D-shapes equal three round-marks plus eighteen D-shapes. If we denote round-marks by x and D-shapes by y, then by elementary algebra

$$4x + 8y = 3x + 18y$$
$$\therefore 4x - 3x = 18y - 8y$$
$$\therefore x = 10y$$

This confirms that, if a truncated oval (D-shape) denotes one, a round-mark signifies ten.

Another tablet, shown below, makes the subject-matter of these documents clear, even though the details escape us.

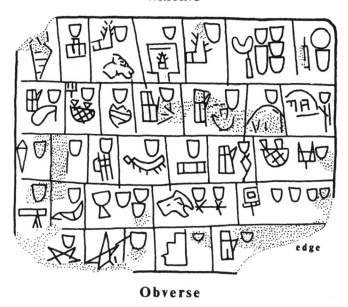

Obverse

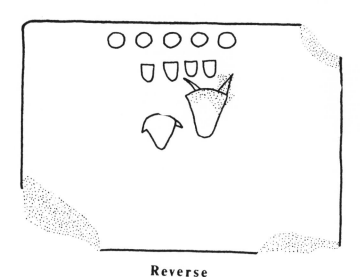

Reverse

Assyriologists conventionally show tablets such as this with the long side vertical (as on the previous page), resulting in all pictograms lying on their backs. The basis of this convention is Sumerian practice later in the third millennium. But we have no means of knowing how a scribe of the

Uruk period held a tablet to read it, and he may well have read it as shown here, with pictograms in their natural stance.

The meaning of the reverse of the tablet is transparent. The two incised pictograms, one probably a calf and the other a horned cow, must mean 'mixed cattle' and the five round-marks and the four D-shapes give their number as 54. The obverse and the edge are divided into five lines of text, each sub-divided into boxes which total 29. The box at the right of the first line contains one round-mark and one D-shape, denoting 11, and the other boxes contain D-shapes totalling 38, bringing the total of the extant numerals to 49. But there must also have been at least one D-shape in the broken box in the top line at the extreme left, and some more must have been lost from the damaged space at the right end of the edge line. Another could have been lost from the box before the last to the left in the fourth line. It is reasonable to suppose that the lost numerals with the extent 49 added up to 54, to equal the numeral on the reverse.

The tablet can therefore hardly have been anything other than an inventory of cattle delivered, either by certain people or from certain places. The pictograms in the boxes on the obverse therefore represent proper names, either of persons or places.

Clearly, this was not a mere extension of some old accounting system using tokens; it was something much more flexible. The beginning of writing did not stand alone; it was one element in a broad cultural advance. This included economic and social changes which brought the first cities into being. Units of agricultural production were becoming more complex, and developing into temple estates; these temple estates, which began to come into being in the late fourth millennium, gradually taking over large areas of what had been communal land held by families, for the next three thousand years were to be the largest unitary landholdings and to lie at the heart of the cities of southern Mesopotamia. This shaped the whole economy. Whereas the working members of an extended family holding would probably have been numbered in scores, or hundreds at the most, the situation soon developed that the labour force of temple estates ran into thousands. These workers had to deliver their products to the temple warehouses, and in return were paid in the form of rations of corn and oil for food and wool for clothing. With such large numbers of people involved, abuses or unfairness could only be prevented by keeping records, wherein receipts and issues were linked to the names of persons.

This brought the problem of how to indicate personal names. Some were easy, even in the earliest stage of writing: for example, such a name as 'Lionheart' would require nothing more complicated than the two appropriate pictographs. But from very early times there were other names, of a type such as 'The-god-has-given-life', which contained elements for which there were no obvious pictographs.

Two different devices came into play to overcome this problem. One was to take a word-sign (technically called an ideogram or logogram)[2] of pictographic origin and extend it to other words by association. This is the kind of thing advertisers have been doing *ad nauseam* in recent years when they have used the heart symbol to indicate 'love', as in 'I ♥ my Mini'. There are many examples of the same process by ancient writers: thus, the sign which was originally a picture of the sun was used to mean 'day', 'bright', or 'white'; the star sign was used to mean 'sky' and 'god'; the foot sign meant 'foot' or 'stand' or 'walk'; the mouth sign with the water sign inside it was employed for 'to drink'; and so on. The other device was a form of punning. It was as though someone wanting to write the name 'Neilson' drew a pair of knees to denotes 'kneel (Neil)' and the sign for the sun to denote 'sun (son)'.

How, it may be asked, do we know this was happening, if we are unable to read the earliest writing? We know it, because by the time writing had reached a stage at which we are able to read it, the effects of these earlier developments are very evident.

In the earliest certainly readable texts from south Iraq, the language was Sumerian. Whether or not the earliest Uruk texts (which we cannot read) also represented Sumerian, we are not sure. We become able to recognize the language as Sumerian, when the stage is reached at which its writers were beginning to represent grammatical elements. To explain this fully would require an outline of basic Sumerian grammar, but as that is not appropriate here, we shall use an analogy.

If one writes '2', this can be read as 'two' or 'second' in English, 'deux' or 'deuxième' in French, 'zwei' or 'zweite' in German, and so on. But if one writes '2nd', '2ème', '2te', these can only be, respectively, English 'second', French 'deuxième' and German 'zweite'. We now turn to see the relevance of this for Sumerian. In most ancient languages, an expression like 'to the owner of the house' would be represented by a word for OWNER and a word for HOUSE plus grammatical particles (prepositions, case-endings, etc.) before, after or between these words. In Sumerian—and in no other language—the grammatical elements would be '*ara*', and the whole phrase would be represented by OWNER-HOUSE-*ara*. Thus, when we find texts containing this sort of construction (or constructions containing other Sumerian grammatical forms known to us) we know that the language on the clay tablet is Sumerian.

But how did the early scribes contrive to write a combination of grammatical elements such as '*ara*', which did not constitute the name of something which could be drawn? They dealt with the problem by isolating the sounds of word-signs from the meanings they bore as logograms. There was a Sumerian noun A which meant 'water', and a verb RA which meant 'to strike'. (This latter was represented by a logogram combining the pictographs for 'sheep' and 'horns', reflecting the fact that the clash of fighting rams must have been a common sight to the Sumerians.) The Sumerian scribes took these two signs, A and RA, and used them to represent the grammatical element '*ara*'. They did this by ignoring the ideas 'water' and 'strike' behind the signs and concerning themselves only with their sounds. Once they had arrived at the system of using signs in this way for phonetic values, one syllable at a time, they could write not only any personal name, but almost anything else they wished.

The Sumerians were not the only language group in south Iraq and may not have been the first inhabitants. However, in the first half of the third millennium, people who spoke Sumerian were certainly culturally predominant there. But before the middle of that millennium, a second linguistic group was becoming of importance—a people who spoke Akkadian, a language of the family called Semitic, to which Hebrew and Arabic also belong. These people took over the writing system as developed by the Sumerians, and their descendants used it for the next two thousand years and more, long after Sumerian had become a dead language.

Alongside developments in the actual system of writing, there were also changes in its appearance. For drawing their signs, the earliest scribes used a pointed stick, and by that technique they were able to produce curves where appropriate. But anyone who tries drawing on clay with a pointed stick will find that problems arise from the stick ploughing up ridges. The Sumerians dealt with this by two changes. They first simplified the signs and drew them as far as possible with straight lines and loose curves giving a linear script. They then found that they could obtain very clear signs by using a sharp edge to impress them instead of a point to incise them. For this purpose they came to use the apex of a reed of triangular cross-section, of a species which occurs widely in Iraq. But this had consequences for the forms of the signs. Firstly, it was no longer possible to draw curves at all. Secondly, every stroke necessarily came out wedge-shaped, for which reason we use the term 'cuneiform' (Latin for 'wedge-shaped') for this form of writing.

It must not be supposed that, either for Sumerian or Akkadian, writing by logograms fell into disuse once it was possible to write words in syllables. The two methods continued in use side by side as long as cuneiform was written. Most cuneiform texts, even if predominantly in syllables, contain some logograms; and, even late in the first millennium

BC, some classes of texts were still written predominantly in logograms. We call such a hybrid system 'logo-syllabic'.

Other logo-syllabic writing systems

We know six later logo-syllabic writing systems; they were probably all influenced by Mesopotamian writing, although, with one possible exception, none was an immediate derivative. Their debt to Mesopotamia is shown by the speed at which these systems developed. Whereas Mesopotamian writing took several centuries to arrive at its developed form, the others were using all the devices of a logo-syllabic system soon after their first appearance. This different time-scale can only be because the Sumerians, working from scratch, had to solve the problems by long experiment, whereas peoples who devised forms of writing elsewhere found the answers ready to hand—ultimately from Mesopotamia.

By far the most important of the other logo-syllabic systems was Egyptian hieroglyphics, written from about 3000 BC down to the fifth century of the Christian era. This is discussed below.

Three of the other logo-syllabic systems have still not been deciphered: one of these comes from southwest Iran, another from the Indus Valley, and the third from Crete. The system from Iran, known as Proto-Elamite, and attested only briefly soon after 3000 BC, was so similar to the Mesopotamian system that a close connection is beyond doubt; either it was directly copied, with modifications, or else both systems derived independently from a still earlier form of writing not yet discovered. The Indus Valley script dates from about 2200 BC;[3] proven trade links with Mesopotamia before that time provide an obvious channel for influence. In Crete, the earliest writing may have begun before 2000 BC; it was probably influenced by the Egyptian system, which itself owed something to Mesopotamia.

Two other important logo-syllabic systems remain to be mentioned: Hittite hieroglyphics and Chinese writing. The former was used in Anatolia (central Asiatic Turkey) and northern Syria between about 1600 and 800 BC: despite the name we give it, it probably had no connection with Egyptian hieroglyphics, although there could have been indirect influence through Crete. It has been deciphered during the past half-century. Finally, there is the Chinese system, still in use, first attested at about 1300 BC; since the principle of writing was very widely known by that time, its introduction is unlikely to have been totally independent of earlier systems.

To return to the Egyptian hieroglyphic system, by the time this first appeared, at about 3000 BC, writing already existed in Mesopotamia. In view of proven contacts between Mesopotamia and Egypt at this time, it is likely that awareness of the Mesopotamian writing system (perhaps through long-distance trade) was a factor in the creation of the Egyptian, although the latter was certainly neither a direct borrowing nor a detailed imitation.

The earliest Egyptian writing occurs on decorated slate slabs known as 'palettes', carved with scenes mainly of warfare. Associated with the carvings are groups of pictographic signs: these cannot be read with certainty, but they are likely to have been either place-names or personal names. One palette, for example (see plate 11), shows buttressed rectangles which obviously represent captured towns; it is a reasonable guess that the signs inside them denoted the names of the places.

The development of writing took different courses in Egypt and Mesopotamia. One factor was different writing materials. We have already seen that the problem of drawing on clay set the Mesopotamian system in the direction of cuneiform and so away from pictorialism. In Egyptian writing, which was predominantly either chiselled on stone, or painted, or applied in ink on papyrus, this did not apply, and for the most formal purposes Egyptian writing retained its pictorial appearance right into the Christian era. However, for many applications of writing, convenience demanded something speedier than pictorial hieroglyphics, and before 2000 BC a cursive form of script, known as hieratic, was developing; in this the original pictorial nature of the signs was no longer clearly recognizable. By the first millennium a form of hieratic still further simplified, and known as demotic, came into use for rapid writing. Hieroglyphic writing continued in use for special purposes down to the end of the fifth century AD, demotic a century longer.

In Egypt as in Mesopotamia the original pictographs came to be used not only as logograms, but also with phonetic values; there were, however, significant differences in detail between the two systems. Both systems developed (with differences of detail) signs of the type we designate 'determinatives' and 'phonetic complements'. A determinative is a sign placed before or after a word to show to what class it belongs, e.g. Man, Woman, God, Wood, City. A phonetic complement is a syllogram normally placed after (sometimes before) a sign to make clear which of several possible readings is intended in the context. Thus, to take a Sumerian example, there was a sign which could represent, inter alia, SILA 'street', HAŠ 'to break', or TAR 'to question'. If the scribe wished to put it beyond doubt that he intended TAR, he might follow that sign with a syllogram pronounced *ar*. By this means he was in effect writing TAR(*ar*),

72

informing his reader: 'I intend this to be read as the logogram which ends in *ar*, namely, TAR'. This device received much wider application after cuneiform writing became used for the Akkadian language.

The differences in the way Egyptians and Mesopotamians used phonetic signs (syllograms) was related to differences in the structure of the Egyptian and Sumerian languages. In Sumerian, nouns and verbs were invariable. Thus, the word for 'mouth' was KA: there was no grammatical situation in which that word might be pronounced KI or KU. The consequence was, that when the Sumerians began using signs to denote their sounds only, divorced from their meanings as logograms, they thought of any particular syllogram as comprising a fixed consonant plus a fixed vowel (and correspondingly for more complex syllograms of the type KUR). But in the Egyptian language, grammatical context did modify vowels in verbs and nouns. For example, the word for 'mouth' was pronounced *r* plus a following vowel, which was not fixed; it depended upon the grammatical context and could vary. Because of this, the Egyptian sign for 'mouth', pronounced *r* plus a variable vowel, came to be thought of, when used as a phonetic sign, as *r* plus any vowel. From this it was only a step to thinking of that sign as basically having simply the sound *r*.

This had a very important consequence. Because there were a large number of monosyllabic nouns and verbs in Egyptian, it came about that for every consonantal sound in the language (Egyptian recognized 24), there existed a sign denoting that consonant plus any vowel. Thus, as early as 2000 BC, it would have been possible to write anything in the Egyptian language by means of twenty-four signs only. That is to say, at that early date the Egyptians already had an alphabet within their grasp. Some scholars actually refer to this as an alphabet. But this implies that the Egyptians had consciously abstracted the concept of signs denoting consonants only, and other scholars demur; they insist that the Egyptians had not gone beyond thinking of the so-called 'alphabetic' signs as syllograms with a fixed consonant and a variable vowel.

Whether these 24 signs constituted a true alphabet or simply an approach to one (a quasi-alphabet, as we shall call it), it is certain that writing by this means would have been much simpler than using the hundreds of different signs available in the full hieroglyphic system. But in practice, the Egyptian scribes used this system mainly as an addition to their already cumbersome combination of logograms, syllograms, determinatives and phonetic complements. They scarcely ever used it as a simpler replacement. Take the word *nfr*, for example, meaning 'good'. The signs for *n*, *f* and *r* were

and the Egyptians could have used them to write *nfr*. But they never did; they most commonly wrote *nfr* as

where the sign to the left is an ideogram of which one pronunciation was *nfr*, and the other two signs were *f* and *r*, added to remove any doubt about the reading. The ideogram by itself would have been quicker than three pseudo-alphabetic signs, but since it did not normally appear alone this was not the reason for its use. The real reason for not simplifying the system was vested interests. The scribes were the experts in writing; every scribe had undergone many years of training to make him proficient in all the intricacies of the scribal art; and the profession enjoyed considerable prestige. Here, for example, is what the scribes themselves thought of their profession:

> *Behold, there is nothing better than writings! . . . I can see no calling comparable. (The office of scribe) is greater than any calling. There is nothing like it on earth.*

It would have been against the interests of this influential group to substitute for their expertise a system of 24 signs which anyone could have mastered in a few months; the resistance of print unions to changing to a simpler technology offers a modern parallel to this attitude.

Changes in writing systems

Writing systems are never likely to be changed by people who are fully proficient in them: modifications come from users of writing who find existing systems difficult to operate. We can actually see an instance of this, in cuneiform writing, towards the end of the third millennium.

Scribes in south Mesopotamia received long years of training to make them expert in writing the two languages of the area, Sumerian and Akkadian. In the second half of the third millennium, Mesopotamian culture spread into north Syria, and with it the writing system. A major city, Ebla, developed there, and adopted the cuneiform writing system. But the Ebla scribes had problems. A long way from the homeland of cuneiform writing, they were less well trained than the scribes of south Mesopotamia. They had another handicap: neither Sumerian nor Akkadian was their mother tongue, since they spoke a West Semitic dialect. One might have supposed that they could have escaped the second problem simply by adapting the system to their own language, but this could never be a complete solution; as an important city within the cultural orbit of south Mesopotamia, Ebla would often need document-ation in Sumerian and Akkadian, for purposes of international com-munications and trade.

These difficulties drove the Ebla scribes towards simplification. South Mesopotamia cuneiform contained several types of syllogram:

consonant-plus-vowel (type ka*),*

vowel-plus-consonant (type ar*),*

consonant-plus-vowel-plus-consonant (type kar*).*

The Ebla scribes moved towards using only syllograms of the *ka* type. For example, there was a godname which south Mesopotamian scribes normally wrote by the syllograms *nin-kar-du*. The Ebla scribes simplified this to *ni-kà-ra-du*. Another example is the word *assammu* (meaning some kind of drinking vessel). This was written in several alternative ways in south Mesopotamia, of which the most straightforward was *as-sa-am-mu*, but the Ebla scribes wrote it as *a-sa-mu-mu*. Now, if we compare the south Mesopotamian writings with those of the Ebla scribes,

South Mesopotamia	Ebla
nin-kar-du	*ni-kà-ra-du*
as-sa-am-mu	*a-sa-mu-mu*

it is evident that in the Ebla writings there is no justification for the *a* of *ra* in the first word, or for the *u* of the first *mu* in the second word. In effect, these signs were used to denote not *ra* and *mu* but simply *r* and *m*. Thus, the Ebla scribes had seen the possibility of using syllabic signs in a way in which only the consonantal element was significant, and were treading the same road as the scribes who produced the Egyptian quasi-alphabet. This was by 2200 BC.

But compared with the problems of other peoples, the difficulties faced by the Ebla scribes were minor ones. The major changes came from peoples who enjoyed a degree of Mesopotamian or Egyptian contacts which made them aware of the advantages of writing, but who were not sufficiently integrated into those cultures to have the benefit of scribes trained in either the Mesopotamian or the Egyptian writing system. These conditions applied above all to Palestine, parts of Syria, and Crete. It was the peoples of these areas who in the second millennium were driven to produce forms of writing simpler than the old logo-syllabic systems.

Logo-syllabic systems, prestigious though they were, were far from efficient. They contained not only hundreds of logograms to be learnt but also many superfluous syllograms. In Mesopotamian cuneiform, for example, apart from the type of duplication already mentioned in connection with Ebla, there was the matter of polyphony. One sign might have several different phonetic values, and several different signs might duplicate one phonetic value. For instance, the same sign could be read alternatively *ud*, *tu*, or *tam* (this is only a selection from a wider range of possible values), and there were several different signs by which the sound *tu* could be represented. An efficient syllabic system would eliminate such duplication: what was needed was a one-for-one equivalence between signs and phonetic values. To achieve this, the system could manage with no more than between 80 and 100 signs (20 or so consonants, each with the choice of from three to five vowels), as against the hundreds or even thousands in an unrationalized logo-syllabic system. Two improved syllabic systems were developed in Crete in the second millennium out of the older Cretan pictographs: the earlier of these, Minoan Linear A, remains undeciphered, although attempts have been made to read it as either West Semitic or Hittite. But the later, known as Minoan (or Mycenaean) Linear B and attested from Knossos and Chania in Crete and Mycenae, Tiryns, Orchomenos, Thebes and Pylos on the Greek mainland, can now be read; it was used to write Greek at a period sometime between about 1450 and 1100 BC, with controversy about the precise limits of date.[4] Another linear syllabic script was used on clay tablets in Cyprus, at about 1500 BC: similarity of signs suggest that this also developed out of Minoan Linear A and it is therefore called Cypro-Minoan. Yet another syllabic system, also undeciphered (despite claims), is attested on inscriptions from Byblos in Lebanon; some authorities date this as early as 1800 BC, others centuries later. Some scholars claim this last as the true ancestor of the Phoenician and related alphabets.

Transition to the alphabet

A simplified syllabic system is a halfway house to a true alphabet. The final step depends upon developing the idea of a symbol to represent not a whole syllable but just a consonant. A simplified syllabic system might end up with three separate signs all beginning with the same letter, as, for example, *ka*, *ki*, and *ku*. Further simplification demanded the replacement of all three of these by a single symbol which could be used for *k* whatever the accompanying vowel. A sign of that kind, which was specific about its consonant but not its vowel, eventually became thought of as representing the consonant independent of a vowel.

Obviously, such a development was restricted to languages whose structure made it possible, without major ambiguity, to represent consonants without at the same time specifying the vowels. For reasons already outlined, this would have been impossible for Sumerian; on the other hand, the structure of languages of the group we call Semitic was ideally suited to it. The Semitic languages best known to the western world are Hebrew and Arabic, but in Palestine and Syria of the second millennium BC the principal Semitic language was Canaanite, of which both Phoenician and Hebrew are descendants.

In Semitic languages, most nouns and verbs are composed of three unchanging consonants, shaped by vowels which vary according to the grammatical form. Since the grammatical form is usually clear from the context, the vowels can in most instances be supplied by any reader who knows the language well, and so need not be written. This principle is to some extent possible even in English; for example, in 'th wmn ws cryng', 'th wmn wr cryng', once one learns from a context what this is about, it is clear that these two entries can only represent 'the woman was crying' and 'the women were crying'. The regularity of Semitic languages makes it far easier to read vowel-less texts without ambiguity. Let us consider Hebrew as an example: *melek*, *malko(w)*, *malke(y)*, *malkah*, *malkat*, *yimlok*, *timlok* mean respectively 'king', 'his king', 'kings of', 'queen', 'queen of', 'he reigns', and 'she reigns', and can be equally well understood if written *mlk*, *mlkw*, *mlky*, *mlkh*, *mlkt*, *ymlk*, *tmlk*. A series of words of this kind lends itself to isolating *m*, *l*, and *k* as elements independent of any vowel. We have seen that the Egyptians virtually achieved this step in the third millennium, and the scribes of Ebla began to move towards it, but neither made consistent use of the principle. So far as present evidence goes, it was experiments in writing Canaanite, in places from Sinai through Palestine to Lebanon and Syria, which during the second millennium produced the first true alphabet. The earlier experimental forms are nowadays referred to as the proto-Canaanite alphabet; the term 'Phoenician alphabet' is restricted to the form which finally became standard.

The earliest form of the proto-Canaanite alphabet yet known is found on texts from various places in Palestine—Shechem, Gezer and Lachish—dated to the seventeenth and sixteenth centuries. There are slightly later examples, of about 1500 BC, from Sinai; these are known as the proto-Sinaitic inscriptions. Other sites in Palestine provide further proto-Canaanite texts spanning the period from the sixteenth to the twelfth century, with increasing convergence towards the fully developed Phoenician script.

The forms of some of the signs in the earliest proto-Canaanite inscriptions leave no doubt about their origin: they obviously derived from pictographs. For instance, the signs

self-evidently began as pictures of, respectively, a head, an open hand, and an eye. Some scholars see the proto-Canaanite signs as specifically borrowed from Egyptian pictograms, which some of them resemble, but the case for this is weak. Drawing, say, a simplified profile of a head gives little scope for variation, and so pictograms in different areas were bound to show some similarity. But in the case of a head there is one possible significant variation—the presence or absence of a beard. The Egyptian hieroglyph 'head' had a beard and the proto-Canaanite pictogram did not; therefore it is most unlikely that the latter derived directly from the former.

The signs in the proto-Canaanite inscriptions, although they clearly show pictographic origin, were not being used as ideograms. This is proved by the fact that their total number did not reach thirty; only an alphabetic writing system can manage with such a small number of signs. The exact number of signs is disputable; this is because in some cases it is unclear whether two shapes which differ slightly represent separate signs or are merely variants of one sign.

We can trace the development of some of the signs from their proto-Canaanite originals right through to the forms they take as letters in the fully-developed Phoenician alphabet. Thus, the sign which began as a picture of a head ends up in the Phoenician alphabet as *r*, the picture of an open hand becomes the sign for *k*, and the picture of an eye becomes used for a Phoenician guttural consonant (in the terminology of Linguistics it should be called a voiced pharyngal fricative), which does not occur in English and which we have to denote in transliterations by ᶜ. In the Canaanite-Phoenician-Hebrew group of Semitic languages, the words for 'head', 'palm of the hand', and 'eye' were respectively *ro'sh*, *kap* and *ᶜayin* (or those words with slightly different vocalization). Thus we have the correlation:

Pictograph	Object denoted	West-Semitic name	Consonantal value
	HEAD	ro'sh	r
	PALM	kap	k
	EYE	ʿayin	ʿ

Obviously, in each of these instances, the original pictograph was an object beginning with the consonant which had to be represented. The same relationship between consonant and original pictograph can be proved for a further seven or eight symbols of the proto-Canaanite and Phoenician alphabets. Evidence on the remaining signs is less clear, but the certain examples show the principle on which the West Semitic alphabet was invented: that is, those who devised it represented a particular consonant by the pictograph of an object beginning with that consonant. This, the acrophonic principle, finds an echo in the nursery in the form of 'B is for ball, C is for cat'.

The Ugaritic alphabet

The earliest inscriptions which can be read, in a script ancestral to the Phoenician alphabet, come from 1250 BC or soon after. But these are not the earliest alphabetic writings. On the coast of north Syria in the second millennium there lay an important trading city, Ugarit, today represented by the mound of Ras Shamra ('Fennel Head'). This site has been under excavation since 1928. Early in their work, the excavators found over 200 clay tablets inscribed in cuneiform. But the signs were quite distinct in shape from those of the cuneiform of Mesopotamia; moreover, instead of the hundreds of signs in the latter system, these did not exceed thirty in number, which showed that the script must be alphabetic. The archaeological evidence dated the tablets to the fourteenth and thirteenth centuries BC, and the first scholars who examined them guessed, correctly, that they were in a language related to the Canaanite-Phoenician-Hebrew group. Decipherment was rapid, and the contents proved to consist in the main of myths connected with Canaanite religion, as known from the Bible.

The signs were composed of groups of impressed wedges, ranging in number from one to seven. Although the letters totalled 30, analysis indicated that three of these must have been added secondarily. The reasons for this conclusion are that, of the three suspect letters, one was used only in foreign words, and the other two were employed to distinguish vowels, whereas apart from this the system was wholly consonantal.

The origin of the Ugaritic signs is controversial. One thing which is certain is that they did not derive directly from pictographs. Because one or two of the signs look a little like Mesopotamian syllograms—for example, Ugaritic *b* looks a bit like Mesopotamian *bi*—some scholars have sought their origin in Mesopotamian cuneiform. But they have not made a valid case. There can be dozens of Mesopotamian syllograms containing a particular consonant: for example, to find something matching Ugaritic *b*, one has the choice of two fairly common Mesopotamian signs pronounced *ba*, two pronounced *bi*, one pronounced *be*, and one pronounced *bu*, and the possible range of shapes for comparison is multiplied severalfold by the fact that some of these had significantly different forms at different periods. In view of this, occasional similarities prove nothing: it would be strange if there were none. Other instances offered of apparent connection between Ugaritic alphabetic signs and Mesopotamian cuneiform are invalid on other grounds. For example, Ugaritic *g* has been linked to Mesopotamian cuneiform *gì* because both are written with a single vertical. But the single vertical did not develop the value *gì* in Mesopotamian cuneiform until long after Ugaritic cuneiform had ceased to be used.

Other scholars have sought to derive the Ugaritic signs from the proto-Canaanite alphabet. If one makes allowance for the necessary differences between impressed wedges and drawn lines, it is possible to see five or six pairs of signs in the two alphabets as of similar shape, but this still leaves more than three-quarters of the Ugaritic alphabet with no demonstrable link with proto-Canaanite signs.

There remains the possibility that the Ugaritic alphabet was an independent invention. G. L. Windfuhr pointed out that the signs are in fact the simplest combinations of three basic components and make such a systematic series that they must have been deliberately invented, not adapted from symbols already existing.[5] The following table (adapted from one published by Windfuhr) illustrates how the signs fit into groups which use simple elements to form a series of patterns of related form of increasing complexity.

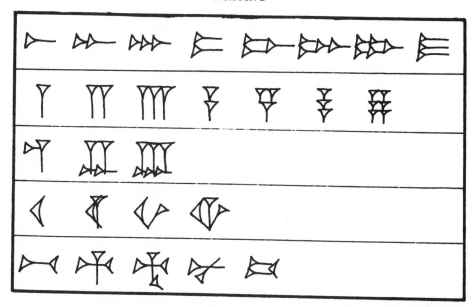

There were three further signs at the end of the alphabet,
⟝ 𝄙 ᔦ, which on grounds unconnected with their shape are
accepted as of later secondary origin, and the first and third of these
clearly do not fit into any of the patterns.

But, even though the actual shapes of the Ugaritic signs were an
independent invention, two key facts show that there was certainly some
link between the proto-Canaanite and the Ugaritic alphabets.

Firstly, the proto-Canaanite alphabet contained just under 30
letters—probably twenty-seven—and this undoubtedly agrees closely,
and probably exactly, with the number of letters in the Ugaritic alphabet,
if we exclude those of secondary origin.

Secondly, there is the matter of the order of the letters. Several Ugaritic
inscriptions set out the letters in the order of a standardized alphabet, and
for the twenty-two letters which correspond to letters in the Phoenician
alphabet, the sequence is that used later for Phoenician and Hebrew.
There are only two ways to explain this; either the Ugaritic scribes
themselves devised the order of their alphabetic signs and this was then
taken over into proto-Canaanite writing and its descendants, or the order
of letters was already fixed in the proto-Canaanite alphabet when the
Ugaritic scribes used it as the basis of their own. The Ugaritic alphabet
gives us a clue to deciding between these two possibilities: we have noted
that it contained three letters added secondarily, and these are placed
together at the end. Clearly, the other 27 letters—those common with the

proto-Canaanite alphabet—had already been fixed in order before the Ugaritic alphabet reached its final form. This strongly suggests that it was in proto-Canaanite that the letters of the alphabet were first placed in the standard order.

The proto-Canaanite, Phoenician and South Semitic alphabets

The Ugaritic cuneiform alphabet was mainly restricted to north Syria, although it was also found at a few Palestinian sites of the thirteenth and twelfth centuries. After the twelfth century it ceased to be used at all; the future lay with descendants of the proto-Canaanite alphabet. The early spread of the latter is evidenced by an inscription, possibly as early as 1050 BC (some scholars demur), found in Sardinia, and another, almost as early, in Crete.

It is difficult to be certain of the exact number of letters in the original proto-Canaanite alphabet. At first the basic shapes were not stabilized, admitting doubt as to whether two slightly different signs represented different letters or whether they were no more than variants on the same letter. There is the further problem that early proto-Canaanite had no rigid convention about the direction of writing: texts might run from right to left, from left to right, either way in alternate lines (boustrophedon), or in vertical columns; and the signs themselves might face either to right or to left or be inverted. There is thus plenty of scope for alternative readings of some of the proto-Canaanite texts.

Such problems have not deterred some scholars from confidently claiming to be able to identify almost all proto-Canaanite signs and to read the inscriptions. The distinguished American Semitist W. F. Albright, for example, in 1966 published what he claimed as an almost complete decipherment of the proto-Sinaitic group of proto-Canaanite texts: there have been others since, scarcely more convincing.[6] An example of one of Albright's supposed translations, and the basis for it, may show the dubious nature of such claims. According to Albright, one of his texts means:

> Itha^c son of Zur, give me an oracle. Thou who didst save [me] from two lio] [nesses, gr]ant me a r[esting-place(?). Swear to bri]ng a sacrifice [. . . a wild] cow.[7]

This translation is weak on lucidity and strong on hypothesis. Albright assumes his Itha^c to have been a dead hero, although he has to jump across the centuries into the Christian period to parallel the name. He sees 38 letters in the four columns of the inscription, but supplies 11 of them conjecturally in breaks. In one instance he assumes that one sign had to be read in both of two adjacent columns. In two instances, he reads as the same letter signs which occur in the text in significantly different forms, and in another instance he reads as *r* a sign which is quite unlike any other instance of a sign taken as *r* in the Proto-Sinaitic inscriptions, where all other examples retain a clearly recognizable pictographic form as a head (*ro'sh*). Most Semitists remain sceptical about the details of Albright's supposed total decipherment.

Shortly before 1000 BC the writing system which began as proto-Canaanite had stabilized into the form which we refer to as Phoenician. Most of the earliest Phoenician inscriptions come from Byblos, the most important being the inscription on the coffin of king Ahiram, of about 1000 BC. Up to a century earlier are inscriptions on bronze arrow-heads, five from Lebanon and three from near Bethlehem, all reading 'arrow of so-and-so'. From early in the tenth century comes a text inscribed on soft stone, called the Gezer Calendar, dealing with the agricultural season; this may have been a student's exercise and in any case shows that Phoenician writing was developing for purposes other than royal inscriptions and marking property.

By the time the alphabetic writing had reached the stage we call Phoenician, the alphabet, originally of 27 letters or thereabouts, had been reduced to 22; all the signs had become linear with no remaining trace of pictographic origin; and the direction of writing had stabilized to be consistently horizontal and from right to left.

The reduction in the number of letters in the alphabet was linked to sound shifts. In all languages, gradual changes result in speech-elements which were originally distinct becoming identical. For example, in English the spellings of 'snuff' and 'enough' show that their final consonantal sounds, now identical, were once distinct. Sound shifts occurred in some dialects deriving from early Canaanite, with the result that some consonantal sounds (technically 'phonemes') ceased to be differentiated from other phonemes. For example, some early Semitic languages, and Arabic to this day, distinguish between two gutturals which we transcribe *ḥ* and *ḫ*, but other Semitic languages, including Phoenician, lost this distinction very early. Sibilants and dentals (varieties of *s*, *d*, *t*) similarly underwent changes. To match such changes, letters were dropped from the original proto-Canaanite alphabet, to give the shorter Phoenician alphabet, which is most widely known in a later form as the Hebrew alphabet.

The Phoenician alphabet was historically the most important descendant of the proto-Canaanite writing system, but it was not the only one. There was another line of descent, in which an alphabet developed which retained all the signs of early proto-Canaanite. Semitic languages are commonly classified in three main groups: East Semitic (mainly Akkadian), West Semitic (Canaanite, Phoenician, Hebrew, Aramaic), and South Semitic (best known from Arabic and Ethiopic). It was the South Semitic alphabet which was the other offshoot from the proto-Canaanite alphabet.

The South Semitic alphabet is found in inscriptions, mainly in stone, from south Arabia from the eighth century BC onwards, and in various later groups of graffiti. The alphabet of these early South Semitic inscriptions consisted of 29 letters; either early proto-Canaanite writing contained more than the 27 signs we usually attribute to it, or the South Semitic adaptors of the alphabet added two signs to represent phonemes found in their dialects but not in Canaanite. Like early proto-Canaanite, the South Semitic scripts were flexible about the direction of writing; this points to derivation directly from the proto-Canaanite writing rather than via Phoenician,[8] and the borrowing must have taken place before the number of letters in the proto-Canaanite alphabet had been reduced to 22. Another feature suggesting separation at a very early date is the order in which the South Semitic alphabet is arranged; it is not that of the West Semitic alphabets. Since the Ugaritic evidence shows that the order of the West Semitic alphabet was already fixed before 1300 BC, and we know that it had been reduced to 22 letters not long after that date, the South Semitic alphabet, which was independent of either of those developments, would appear to have split off before 1300 BC. This leaves it a period of development of at least 500 years before the first South Semitic inscriptions yet known.

Transmission of the alphabet to the Greeks

Widespread Greek tradition holds that the Greek alphabet was borrowed from the Phoenicians. According to Herodotus, Phoenicians brought it to Greeks:

> *Those Phoenicians who came with Cadmus . . . introduced letters* (grammata*) into Greece, which, as it seems to me, were formerly unknown to the Greeks. At first they were such as the Phoenicians used, but in course of time they became changed both in sound and in shape.*

Herodotus goes on to say that

> *at that time most of the Greeks in the region were Ionians, who were taught these letters by the Phoenicians.*[9]

Since the Ionians were the Greek colonists on the west coast of Asia Minor, this defines more exactly where Herodotus supposed the borrowing to have taken place.

Diodorus Siculus writes to the same effect as Herodotus, without specifying the Ionians.[10] The elder Pliny records a rather more detailed tradition of the introduction of the Phoenician alphabet into Greece, saying that

> *Cadmus brought into Greece from Phoenicia sixteen letters, to which Palamedes added the four characters* Z Ψ Φ χ *during the Trojan war, and after him Simonides . . . added* Y Ξ Ω Θ.[11]

Apart from the classical tradition, several factors prove beyond doubt a direct link between the Greek and Phoenician alphabet. The names of most letters in the two alphabets (*alpha/aleph, beta/bet, delta/dalet,* etc.) are obviously related; the order of the letters is the same; and the shapes of the earliest Greek letters are identical with or close to those of Phoenician letters. The borrowing could not be by Phoenicians from Greeks, because the letters are attested much earlier in Phoenician than in Greek, and the names of the letters make no sense in Greek but are meaningful in Phoenician (e.g. aleph = ox; bet = house; dalet = door; etc.).

Despite the unanimity of classical tradition, some scholars question the view that the Phoenicians were the direct source of the Greek alphabet. Their argument rests heavily on the names of the Greek letters. In the Phoenician language, the names of the letters were (ignoring exact vocalization, which might differ with time and place) of the form *aleph, bayt (bet)*, etc., with no final -a. In the Greek alphabet, nine or ten of the letters *alpha, beta, gamma, delta, eta, theta, iota, kappa, lambda* and *sigma* (if it was a modified derivative of *samek*) have names clearly related to the name in Phoenician but with an added final -a. The final -a in all these letter names cannot be explained from the Phoenician language, but it does appear to correspond with the termination -a which the West Semitic language Aramaic used for nouns in the defined state (approximately the equivalent of nouns with the definite article). Some scholars therefore conclude that it was the Aramaeans (p. 19), the primary speakers of the Aramaic language, who transmitted the alphabet to the Greeks.

This theory rests on an unjustified assumption. It assumes that race, language and habitat necessarily run parallel. But Aramaic was spoken by many people who were not Aramaeans. The ports along the coast of Phoenicia and Syria have always been very cosmopolitan, and in some of them, as early as the second millennium, languages regularly spoken included not only Canaanite but also Egyptian, Akkadian, Hurrian, Ugaritic and several others. Because the first-millennium Phoenician ports were trade terminals and the Aramaeans were traders across the area from Mesopotamia to the Levant, there must have been many non-Aramaean merchants in the Phoenician ports who spoke Aramaic. Even if the names of some of the Greek letters came under Aramaic linguistic influence, this could have happened amongst Phoenicians in a Phoenician city; there is no need to assume that the Greeks who first borrowed the alphabet were in direct contact with Aramaeans.

There are some letters in the Greek alphabet, undoubtedly borrowed from Semitic, whose names do not show Aramaic forms: these are *mu, nu, pi, rho* and *tau*. *Chi* is perhaps to be added to these. There is also the old *digamma*, of which an earlier name was *vau*, which is generally taken as derived from Phoenician *waw*.[12] *Zeta* appears to show an Aramaic *-a*, but the name for *z* in Phoenician does not contain a *t*, and *zeta* in Aramaic means 'olive', which would not be appropriate for the name of this letter; the letter name *zeta* must therefore be a development within the Greek alphabet, perhaps by analogy with *eta* and *theta*. *Rho* is particularly significant. The name of the letter in the Semitic alphabets undoubtedly comes from the word for 'head', in one of several forms all going back to early Semitic *ra'sh*. In Phoenician, but not in Aramaic, there was a sound-shift, so that *ra'sh* became *ro'sh*. The *-o* vowel of Greek *rho* shows therefore that it was specifically of Phoenician origin and cannot have derived from Aramaic.

The factor common to those Greek letters, for which it is not possible to claim the influence of Aramaic, is that they all end in vowels. This suggests the possibility that the *-a* on the end of *alpha, beta*, etc. was added to Phoenician names by the early Greeks themselves, to produce a uniform series of letter-names all ending with a vowel. Names of other letters in the Greek alphabet do not affect the argument. Although *epsilon* was derived from Phoenician *he*, *upsilon* from Phoenician *waw*, and *omicron* and *omega* ultimately from Phoenician *'ayin*, the names of these letters are of later origin within Greek. Of the remaining letters, *xi, phi, psi*, and *chi* (if direct derivation from Phoenician is not accepted for it), were secondary developments within Greek from letters already borrowed from Phoenician.

The other main argument in support of an Aramaic origin for the Greek alphabet is based on the Greek vowel letters. This is touched upon later.

The latest possible date for the Greek adoption of the alphabet is fixed by the date of the earliest Greek inscriptions. At present none is known earlier than 750 BC, but there are about ten from between that date and 700 BC, mainly on sherds and clay vessels, from sites ranging from near Naples to the Greek mainland and islands. This wide spread shows that by 700 BC Greek writing was well established. The earliest example of the Greek alphabet written out in order is scratched on an ivory tablet found in Etruria in Italy, datable to between 700 and 650 BC.

But the date of the earliest finds does not necessarily fix the date at which the Greek alphabet first came into use. One feature in particular has been urged in favour of a much earlier date of borrowing. We have seen that Phoenician script had standardized its direction of writing as right to left before 1000 BC, and prima facie one would expect that if the Greeks borrowed the alphabet after that date they would conform to Phoenician practice. But archaic Greek inscriptions do not: amongst the twenty or more Greek inscriptions from between 750 and 650 BC, some are written from right to left, others from left to right, and still others boustrophedon. A further point which some scholars regard as very telling is that some of the archaic Greek letters are written inverted or with some other odd stance, just as in proto-Canaanite but not in Phoenician. This marked variability in direction of writing and stance of letters is urged as proof that the beginning of Greek script went back to before 1050 BC, when proto-Canaanite, which had fluctuation in its direction of writing, was still in use.

This argument looks only at ancient epigraphy: it entirely disregards evidence about human behaviour in relation to writing. As any experienced infants teacher will confirm, it is no unusual thing to find that a child learning to write, although he has never seen any kind of writing except that which runs from left to right, produces mirror-image writing, with the letters reversed and whole words running from right to left. This condition, an aspect of dyslexia, has been investigated by psychologists. One authority writes:

> *my colleagues and I have begun to . . . challenge . . . the notion that the condition stems primarily from visual deficits. . . . We have been finding that dyslexia is a subtle language deficiency. The deficiency has its roots in other areas: . . . inability to represent and access the sound of a word in order to help remember the word; . . . inability to break words into component sounds; poor vocabulary development, and trouble discriminating grammatical and syntactic differences among words and sentences.*[13]

These are precisely the difficulties which would have faced Greek merchants attempting to apply a Phoenician writing system to the representation of their own language for the first time. As to the anomalies in stance of letters, these are characteristic of the unskilled writer, and anyone who cares to examine graffiti in London or Paris will soon find many examples of anomalous stance which do not go back to 1050 BC. The variability in the direction of writing and the stance of letters, amongst the earliest examples of Greek script, could well have been the result of these factors: it is not necessary to posit two or three centuries of borrowing for which there is no epigraphic evidence whatever.

A technical epigraphic point has also been used to support Greek borrowing of the alphabet at about 1100 BC rather than about 800 BC. In the proto-Canaanite and Phoenician alphabets, the shape of letters underwent small changes in the course of time. For example, the tail of *k* was shorter later than it had been earlier. In some letters, the shape of the earliest Greek letters seems to be nearer to Phoenician forms of 1100 BC than those of 800 BC. Again, this argument disregards human behaviour. I have tried the experiment of asking non-epigraphists to reproduce a Phoenician *k* in the form of 800 BC. In most cases they exaggerate the length of the tail, making it closer to the form of 1100 BC (which they had not seen). The fact is that the earliest users of the Greek alphabet were not expert scribes, and did no more than approximate to the shapes of the current Phoenician letters.

Proponents of an earlier date for the Greek adoption of the alphabet use yet another argument. There are small local variations in the early Greek scripts, and these are assumed to indicate several separate lines of development from the alphabet as originally borrowed, implying an earlier Greek proto-alphabet. But even if this argument is valid, a century would give ample time for variations to arise at the hands of Greek scribes who were by no means experts, so that, with the earliest extant Greek inscriptions at 750 BC, the original borrowing need have been no earlier than 850 BC, which accords with the traditional view.

The major new principle in the Greek alphabet was its consistent use of specific symbols for vowels. The Semitic language had certain consonantal phonemes which did not occur in Greek, and the Phoenician symbols for these were therefore not needed for Greek consonants. The Greeks took over some of these letters to denote vowels.

The consistent representation of vowels, although a new principle, may have been suggested by the way in which the Semitic alphabet was already being used. From early in the first millennium the same alphabet was being used for writing both Phoenician and Aramaic, though with slight differences. The main difference is usually expressed something like this: 'Phoenician inscriptions were entirely consonantal, whilst Aramaic, Moabite and Hebrew were not'. The Greek representation of vowels is then used to support the view that the alphabet was borrowed not from Phoenician but from Aramaic.

Aramaic, Moabite and Hebrew used the symbols for *h*, *w* and *y* to represent not only those consonants but also the vowels (respectively) *a* or *e*, *u* and *i*. This practice was not current in Phoenician. But even in Phoenician, the connection between writing and pronunciation might well have led a Greek merchant of the early first millennium BC, with no more than a rudimentary understanding of the Phoenician writing system, to conclude (wrongly) that a particular consonantal symbol represented a vowel. The following examples from early Phoenician inscriptions show how this could have happened; in each case the stated pronunciation is approximate, with slight variations according to period and place:

'hrm (personal name), pronounced Ahiram, could suggest (wrongly) that the symbol for ' denoted *-a-*. (It was ultimately this symbol which was used in Greek for *a*.)

'dny, 'my lord', pronounced *adoni*, would not only reinforce the idea that the symbol for ' denoted *a*, but would also suggest that the symbol for *y* denoted *i*. (It was ultimately this latter symbol which was used in Greek for *i*.)

yrḥ, pronounced *yarḥ*, 'month', has a form *yrḥw* in the Gezer Calendar. The grammatical nature of the ending is disputed, but whatever it was, the sound it added to *yrḥ* would have been in the range *aw/au/o/u*. This could suggest to a Greek that the symbol *w* denoted either *o* or *u*. (It was this symbol which became used in Greek for *u*, *upsilon*.)

Thus the Greeks could have derived these three vowel symbols from Phoenician usage just as well as from Aramaic.

The Greeks took two further Semitic consonantal symbols, un-needed for Greeks, to represent vowels, although neither had been used as vowel letters in any Semitic languages. The two were the voiced pharyngal fricative ᶜ (*ᶜayin*) and its unvoiced counterpart *ḥ* (*ḥet*). The basis of the Greek use of the former could have been that in Phoenician (as in Hebrew) an *a* vowel following ᶜ often sounded as *o*. Since the ᶜ had no significance to Greek ears as a consonantal phoneme, this circumstance would suggest to a Greek, ill instructed in Phoenician linguistics, that ᶜ represented *o*. Similarly the frequent use of *ḥ* (meaningless to Greek ears) to introduce a vowel which sounded as *e* would suggest that the symbol for *ḥ* actually represented the vowel *e*.

Dead ends in writing

The development of writing is littered with barren lines: scripts arose which were employed for a few centuries but left no descendants. Some have been deciphered and provide important information about the societies in which they originated. Others can be understood but tell us little; yet others remain undeciphered, dumb engimas.

The earliest undeciphered writing is proto-Elamite. This first appeared in the *Jemdet Nasr* period (the final phase of *Uruk*), in the first century of the third millennium, in southwest Iran at Susa, capital of the kingdom later known as Elam. From there it quickly spread along trade routes up to 500 miles eastwards and northwards: examples have been found at Sialk, Tepe Yahya, Shahr-i-Sokhta and Shahdad in Kerman province. This writing, drawn on hand-sized tablets of clay, was so similar to that of *Uruk*, in method of production and general appearance, that a connection cannot reasonably be doubted; either proto-Elamite script was directly based on the *Uruk* writing, or both forms of writing derived from the same unknown precursor.

Like the signs of the *Uruk* writing, those of the proto-Elamite system were basically pictographic, comprising outline drawings of animals and vessels and the like, but the pictographs in the two systems were not identical. The number of proto-Elamite pictographs on extant tablets totals about 630.[14]

In a purely pictographic script, it is sometimes possible to guess the meaning of a text, if it has a framework of obvious number symbols. Thus, when we see this kind of thing on a tablet,

it is evident that it is an economic record about deliveries of strings of horses, with the differences in the manes perhaps indicating sex or stage of maturity.

But guessing the meaning is not reading, in the sense of interpreting the written signs as words; no purely pictographic script, or script written in logograms derived from pictographs, can be read until one knows in what language it is written, and even then there can be doubts. As there is nothing in the proto-Elamite script to tell us what language it represented, it is impossible to read it.

We saw earlier that, in south Mesopotamia, the *Uruk* pictographic script developed early in the third millennium into a logo-syllabic system which was used to write at first Sumerian and later Akkadian. Simultaneously, the forms of the signs evolved to become first linear and then cuneiform.

It is not certain whether proto-Elamite underwent changes similar to those of the *Uruk* system, or whether it just died. After the proto-Elamite pictographic writing early in the third millennium, there is a big gap in evidence of writing in Iran until the twenty-third century, when we meet a linear script. This linear script has been found in only 18 inscriptions, 11 of them on stone, one on a silver vase, and six on potsherds. Known symbols in this script amount to only about 80, but in view of the very limited number of extant texts this may not be all that were in use. The direction of writing was not yet standardized, but was mainly from top to bottom with columns running from right to left.

This linear script was finally deciphered in 1961, with the help of a bilingual inscription, of which one version was in Akkadian cuneiform.

The decipherer showed the language to be an early form of Elamite, which is known from later texts. The script proved to be almost entirely syllabic, with syllables mainly of the consonant-plus-vowel or vowel-plus-consonant type; there were a very few logograms, just sufficient to admit its classification as a logo-syllabic script.

Did this linear writing develop from the proto-Elamite pictographic script, or was it of independent origin? The historical situation offers a clue. By the twenty-third century Elam had close political relations with Mesopotamia; and during that century an Elamite king—probably the predecessor of the one with whom the texts in linear script are connected—made a treaty of alliance with Naram-Sin, the powerful king of Agade. This treaty was written in the Elamite language, but in the script of Mesopotamia. A statue found at Susa is also relevant, for it bears a Sumerian dedication 'for the life of Naram-Sin, king of the four regions'. This leaves no doubt that, a generation before the Elamite linear script, Mesopotamian script was already in use in Elam. This, with the total absence of evidence for native Elamite script between proto-Elamite pictographs and the twenty-third century, makes it very probable that the Elamite linear script was simply an adaptation of current Mesopotamian writing. After this one experiment at creating a specifically Elamite script, Elamites almost exclusively used Mesopotamian cuneiform as their writing system, mainly in the Akkadian language, until almost the middle of the first millennium BC.

Another find of an apparently very early form of writing once occasioned a flutter of excitement amongst archaeologists. This comprised three inscribed clay tablets found at Tartaria in Rumania, bearing signs said to be comparable with those of late *Uruk* (*Jemdet Nasr*). Extravagant claims were made: one interpretation of the find was that Sumerian civilization had already spread as far as Rumania by the beginning of the third millennium; and there was an even bolder alternative suggestion that the very roots of Sumerian civilization were connected with Rumania. But the excitement has faded: stratification suggests that the date of the Tartaria tablets may not be as early as once supposed, and some of the Tartaria signs are at least as similar to signs in the earliest Cretan script (end of the third millennium) as to late *Uruk* signs. Some scholars have made valiant attempts at interpreting them, but it is possible that the Tartaria signs were not true writing at all: they may simply have been copied for use as magical amulets. This would, of course, presuppose trade contacts between settlements in Rumania and either Crete or Mesopotamia.

Leaving aside the disputable Tartaria tablets, the oldest undeciphered script after proto-Elamite comes from sites in the Indus Valley, now in Pakistan. Predominantly this writing is on stamp-seals of ivory or stone, dated within the second half of the third millennium. The signs give the impression of being of pictographic origin, but the original forms are not easily recognizable; the calculation of their total number depends upon the method of analysis, and estimates range from about 250 to 400, which suggests a heavy representation of ideograms.

With any inscription in an unknown language and script, the briefer it is, the more difficult is its decipherment. In the extreme case, an isolated sign in an unknown script and language could denote anything whatever. The longer an inscription is, the easier it becomes to deduce the pattern of its elements and thus to obtain some insight into the nature of the writing system and perhaps of the language. The brevity of the Indus Valley inscriptions makes their decipherment extremely difficult, and it has not yet been achieved, despite ambitious (and conflicting) claims by several scholars. There are two main lines of approach to decipherment. One assumes that the Indus Valley population must have been ethnically related to the pre-Aryan population of India, and looks for their language in the Dravidian group, commonly held to be the oldest language group in India. The other starts from the known contacts of Indus Valley culture with south Mesopotamia, and assumes that the script must be related to Sumerian writing.

Cretan writing systems

When Sir Arthur Evans began his excavation of Knossos in Crete at the end of the nineteenth century, he did so hoping to find evidence of ancient writing. He had already recognized primitive Cretan writing of a kind, in the form of groups of pictographic symbols on ancient seal-stones found in the ground and worn by peasant women. His excavations yielded not only further engraved seal-stones, but three kinds of writing on clay, one pictographic and the other two predominantly linear. He called the script on the seals Hieroglyphic A, the pictographic writing on clay tablets and other objects Hieroglyphic B, and the two linear scripts Minoan Linear A and B. More recently it has become accepted that the so-called Hieroglyphic B probably represented the same language and writing system as Hieroglyphic A, differing only by adaptation to a different surface and technique of writing. This script is now known as Cretan Pictographic.

Cretan Pictographic
Just over 90 signs are known, either clearly pictographic or of pictographic origin. There may be some limited Egyptian influence in the form of a few of the signs, but most are of independent origin.

Example of Cretan pictographic

Archaeological indications are that it was used on clay—sealings on jars, labels and oblong tablets between about 1900 and 1700 BC, on seal-stones rather earlier. It remains undeciphered.

Minoan Linear A

This script, which flourished mainly between about 1700 and 1550 BC, developed out of Cretan Pictographic script as the original pictographs became less naturalistic and took a linear form. The connection between the pictographic and linear scripts does not necessarily mean that the later writing system was used for the same language as the earlier, but it could have been. Linear A has been found at about twenty sites in Crete, mainly in very brief isolated inscriptions, on such objects as steatite lamps and vases. The largest group of texts, which are also the latest in date, comprise 168 clay tablets from Agia Triada in the south of Crete. Two clay cups bear Linear A inscriptions written in ink made from the secretion of the cuttlefish, which was later the source of the pigment sepia; analogy with later practice elsewhere suggests that these inscriptions were magical incantations. The texts on the lamps and vases are likely to be dedications, and the large representation of numeral signs in inscriptions on tablets shows them to be mainly accounts.

In addition to numerals, Linear A contained about 100 signs. About 12 of these occur by themselves before numerals and are probably logograms, that is, signs denoting complete words, mainly types of commodities. The other eighty or so signs must be syllograms. The existence of empty spaces to the right in incomplete final lines show that the script was written from left to right. Linear A shares some signs with Linear B, which can be read, and this potentially provides a starting-point for attempts at its decipherment. Some scholars have claimed success, but with such widely differing presuppositions (one main group sees the language as Semitic and the other makes it Hittite) that their claims remain in doubt. The following is an example of Linear A script.

Minoan Linear B

Since the appearance of the original Linear B tablets at Knossos, inscriptions have been found at Pylos, Orchomenos, Thebes, Mycenae, Tiryns and Eleusis in mainland Greece and most recently at Chania in Crete. The largest group of texts remains the nearly 4000 from Knossos, to which must be added over 1200 from Pylos. The other sites have contributed a few each. They are dated, according to how one interprets the archaeological evidence, between 1450 and 1200 or between 1375 and 1100 BC.

Linear B is superficially similar to Linear A script; twenty-eight signs in the two scripts are virtually identical, and another twenty or so show sufficient similarity to establish a direct connection.

Despite the description of Linear B as a linear script, it contains many signs which clearly show their pictographic origin, such as an arrow, bowl, chariot, cup, horse, man, pig, pot, spear, tripod, wheel. Many of these pictograms stand alone followed by numerals; this suggests that they were being used not as syllables but as logograms (whole words). Some other signs which are less easily recognizable as pictograms similarly stand alone before numerals, and these may reasonably be interpreted as logograms which had developed away from their original pictographic form. Together these logograms amount to more than half of the almost 200 signs in Linear B. There remain just under ninety signs which must be syllograms.

The first significant step towards the decipherment of Linear B was taken by an American scholar, Dr Alice Kober. She showed that it was possible to identify patterns within groups of symbols. To illustrate her method and conclusion, let us use capital letters to represent Minoan B signs. Dr Kober showed that signs were grouped, inter alia, in this way:

ABCX	DEFX
ABCY	DEFY
ABZ	DEZ

Clearly ABC, DEF must represent noun or verb stems, and x and y must represent inflexional endings, with z an ending which modifies the end of the noun or verb stem; or (less probably), the nouns or verbs are ABZ, DEZ in the uninflected form, and the inflexional endings x and y modify the end of the stem. Dr Kober identified several other patterns in groups of three but the same principle covers them all.

The gifted amateur, Michael Ventris, used this, combined with a statistical analysis of the frequency of each sign in various positions, as a starting point for a brilliant decipherment of Linear B. He developed his approach with such skill that in 1951 he was able to set out a majority of the syllabic signs in a grid of five columns of vowels and fifteen lines of consonants, and shortly afterwards succeeded in deciphering sequences of words and showing that the language was an early form of Greek, in fact, Mycenaean Greek.

The Phaistos Disc script

This script, known from one example only, shows several very unusual features. One oddity is the object which bears the writing. This is a terracotta disc about the size of a tea plate, found at Phaistos, and dated to about 1600 BC or a little earlier. It is inscribed spirally on both sides, with very naturalistic pictograms (see plate 7). The text on Face B runs continuously from the centre to the outer rim. On Face A the text likewise runs from the centre as far as the line before the outer rim; here a box drawn across the two outer lines appears to constitute a stop, leaving the rim line to be read independently. Some scholars argue that the inscription runs from the rim to the centre, but this is disputable, since one of the pictograms is a running man, who is only running forwards if the text is read anti-clockwise from the centre outwards. A running-man sign on the rim line of Face A is also running anti-clockwise.

The strangest feature of this writing is that the signs were not made with a stylus but impressed individually with stamps: this makes it a remote precursor of printing. Some signs are stamped inverted or misaligned. The signs are manifestly of pictographic origin; besides the running man already mentioned, there are clear pictures of a head, a head with a cockscomb haircut, a bird, a fish, and what some would take as an animal's pelt and others as an ingot. The following illustration reproduces a section of the text with examples of some of these.

The signs are wholly distinct from those in the Cretan pictographic scripts.

The text on each face is divided by lines into sections containing between two and seven signs, most commonly four or five. This grouping of the signs shows that the system cannot be primarily logographic. The disc bears a total of 241 signs, but the number of different signs is only about 45. The uncertainty of the exact number is because one or two of the signs occur with or without an added oblique line, and if that line was intended as a modifier this could bring the number up to 50. Since an alphabet is most unlikely to have more than forty signs (there are seldom more than 30), the system must be syllabic.

Several people have claimed decipherments, more fantastic than convincing. On a more scientific level, W. Nahm has published a preliminary grammatical analysis, without claiming the ability to translate the document as a whole. Translation is unlikely without the finding of either a bilingual or substantial additional texts in the same script.

Cypriot Scripts

In the middle of the nineteenth century coins and other objects came to light in Cyprus, inscribed in an unknown linear script, written from right to left. The inscriptions showed the script to contain about 54 signs, too many for an alphabet and too few for a logographic system; clearly this writing was in syllograms. The honour of deciphering this script fell to the brilliant pioneer assyriologist George Smith, after the discovery of a bilingual, dating from about 388 BC, which gave the Phoenician equivalent of the Cypriot script.

Over 500 texts in this script are now known, ranging from the eighth to the third centuries BC, with most from the fifth and fourth. George Smith proved that in the majority of texts available to him this script was employed for writing Greek, although it was far from efficient for this purpose. For example, in the Greek language *g*, *k* and *kh* are morphemicially distinct, as are the group *d*, *t*, *th* and the group *b*, *p*, *ph*. But the Cypriot script made no such distinctions: the same sign was used, for example, for *do*, *to* and *tho*. In addition, it was unable to indicate a consonant without a following vowel, and it did not denote nasals before dentals. Thus the word *anthropos*, 'man', had to be written with the syllables *a-to-ro-po-se*. Obviously then, the Cypriot script was not invented for writing Greek. It was therefore not surprising to find that there were some inscriptions in this script which were not in Greek but in an unknown language.

Subsequently, other substantially earlier inscriptions, on clay balls, pottery, copper ingots and clay tablets, were found in Cyprus, mainly at Enkomi, from about 1500 to 1150 BC. Analysis of this script showed that, on the one hand, it was ancestral to the Cypriot script of the first millennium, and, on the other, that it was derived from the linear scripts of Crete. It has therefore become known as Cypro-Minoan. Just over 100 Cypro-Minoan inscriptions are now known, all very brief and none of more than eight signs. The total number of different signs, in addition to symbols for numerals, amounts to 63, indicating that the system is syllabic. As usual with inscriptions of extreme brevity, decipherment is a very difficult task. One scholar has claimed partial success, taking the language as a form of Hittite. A text with a related script, longer than those from Cyprus, occurs on a clay tablet at Ugarit, c.1400 BC, and further such finds would contribute considerably to decipherment.

Proto-Byblian Script

In 1929 archaeologists at Byblos came upon a fragment of a stone stele engraved in an unknown script; some of the signs were clearly of pictorial origin. Subsequent discoveries brought further specimens of the script, so that twelve examples are now known. The total number of distinct signs has been various estimated but was probably about a hundred. The dating is disputed, but was probably between 1800 and 1400 BC.

Some of the signs suggest Egyptian hieroglyphics, although others have become purely linear. In view of the close trade links between Egypt and Byblos since the third millennium, it is not impossible that this script originated under Egyptian influence. Some scholars see this as the ultimate ancestor of the proto-Canaanite and Phoenician alphabets, but the evidence is not compelling.

5

Education

In the modern world no skill is more highly valued than literacy. The word 'education' is normally used in the limited sense of literate education; and the percentage of literate citizens has become a yardstick of the social progress of developing countries. In this high, perhaps exaggerated, esteem of literacy, we are reflecting attitudes of the ancient world. In both Babylonia and Egypt literacy was held in honour, and from both regions the scribes have left us self-admiring descriptions of the importance and dignity of the scribal office. Literary proficiency was so highly regarded that even kings claimed it, or had it attributed to them. Shulgi, for example, a notable Sumerian king of just after 2100 BC, spoke proudly of his literacy:

As a youth, I studied the scribal art in the Tablet-House, from the tablets of Sumer and Akkad;
No one of noble birth could write a tablet as I could.

This remained the royal attitude throughout Mesopotamian history; as late as the seventh century we find the last of the great Assyrian kings, Ashurbanipal, boasting that he had 'explored the entire scribal art, the knowledge of all the experts', and that he could read complicated texts both in Akkadian and in the long dead language Sumerian.

The scribe and scribal education in Egypt

Literacy was a claim equally made in Egypt, both for high officials and for kings, even before the middle of the third millennium. The chief executive of the Third Dynasty king Zoser, the man responsible for building the Step Pyramid, called himself 'Chief of the King's Scribes'. Sneferu, the first king of the Fourth Dynasty soon after 2600 BC, was also literate, for a text speaks of him writing on papyrus. A Fifth Dynasty official quotes a letter of commendation which his king had written with his own hand. The third-millennium Pyramid Texts, carved on the tombs of early Egyptian kings to provide for their wellbeing in the afterlife, contain further evidence of royal literacy, in spells to ensure that the deceased king, as he entered the afterworld, should become the scribe of the god Re^c; this only made sense if it was taken for granted that kings were literate. From over a millennium later, a temple scene at Abydos shows a prince holding a papyrus scroll, and describes him as 'reading out praises'; the prince in question later became the great pharaoh Ramesses II (1290–1224). Scribal equipment figured among the contents of the tomb of Tutankhamun (c. 1340 BC), and Ramesses IV made a special boast of having studied all the texts of the House of Life (pir-ankh, the academy of the scribes).

To be a scribe in Egypt was to hold a position of respect. High officials, such as a chief magistrate, might be content simply to use the title 'scribe'. A Nineteenth Dynasty text recommends the profession of the scribe, and tells how a man of that kind goes out looking sleek, dressed in white, and finds himself greeted by men of standing.

The high conceit which Egyptian scribes had of the importance of their profession was not without some basis, for the scribal office could open the way to the highest posts in the land. The earliest biographical text that we possess is of a Third Dynasty worthy, Methen, who tells us that he began his career as chief scribe of a food depot. From that he graduated to become a local governor and a junior judge. A series of subsequent promotions left him as ruler of a large town, districts in the Delta, parts of the Fayum oasis and one of the nomes, with the final delight of a house covering two acres, set about with trees and orchards and with its own lake.[1]

But not all scribes moved in such exalted circles. In one case it is possible to trace a scribal family from father to son for six generations, and whilst they were men of respectability, administering the people working on the tombs of the New Kingdom kings in the Valley of the Kings near Thebes, they were not of particular distinction. One of them even served as an ordinary workman before succeeding to the office of scribe.

The original creative impulses of the civilizations of Egypt and Mesopotamia did not depend upon writing, but writing quickly followed as one of the consequences of those impulses, and the consolidation and extension of those emerging civilizations rested heavily upon scribal activity. This was not only a matter of recording literature and historical records for posterity; many aspects of those societies could not have operated at all without the services of scribes. Public works and taxation required census lists and other records; the army could not function efficiently without trained personnel to work out its ration requirements; building operations needed scribes to calculate such things as the quantity of earth to be moved, or the amount of stone required and the sizes and shapes to which it was to be cut, or the manpower necessary to move an obelisk: these necessitated instruction in arithmetic and geometry. Communication between the king and his officials, upon which the administration of the state depended, was mainly by letters dictated to scribes; business contracts and court decisions had to be recorded in writing; and international diplomacy required written treaties. An Egyptian scribe might find himself sent on a mission to Syria, and to cope with this he would require a detailed knowledge of the geography of the country. Again, the manifold aspects of religious life—hymns to the gods, prayers and laments, spells and rituals to safeguard against evils— required the services of writing; and the maintenance of the calendar depended upon calculations undertaken by scribes.

In both Mesopotamia and Egypt, scribal training involved a long period of formal education, but our knowledge of details is patchy. Diodorus Siculus transmits a summary of formal education in Egypt in the first century BC:

> *The priests teach their sons two kinds of writing, that which is called 'sacred' and that which has more general application for information. They devote particular attention to surveying and arithmetic. For the river, by changing the countryside in various ways every year, creates all kinds of disputes about boundaries between neighbours, which are not easy to sort out accurately except by a surveyor establishing the facts through his expertise.*[2]

Some of the assumptions Diodorus makes are questionable. He could be understood to imply that knowledge of Egyptian writing was limited to priests, but this was certainly not the case. He also speaks as though the teaching of writing was exclusively from father to son, whereas it is certain that there were schools where formal teaching took place. However, Diodorus was undoubtedly correct in implying that there was a strong hereditary element in the scribal profession. This hereditary element is reflected in a text, the *Instruction of Ptahhotep*,[3] which describes how the ageing vizier of a king of the Fifth Dynasty, in the twenty-fourth century BC, set about training his son to succeed him in his office. But this text is concerned with the general behaviour expected of a high official, not with formal education. There is no implication that the son of a high official received no training until his father took him in hand; on the contrary, the duties of the vizier could not have been carried out without a high standard of literacy, and so the text carries the implicit assumption that the son already possessed the basic skills of reading, writing and numeracy before his father began giving him his final polish.

In Egypt the scribal craft was predominantly a profession for men, but there are occasional references to female scribes. We also know that princesses learnt to write. We have no precise information about the age at which scribal education began[4] but boys were already attending 'the teaching room' (i.e. school) while they were still heavily dependent upon their mothers. We deduce this from a text called *The Maxims of Ani*, which exhorts a man to be good to his mother because, after suckling him as a baby for three years and clearing up his messes, she then put him to 'the teaching room' where he was taught to write. This suggests an age of perhaps as young as four and certainly not more than six.

In the early stages pupils wrote on the cheapest material available, ostraca, that is potsherds and flakes of limestone. The first stages of writing used the simpler hieratic script, not hieroglyphics. The 'teaching room' was strictly a day school, for we learn that the mother waited at home each day for her young son to give him bread and beer. In the New Kingdom at least, school classes were often held outside, to judge by heaps of ostraca bearing exercises of a few lines each, mostly extracts from three particular compositions. The elementary scribal training lasted for four years, after which the trainee scribe went on to more advanced work. Teachers kept their pupils to their tasks by the sanction of corporal punishment: it was said that 'a lad's ear is on his back and he listens when he is beaten'.

Ancient Egyptian sources give us nothing very specific about schools for older pupils, although we know that some cities contained educational institutions, to which men of substance sent their sons. A Middle Kingdom work called *The Satire on Trades* (p. 102) begins with a man sailing south from the Delta to place his son in the scribal school at Memphis among the sons of notables. Since the principal government departments and temples needed administrators and clerks, it is likely that many of them organized the training of suitable boys for this. When the Persians took Egypt over in the late sixth century, king Darius established academies to train his civil service, in continuation of older Egyptian practice; the text describing this specifically says that he only accepted trainees of good family, but this elitism derived from Persian and not Egyptian attitudes; at earlier periods boys of humble origin could and did become scribes, and in a text from the end of the third millennium a king instructs his son: 'Do not prefer the wellborn to the commoner'.

Once settled in their schools, students had to cope with two main tasks: one was to learn certain ancient literary works by heart, and the other was to become competent in writing to a degree at which they could compose letters and official documents. Learning by heart was achieved by the class members reciting aloud in chorus: we have a text which refers to someone's old school friend as 'the man with whom you once used to chant the writings'. Skill in penmanship and drafting documents was acquired by constant practice in writing out texts: the ancients would have applauded Francis Bacon's dictum that 'writing maketh an exact man'. In the New Kingdom period (1554–1080 BC) the texts used for this purpose were mainly of two kinds. Some were documents of recent origin in the form of specimen letters from one scribe to another, obviously useful as models for the real letters that the trainee scribe might one day be required to compose. The other type of practice material consisted of passages from literary works which had their origin in the Middle Kingdom (beginning of the second millennium), and were in a form of Egyptian which by the time of the New Kingdom was no longer the living tongue. To help the trainee scribe master these, there was instruction in ancient grammar, of which relics remain on hieratic ostraca bearing lists of verbal paradigms. Some of these literary texts were manifestly designed to heighten the motivation and increase the self-esteem and group solidarity of the trainee scribes. One such composition, known in modern times as *The Satire on Trades*[5] (although some scholars question whether it had any satirical intent) pointed out how happy was the lot of a scribe compared with what manual workers had to endure; for example,

> *I watched the coppersmith at work at the mouth of his furnace. His fingers were like crocodile's claws. He stank worse than fish offal.*
>
> *The weaver in the workshop is worse off than a woman, (having to crouch) with his knees against his chest, (so that) he cannot breathe. If he shirks his day's weaving, he is beaten with fifty lashes. He has to bribe the doorkeeper with food, to let him see the light of day.*

Other compositions, from the late second millennium, set out to discourage pupils from taking up anything but the scribal profession:

> *You set your mind on working in the fields and neglect texts. Do you not consider how things are with the farmer, when the harvest is taxed? Grubs have taken half the corn, the hippopotamus has eaten from what is left. There are mice in the field and the locust swarm has come. Cattle munch and birds steal. . . . What remains to reach the threshing\floor, the thieves make off with.*
>
> *Now the scribe lands on the bank and wants to register the harvest. His attendants carry sticks, the Nubians [used as police] wield truncheons. They say: 'Hand over corn!' (The farmer answers:) 'There is none here'. He is stretched out and beaten. He is bound and thrown into the water. . . . His wife is bound in his presence. . . . His neighbours abandon them and take to flight.*
>
> *But the scribe organizes the work of everyone. For him there are no taxes, for he pays his dues by writing.*

Let me tell you how the soldier fares. . . . Let me tell you how he goes to Syria, and how he marches over the mountains, his bread and his water carried on his shoulder like the load of an ass. . . . His drink is foul water. . . . If he gets back to Egypt, he is like worm-eaten wood, sick and bedridden.

O scribe, perish the thought that the soldier fares better than the scribe!

These were amongst the texts from which trainee scribes learnt. We do not know how they most commonly wrote their exercises, whether from dictation, from memory, or by copying from written texts, but the last method was certainly customary for at least one work. The work in question was a composition called *Kemyt*, of which there are many copies, evidently the work of learners. At the time these were written, the usual direction of writing was horizontally from right to left, but despite that every single extant copy of *Kemyt* is set out in vertical columns. Had the students been writing from dictation or memory, some of them would have been sure to lapse into the current direction of writing, even if instructed otherwise. That they invariably used the archaic system of vertical columns can only be because they were copying by sight from master documents set out in that form.

This proof of copying by sight in one case does not mean that dictation was never used as a teaching method. Indeed, it must have been an essential part of the scribe's training. There are many scenes in Egyptian art which show an administrator making decisions about assessment and collection of taxes, with a scribe taking his decisions down; scribes could only have done this if they had learnt the skill of writing direct from the spoken word.

For their writing, the scribal students used red and black pigments applied by means of a reed brush. Various materials were available as writing surfaces. We have already noted that the trainee scribe usually wrote on flakes of limestone or pottery sherds, but for more formal occasions writing boards were available. These were slabs of sycamore up to 20 by 15 inches in size, with a skim coating of gypsum plaster, from which an exercise could be rubbed off to allow reuse. The most expensive and prestigious writing material, papyrus, would only have been available in scroll form to expert scribes, although learners might have been given small pieces for practice.

Major states needed communication with other countries, and this required interpreters. Some Egyptian scribes must certainly have been trained for this; there is little direct evidence from earlier periods, but for the first millennium we know that the Egyptian king Psammetichus sent boys to live with Greek settlers in the Delta to train them as interpreters. We also find mention of the teaching of Egyptian to Nubians, Syrians, and other foreigners. Interpreters accompanied the army, and from the Eighteenth Dynasty, there were Greek interpreters at the Pharaoh's court.

In the second millennium, the language of international communication was Akkadian cuneiform, used far beyond the region in which it was a language of everyday speech. It was, for example, used in correspondence between Egypt and the Hittites. Either both countries had scribes highly competent in Akkadian cuneiform, or (less probably) both courts employed bilingual Babylonian scribes. One letter to the Pharaoh, exceptionally written in Hittite, addresses the recipient scribe directly and requests a reply in the same language, indicating that some Egyptian scribes could both read and write Hittite. A literary composition of the thirteenth century attests the knowledge of foreign languages amongst Egyptian scribes; the writer takes the opportunity of working in odd phrases to demonstrate his mastery of Canaanite. For example, after describing how the scribe of the commissariat arranges provisions for an expeditionary force sent into Palestine to crush a rebellion, he attributes to the Beduin looking on, the comment *sopher yodea!*, Canaanite for 'a shrewd scribe!'.

Scribal education in Mesopotamia

Already in the second quarter of the third millennium, some kind of formal scribal education must have been taking place in Mesopotamia, for tablets of this period found at Ur contain word-lists of a type which later developed into standard material for scribal training. Formal scribal education may have been operating even earlier, since tablets from Erech, from the beginning of the third millennium, include texts which seem to be ancestral forms of those word-lists.

As in Egypt, most scribes at all periods were men. But female scribes are occasionally mentioned, and the idea of females practising in this profession was quite acceptable, for epithets like 'the scribe who knows the tablets' and 'supreme scribe of the underworld' were applied to some goddesses. Some third-millennium women, particularly royal women, were literate, and one, the daughter of Sargon of Agade, who was high-priestess of the Moon-god in Ur, gained distinction as a major poet, and some of her compositions have been preserved.

As one might expect from the difficulty of the cuneiform system, literacy outside scribes and administrators was not widespread. In Sumer just before 2000 BC, king Shulgi, who boasted of his own literacy and had himself written some hymns, obviously did not expect the lower classes to be able to read, for he gave instructions that scribes should read his hymns out to singers so that they could perform them.

At some periods, when scribes signed documents, they added the names and professions of their fathers after their own names, and from this we learn something about the class to which they belonged. At the end of the third millennium they were mainly sons (or, rarely, daughters) of well-to-do people, such as city governors, temple administrators, army officers, tax officials or priests. We also find references to poor orphan boys being adopted by generous patrons, who, as the height of their kindness, put them to learn the scribal art.

In some instances the fathers were themselves designated scribes, and it is probable that all men who held senior professional positions had received some scribal training, and might, in the absence of any other title, call themselves scribes. Indeed, one distinguished American scholar, Albrecht Goetze, made the plausible suggestion that the Sumerian term *dub.sar*, literally 'scribe', was the equivalent of 'Esquire' or 'BA', applied to any educated man, and did not necessarily imply that the person so designated actually specialized in scribal functions as a profession.

The first Mesopotamian schools of which we have positive knowledge were two established by king Shulgi at Nippur and at Ur in the last century of the third millennium. But for Shulgi to be able to refer to them without further explanation, they must have been well-known before this. It has often been assumed that there were schools attached to temples, but this has not been proved, although it is not impossible. But wherever the finding-place of literary tablets can be related to specific buildings, most have come from private houses.

The Sumerian name for school or scribal academy was *edubba*, literally 'Tablet House'. Most of our direct information about scribal education within the *edubba* comes from texts from the first half of the second millennium, but the circumstances those texts reflect must already have applied in the third.

The head of a school was in Sumerian called either 'Father of the Tablet house' or *ummia*, which had the implication 'expert'. If one requires a current Anglo-American equivalent, Headmaster probably comes nearest. He was held in high respect, and when he honoured parents with a visit, he was received with great deference. One text has a pupil say to his Headmaster: 'You have opened my eyes as though I were a puppy; you have formed humanity within me.' There were specialist masters for Sumerian, Mathematics ('scribe of counting') and Surveying ('scribe of the field'), but for routine matters pupils seemed to have received their instruction mainly from someone called literally 'Big Brother'. 'Big Brother', who had less authority than the Headmaster and assistant masters, probably corresponded to the pupil-teachers who used to assist in British schools—i.e. he was a good pupil who had graduated and stayed on as an apprentice teacher. The duties of 'Big Brother' included preparing tablets for the junior pupils to copy, correcting their copies, and hearing the texts they had learnt by heart.

From 2600 BC onwards, we find, from such sites as Erech, Ur, Shuruppak, Nippur and Abu Salabikh, cuneiform extracts from standard works, which are commonly known as 'school texts'. Sometimes the copy is the work of an expert, making this term a misnomer, but some are manifestly student exercises. This is obviously the case when one finds a tablet bearing the same text copied out several times by different hands, or with a piece of a literary text on one side and mathematical problems on the other. Tablet collections in modern museums contain many examples of student exercises, in some of which an expert's original is accompanied by the learner's copy. Typically the teacher's text was on the left side, and the learner's on the right. Occasionally one finds a pupil's exercise with the teacher's corrections, and even the whole thing crossed out by the exasperated teacher.

The evidence of these students' copies suggests that the curriculum was largely a matter of endless copying out of exercises, and memorizing. Amongst the texts were long extracts from what we call 'synonym lists', in effect dictionaries. These might give the Akkadian equivalents for Sumerian terms, or explain rare Akkadian words or vocabulary from foreign languages. In some respects they had similarities with Roget's *Thesaurus*. Here is the transliteration of a brief extract from such a text:[6]

e-me	KA×ME	*li-ša-nu*	[tongue]
nu-un-du-un	KA×NUN	*šap-tu*	[lip]
su-um	KA×SA	*zi-iq-nu*	[beard]
mu-un-su-ub	KA×X	*li-e-tu*	[cheek]
ú-su-ug	KA×Ú	*ú-suk-ku*	[cheek]
....	....	....	....
gu-ú	KA×GAR	*a-ka-lu*	[to eat]
ni-ga	KA×GAR	*ú-kul-tum*	[provisions]
ša-ga-ar	KA×GAR	*bu-ú-ru*	[hunger]
na-ag	KA×A	*ša-tu-ú*	[to drink]
im-mi-in	KA×A	*ṣu-ú-mu*	[thirst]

Restorations from parallel texts are not indicated. The different type founts simply represent the conventions of modern assyriologists, who use capital Roman to identify a Sumerian sign, lower case Roman to indicate the Sumerian word which the sign denotes, and italics to indicate Akkadian meanings.

The second column gives the Sumerian ideogram. A writing of the form KA×A denotes 'this is the sign KA [ideogram for 'mouth'] with the sign A [ideogram for 'water'] inserted'. In this case nag (written syllabically na-ag); and immin (written im-mi-in) are two different Sumerian words which KA×A can represent, and *šatû* (written syllabically *ša-tu-ú*) and *ṣūmu* (written *ṣu-ú-mu*) are the Akkadian equivalents of nag and immin respectively. Texts of this kind and of the class illustrated on page 109 have been invaluable in the modern understanding of Sumerian and Akkadian texts.

Other types of texts copied included model letters, omens, and texts about school life. Clearly, the pupils had to keep hard at it: in one text a pupil reports on his activities:

> *This is the monthly scheme of my school attendance:*
> *My free days are three each month;*
> *My religious holidays are three each month;*
> *For twenty-four days each month*
> *I must be in school. How long they are!*

Some of the pupils may well have found the system tedious and harsh; mention amongst the school's personnel of 'a man in charge of the whip' suggests rigid discipline, a conclusion supported by reference to corporal punishment and boys being locked up for bad behaviour.

Many of the texts which the pupils had to learn and copy out were long lists categorizing various aspects of the world; they might cover almost anything, from lists of deities to lists of trees, countries, animals or minerals. Some of the lists gave the equivalents in Akkadian, and sometimes other languages, of Sumerian words, making them in effect the first dictionaries. There were also lists of grammatical forms to assist with the mastering of the Sumerian language.

However, the most interesting school texts known to us are those in which the scribes themselves gave a picture of school life, perhaps with an element of satire and exaggeration. The most instructive of these is a text which represents a qualified scribe reminiscing about his school days.[7] It begins with someone asking him: 'Son of the tablet house, where did you go when you were young?' 'I went to the tablet house [i.e. school],' he replied, and he then proceeds to give an account of a typical day. He says:

> *I recited my tablet, ate my food, prepared my new tablet and wrote it out and completed it. . . . In the afternoon my exercise tablets were brought to me. When school finished, I went home, went indoors, and found my father sitting there. I recited my tablet to him and he was highly pleased.*

But things did not always run so smoothly. On another morning, he tells us,

When I got up in the morning, I went to my mother and said to her: 'Give me my food, I want to go to school.' My mother gave me two rolls and I set off.

Unhappily, despite his hurry, the boy was late, and was rewarded with a beating. This was only the first of several. The Headmaster beat him for a bad exercise of the previous day and he earned further beatings for being untidily dressed in the street and for misbehaving in class. Things came to such a pass that the boy urged his father to take steps to sweeten the Headmaster. The father duly invited the Headmaster to dinner, treated him with great honour, and expressed his gratitude for what the Headmaster was doing for his boy. As had been hoped, the Headmaster responded graciously, and, all charm, foretold a great future for the boy. (When I was teaching at Baghdad University in 1956–7, I encountered a remarkably similar approach in respect of one of my worst students.)

Another section of these texts about schoolboys shows the boy's father pointing out all the advantages he had given his son, and upbraiding him for his idleness and ingratitude.

Why did the expert scribes compose works like this for their pupils? Part of the object was no doubt to set before the pupils how fortunate they were in comparison with those who had not been sent to the *edubba*, and to instil in them a due sense of gratitude to their parents and of responsible conduct towards their teachers. But the scribes were also cleverly framing the texts to serve another purpose. An abridged translation of the beginning of one of the texts will demonstrate what they were doing. Brackets are used to identify the speakers, which are implied but not explicitly stated in the original Sumerian:

[Father]	*Where have you been?*
[Son]	*I haven't been anywhere.*
[Father]	*If you haven't been anywhere, why are you loafing around? Go to school, stand before your headmaster, recite your exercise, open your satchel, write your tablet, let Big Brother write your new tablet for you. . . . Now then, do you know what I said?*
[Son]	*I know, I'll tell you.*
[Father]	*Now then, repeat it to me.*
[Son]	*I'll repeat it to you.*
[Father]	*Come along, tell it to me.*
[Son]	*You told me to go to school, recite my exercise, open my satchel, write my tablet, have Big Brother write my new tablet for me . . .*

What the writer of this text has done here (and a similar device occurs in other texts) is to invent an ingenious and painless way of teaching grammar. He has achieved this by providing an amusing framework in which set words and phrases undergo changes of grammatical form, for example, indicative to imperative, second person to first person, and direct speech to indirect speech.

Sumerian was probably dead as a spoken language by the early second millennium, but it had enormous prestige, like Latin in our own culture until very recently, and a main task in the schools was to learn to read and write Sumerian. One of the teaching methods was to give the pupils lists of grammatical forms to copy. These were intelligently devised, with translations into Akkadian, to show how the Sumerian language conjugated its verbs or declined its nouns. The following is an abridged extract from a text of this kind:

Sumerian	Akkadian	Meaning
te.a.na	ṭe-ḫi-šum	Approach him!
in.na.te.e.en	te-et-ḫi-šu-um	You approached him
ba.an.na.te	i-ṭe-ḫi-šum	He will approach him
ba.an.na.te.en	e-ṭe-ḫi-šum	I shall approach him
in.na.te.e.en	te-eṭ-ḫi-šum	You approached him
gub.ba	i-zi-iz	Stand!
ga.gub	lu-zi-iz	Let me stand
he.gub	li-zi-iz	Let him stand
al.gub	i-za-az	He will stand
al-gub-bé.en	a-za-az	I shall stand
nu.gub	u-la i-za-az	He will not stand

Scribes also needed to learn the technical terminology for the many crafts that formed part of ancient life. As a case in point, there are scribal texts about glass-making. These give the terms for the various ingredients and processes, but omit many practical details essential for the actual making of glass. But it was the terminology and not the practical glass-making which the scribes came to think of as the important thing. In course of time the attitude grew up amongst scribes in both Mesopotamia and Egypt that knowledge consisted not in practical activities incorporating observation and experiment but in the texts they copied and transmitted. This became a serious obstacle to scientific progress. In medicine, for example (p. 255), the Egyptians had made considerable advances by the middle of the third millennium, but the texts incorporating this knowledge became loaded with the unchallengeable authority of scripture and blocked any attempt to go beyond it. Mesopotamians made less spectacular early discoveries in this field, but such progress as they did make had, by the second millennium, equally become enshrined in authoritative texts which blocked any further advance. The same principle applied to every branch of knowledge; in geography, for example, Mesopotamian scribes in the third millennium had drawn up lists relating different mountain ranges to different forest species. Scribes went on copying and recopying these lists into the second and first millennia, long after the identity of some of the mountain ranges had been forgotten and some of the forests had been destroyed, and never with any attempt to check the information physically and bring it up to date.

We have no texts which list the curriculum of Mesopotamian scribal schools, but we can infer its main contents from the tasks which trained scribes might be called upon to do.

Firstly, they must have learnt to write cuneiform in various scripts. Signs chiselled into stone took rather a different form from those impressed into clay tablets, and even for clay tablets the scribes would have to learn to write more than one script, since at all periods there were distinct forms for Babylonian and Assyrian. There were also archaic scripts which the high fliers amongst scribes would have to master; ancient texts written in such scripts might turn up in a library and need to be copied and transposed, and it was regular procedure in repairing an ancient temple to hunt out and read the inscriptions which the builders of old had buried in the foundations, written in a script of long ago. Occasionally scribes might be called upon to use their skill in archaic texts for less reputable reasons. Temples sometimes had a document drawn up and then 'discovered', to support a false claim for a grant of land or exemption from taxes supposedly awarded by a king long past.

Amongst subjects with which scribal students had to deal, in addition to the Sumerian language and copying texts, the most important were the writing of legal and administrative documents, and mathematics, including geometry. Mathematics involved learning to solve problems, of a kind which might be relevant in later duties, for example, calculating the amount of earth required to build a ramp for a siege.

There were also technical processes which scribes needed to learn, in particular, tablet production, from raw materials to the baking of inscribed documents intended for libraries. The basic material was clean clay; this had to be wetted to the appropriate degree and kneaded to the correct consistency. Often ground limestone was added to improve the texture: in some Babylonian tablets the proportion of limestone is so high (up to 30 per cent) that a tablet fragment effervesces violently in dilute hydrochloric acid. Various techniques were used for preparing a tablet from the kneaded clay mixture. Sometimes the clay was rolled out into a long thin cylinder; from this lengths were cut off, rolled up lengthwise and pressed out into a slightly convex oblong. (The process is put beyond doubt by the spiral coiling visible inside some broken tablets). The scribe would then run a concave terracotta cylinder, about the size of a thimble, along the edges to shape them; cylinders of this kind were found with tablets at Nimrud in 1952. Another method of production, especially for larger tablets, was to spread a final surface of fine clay over a core of coarse clay. Tablets for preservation in libraries were often baked, a process which required careful control to avoid cracking.

We have evidence of scribes at work in these processes from an early second-millennium building at Isin in Babylonia. One room, evidently a workshop, contained clay in different stages from mere lumps to blank tablets ready for use. In another room the inscribed tablets were filed. Finds elsewhere show tablets stored either in earthenware jars or on shelves.

Clay was not the only material used for cuneiform writing by professional scribes. Also available were writing boards of wood or ivory, covered with a coating of wax, sometimes hinged as a triptych, or more accurately polyptych, since there could be more than three leaves; this device was later taken over by the Romans. On these the writing could be erased for reuse. The handling of these materials was another skill the scribes must have learnt at some point in their training.

Scribes outside Mesopotamia and Egypt

South Mesopotamia and Egypt were the regions where the scribal tradition developed and the main sources of information for it. But the tradition spread, and we can sometimes see scribal schools at work in other parts of the ancient Near East. Everywhere where cuneiform writing came into use, the scribal tradition followed. The earliest major use of cuneiform outside Mesopotamia was at the city of Ebla in north Syria in the second half of the third millennium, and there we find quantities of the usual kind of lexical texts, sometimes adapted to take account of the local West Semitic language. Lexical and literary texts found at Boghazkoi, the site of the second-millennium Hittite capital, show a scribal tradition there also. One scholar interprets a scene on a late Hittite stone relief as showing a young prince holding an exercise book, but it is more likely a writing board.

There was also abundant evidence for a scribal tradition on the coast of Syria in fourteenth-century Ugarit. There we find, in the 34-roomed mansion of a certain Rap'anu, a high royal official, a library with cuneiform lexical texts constituting virtual dictionaries for scribes. Obviously Rap'anu owed at least part of his eminence to the fact that he was highly literate. Some of Rap'anu's texts contained Hurrian equivalents of Sumerian and Akkadian terms; presumably these were required for administrative purposes. The following gives a few simple lines of one such:

Sumerian	Hurrian	Akkadian	Meaning
šà	ti-iš-ni	lib-bu	[midst]
šà-bi	"-di	lib-ba-šú	[its midst]
šà-bi-se	"-di-e	ana lib-bi-šú	[to its midst]
šà-bi-se in-gar	"-ki-e	ana lib-bi-šú iš-kun	[he put to its midst]
....			
uš-sag	zi-ia-ri	šid-du pu-u-tum	[principal side (of a field, etc.)]
uš-gid-da	"ki-ra-i	šid-du ar-ku	[long side]
uš-ku-da	"aš-ḫu-we	šid-du ku-ru-u	[short side]

The ditto marks represent pairs of vertical strokes, used in cuneiform with that sense.

Another substantial library was found in Ugarit in the house of a person whose title identified him as the chief priest (*rb khnm*, exactly the same term as in Hebrew). Understandably, its contents were mainly mythological and religious texts, but the presence of exercise tablets shows that the library was also the centre of a scribal school.

There was some use of cuneiform Akkadian on clay tablets in Palestine, at least in the half century after 1400 BC, and one scholar thought he had found evidence for a school there, based on a letter which he interpreted as sent to a parent in Shechem by a teacher whose fees were in arrears. Unfortunately, this interpretation was based on a misunderstanding of several crucial words.

It is noteworthy that the most extensively used script of Cretan origin, Linear B, never advanced significantly beyond economic and administrative applications, a stage which both Egypt and Mesopotamia had passed by 2600 BC. There is also very little evidence for scribal schools. Either the absence of more sophisticated writing made scribal schools of minimal importance, or conversely the little importance attached to scribal schools discouraged the development of writing for wider purposes.

There must, however, have been some form of training for the writing of Linear B, even if not in the form of schools propagating a scribal tradition as in Mesopotamia and Egypt. One piece of evidence for scribal education, not hitherto recognized as such, comes from a Linear B inscription found at Pylos. A leading authority on Linear B describes the test in question as 'the most disgraceful piece of handwriting to have come down to us', basing this condemnation on the large number of erasures, corrections, omissions and misshapen signs it contains. Puzzled at all these defects, he suggests that they arose because the writer was taking the minutes of an 'unusually stormy meeting' to pick victims for human sacrifice. It could be that if the Senior Common Room of a British university had occasion to select a victim for human sacrifice they would deliberate on it in a stormy committee, but that was not the way of the ancient world: decisions on such matters were made directly by the gods themselves, by omens. The scribal imcompetence on this particular tablet gives it away for what it is—a student exercise. There must therefore have been some kind of scribal training at Pylos.

6

Living in Cities

Cities were not synonymous with city-states. A city was a heavily populated settlement, typically of a hundred acres upwards, characterized socially by a complex economic structure and loyalties based on the urban community rather than the tribe, and physically by public buildings and a strong perimeter defence wall. A city-state was a unitary administrative region which might be as large as an average English county and contain several cities.

It was in south Mesopotamia that cities began, and it was there that the greatest concentration was always found in the pre-classical world. North Mesopotamia, Syria, Anatolia and parts of western Iran all developed some large cities, but a far greater proportion of the population in these regions continued to live in villages outside the administration of a city than in south Mesopotamia.

Egyptologists differ as to the situation in Egypt. Some argue that urbanization was very late to develop there, and regard what we think of as cities there as cult-centres and administrative headquarters, rather than concentrations of population. It is not disputed that some places, such as Memphis and Heliopolis, were the focus of their area, but the issue is whether or not they had a large residential population. Did the majority of the local agricultural population live in villages on their land and come into the urban centre for festivals, or did they live in the urban centre, and walk out each day to their land, as they certainly did in south Mesopotamia? John A. Wilson, a major authority on early Egypt, concluded that all communities in early Egypt remained 'agricultural villages of greater or less degree', and expressed the view that it is not until the middle of the second millennium that Egypt had any city, in the modern sense. The opposing view is presented by Barry J. Kemp,[1] who points to the clear archaeological evidence for the existence of walled towns at several places in Upper Egypt well before the end of the third millennium. But urban life and agricultural background were not mutually incompatible. Specialization of labour certainly occurred widely, but down to the first millennium the typical inhabitant of ancient Egypt or ancient Mesopotamia (and other lands) was a farmer or a shepherd or a cowherd. He might live in a city, but his gods and his rituals were concerned mainly with the fertility of the land and the fecundity of the flocks and herds, and much of the legal system was concerned with rights over land.

Ancient cities everywhere lived by their agriculture. If an enemy gained control of the city's fields, that city was doomed. We see this with the fate of Megiddo in 1468 BC, when an Egyptian army arrived at the time of wheat harvest and took the lot, 450,000 bushels in all. The city was starved into surrender within seven months.

As cities developed in Mesopotamia, they began to take on a pattern which was clearly not the result of random growth. Archaeologists, poring over the layout of ancient cities and noticing such features as the presence of squares or the grouping of buildings into quarters, sometimes treat them as the beginning of town planning. I have even noticed a case where a long alleyway a mere four feet wide was spoken of in such terms. But these things were not town planning. There was no town planning in third-millennium Mesopotamia in the sense that someone had deliberately thought out a scheme for the different quarters and streets: the pattern which developed, although it sometimes looks deliberately organized, was a secondary consequence of other factors, mainly social stratification. The power of the ruler, and the growing wealth of the temple, were reflected in major building complexes which gave the city a clearly defined centre. Temple officials would naturally tend to develop a kind of close near the temple, and merchants would correspondingly set up an enclave in the area where trading was most active, probably not far from where trading ships anchored on the river. The plan of the city in early Mesopotamia was thus an organic outgrowth from the form in which society was developing, not an imposed design.

There are a few possible hints of conscious town planning in third-millennium Egypt. The hieroglyphic sign for town, $\oplus$, appears to represent an enclosure in which two straight roads intersect to divide the enclosed area into quarters; if the sign was anything more than a stylized representation, it could imply that the Egyptians thought of a town as a settlement planned in regular form, and certainly the early towns at Hierakonpolis and El Kab were oval or circular in outline.[2] Archaeological excavation shows the workmen's village at Kahun to have been laid out on a regular grid, and the same was true of the corresponding housing units at El Amarna and Deir el Madineh.[3] These were of course large housing estates and not cities. The city of El Amarna, built just after

1400 BC, shows some degree of planning, in that it was based on three roads running roughly parallel with the river and each other.[4] The buildings were in several well-defined sectors related to the roads, but beyond that there was little evidence of overall town planning, and the considerations against drawing too far-reaching conclusions from a degree of regularity perhaps apply as much here as to early Mesopotamian cities.

If Memphis really was built as a capital from scratch by Menes when the two former kingdoms of Upper and Lower Egypt were unified, and if, as tradition has it, the work involved the damming and diversion of the Nile, this was certainly an artificial planned creation. But we do not know this as a fact. What Menes planned and built may have been no more than a fortified palace, around which an administrative city and cult-centre gradually grew up in the following centuries.

For the boldest claims of conscious town planning in the third millennium we have to turn to the cities of the Indus Valley civilization. Sir Mortimer Wheeler, who excavated Mohenjo-daro, held that, not later than 2300 BC, the street plan was set out on a grid. According to him, there were broad streets running north to south, crossed by others at right angles, forming blocks of about 400 by 200 yards; these were subdivided by lanes parallel to the main streets. But not everyone agrees. Later archaeologists say that there is no proof of the supposed grid pattern, and allege that the only basis for Sir Mortimer's conclusions was a single street running north to south, helped out by a good deal of imagination. Something deceptively like a grid pattern, they say, could come about without any central planning. For example, there might be a tradition that houses should be orientated in a certain direction (compare the traditional layout of a church with its long axis east to west), and this in itself would produce a striking regularity.[5]

But this argument ignores how human beings actually behave. Firstcomers may well build houses on a traditional layout, well spaced, but without a strong authority in a city, squatters will quickly seize any empty spaces to build temporary shelters which eventually become permanent houses; and owners of the older houses will infill with extensions. Without planning in some form, the layout at Mohenjo-daro in its heyday would have been much more irregular than excavation shows it to have been; even if Sir Mortimer Wheeler's grid plan owed something to his imagination, there is far more regularity in the layout of the buildings in relation to each other and to minor streets than would be compatible with random building. What happened in the final phase of Mohenjo-daro reinforces this conclusion; then the layout degenerated into an amorphous cluster of hovels. It was no less difficult in an ancient

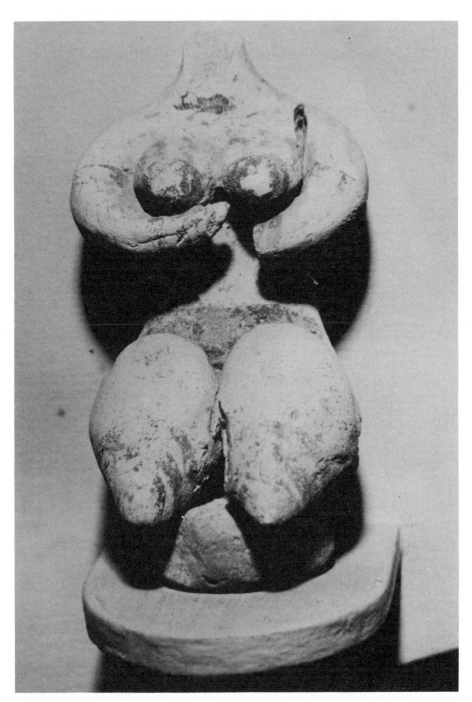

1 Prehistoric fertility figurine

2 **Above** *Mosque inside ruined church inside ruined Egyptian temple at Luxor*

3 **Below** *Step pyramid at Saqqara*

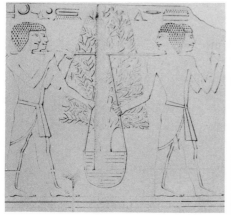

4 Transplanting a myrrh tree from Punt to Egypt

5 Houses on stilts in Punt

6 The Queen of Punt

7 *The Phaistos Disc*

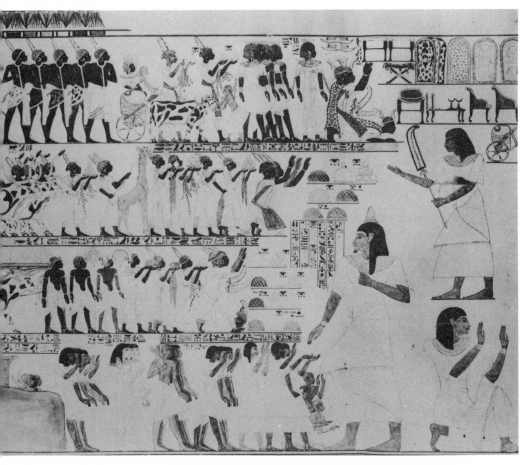

8 Delivery of tribute from Nubia

9 *From the tomb of Kemsit: delivery of products from the owner's estate*

10 Tablet inscribed in Minoan Linear B

11 Part of a Predynastic slate palette, showing symbols of captured Egyptian towns

12 Egyptian slate palette, c. 3000 BC; King Na℉mer conquers his enemies

13 Excavated site of Indus Valley city Lothal, showing evidence of town planning

14 Showing accuracy of masonry in blocks of the Great Pyramid

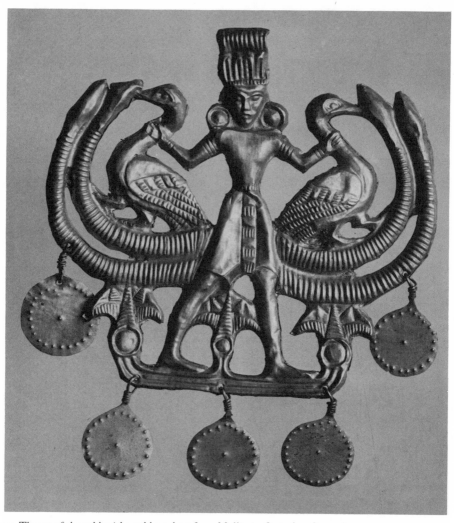

15 The art of the goldsmith: gold pendant from Mallia in Crete (c. 1650 BC)

16 The stele bearing Hammurabi's law code

17 **Above** *Palm trees in natural habitat*

18 **Below** *Palm trees under cultivation*

19 **Above** *The Great Sphinx of Giza*

20 **Below** *Remains of the ziggurat of Borsippa, possibly the original Tower of Babel*

21 **Above** *Colossi near Luxor*

22 **Below** *The enclosure of Etemenanki and Esagila in Babylon (Reconstruction by E. Unger)*

24 **Above** *Letter to the king in Assyrian cuneiform, eighth century* BC

23 **Left** *Snake symbol on the temple of the Yezidis (miscalled 'Devil Worshippers') in north Iraq*

25 Funerary furniture: the chair of Tutankhamun, showing the pharaoh and his queen

town than in a modern one to prevent encroachment upon empty land; and therefore the degree of regularity shown at Mohenjo-daro—even though less than Sir Mortimer claimed—points to a central authority with some concept of a town plan and willing and able to prevent the landless or greedy from building on empty public spaces. When in the early seventh century BC Sennacherib rebuilt Nineveh as a planned city with improved streets and at least one wide boulevard, the likelihood of encroachment was so real that the king made it a capital offence (see pp. 120f.).

Evidence on town planning from other cities of the Harappan civilization is not wholly consistent. Lothal certainly shows a regular plan (plate 13), but one of the more recently excavated Harappan sites, Banawali, undoubtedly had roads which were neither straight nor laid out even approximately on a grid. But this city was on the eastern fringe of the Harappan cultural area, and it may have been subject to other influences than Harappan.

One of the great advantages of life in cities was security. The city organization gave the citizen protection from violence against the person and from economic exploitation: dwellers in cities were much freer than people tied as serfs to the estate of a great landowner or a temple estate. A comparison of the lot of the city dweller with that of the peasant in the countryside makes this clear.

Everywhere, in the course of time, more land went to the temple and more to wealthy officials. It happened in Mesopotamia, it happened in Egypt, where royal estates and temple estates came to control the lives of tens of thousands of peasants, and Isaiah castigated the same evil in Judah:

> Woe unto them that join house to house, that lay field to field, till there be no place, that they may be placed alone in the midst of the earth! (5:8)

With two classes of winner, there had to be losers, and the losers were the peasants in the villages. They either became serfs tied to the land, or they were dispossessed completely and had to serve as hireling labourers. But in the cities there was substantial specialization in labour, not only of administrators and skilled craftsmen such as jewellers and metalworkers, but also of humbler occupations such as weavers, laundrymen, butchers, makers of sun-dried bricks, ferrymen, gardeners and tenders of date orchards, and so on, and this gave opportunities by which those who had lost their land might live as hired labourers.

The city also gave its citizens protection from external attack. In outlying regions villages were always liable to raids from outside the country, and even well inside the countries villagers were liable to the depredations of passing troops; as an illustration of this we find an Egyptian Old Kingdom military administrator boasting that he was able to prevent his troops from extorting food or clothing from the civil population;[6] the implication is that there were other military administrators whose troops were not under such tight control.

Because of these factors, people felt a deep emotional attachment to their cities. When Ur was devastated at the end of the third millennium, a poet expressed the current feeling in a lamentation, in which he showed by his enumeration of the different parts of the city—its encircling wall, its great gate, its roads and avenues, its houses, its temples, the places where the citizenry were wont to take part in games and festivals—that every feature was dear to him. In the biblical Song of Solomon, the lover can find nothing finer than a city with which to compare his sweetheart: 'Thou art beautiful, O my love, as Tirzah, comely as Jerusalem' (6:4), and the psalmist's love of Jerusalem is warm with religious fervour: 'Pray for the peace of Jerusalem: they shall prosper that love thee. Peace be within thy walls, and prosperity within thy palaces' (Psalm 122:6–7).

Ancient town plans

We have a contemporary plan of an ancient city. A cuneiform map of the city of Nippur, in the middle of Babylonia, from about 1500 BC, shows that someone was interested in its layout, although the interest may have been military. The map, drawn to scale, shows the city bounded to the southwest by the Euphrates, which formed a formidable first line of defence; other city walls were protected by moats. One side of the tablet is broken away, so that the line of the wall on that side is lost, but three walls still shown contain between them seven gates. The layout of the city was far from square, as two of its walls joined at an acute angle, and the walls were far from straight: the line of the southwest wall was dictated by the Euphrates, and the others presumably by the immediate terrain. In addition to the walls and waterways, which include a canal running through the middle of the city, the map shows some of the principal temples, and also a park, at the southern end of the city where two of the walls met. No ordinary houses are marked on the map, nor certain public buildings which we know existed. If we knew why some buildings were shown and not others, we might understand the purpose for which the map was produced. One suggestion, based on the way in which the map emphasizes the walls and gates, is that it was prepared for defence against an expected attack, but it is difficult to see how it could have helped in that, since the map could have told the native defenders nothing that they did not already know from long residence in the city. It would have been of much more use to people planning an attack.

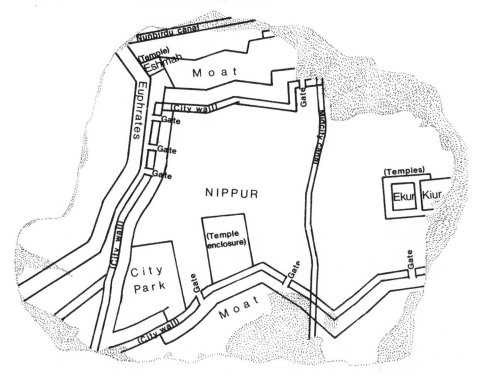

The Nippur Map, c.1500 BC, with translation of main features originally labelled in cuneiform (bracketed words not on original)

Our best pre-classical account of the planning of a city comes from the Assyrian king Sennacherib. He tells how he rebuilt Nineveh at the beginning of the seventh century, concentrating upon his palace, the city's defences and its park land. In his account, which he left in slightly different versions on several monuments, he speaks first of the venerable antiquity of Nineveh, and then says of his royal predecessors,[7]

> No one among them had set his mind or given thought to widening the site of the city, to building a wall, to straightening the streets, to digging canals or planting orchards. Nor had anyone considered applying his skill to the palace therein, where the private quarters of my royal residence were too small and their workmanship was not in good taste. But I, Sennacherib, king of the world, king of Assyria—it came into my mind to perform that task in accordance with the will of the gods.

He used conquered peoples as a pool of slave labour. Not only was the old palace too small and in poor taste, but also it had been damaged by the repeated flooding of a stream that ran through the middle of the city. He diverted the stream, pulled down the old palace and built a larger and more splendid one. He sent out prospectors into the mountains to discover new sources of large timber and alabaster. He personally devised (so he claimed) an improved method of casting large bronze statues. He provided a safe water supply for his palace, not from streams but from wells, raising it by buckets fixed on an endless bronze chain turned by a winch. He more than doubled the size of his city by enclosing new land, making its circumference over six miles, and round it he built a great inner wall with fifteen gates. Beyond, an outer wall stood sentinel, defended with a moat some 150 feet wide. It left the Tigris north of the city, swung round it to the east, and rejoined the river at the south: Nineveh was the strongest defended city of antiquity. Some of the additional land taken into the city boundaries, Sennacherib allotted to the citizens in two-acre sections for orchards, and the rest he made into a great wildlife park, part of it marsh, where he encouraged colonizing by birds, wild pigs and other animals. This provision of open spaces within cities was typical of regions where geography made it possible, particularly Mesopotamia. Some open spaces were doubtless busy market squares, but (as laws make clear) others were so secluded that a woman might be in danger of being raped there.

In his new park, Sennacherib planted all kinds of foreign timber trees, aromatic plants, and cotton bushes, and managed his plantations as a source of building materials and cotton for weaving. To provide the water which this enterprise needed, Sennacherib cut canals to tap mountain streams thirty miles away. Remains of a massive aqueduct, part of this major engineering achievement, still stand. A similar system brought water to the city of Arbail (now Erbil). Inside Nineveh, Sennacherib enlarged its squares, pulled down buildings to let light into alleys and narrow streets, straightened some streets and widened others to make a main ceremonial avenue ninety-three feet wide; as paving for this he probably used limestone blocks, as he certainly did for his palace courtyards. Remains of a similar main avenue leading to the acropolis were found twenty miles further south at the ninth century capital Calah (Genesis 10:11–12); the surface of that road was cobbled. Sennacherib was proud of his new avenue and determined to preserve it uncluttered:

I widened its streets as a route for the royal processional way. . . . In order that the royal processional way should not in after days be reduced in width, I had markers made to stand facing each other. I fixed the width of the royal processional way at 93 ft. . . . If ever any person living in the city pulls down his old house and builds a new one, and the foundation of that house encroaches on the royal processional way, they shall hang that man upon a stake over his own house.

The final sentence contains Sennacherib's only mention of citizen's housing, but it is sufficient to show that, provided they kept clear of public land, citizens were free to build their dwellings wherever they wished, and to whatever plan.

In various sites, archaeologists have found many impressive houses. For example, excavation on the island of Thera, a site of second-millennium Minoan civilization, revealed town houses of two or three storeys, and in the Diyala region in third-millennium Mesopotamia there were spacious houses with identifiable lavatories, consisting of a brick platform with a wide slit. And paintings in tombs of Egyptian notables show fine houses set in a garden with a small ornamental lake and a surrounding of trees. But buildings of this kind were not the houses of ordinary people: these were the dwellings of a well-to-do minority—priests, scribes, administrators, courtiers, great landowners, merchants. The houses of ordinary peasants, who formed the mass of the population everywhere, were very simple one-storey structures of one or two rooms, with a minimum of equipment. The building material would depend upon what was locally available; in Egypt and Mesopotamia it was mudbrick, built into the kind of peasant hut, called *serifah*, still common in Iraq up to the middle of the twentieth century AD.

Water supply and sewage disposal

Writing on ancient history is flawed if it ignores three physiological facts basic to human life: humans need water to survive; human communities need a clean water supply to flourish; human beings produce potentially harmful excretions. The health of the community is directly linked to its ability to dispose of human waste without contaminating its water supply. To ignore drains is to distort history. Ancient records tell us from time to time of cities or whole countries decimated by epidemics; these were certainly not all waterborne, but some may have been, and the differences between a prosperous city and one in decay may well sometimes have been linked to differences in their supply of clean water and their means of sewage disposal.

No large city could exist away from a major perennial watercourse. Hence clusters of large cities were limited to the banks of channels of the Euphrates in Iraq and of the Nile in Egypt. Lesser cities could prosper if they had the benefit of abundant springs, wells or water brought by aqueducts, sometimes supplemented by rainwater collected in cisterns.

Jericho came into being in the Neolithic period as one of the first towns, if not the very first, because of an abundantly gushing fountain, which gives the city its life to this day. Jerusalem lived by a spring at its southeast corner, later supplemented by water fed in by an aqueduct from the south, for which Hezekiah was famous:

> The rest of the acts of Hezekiah, and all his might, and how he made a pool [i.e., reservoir] and a conduit, and brought water into the city, are they not written in the book of the chronicles of the kings of Judah? (2 Kings 20:20)

Remains of these works are still to be seen in Jerusalem.

The obvious sources of drinking water in Mesopotamia and Egypt were the great rivers and their canals, and in many cities these remained the main source, even sometimes for royal purposes, well into the first millennium, even though by that time some palaces, particularly in Assyria, were drawing their water supply from deep wells, secure from pollution. As early as the second millennium palaces in both Crete and Ugarit had piped water; the water supply for the Knossos palace was brought by aqueducts from a spring in the mountains seven miles away, and carried under the palace floor through terracotta pipes, sealed at their joints. At El Amarna in middle Egypt there were communal wells in some quarters, and the better houses had their own; since the city was built for Amenophis IV from scratch after 1400 BC, this probably reflected the ideal of domestic water supply which had developed at that time, although the chief consideration may have been the convenience of not having to make journeys to the river, rather than recognition of possible implications for health. In some parts of the ancient Near East, particularly such areas as the more arid parts of south Palestine, seasonal rains were caught and stored in cisterns.

The potential health risk in drinking from the rivers depended upon whether or not human habits were likely to contaminate the water. Royal palaces, and houses of the more wealthy citizens, often, even as early as the third millennium, had indoor lavatories; in Egypt, there were lavatories in bathrooms even in some Second Dynasty mastaba-tombs. In most places, lavatories were set against outside walls, with a seat over a drain leading in some cases (as at Knossos) to an elaborate system of sewers for waste disposal, the effluents being discharged at a distance, frequently into a river. The most advanced of the cities of the Harappan culture in the Indus Valley had municipal sewage systems, although this was not invariable, and in some Harappan cities, such as Banawali on the eastern fringe, there were no city drains, and the effluents ran into large jars in the street, presumably to be cleared away by scavengers.

But these refinements of life for the wealthy few did not affect the great mass of the population. Even where major cities had developed, the majority of the population were still peasants, and even those not directly linked to agriculture remained in close touch with the countryside. Archaeology shows that the dwellings of ordinary workers and peasants certainly had no lavatories, and there were no communal ones. But cities always had orchards and often fields within their city walls, as well as fields immediately surrounding them; and so, in the absence of public lavatories, most of the population would go out into the fields to defecate, as they still do today in many parts of the world outside the most advanced.

In Egypt and Mesopotamia this would not necessarily present a health hazard, as the hot sun dries and sterilizes ordure within hours. But too close proximity to a watercourse or well, or waterlogging of the ground, could result in contamination of drinking water by disease organisms or by the ova of parasitic worms. Contamination of the latter kind was certainly endemic to ancient Egypt (p. 243) and most Egyptians seem to have been infested, from drinking contaminated water.

Another waterborne debilitating disorder, always endemic to the Nile, and now and perhaps in ancient times also to the Euphrates, was bilharzia (schistosomiasis), a kind of liver fluke in humans caused by a parasite of which the intermediate host is the water snail. The parasite swims in the water and enters exposed skin, so that peasants working with hands or feet in a river or canal or irrigation ditch are always at risk.

There were circumstances in the ancient Near East where great care was taken to provide a pure water supply. This was the case at the Hittite court. There, water for the king had to be strained, and it was recorded that once when the king found a hair in his water jug, the guilty water carrier was put to death. But the primary concern in this situation was not hygiene in our sense; the concern here was the ritual purity of the king and his protection against possible black magic. Yet the result was to ensure to the king a source of water as free as possible from contamination. But the fact that polluted water could be dangerous was well recognized everywhere; Mesopotamian texts refer to the risk of death from drinking bad water, and the Israelites used deliberately polluted water as a test of the virtue of a suspect wife (Numbers 5:16–22). Probably everywhere in the ancient Near East and Egypt the requirements of ritual purity had considerable side benefits in eliminating some of the worst threats to the safe water supply.

Waterborne diseases and parasites were by no means the only health hazards in ancient cities, and perhaps not the worst ones. In most places there was no municipal rubbish collection, and refuse, including food offal, was often simply thrown out into the streets. The only possible indication of any form of municipal arrangements for refuse disposal comes from the third-millennium cities of the Indus valley, where there are architectural features in some better-class houses which archaeologists have interpreted as rubbish chutes. But even if they were just that (and other interpretations are possible), there is no proof that the jettisoned rubbish did not simply lie in the streets as in many other cities.

The usual treatment of street rubbish was that it was cleared up by scavenging pigs and dogs. These animals certainly wandered about in Babylonian cities, and in the Hittite area it was taken as a matter of course that such scavengers would roam around even inside the palace of the king, the only restriction on them being to prevent them crossing the threshold of the place where the food of the king or the god was prepared. The scavenging pigs were themselves eaten in due course (except by such people as the Israelites, who held the pig as taboo), and if not thoroughly cooked, as with the barbeque type of cooking often used was likely to be the case, the flesh transmitted dangerous Trichinella worms. Rodents also flourished in the constant presence of waste food, and rats carried the fleas which were the vector of bubonic plague.

For long, south Mesopotamia had the most heavily populated cities, and the greatest concentration of them. Conditions were ideal for the outbreak of epidemics, including bubonic plague. Epidemic disease was such an accepted part of the scheme of things that there were prominent plague gods, whose duty was to punish cities by this affliction. The word for epidemic disease was *mutanu*, meaning literally something like 'certain death', from *mutu*, the ordinary word for 'death'. The term denoted fatal pestilence generally rather than any specific disease, and could be applied to animal epidemics as well as to human. Akkadian texts abound with references to *mutanu*. An Old Babylonian letter reports 'There is at present pestilence in the city, but it is not the pestilence of the god Nergal'. Obviously Nergal's pestilence was some specific epidemic, perhaps bubonic plague. An omen speaks of plague gods marching with the troops, perhaps a reference to typhus, since that disease often breaks out in armies. Other texts speak of affected cities with daily deaths, whole countries hit by a fatal epidemic, and epidemics continuing for years. One of the Akkadian myths, *Erra*, was written in consequence of an outbreak of plague at Babylon, and was believed to be efficacious against further such visitations.

The late fourteenth-century Hittite king Murshilish in a prayer to the gods of Hatti-land gave an account of the course of such an epidemic, probably either bubonic plague or typhus. It began with a military attack by Hatti-land on Amke, a part of Syria held by Egypt. The Hittites won the war and brought back Egyptian prisoners. But then fatal plague broke out among the prisoners and spread to the Hittites. At the time of the prayer it had raged for twenty years, taking a heavy toll on the population. Ploughmen, cowherds and shepherds, and female workers were all affected, leaving the country so weakened that peoples on its northern fringes were beginning to attack it.

The Bible reports several large-scale fatal epidemics, attributing them to divine anger. The best known was that which has become mythologized as the death of the Egyptian firstborn (Exodus 12:29–30). Numbers records two mass deaths from disease during the desert wanderings, one in 11:33–34, linked, perhaps only coincidentally, with eating quails, the other in 16:46–49. Another fatal epidemic broke out in the Philistine city of Ashdod and spread to the four other Philistine cities and eventually to some of the Israelites (1 Samuel 5:6–6:19), and in the reign of king David an outbreak of mortal disease hit all Israel (2 Samuel 24:15–16).

The fatal epidemic which, according to the Bible (2 Kings 19:35–36 with the miraculous interpretation omitted), broke out amongst Sennacherib's army at the siege of Jerusalem, is not likely to have been either bubonic plague or typhus, or it would surely have spread to the Israelite population, and there is no mention of cases there. One credible suggestion is that the Assyrians became heavily infected with malaria on their passage to Jerusalem through north Palestine (parts of which were prominently signposted as dangerously malarial as late as the 1940s AD), and the cold nights of hilly Jerusalem brought on fatal attacks; during the first World War precisely the same kind of mass deaths occurred overnight amongst a contingent of British soldiers affected with malaria and sent to recuperate in Jerusalem.[8]

Other health hazards were burial practices. In some places in ancient Mesopotamia and Palestine the dead were shallowly buried under the floors of houses, with dangers obvious to us if not to the ancients. The Jews in Jerusalem minimized the risk from dead bodies by burying the common people outside the city in the Kidron valley; only kings were buried within the city walls.

City government

Ancient oriental cities, like their successors until recent times, tended to be zoned. There was always a separate temple area, but in addition there usually grew up also separate quarters for the people of different crafts and trades, such as merchants, metal-workers, carpenters, butchers, and so on; in a city important for international commerce there would also be enclaves for different groups of foreigners (see, e.g., 1 Kings 20:34).

However powerful the central royal administration, social organisms of this kind would give rise to problems which could only be dealt with at the local level. Some form of policing was also essential, and necessarily locally based and administered, although at some points this could impinge upon the central government. The security of the goods and persons of strangers was a case in point: everywhere responsibility for apprehending robbers or murderers of strangers, or, failing that, paying compensation, lay in the first instance with the city authorities, but if the city authorities failed in these responsibilities the royal power could and would intervene. Other matters which were usually dealt with locally included family disputes or matters of inheritance or disputes between citizens where there were no elements affecting the rights of the king or the temples. Another area of necessary involvement of local government was the selection of citizens to undertake labour or military service for the state: here again, enforcement of such corvée duties was in the hands of the central government, but in practical terms it was only the local authorities who were in a position to identify those citizens who had liability.

Thus, everywhere there was necessarily some form of local city government, under a body often known as the Elders. These were in no sense elected representatives of the community as a whole. Normally, unless the royal authority or the temple had acquired such power locally that they were in a position to pack the local administration with their own nominees, the members of the local city administration held their positions on an hereditary basis, as the heads of old local families.

Nowhere in the pre-classical world was there democracy in the modern sense, or, with the possible exception of earliest Sumer, in the sense which the Greeks gave to the term. Power was concentrated within three groups: the king, the temple authorities, and senior members of ancient or wealthy families; the exercise of power depended upon the balance between these. Most commonly the scales were heavily tilted in favour of the king.

In some cases the local authorities were entirely dominated by the royal power. In view of the monolithic rule of the pharaoh in Egypt, one would expect this situation there. Even when there was a weakening or collapse of the central power, the administrators of individual cities seem never to have come to prominence; in such circumstances it was always the governors of the provincial divisions called nomes who came to the fore.

Another area where city administrations seem to have been particularly weak in resisting royal domination was Israel. Factors underlying this probably included the smallness of the country and the fact that in the northern kingdom of Israel the royal power virtually controlled the national religion, even though individual prophets (outside the religious establishment) could at times challenge the king. Several instances are recorded of city administrations making immediate obsequious submission to demands from the royal power, unjust though they were. The extent to which the royal court could dominate the local authorities of a city is shown by the story of Naboth's vineyard in 1 Kings 21. King Ahab wanted Naboth to sell him his vineyard, but Naboth declined. Thereupon Jezebel, Ahabs's wife, wrote to the local authorities in Naboth's city, instructing them to bring a false charge of blasphemy and treason against Naboth, and to condemn and execute him. They did exactly as they were told. Later, the elders of Samaria, cowed by the usurping king Jehu, who challenged them to let it be known if they proposed to support a legitimate successor from the dynasty he had just supplanted, capitulated at once, even to the extent of murdering all Jehu's potential rivals (2 Kings 10:1–7).

But in other parts of the ancient Near East, some city authorities, despite the ever-increasing royal power, to the end succeeded in retaining a measure of local independence. Some of the cities in Mesopotamia were aware that they could trace their existence back to primeval times, which gave them the authority of ancient custom, and to that they sometimes added the ability to turn particular political developments to their advantage. There were occasions when a ruler was in difficulties, particularly from rebellion or attempted usurpation, and at such times he needed the active support of the great cities. In such circumstances he might buy the desired support from a city with the promise of its future exemption from certain taxes or liability to the corvée. When Babylon was in revolt against Assyria in 734 BC, we find the representative of king Tiglath-Pileser III promising, in return for the city's submission, to recognize all Babylon's ancient charter privileges. Thirteen years later Sargon II obtained the throne of Assyria in an insurrection, by winning the support of the ancient Assyrian capital Ashur by granting a charter of new privileges. Because of such factors, no Mesopotamian king, however powerful, could finally snuff out the rights of the city authorities.

The kind of bargain just illustrated between ruler and ruled is not to be thought of as a social contract, since every king everywhere claimed to reign by divine right, not by consent of his subjects. Such situations did, however, serve as a means by which city administrations, emasculated though they might be, were able to bring to bear upon the central government the pressure of public opinion.

Even in Israel, at a time when society was still predominantly tribal rather than urban, we see a corresponding situation. At the death of Solomon, the representatives of the people came to bargain with his son Rehoboam for a reduction in the harshness of the corvée (1 Kings 12:1–16); when he was foolish enough to reject this demand, he lost the greater part of his father's domains.

7

Trade

Two factors are essential for the development of trade: a surplus of goods of one kind and an unfulfilled demand for those of another. Very early, surpluses became a feature of the river valley civilizations of Egypt and Mesopotamia: they had an almost permanent over-abundance of grain. Abnormally high or low river floods might temporarily disturb this situation, but reserves stored from good years were almost always sufficient to tide over, as the biblical story of the Pharaoh's seven good and seven bad years recognizes.

Biologically, humans have no real needs beyond an assured food supply and protection from the elements, but society quickly creates others. In both Mesopotamia and Egypt, the beginning of civilization saw the rise of a ruling minority marked off by wealth, power and esteem. This was a potent factor in the development of new needs and thereby trade. In any socially stratified society, the top group behave in a way which demonstrates and reinforces their status. One conspicuous marker of high social status is possession of the rare and beautiful, either worn on the person or brought into association with aspects of life controlled by the top stratum; in Egypt and Mesopotamia it was religious buildings and images which offered the readiest opportunities for display of the wealth controlled by the governing class.

Amongst the most beautiful and conspicuous of easily portable objects available to early man were coloured stones and nuggets of gold. The quest to obtain such precious materials had important consequences, dictated by the geographical and geological circumstances of the two primary cultural areas.

In Egypt, gold was to be found within the country itself. Throughout the ages the waters of the Nile had worn down gold-bearing rocks in the far south, and here and there in the shallows of the river, eddies had deposited gold in the form of dust or nuggets. Random discoveries would have sufficed to create a demand for the beautiful metal, but the only way to achieve an assured supply was by the laborious crushing and washing of gold-bearing rock. This brought about the development of mining, involving not only the application of appropriate technology but also the organizing of gangs of forced labour to undertake the disagreeable work.

Sources of the precious stone amethyst were available to Egypt in the eastern desert and the far south, and turquoise in Sinai. Exploitation required the organization of labour gangs, logistical operations for provisioning in a desert area, and military measures to safeguard personnel and routes, but none of these occasioned major problems.

Trading in precious commodities in Mesopotamia

South Mesopotamia was completely lacking in both native sources of metals (precious and otherwise) and in precious stones. But beyond the Zagros to the east there was a wealth of such things: there it was possible to obtain gold, silver, tin, copper, lapis lazuli and carnelian. From at least the beginning of the third millennium, this provided a major incentive to trade.

The most important of these materials as a marker for ancient trade is lapis lazuli. This is a beautiful dark blue stone, chemically a form of sodium aluminium silicate containing sulphur. From the very beginning of civilization, it was much prized for ornamentation by the peoples of both south Mesopotamia and Egypt. But how did they obtain it? The nearest known source was Badakhshan, in north Afghanistan, 1400 miles away from Mesopotamia in a straight line across many difficult mountain ranges and deserts, and almost twice as much by any practicable route. Theoretically, the ancient civilizations might have known some nearer source which has since been worked out, but any such workings should have left evidence identifiable archaeologically, and no such evidence has been found.

What have been found are sites in Iran which in the middle of the third millennium were evidently centres for the lapis lazuli trade. At one, Shahr-i-Sokhta in Sistan (eastern Iran), there was a workshop containing blocks of lapis lazuli up to two kilograms in weight, together with utensils for stone working, and chips and beads of lapis lazuli. Another mineral worked there was the beautiful red stone carnelian, and for this the nearest source was the Hindu Kush. Turquoise was also present, but as this is of fairly common occurrence in the Near East, it is less helpful for tracing trade routes. A second site, Tepe Hissar in north Iran, provides similar evidence of a similar date. Both Shahr-i-Sokhta and Tepe Hissar lie between south Mesopotamia and the source of lapis lazuli in

Badakhshan and of carnelian in the Hindu Kush, which makes it a reasonable conclusion that both were entrepots for international trade, on alternative routes.

There were several ways in which lapis lazuli could have reached south Mesopotamia. Merchants from Mesopotamia might have journeyed to its place of origin to fetch it, or it might have been passed on from settlement to settlement. A third possibility is what economic historians call Central Place Trade. In this, producers sent their goods to some centre, from which the final users obtained them, either by direct missions or through further intermediate settlements. Shahr-i-Sokhta and Tepe Hissar could well have been central places in this sense for the distribution of lapis lazuli and carnelian.

We are not limited to archaeological evidence; there are Sumerian epics which reflect third-millennium trade in lapis lazuli and carnelian. Although these texts, one called *Enmerkar and the Lord of Aratta*, and two others linked to a hero Lugalbanda, are known only from copies from the early second millennium BC, their contents show them to derive from nearly 1000 years earlier.[1]

The heroes Enmerkar and Lugalbanda were two of the Early Dynastic rulers of the city-state of Erech in south Mesopotamia. The epic about Enmerkar introduces another city-state, Aratta, that lay to the east across seven mountain ranges. It was a notable source not only of gold and silver, but also of lapis lazuli and carnelian, just as Shahr-i-Sokhta and Tepe Hissar were. One or both of those sites may actually have been part of the territory of Aratta.

Enmerkar wished to bring glory upon himself by adorning the temple of Inanna, the great goddess of Erech, with lapis lazuli and carnelian, and the epic tells how this was achieved. Surmounting the difficulties of distance and terrain, Enmerkar sent out an ambassador to the ruler of Aratta, to negotiate his needs. But the ruler of Aratta had his own ideas of personal glory: it was, he claimed, not Enmerkar but himself whom Inanna had chosen as her chief earthly representative, and at first he refused the request. Here already we see states competing for cultural prestige. The conflict of interests was only resolved after protracted negotiations, involving challenges which ranged from the solving of riddles to the threat of military force. But the final result, and the essential heart of the epic, was that eventually Erech sent a donkey caravan laden with grain as payment, and duly received in exchange the desired precious metals and stones. This shows that already, by perhaps 2750 BC, direct trading between states, by organized caravans, was taking place. The epics linked to Lugalbanda tell the same story, of Erech's dependence upon Aratta for precious stones and metals, and its determination to gain those resources, by trade if possible, by force if not.

The lapis lazuli routes did not terminate in Mesopotamia. Finds show that even before 3000 BC this precious stone was reaching Egypt, and subsequently it was extensively used there for beads, amulets, scarabs, and inlays in jewellery. There is no doubt that it came by way of Mesopotamia, since finds of lapis lazuli in Egypt include objects inscribed in cuneiform, such as cylinder seals from about 1800 BC and in the first millennium an inscribed lapis lazuli bead from a king's tomb.

Trade in timber

The beginning of the third millennium saw the building of many major temples in both Mesopotamia and Egypt. This created a need for large strong timber. Neither country was without native trees—Egypt had acacia (much used for boats; forests of it remained up to the early nineteenth century AD), sycamore and tamarisk; and south Mesopotamia date palm, poplar and willow—but none of these timbers had the strength and size suitable for major buildings. Both countries therefore had to look outside their own boundaries for large timber. This is not a commodity likely to be passed from settlement to settlement over long distances, and therefore the only way of getting it was to send expeditions abroad to fetch it or to compel natives of the producing area to bring it.

Mesopotamia had no real problem. East and north, within sight of the plains, was a semi-circle of forested mountains, which offered what seemed to be an inexhaustible supply of large, strong, and in some cases beautiful, timber—cedar, fir, pine, walnut, oak, oriental plane. Where these grew, there was no organized population likely to exploit this timber as a matter of trade, and in the beginning the only way the Mesopotamians could obtain it was to go themselves, fell it and bring it back. To set out for the first time to tackle a wild unexplored mountain forest, full not only of wild beasts but also of the supernatural terrors created by early man's imagination, must have been a daunting undertaking, and we find a lively reflection of this in the *Epic of Gilgamesh*. This, the widest diffused of all epics of the pre-Greek world, is known in recensions from the third to the first millennium.[2]

Gilgamesh was another Early Dynastic ruler of Erech, not the first founder but the man who in tradition brought it to its full walled splendour. The epic relates how he and his bold companion Enkidu set out to challenge the cedar forest. Enkidu, formerly a wild man, warned Gilgamesh of its terrors:

I came to know it, my friend, in the hills,
As I roamed there with the wild beasts.
For ten thousand leagues the forest extends.
Who would dare enter there?
(There is) Huwawa:—his roar is the flood-demon,
His mouth is fire,
His breath is death!

But Gilgamesh was not to be moved from his purpose. The heroes journeyed to the cedar mountain and

Gilgamesh took [the axe and] felled [a cedar]
[Huwawa] heard and was enraged:
'Who has felled a cedar growing in my mountains?'

The Old Babylonian (early second millennium) form of the epic describes the killing of Huwawa, guardian of the forest:

Gilgamesh struck the guardian, Huwawa, to the ground.
For two leagues the cedars resounded. . . .
Enkidu killed [the guardian] of the forest,
At whose word Hermon and Lebanon trembled. . . .
(Then) Gilgamesh cut down the trees.

Huwawa, a kind of ogre, represented both the mythical perils of the unexplored forest and the real danger of the tribes of the mountains. The first contacts with the mountain dwellers must have been hostile, but in due time their encounters with the more advanced Mesopotamians tamed them, so that subsequently the Mesopotamians were able to use them as labour gangs for felling and transporting timber.

Obtaining good timber was a different matter in Egypt. There was indeed a source in Nubia in the south, but at the beginning of the Dynastic period the major building projects were in the neighbourhood of what is now Cairo, and Nubia lay many hundred miles upstream beyond the rapids of the First Cataract. But within easy access by sea were cedar, cypress and pine from the mountains of the coastal strip of Syria (including what in political terms is now the state of Lebanon). All three of these timbers were already being used in small quantities in Egypt in Predynastic times, before 3000 BC, and they became of considerable importance later, for such purposes as columns of temples, ships, doors for temples and tombs, and coffins. From the third millennium right through to the first we find very frequent evidence of sea trade between Egypt and the ports of Syria, with timber always the chief commodity sought by the Egyptians. The port principally used by Egypt was usually Byblos, a beautifully sheltered haven about twenty miles north of Beirut. The connection developed so early that it entered the realms of myth. The myth of Osiris told how, after that god-king had been slain by his wicked brother, the coffin in which he lay was washed ashore at Byblos, where a tree grew round it. Isis, the wife of Osiris, in sorrowing quest of her husband's body, found that tree and brought it back to Egypt.

Archaeology confirms the very early date of the link presupposed by the myth, through Predynastic Egyptian objects excavated at Byblos. An Egyptian trading presence there in the twenty-seventh century is proved by the finding of a piece of a stone vase bearing the name of Khasek-hemwy, an Egyptian king of the Second Dynasty. The Palermo Stone (a fragment of inscribed diorite recording events of the reigns of early Egyptian kings) mentions during the reign of the Fourth Dynasty king Sneferu (soon after 2600 BC) 'the bringing of 40 ships filled with cedar wood', presumably from Syria, and the entry for the following year records the building from cedar wood of a ship about 150 feet long. A Fifth Dynasty relief shows ships which, as they carried bearded Asiatics in addition to the Egyptian crew, had obviously just returned from Syria; the cargo is not indicated but was presumably timber. The timber trade with Syria was considered so vital that when social and political conditions temporarily cut trade with Byblos, we find an Egyptian lamenting the loss of the proper wood for coffins.

But not all timber used in Egypt came from Syria: there was one species, found as early as the First Dynasty, which could not have done so. This was ebony, of which the only sources available to ancient Egypt lay to the south. Another marker for early Egyptian trade to the south was gum-resins, used as incense in temple worship, and also employed in embalming. The two principal gum-resins were frankincense and myrrh, which derive from various species of a genus of trees occurring only in south Arabia, Somaliland, north Sudan and Ethiopia. These two substances are very commonly mentioned in Egyptian texts from the Fifth Dynasty onwards, and to meet the needs of the temples for incense, there must have been regular trade with regions to the south of Egypt from at least the middle of the third millennium.

Trade with Nubia and Punt, and beyond

For the Egyptians, the most exotic of the southern lands was that which they knew as Punt (some scholars vocalize the name as Pwene or Pwenet), probably part of Somaliland. The first mention of an expedition to Punt occurs on the Palermo Stone, which records the bringing of 80,000 measures of myrrh from that country in the reign of the Fifth Dynasty king Sahure; under king Isesi later in the same dynasty there was a second expedition, of which the event most memorable for the Egyptians was the bringing back of a dancing dwarf. Sixth Dynasty inscriptions reveal the route by which the Egyptians reached Punt: they went by way of the Red Sea, as we learn from mention of an official being killed by Asiatics on the northern Red Sea coast when building a ship for an expedition to that land. By this time such voyages were common, and one Sixth Dynasty official records taking part in eleven expeditions.

In Egypt, foreign trade was always under state control. The importance attached to central control of trade is illustrated by the efforts made to reestablish contacts with foreign parts when a strong government took over after a period of decline. We see an instance of this just before 2000 BC, when the Eleventh Dynasty reunified Egypt after a time of chaos. For nearly two centuries the Egyptians had not visited Punt. Now, in 2002 BC, a large and highly organized expedition was sent out to resume trade, under a royal minister, Henu. Having recruited 3000 men in Upper Egypt, he marched them from the Nile to the Red Sea, across 90 miles of desert. A commissariat provided daily rations of 20 loaves per man and two jars of water, from wells dug along the route. Foreseeing the problems which the rough terrain would cause, Henu took along a pack train of donkeys carrying replacement sandals. There was also the problem of security: the preceding anarchy had left the deserts open to hostile nomads, and soldiers were sent ahead to clear the route of possible marauders. On reaching the Red Sea, Henu had a seagoing ship built,[3] which carried the trading cargoes down the Red Sea to Punt, where they were bartered for the goods which Egypt required.

We hear of several subsequent voyages to Punt, but the most informative account, at about 1500 BC, comes from Hatshepsut, the remarkable aunt and stepmother of Tuthmosis III, who made herself ruler of Egypt before he took over. Hers was a large-scale expedition of five sailing ships; the importance she attached to it is shown by the prominence she gave to it in her reliefs and inscriptions. The expedition had an undoubted commercial basis but received a theological justi-fication: it was said that the god Amun loved Punt and wanted his temple planted with a grove of myrrh trees from that land, reflecting the ambitious experiment of attempting the cultivation of myrrh in Egypt. We are not told how Hatshepsut's crews reached the Red Sea; it has sometimes been suggested that a navigable canal linked the Nile to the Red Sea at this time, but this lacks proof. The reliefs depict the expedition duly arriving in Punt, where the Egyptians won the favour of the local chief, who is shown with his wife and their children amidst the round-

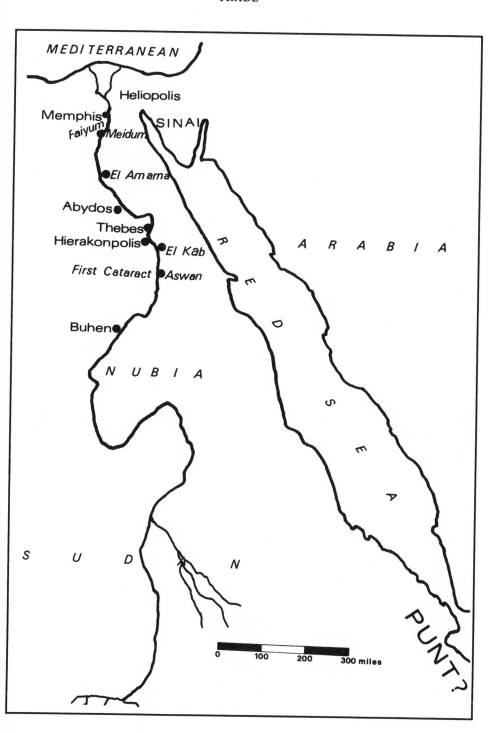

Ancient Egypt and regions to the south

domed huts on stilts (plate 5) in which the natives lived. Either the artist caricatured the chief's wife or the poor lady was suffering from a deforming disease (plate 6). The artist also shows the Egyptians presenting the natives with strings of beads, axes, daggers and bracelets; in return they had their ships loaded with myrrh-resin, myrrh trees with their roots wrapped in sacking (plate 4), ebony, ivory, cinnamon-wood, eye-paint, monkeys, panther skins and slaves.

But the Red Sea was not the only route to the south; the Egyptians always attached importance to trade up the Nile. Their natural southern border was the region known as the First Cataract, where rocks and rapids obstruct the river, but as early as the third millenium the Egyptians took measures to create a navigable waterway through that obstruction. Just after 2300 BC a Sixth Dynasty ruler entrusted an official, Uni, with the task of overcoming this obstacle to transport. He did so by digging five channels for the safe passage of ships. Trading expeditions were then able to penetrate by river far to the south, perhaps as far as Sudan, where they bartered such Egyptian products as oil, honey, clothing and faience for ivory, ebony and panther skins. Egyptian military control followed the trade missions, so that subsequently goods came into Egypt from the south not only by barter but also as tribute. A tomb painting of the middle of the second millennium shows natives of Nubia bringing such tribute, which included not only such typical goods as logs of ebony, elephant tusks, panther skins, and baskets of gold rings, but also a live giraffe with a monkey on its back.

But the behaviour of the Nile makes the rapids at the First Cataract a recurrent problem, and after the original clearance of the channel several later kings had to send officials to clear the passage again. In the nineteenth century the Twelfth Dynasty ruler Sesostris III had the work done on such a scale that the largest Egyptian ships could sail upstream towards Nubia. He also made provision for his ships to be dragged through the Second Cataract to enable him to campaign in the Sudan. Just after the middle of the second millennium, Tuthmosis III produced a permanent solution of the problem of the First Cataract, by making the local fishermen responsible for an annual clearance of the passage.

Before the end of the third millennium, Egyptian trade with Syria was spreading well inland from the coastal fringes where it began. One of its partners, proved by Egyptian hieroglyphics excavated at the site, was Ebla, a city of inland north Syria which between about 2400 and 2250 BC was a major trading centre linked to south Mesopotamia. A temple in Upper Egypt, dated by an inscription to about 1900 BC, yielded four bronze caskets which amongst other things contained cylinder seals, some of Mesopotamia origin and others from still further away, from eastern

Iran. How they reached Egypt we do not know, but they indisputably prove long-range links. Links from even further afield are shown by a seal impression on a jar found in Nubia in a level dated to about 2200 BC; the seal impression is one which can only have originated between east Iran and the Indus valley.[4]

Mediterranean sea trade

The evidence of art suggests trading links between Egypt and Crete from at least the beginning of the second millennium. Paintings in each country show vessels characteristic of the other, and some motifs occurring in Egyptian art appear to derive from patterns on Cretan textiles. The Cretans in turn borrowed from Egypt, and in their splendid paintings usually adopted the Egyptian convention of painting men brown and women white. Here unquestionably trade was a vehicle for cultural influence. Navigation between Egypt and Crete would have presented little difficulty, as a sea current flows northwards from the Nile Delta to take a ship to Crete with the minimum of trouble, and in summer a steady north-west wind blows for the return journey.

But the main centre of trade in the eastern Mediterranean was always Syria, the natural link between Egypt, Mesopotamia and Asia Minor. Egyptian trade missions to Syria were almost invariably by sea; although there was a land route through Palestine, this involved a difficult journey across the Sinai desert, demanding the organizing of water supplies and sustained military action against marauders. The Egyptians did indeed, as early as the third millennium, make intermittent attacks to subdue their eastern neighbours, but it was not until their imperial expansion into western Asia in the middle of the second millennium that they firmly established control over Palestine; before that time Egyptian land trade with Syria must have been exceptional.

Trade was of course a two-way affair, and Syrian ships plied to Egypt as Egyptian ships did to Syria. A painting in the tomb of a mayor of Thebes gives us a vivid picture of this in the latter part of the second millennium. Ships manned by Syrian sailors are discharging cargo in an Egyptian town, presumably Thebes, and a port official is recording details of some of the crew. The main merchandise consists of large jars of wine or oil, and vases of precious metal, sold, as the picture indicates, not to private individuals but through the owner of the tomb, who in his lifetime was a government official in charge of the municipal store-houses. This is what we would expect from highly centralized Egypt, where all major foreign trade, where not actually organized by the state, was carefully controlled by it. However, the system did provide for a degree of small-scale private trading, for we see sandals, textiles and foodstuffs being sold in waterside shops.

This raises the question of how, in the absence of coinage, private purchases were paid for. An Egyptian document arising from a lawsuit shortly after 1300 BC gives us a partial answer. It recounts how a merchant had gone from house to house offering a Syrian slave-girl for sale, until finally the wife of an official bought her. The price was agreed in terms of silver, but it was paid in various cloths, garments and bronze vessels, each item being separately valued. The text specifically mentions that the bronze vessels were obtained from neighbours. This suggests that neighbours were accustomed to borrow and lend amongst themselves, keeping a tally of debits and credits, so that when it suddenly became necessary to pay for a purchase made outside the community, the purchaser could call for goods from those with whom he or she had a credit balance.

Between 1600 and 1400 BC, the Syrian trading centre about which we are best informed was Alalakh, some 25 miles inland on the most northerly point of the Orontes river; it was successively under the control of Egypt, the Mittannians of north Mesopotamia and the Hittites. Subsequently it was superseded by the coastal city of Ugarit, about 60 miles to the south-west.

Egypt had a perennial need for timber from Syria, and other common imports were cedar oil, olive oil and wine; these were paid for by such exports as pottery, glass, jewellery and perfumes. Although, as we have seen, all this was predominantly state trading on Egypt's side, there was a degree of private trading. During the latter part of the second millennium private Egyptian trading included slaves, who may in the first instance have been obtained by pirate raids on Mediterranean coastlands. Pirates certainly infested the eastern Mediteranean, so much so that at about 1400 BC the Egyptian king Amenophis III was forced to set up a marine police force to patrol the Delta area, to deal both with pirates and with smugglers attempting to evade the payment of the customs duties to which imports into Egypt were liable.

Imperialism and trade

We return to the third millennium to trace another development significant for the pattern of international trade. In the twenty-fourth century, political changes took place in Mesopotamia with far-reaching consequences. Political institutions had developed to a stage in which for the first time a ruler had not only the will, but also the power, to attempt to control the trading pattern of distant regions by the threat of military aggression. Thereby the first major empire arose. The empire in question was founded by a certain Sharrum-kin, more commonly known as Sargon, who from his base at Agade, not certainly identified but somewhere not far from later Babylon, first mastered all south Iraq and then followed the old trade routes up the Euphrates to gain control of two major commercial centres, Mari on the middle Euphrates and Ebla in north Syria, cities which owed their existence to their strategic position on trade routes. Although hitherto politically independent, these cities had, by contact with merchants from south Iraq, developed cultures that were essentially Sumerian-based, an illustration of the part played by trade in the spread of civilization. According to later literary tradition, not to be dismissed out of hand even though it may have embroidered details, Sargon went beyond north Syria into Asia Minor, where he gave his protection to merchant colonies from Mesopotamia. The objective of the imperial ruler was primarily economic: he sought to compel cities to modify their trading pattern to the benefit of the imperial centre. Although conquest and destruction were not the primary aim, this policy inevitably brought military conflict, and eventually Sargon's principal successor, Naram-Sin, came to regard Ebla as an outright rival which had to be destroyed by military might.

Sargon and his successors also drove along the eastward trade routes in their expansionist aims, and gained some success as far east as Elam (south-west Iran). But military coercion had its limitations. It could increase the flow of goods to the imperial centre only from areas that could be firmly held: outside that area it was counter-productive. Merchants not yet in the Sargonic orbit would not willingly surrender their trading arrangements to the control of a military aggressor, and from such areas there was a reduced trade flow. The land routes across Iran withered. Excavation illustrates this: although Shahr-i-Sokhta remained a major site in the second half of the third millennium, its trade in lapis lazuli, so important earlier, had come to an end. But, to counter this decline, there was a development of sea trade along the Persian Gulf, so that we find Sargon of Agade speaking of 'ships from Meluhha, Magan and Tilmun moored at the quay of Agade'; whilst a later poem, looking back to the splendours of the time of Naram-Sin, refers to 'mighty elephants and apes, beasts from distant lands, jostling in the great square', and such exotic creatures can hardly have been imported except by sea from India. In highlighting thriving waterborne trade as one of the glories of his capital, Sargon showed a shrewd sense of values. In Mesopotamia the bustle of riverine trade was always the life-breath of the city, and when it ceased the city died. A later text reflects this truth in the words in which it evokes a city which had become a ghost town from its loss of trade: 'Asleep is the ferry, asleep the quay, the sailors all lie sleeping.'

The identity of Meluhha, Magan and Tilmun gives problems. Tilmun is the easiest to settle: basically it was the island of Bahrein, with possibly also part of the adjacent Arabian coastal area.[5] Excavations show that, in the third and early second millennia, Bahrein and nearby coastal Arabia had contacts with Mesopotamia on one side and Oman and the Indus valley on the other.

Meluhha is a bigger problem. By the late second millennium the name was applied to Nubia, south of Egypt. If this had always been its designation, third-millennium references to Meluhha would relate to sea journeys along the southern coast of Arabia to Africa. But it seems more likely that the name Meluhha only became applied to Africa after Babylonia had lost contact with the area it originally denoted. The shift of name was probably encouraged by the fact that Africa was a source of imports of the kind typical of the original Meluhha, notably ivory and ebony.

Archaeological evidence now leaves little doubt that the third-millennium Meluhha was some region or port connected with the civilization in the Indus valley, which we know from such excavated sites as Mohenjo-daro, Harappa and Lothal. Third-millennium links between Mesopotamia and the Indus valley are indisputable. Various objects have been excavated in Mesopotamia and south-west Iran bearing representations of Indian humped bulls, and seals characteristic of Mesopotamia and the Persian Gulf have been discovered at Mohenjo-daro and Lothal.

The third term, Magan (alternatively read Makkan), must have represented some coastal area between Bahrein and the Indus valley; probably Oman, or the Iranian coast opposite.

We know nothing further of Sargon's trade with Tilmun, Magan and Meluhha, but documents from the period of the Third Dynasty of Ur, just before 2000 BC, show south Mesopotamian merchants trading along the Persian Gulf. Officials in Ur financed them with goods from the temple warehouses, such as garments, wool, oil and leather products, which the merchants took by boat to Magan to buy copper. The following typical document illustrates the procedure:

> *Lu-enlilla has received as goods for the purchase of copper, 60 talents [over a ton and a half] of wool, . . . from the warehouse, 70 ushbar-garments from Ur-shulgira, 6 kur [about 330 gallons] of good quality linseed oil from Lugal-gab, 180 leather goods from Ur-shulpae, belonging to the temple of Nanna. . . . Merchandise put in a ship for Magan. . . .*

The goods brought back included, in addition to copper as the main cargo, beads of precious stones, ivory, and onions. On whichever side of the Persian Gulf Magan lay, it must have been an entrepot for international trade rather than a primary producer, since the ivory and some of the precious stones could not have originated there.

After the collapse of the III Ur empire, direct contact with Magan was lost; now it was Tilmun which became the principal partner in Mesopotamian sea trade, with Ur still the main river port. A group of business documents and letters in Sumerian and Akkadian, from the century 1900–1800 BC, shed light on this trade. The trading voyages were now financed not by temples but by private entrepreneurs and possibly also by the royal authorities. Contracts stated the silver value of the trading goods provided, and the amount of copper to be brought back, in this way:

Lu-meshlamtae and Nigsisanabsa have borrowed from Ur-ninmar 2 minas of silver (in the form of) 5 gur of oil and 30 garments as capital for a partnership for an expedition to Tilmun to buy copper. After safe return of the expedition, he [i.e. the creditor, Ur-ninmar] will not recognize any loss incurred by the merchants; they [the seafaring merchants] have agreed to satisfy Ur-ninmar with 4 minas of copper for each shekel of silver as a just price.

They have sworn by the king. Before [five named witnesses].

Such terms ensured the financial backer a risk-free fixed return, but no share in profits. But some entrepreneurs obtained even better terms; they not only had repayment of their capital guaranteed, but also received a full share of the profits instead of a fixed return. The procedure they used was to enter into a contract with the merchants, on terms which made the capitalist a full partner with the right to share in full in any profits but at the same time left each of the merchants individually responsible for full repayment of the entrepreneur's capital. The entrepreneur could only face risk to his capital if every one of his partners became destitute.

We have some of the correspondence of a leading merchant in the Tilmun copper trade. His name was Ea-nasir. Although in a big way of business, Ea-nasir had his problems. We find, for example, a customer complaining that he had failed to supply him with copper of the quality required:

Thus says Nanni to Ea-nasir:

When you came, this is what you said: 'I will deliver satisfactory ingots to Gimil-Sin [Nanni's agent].' You told me this when you came, but you haven't done it. You put unsatisfactory ingots before my messenger, and you said 'Take it or leave it'.[6] Who am I that you treat me in such a way, that you show contempt for me in this way? This between gentlemen like us! . . . Who is there amongst Tilmun traders who has done anything like this to me? . . .[7]

The writer goes on to warn that he will insist on his right to select his copper ingots from Ea-nasir's stock one by one, to ensure that he gets good quality.

Several other letters also contain complaints against Ea-nasir, or indications that he had failed to fulfil bargains. It may be that he was downright unscrupulous, but it seems more likely that he was having difficulty in importing sufficient good quality copper to meet the demand. Other texts show that a major part of his business was providing copper for the palace, and possibly this had to take priority, leaving his private customers to bear the brunt of any shortages.

The copper imported from Tilmun was brought back either in the form of ingots of up to two hundredweight (100 kilos) or as manufactured objects. One text mentions a total of 13,000 minas of copper, which would be six to seven tons. It was subject to heavy customs duties, levied by the administrative authorities, acting through the temple of Shamash. Trade was very much under royal supervision in the early second millennium; there were check points along the Euphrates, which merchants plying by ship were unable to pass without a formal permit called 'tablet of the king'.

Even when the temples did not directly finance foreign trade, they still had a part to play, for they controlled the standard systems of weights used in Babylonia. Tilmun used a different system, and as some deliveries of copper are entered in both forms, we are able to calculate that the unit used at Tilmun equalled 2⅔ Ur minas. Since the Ur mina weighed about 480 grams (just over one pound), the Tilmun unit was about a kilo and a quarter. The Tilmun weight standard was also used in the Indus valley, another piece of evidence supporting its equation with Meluhha.

The nature of most of the imports from Tilmun shows that, even more than Magan, Tilmun was an international entrepot rather than a primary producer. There are no major deposits of copper ores in the region of Bahrein, so that copper could not have been produced locally. The same applies to most of the other principal imports from Tilmun—lapis lazuli, carnelian, timber, and ivory in various forms including combs, a characteristic product of the Indus valley. (An import called by a term meaning literally 'fish-eyes' might have been a native product of Tilmun, if this referred to pearls.) This function of Tilmun as a major international trading entrepot may be not unrelated to a Sumerian tradition which saw Tilmun as a holy land free from strife. This reputation has no obvious basis in religion, and it may have originated in Tilmun having been from prehistoric times a neutral meeting-place to which merchants from many lands could brir.g their wares in the assurance of being free to barter there unmolested.

Merchant colonies in Anatolia

At the very period, around 1900 BC, that merchants in south Mesopotamia were trading down the Persian Gulf, at the opposite end of Mesopotamia merchants from Assyria were operating an extensive caravan traffic between Ashur on the middle Tigris, and trading colonies in Cappadocia (central Anatolia, Asiatic Turkey). The most prominent colony was at Kanesh (modern Kultepe near Kayseri), about seven hundred miles away across the Taurus.

Kanesh has yielded some 14,000 clay tablets (not all published yet), consisting of archives of the Assyrian merchant colony there. The texts give the names of more than twenty other such colonies, but very few of them have yet been identified. The economy was based on the export from Ashur of tin and textiles, which the agents in Cappadocia sold to the local populations, sending the proceeds back to Ashur.

Anyone who has ever made the journey between Ashur in north Iraq and Kayseri in Turkey will know that there are difficulties. The roads are bad in places, there are arid regions and mountains to cross, security is not all that might be desired, and there can be trouble at borders with rapacious customs men. All these adverse considerations must have applied with far greater force in 1900 BC. Yet the Assyrians kept regular caravans running between Ashur and Kanesh for several generations.

Like other international trading centres, Ashur did not rely on its own primary production. Iraq has no sources of tin, and this must have come from somewhere further east, possibly as far away as eastern Iran, where tin ores do occur. The best quality textiles exported from Ashur originated in Babylonia, although others may have been of local Assyrian manufacture.

Transport was by donkey. A merchant would have up to about twenty animals of his own, but several merchants would join together for security, so that a caravan could total up to 200 beasts. A donkey's load would be up to 100 kilos, with the tin carried in two balanced panniers and textiles slung over the top. The textiles were mainly bales of woollen cloth, but some could be in the form of made-up garments. The goods were sealed to prevent pilferage on the way. Documentation in the form of inscribed clay tablets accompanied the consignments, which were checked on arrival against the manifest.

These caravans travelled some 12–15 miles a day. On some parts of the route there were towns, inhabited by Assyrians, serving as staging posts, and at one, about halfway along the route, it was possible to hire fresh donkey-drivers. But there were desolate stretches where the travellers faced danger from bad weather, wolves and robbers, and we hear of not only men, but also donkeys, dying en route. Taxes were payable during the journey and on arrival at Kanesh, totalling ten per cent or more of the value of the consignment. Caravan leaders received an allowance on setting out, and kept diaries recording expenses, rendering an account to the financier at the end of the journey.

On arrival at Kanesh, the goods were registered with an organization called the *karum*: the word meant literally 'quay' but was used here of a kind of merchants' guild based at the commercial centre, with written rules of procedure (partly preserved) and means of controlling its members and ensuring their commercial integrity. The goods were then sold, usually to be paid for in silver. The proceeds might be sent back to Assyria as silver, to be laid out on further tin and textiles for further journeys, or more often they were used to buy copper, in consignments of up to five tons.

The Assyrian colonies in Cappadocia finally came to an end in the eighteenth century, possibly from major political upheavals. Whatever the cause, the effect was the temporary cutting off of supplies of Anatolian copper to the Near East.

Royal exchange of gifts

Mari on the middle Euphrates was of high significance for international trade in the early second millennium. It was one of the wealthiest of cities, a status reflected in its enormous palace covering more than six acres, with bathrooms equipped with full-sized terracotta baths, and frescoes on plastered walls. This great wealth came from the city's control of trade along the Euphrates from the Persian Gulf to Syria and the Mediterranean. Along that route passed timber from Lebanon, wine and olive oil from Syria, cloth from Crete, and copper from Cyprus, most of them destined for Babylonia. From the other direction, en route to Syria, came tin from Iran and lapis lazuli from Afghanistan.

Correspondence of around 1800 BC found at Mari tells us a great deal about the conventions on relationships between rulers. One aspect of this was the royal exchange of gifts, which in later centuries came to play an increasingly important part in international trade. This is particularly well illustrated in fourteenth-century cuneiform letters found at El

Amarna in central Egypt, a new capital founded by the Egyptian king Amenophis IV (also called Akhenaten). One of these letters, from the king of Babylonia to the king of Egypt, makes an explicit proposal to use royal exchange of gifts as a mechanism of international trade:

> *Just as formerly you and my father were on good terms with each other, so now let I and you be (like that) with each other. Let no adverse matter come between us. Whatever you want, write to me, so that they may bring it to you, and whatever I want from your land, let me write and let them bring it to me.*[8]

Other letters from the same group show us how this operated. Amenophis III writes to the Babylonian king to say:

> *I have had sent to you as a present for the new house . . . one ebony bed, inlaid with ivory and gold; three ebony beds, inlaid with gold; one ebony headrest, inlaid with gold; one ebony armchair, inlaid with gold; five ebony chairs, inlaid with gold; . . . Altogether these contain gold to the weight of seven minas and nine shekels. The weight of silver is one mina eight shekels.*[9]

The precise valuation which Amenophis puts upon the goods makes it clear that this was no gratuitous gift; it was disguised trading, which expected goods of equal value in return.

Here is another example. The king of Babylonia is writing to Amenophis IV:

> *Since they have told me that the road is dangerous, water scarce and the weather hot, I have not sent you many fine presents. I have sent my brother four minas of fine lapis lazuli as an interim present. I have also sent my brother five teams of horses. When the weather improves, I shall send my brother many fine presents by a later emissary who will be coming. Anything my brother wants, let my brother write to me.*

The Babylonian king then turns to what he would like in payment:

> *I have embarked on a (building) project, and so have written to my brother. Let my brother send me much fine gold, so that I may use it for my project.*

Then comes an indication of problems which could arise in long-distance trading of this kind:

> *The gold which my brother sends, he should not entrust (arrangements for it) to any subordinate. Let my brother see to it personally [literally, let the eye of my brother see (it)], and let my brother (himself) seal and send it. The former gold which my brother sent, because my brother did not see (to it himself) but a subordinate of my brother sealed and sent it, the forty minas of gold which they brought, when I put it into the kiln, it did not come out in the proper amount.*[10]

The quantities of goods mentioned in the foregoing texts are trifling compared with those in one inventory of a consignment sent by Amenophis IV to the Babylonian king. The extant part of the text runs to over three hundred entries: there were over a thousand pieces of clothing; huge numbers of jugs, bowls, basins and other vessels of stone; a similar wealth of ornaments and vessels of ivory and ebony; hundred of bronze mirrors and vessels and tools of the same metal; and objects such as amulets, rings, anklets, vessels of many types and sizes, chests, statues, chariots, bedsteads, and chairs, either of solid gold or silver, or overlaid with those metals. The quantity of gold alone was given as 1200 minas, that is over half a ton, which at the 1988 gold price would be worth over £4,000,000.[11]

But the direct links between the two kings were only the most conspicuous elements in a much more extensive network of trading relations between the territories controlled by Egypt and Babylonia. We find, for example, the Babylonian king asking for the intervention of the Pharaoh, who was overlord of Palestine, on behalf of Babylonian merchants who had been robbed and murdered when trading there.

My merchants . . . were held up on business in Canaan. . . . In the city of Hinnatun in Canaan, [named men] of Acco killed my merchants and took their silver. . . . Canaan is your land and its kings are your vassals. I have been robbed in your land. Make enquiries and repay the silver that they took. And, as to the people who killed my servants, kill them and avenge their blood. For if you do not kill these people, they will come back and kill either a caravan belonging to me or your messengers, so that communications [literally, a messenger] between us will be cut off.

There were occasions when the circumstances of royal exchange of gifts did not result in the amity aimed at. We see an example of this in some letters, probably of the thirteenth century BC, written to the vassal king of the north Syrian city of Ugarit by his representative at the court of his overlord, the Hittite king. As we have seen, lapis lazuli was in great demand by the wealthy, and the only source of it was distant Afghanistan. But Ugarit was at this time the principal trade terminal on the Syrian coast, and thereby the sort of place where lapis lazuli might be available. Other rulers would therefore expect the king of Ugarit to be able to provide it, and it seems that when he could not do so, he resorted to unethical business practices. In this correspondence we find he had been caught out, and had given severe offence to his overlord.

The first letter reads

To my lord, the king of Ugarit, say: thus says your servant Takuhli. From afar I fall twice seven times at the feet of my lord. . . .
What is this business about which you have kept sending messages to the king,

saying, 'Herewith I have sent you lapis lazuli'? The king is very angry. The king has quarrelled with me, saying, 'Is this man having a joke with me, that he has picked up stones from the ground and sent them, saying "Herewith I have sent you lapis lazuli"?'

Is it true about that lapis lazuli that you sent? Better that you did not send at all than that you should take and send such stones—(mere) frit! . . . Now, do find lapis lazuli from somewhere, and send it to the king, so that the king may not be angry against my lord.[12]

There was a second letter on the subject. The king of Ugarit had written to his man to admit that he was unable to obtain any lapis lazuli. This had made the Hittite king very displeased. The representative urged the king of Ugarit to keep trying, because

The king greatly desires lapis lazuli. If you send the king lapis lazuli, then you will see that the king will surely do something good for you.[13]

Another accusation of sharp practice occurs in one of the El Amarna letters. Tushratta, king of Mittanni, north of the middle Euphrates, was writing to the Egyptian king. The Egyptian king's father, who had recently died, had, so Tushratta claimed, promised him statues cast in solid gold, and, he added,

my emissaries, when they were dwelling in Egypt, saw with their own eyes the gold for the statues; and your father had them cast, made and completed in the presence of my emissaries.

But subsequently there must have been a substitution, for Tushratta complains

You have not sent the solid statues which your father was going to send, but you have sent ones of wood, overlaid.[14]

Another diplomatic and trading partner of the king of Egypt in the second half of the second millennium was Cyprus, known in the ancient world as Alashiya. Cyprus, which has important deposits of copper ore, had begun to produce the metal by 2300 BC, and by 1800 BC it was exporting it as far as Mari on the middle Euphrates. In the El Amarna letters (fourteenth century) the king of Alashiya sent an initial missive to the king of Egypt on his accession promising him 200 talents (above five and a half tons) of copper, and requested the opening of diplomatic relations by the exchange of emissaries. In a later letter he had actually sent half the copper promised, and requested in exchange an ebony bedstead inlaid with gold, a chariot and team of horses, various garments, pieces of ebony, and oil. In yet another letter, the king of Cyprus showed himself to be a major supplier of copper to Egypt, as he had sent 500 talents (over 14 tons). However, he was at present unable to send any more, owing to an outbreak of plague ('the hand of the god Nergal'), which, as he put it, 'has killed all the men of my land, so that there is no one to produce copper'; his own son had also died.[15]

The king of Alashiya had his own merchants and his own ships trading with Egypt, and one of his letters seems to be a kind of passport for them. After the initial greetings to the king of Egypt, it reads:

> These people are my merchants, my brother. Send them (back) safely and quickly. As to my merchants and my ship, anyone (responsible for) making claims on your behalf must not make a claim against them.[16]

A north Syrian trading port

On the coast of north Syria, for two centuries from about 1400 BC, the richest mercantile centre was Ugarit. This city gives us much information on trade in the eastern Mediterranean, and it is particularly enlightening because it was never more than a minor state, so that the picture it draws is not complicated by power politics. Some of the information is derived from archaeological remains, but most comes from inscribed clay tablets. These tablets were of two kinds; some were in the syllabic writing of Akkadian cuneiform, and others were written in the alphabetic cuneiform script invented in Ugarit itself (pp. 79–82).

The documents mention a great range of trading goods. There were foodstuffs such as wheat, barley, emmer, olives, raisins, figs, dates, honey, cheese, cummin, wine, and olive oil; other vegetable products included linseed oil,[17] aromatic oils, incense, and reeds. Flax was traded there. So was wool, particularly purple wool, for Ugarit was already a centre for the production of purple dye, anticipating in this the industry for which the ports of Phoenicia, further south along the coast, were later to become famous; purple wool was sent as tribute to Hatti-land. Traders dealt in a wide range of textiles, such as cloths, carpets, sashes and garments of linen and wool. Metals such as copper, bronze, tin, lead and iron (still rare and valuable) have been found in excavations or are mentioned in texts, as ingots or in the form of weapons, vessels or tools. Livestock markets at Ugarit dealt in horses, donkeys, mules, cattle, sheep, and geese and other birds. Timber was an important export from Ugarit: a foreign customer would specify the variety and dimensions of the timber he needed and the king of Ugarit would send logs of appropriate size. We find this procedure reflected in the following letter:

Thus says the king of Carchemish[18] to Ibirani king of Ugarit:
Greetings to you! Now the dimensions—length and breadth—I have sent to you.
Send two junipers according to those dimensions. Let them be as long as the
(specified) length and as wide as the (specified) breadth.[19]

Miscellaneous objects of commerce included baskets, sacks, ropes, tongs, scales, hammers, lapis lazuli and other precious stones, glass, beads, and cosmetics. Carpenters produced beds, chests and other wooden furniture, and we hear of other craftsmen such as bowmakers and metalworkers. There were also shipbuilders, who produced ships not only for Ugarit's own merchant navy but also for sale to other maritime cities such as Byblos. As a final traded commodity, there were slaves.

Some of the objects of trade came from a great distance. Myrrh, for instance, originated in the southwestern corner of Arabia, and lapis lazuli came from Badakhshan in northern Afghanistan; both regions were about 1700 miles in a straight line from Ugarit, and substantially more by the practicable routes. One of the timbers was ebony, which had to be imported from central Africa via Egypt.

The texts from Ugarit contain many references to merchants, both native and foreign. Some of the native merchants were very wealthy: we meet one who owned several landed estates and had two villages granted to him by the king. Some merchants belonged to the class called *mariannu*, a title granted by the king bestowing status next after the royal family; such noblemen owned chariots and teams of horses for use in war.

Ugaritic merchants received official status and grants of land in consideration of their undertaking trading activities on behalf of the king. We see this clearly stated in the following document, written in Akkadian cuneiform:

. . . Amistamru . . . king of Ugarit took the houses and fields of Abutena and gave
it to Abdi-hagab son of Shapidana, and his sons for ever. And he shall perform the
service of duties as a merchant. Moreover, as long as Abdi-hagab performs
merchant duties, no one shall take (the grant) away from Abdi-hagab and his sons
and grandsons for ever. The seal of the great king. Iluramu (was) the scribe.

But, although in the first instance merchants acted on behalf of the state, one would be surprised if, in view of the opportunities they had, they did not engage in trade on their own account and to their own profit; indeed, there is specific evidence that they did so.

Ugarit was both a terminal for land routes from Anatolia and inner Syria and Mesopotamia, and also a sea port, and many merchants from Ugarit went on trading journeys abroad, either overland by donkey caravan, or by sea. To destinations such as Cyprus and Crete, sea travel

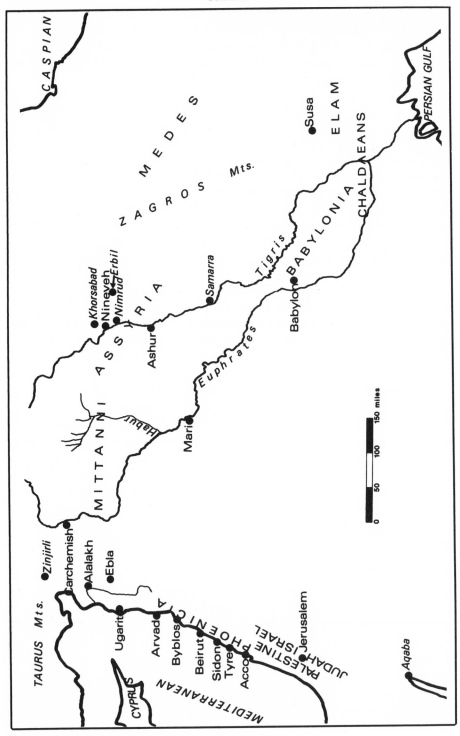

Mesopotamia, Syria and Palestine

was the only possibility, and it was by far the most convenient way of reaching Egypt and the southern coast of Asia Minor and other ports along the Levant. Copper, for example, was shipped to Beirut, and ships from Ugarit often touched at Byblos. We have a letter, written on a clay tablet in alphabetic cuneiform, in which the king of Tyre reports the loss at sea in a storm of a ship from Ugarit, en route for Egypt. In another document, we hear of a merchant's ship arriving in Ugarit from Crete, when it automatically came under the protection of the king and was exempt from customs duties. Another document constituted a passport for a man and his son, issued by the king, authorizing them to use the routes to Egypt and the land of the Hittites, clear proof of the royal supervision of trade.

Groups of merchants might enter into partnerships for foreign ventures: we find, for example, four merchants jointly subscribing a total of 1000 shekels of silver for a trading expedition to Egypt. Being a merchant abroad was not without its risks. At least nine documents from Ugarit deal with compensation for foreign merchants killed either there or in other cities. Townsmen were responsible for the safety of foreign merchants doing business in their town, and if a merchant were robbed and murdered and the criminals were not caught, the citizens themselves had to pay compensation.

Ugarit was a thoroughly cosmopolitan city. Foreign nationals recorded there, mainly merchants but also diplomatic personnel, included Egyptians, Hittites, Hurrians, Assyrians, Cretans, Canaanites and Cypriots. The spread of languages used in inscriptions matched this. Some of the foreigners were apparently in the service of the king of Ugarit. Thus, one Egyptian received a royal grant of land, and another Egyptian and his sons were said to be liable to state service in connection with Egypt and Hatti-land, which probably meant that, in return for a grant of land, they serve as commercial agents for the king of Ugarit in Egypt and Hatti.

International trade brought large numbers of foreign merchants into some commercial centres, where some were tempted to become permanent residents and buy up property. This could create friction. We see the Hittite Great King Hattushilish III (early thirteenth century BC) attempting to deal with such a situation, in which some of his agents, merchants from Ura, a centre of trade somewhere in Anatolia north of Syria, were making themselves unpopular. His vassal, Niqmepa, king of Ugarit, had complained, and Hattushilish was now writing to tell him of the measures he proposed to take:

Since you have said to me, 'The merchants of Ura are very heavy upon the country of your servant', now the Sun-god, the Great King, has made an arrangement for the people of Ura with the people of Ugarit. Let the people of Ura do their mercantile activities within Ugarit in the summer, and in winter time they shall send them out from within Ugarit to their (own) country. They shall not dwell within Ugarit in the winter, and they shall not acquire houses or fields with their silver.[20]

A further provision followed, to cover the problem which might arise from a merchant of Ura having his funds wholly tied up in Ugarit so that he could not leave.

At about 1200 BC the Hittite empire was overthrown by a mass movement of population into Asia Minor, and the north Syrian cities, including Ugarit, shared in the disaster. This increased the commercial importance of the Phoenician trading centres, particularly Tyre, Sidon and Byblos, further south along the coast; from about 1100 BC, they began to become the sea traders par excellence.

The Phoenicians

The Phoenicians, one of the most important factors in first-millennium international trade, were ethnically descendants of the Canaanites, who had earlier occupied much of Palestine but by the end of the second millennium had become restricted to the coastal fringe from Tyre northwards, now known as Lebanon.

Geography determined the primary economy of Phoenicia. It lay between great cedar forests and the Mediterranean Sea: its timber potential had always made the region of economic interest to the great powers of Mesopotamia and Egypt, and the sea provided an escape route from total economic domination by those two powers. The people of the area had long engaged in sea trade, and by early in the first millennium the Phoenicians were beginning to outstrip all other peoples in this activity. They developed an improved type of ship capable of making longer voyages, and the Bible mentions 'ships of Tarshish', which are generally taken to mean ships capable of trading with distant Spain. Under the stimulus of their Phoenician neighbours, the Israelites also began to engage in naval activity from the beginning of the first millennium. The coastal tribes of Zebulon and Dan had been involved with shipping almost as early as the Phoenicians (Genesis 49:13; Judges 5:17), but these were minor peripheral tribes, and when Solomon, in his attempts at economic expansion, built a commercial navy in the tenth century BC, it was, as 1 Kings 10:22 tells us, the Phoenician king Hiram of Tyre whose assistance he invoked to man his ships. Solomon's navy joined with Tyre's to operate from the Gulf of Akaba, on voyages which might take up to three years for the round trip, to a place called Ophir. Thence they brought back silver, gold, precious stones, valuable hardwood, ivory, apes and peacocks (if Hebrew *tukkiyyim* is correctly so translated). The length of time taken, and the goods obtained, suggest that the mysterious Ophir may have been India. Others would take it as some port in south Arabia.

But cooperation with Israel in the Gulf of Akaba was only a brief incident in the trading activities of the Phoenicians; their main activities were in the Mediterranean. Besides timber production, Phoenicia had another industry which brought great wealth. The sea along its coast was the habitat of a shellfish (*murex brandaris*) which secretes a substance yielding a purple dye, and the Phoenicians exploited this to make themselves the main Near Eastern centre of dyed textiles: so valuable was this dye, that robes of this colour became a mark of royal rank, whence the expression 'born to the purple'.

Classical authors speak of a Phoenician expansion into the western Mediterranean as early as the twelfth century, attributing the founding of Cadiz to these people before 1100 BC, but archaeologists have so far found no evidence to support such an early date for Phoenician colonies. It is true that a bronze statuette of Phoenician type and datable to about 1000 BC was found in the sea off Sicily, but this may have been dropped there centuries after it was made. However, the biblical story about Solomon and Hiram of Tyre puts it beyond doubt that by the tenth century the Phoenicians were the recognized experts in operating ships on long voyages.

The first definite proof of a Phoenician presence further west in the Mediterranean comes from a Phoenician inscription of the ninth century found in Sardinia, and on the basis of this there is no reason to reject the traditional date of 814 BC for the founding of what was to become the greatest Phoenician colony, Carthage in north Africa; Phoenician pottery of about 800 BC, found in that area, further supports that date. Several Phoenician settlements in the western Mediterranean can be archaeologically dated to not later than the eighth or seventh centuries: for Cadiz the evidence points to a date not later than the eighth century, perhaps earlier. By tradition the most important settlement in Spain was called Tartessus, possibly the biblical Tarshish, somewhere in the south, but the site is not archaeologically identified. A colony on the island of Ibiza was according to tradition founded in the seventh century. What the Phoenicians were after in Spain were silver and tin, and there is a persistent classical tradition that by the mid-fifth century they had extended their quest for tin as far as the British Isles (Cornwall and Ireland).

Archaeological evidence thus has Phoenician colonization beginning its main phase in the late ninth century, and intensifying in the eighth and seventh. This ties up with political history. Assyria expanded to the Mediterranean coast in the ninth century, tightened its hold over all Syria and Palestine during the following century and totally dominated the region by 720 BC. When the Assyrians first arrived, the Phoenician cities (Tyre, Sidon, Byblos, Arvad, and others) were already thriving commercial communities. By hastening to pay a rich tribute of gold, silver, tin, bronze, coloured linen, and ivory, they escaped attack, but the undoubted Assyrian ability and obvious intention to control their mainland trade gave the Phoenicians a strong incentive to develop their maritime potential; from this time they increasingly traded with other coastal regions and with more westerly parts of the Mediterranean, and began to found colonies away from Assyrian control. By the time of Homer, not later than the eighth century, the Phoenicians were well known to the Greeks as seafarers who ranged the Mediterranean, for in the *Odyssey*, Odysseus tells a story of how he was taken up by a Phoenician sea-merchant in Egypt, carried to Phoenicia, and then put on a ship for Libya.[21]

Just before 700 BC, Isaiah spoke of Tyre, the greatest of the Phoenician cities, as 'the merchant of the nations' (23:3),[22] but for Phoenician trade in its heyday, no better summary could be asked than that given by Ezekiel over a century later:

The inhabitants of Sidon and Arvad were your rowers; skilled men of Zemer were in you, they were your pilots. The elders of Gebal [Byblos, north of Beirut] and her skilled men were in you, caulking your seams; all the ships of the sea with their mariners were in you, to barter for your wares. . . . Tarshish [Spain?] trafficked with you because of your great wealth of every kind; silver, iron, tin, and lead they exchanged for your wares. Javan [Greece], Tubal [in Asia Minor] and Meshech [Phrygia] traded with you; they exchanged the persons of men and vessels of bronze for your merchandise. Beth-togormah [in Asia Minor] exchanged for your wares horses, war horses, and mules. The men of Rhodes traded with you; many coastlands were your own special markets, they brought you in payment ivory tusks and ebony. . . . Judah and the land of Israel traded with you; they exchanged for your merchandise wheat, olives and early figs, honey, oil, and balm. Damascus trafficked with you for your abundant goods, because of your great wealth of every kind; wine of Helbon, and white wool, and wine from Uzal [south-east Turkey] they exchanged for your wares; wrought iron, cassia, and calamus were bartered for your merchandise. . . . Arabia and all the princes of Kedar were your favoured dealers in lambs, rams and goats; in these they trafficked with you. The traders of Sheba [south Arabia] and Raamah traded with you; they exchanged for your wares the best of all kinds of spices, and all precious stones, and gold. . . . The ships of Tarshish [i.e., sea-going ships] travelled for you with your merchandise. (Ezekiel 27:8–9,12–15,17–19,21–22,24)[23]

But the Phoenicians went even further afield than the prophet knew. According to Herodotus, a decade or so before Ezekiel's description of the Phoenician seafarers, one group of their sailors, on the orders of the Egyptian king Necho, had undertaken a voyage of discovery southward from the Red Sea to find if Africa could be circumnavigated. (Herodotus called it Libya, extending the name used for north Africa to designate the whole continent.) The Phoenician explorers succeeded, returning after three years via the Straits of Gibraltar.[24]

8

Law

Everywhere in the ancient Near East, the giving of justice was an essential function of the ruler, whether king or tribal leader. Social injustice was an offence against the gods. Ancient Israel was one of the slowest of ancient Near Eastern societies to develop to statehood, and kingship did not arrive there until the eleventh century BC, but long before that time we find Israelite leaders who were lawgivers and judges. The first and greatest was of course Moses, and so important was his function of administering justice that at one stage his activities in settling disputes were occupying the whole of his time (Exodus 18:13–26). His father-in-law, concerned for his health, advised him to limit his personal involvement to major cases, delegating minor cases to 'able men from all the people, such as fear God, men who are trustworthy and who hate a bribe'. This was duly done: these other men 'judged the people at all times; hard cases they brought to Moses, but any small matter they decided themselves'.

Under the early Israelite monarchy the ruler's responsibility to give judgement either himself or through his delegate was still strongly felt; David's son Absolom exploited this situation to gain popular support before his rebellion:

> Absolom used to rise early and stand beside the way of the gate; and when any man had a suit to come before the king for judgment, . . . Absolom would say to him, 'See, your claims are good and right; but there is no man deputed by the king to hear you. . . . Oh that I were judge in the land! Then every man with a suit or cause might come to me, and I would give him justice.' (2 Samuel 15:2–4)

The Bible was long held to contain the world's earliest laws, comprising not only the Decalogue but also a large collection of other laws attributed to Moses. These laws take one of two forms, called respectively apodictic and casuistic. Apodictic laws are absolute prohibitions, such as 'Thou shalt not kill'. Casuistic laws are those of the type 'If a man delivers to his neighbour money or goods to keep, and it is stolen out of the man's house, then, if the thief is found, he shall pay double' (Exodus 22:7).

Many biblical laws do not relate to the circumstances of the time of Moses: examples are those about land tenure or vineyards or corn stacks catching fire (Exodus 22:6). Those whose critical judgement has been frozen by the icy kiss of religious dogma settle the difficulty by taking these as laws given by God in advance for the time of the settlement in Palestine, but they do not explain why God should have limited his legislative foresight to minute details of the four centuries of the Israelite monarchy, down to details of which fabrics might or might not be worn (Leviticus 19:19), and given no guidance on major problems which were to arise in later ages, such as motoring law or the use of gas in warfare. But others take the evidence as showing that lawgiving in Israel did not end with Moses, but was an evolving process which went on right into the Monarchy period.

Laws of Hammurabi[1]

At the very beginning of the twentieth century, the traditional belief in the chronological priority of the biblical laws was rudely shattered. In late 1901 and early 1902, French archaeologists digging at the site of Susa in south-west Iran found large inscribed fragments of the black stone basalt, which, rejoined, made up a stele about eight and a half feet high (now in the Louvre, plate 16), which proved to contain the law code of the Babylonian king Hammurabi, early in the second millennium. Elamites had taken it off to Susa as a war trophy in antiquity. Not only were these laws indisputably earlier than the earliest date from which the laws of Moses could have derived, but also parts of the subject matter coincided with the subject matter of the Mosaic laws. Thus, both Hammurabi and Moses legislated for the case of a person reduced to slavery for debt:

> Hammurabi's Laws, §117: *If a debt has brought about the seizure of a man and he has delivered his wife or his son or his daughter for silver, or has delivered them as persons distrained for debt, for three years they shall serve in the house of the buyer or distrainer; in the fourth year their freedom shall be established.*
> Deuteronomy 15:12,18: *If your brother, a Hebrew man, or a Hebrew woman, is sold to you, he shall serve you six years, and in the seventh year you shall let him go free from you. . . . It shall not seem hard to you, when you let him go free from you; for as double the hire of a hireling [RSV, 'at half the cost of a hired servant'] has he served you six years.*

Obviously, the two laws give essentially the same kind of solution for the same problem. It was initially argued that the biblical prescription of six years' servitude rather than three, together with the reference to 'double the hire', showed that the biblical legislator was aware of Hammurabi's law and had deliberately modified it in favour of the slave-owner. A controversy developed, in which some claimed that the biblical laws were directly derived from those of Hammurabi. More detailed research showed that this view was untenable, and that such similarities as there were resulted from the need for both to deal with similar social and economic problems in accordance with customs widespread in the ancient Near East.

Altogether nearly 300 clauses of laws are now known, sandwiched between a prologue and an epilogue. Some of the clauses were erased from the stele in antiquity, but can be restored from clay tablets containing part of the code. The subjects covered comprise the following:

Administration of justice (5 sections).
Offences against property (20 sections).
Land tenure (about 50 sections).
Trade and commercial transactions (nearly 40 sections).
The family as a social institution (68 sections). [These laws cover such matters as adultery, marriage, concubinage, desertion, divorce, incest, adoption, inheritance].
Penalties for assault (20 sections).
Professional services (16 sections). [These concern rates of payment, and penalties for unsatisfactory performance of services].
Draught-oxen (16 sections).
Agriculture (11 sections).
Wages and rates of hire (10 sections).
Ownership of slaves (5 sections).

All the laws are in the casuistic form: as an example, one of the shortest reads

If a man has kidnapped the son of a free man, he shall be put to death.

Hammurabi makes it clear in the prologue and epilogue to his laws that they were positioned in a public place, where people could read them or have them read to them:

Let the oppressed man who has a cause go before my statue called 'King of Justice', and then have the inscription on my monument read and hear my precious words, that my monument may make clear his cause to him, let him see the law which applies to him [literally, 'let him see his case'], and let his heart be set at ease.

Hammurabi's laws were not statutes: we never find them quoted in Babylonian courts, even though we have thousands of court records. In the prologue and epilogue, what we call the laws are designated by a term which means 'decisions'. This terminology, and the form of the clauses, suggests that in many cases they actually were royal decisions. On the other hand, they were not purely real royal decisions. Rather, they were specimens of what a sound royal decision should be, as a basis for the administration of justice. This is clear from the advice Hammurabi gives his successors in the epilogue:

> *To the end of days, for ever, may the king who happens to be in the land observe the words of justice which I have inscribed on my stele. . . . If that man has the sanction (of the gods) and so is able to give his land justice, let him pay heed to the words which I have written on my stele, and let that stele show him the accustomed way, the way to follow, the land's judgements which I have judged and the land's decisions which I have decided.*

Not all the so-called 'decisions' in the laws were real decisions at all; some must have been extensions to fit hypothetical cases, by analogy from some actual decision. There is a very evidence instance of this in a group of laws concerning a man striking a pregnant woman. The first two clauses of this group read:

> *§209: If a man has struck the daughter of a free man and caused her to cast that which was within her womb, he shall pay ten shekels of silver.*
> *§210: If that woman died as a result, they shall kill his daughter.*

At this time Babylonian society was tripartite: in addition to full free citizens, there was a client class and there were slaves. This group of laws goes on to prescribe penalties if a man caused the miscarriage of a lower class woman or a slave, and the more severe penalties which would be appropriate if such a woman died as a result. It is most unlikely that Hammurabi ever had before him six distinct cases about striking different classes of women with different consequences, and we may reasonably conclude that there was one real case he had to decide upon, and that when the laws were drafted his decision in the one real case was expanded to make provision for the other five possibilities. It is this kind of systematization which makes it legitimate to think of the laws of Hammurabi as not just a random collection but in some sense a code.

The laws were not intended to effect major alterations in the social structure and general legal practice of the land, but in some places they must have appeared in a limited sense as a reform. Previously, different cities in south Mesopotamia had had different customary ways of dealing with certain problems; now Hammurabi's law laid down a uniform code of practice for his whole kingdom, and for some of the cities this must have involved changes of long-established practice.

We have mentioned that the laws of Hammurabi were never quoted in Babylonian courts. Yet there are hints that, although never quoted, they continued to play a part in court decisions centuries after they were promulgated. A case in point was a trial at Erech in the late sixth century BC, in which two workmen were accused of having stolen two ducks belonging to the temple. For what might seem a trivial offence, the proceedings were remarkably highpowered, since there were present not only the principal administrators of the great temple of Eanna but also representatives from the capital, Babylon. One can hardly understand what all the fuss was about, without assuming that the authorities still acted according to the laws of Hammurabi, of more than a millennium earlier. In those laws, there were two clauses which might have had relevance to the present case:

§6: *If a man has stolen the property of a god or of a palace, that man shall be put to death.*

§8: *If a man has stolen an ox, a sheep, an ass or a pig or a boat, if it belongs to a god or if it belongs to a palace, he shall pay thirty-fold.*

There is a slight difference in the wording between the two clauses: §6 implies that the property was stolen actually from the dwelling of the god or from the palace; whereas §8 covers the case in which the property belonged to, but was not actually inside, the temple or palace: the former case alone was sacrilegious and involved the death penalty. Thus the issue in the sixth century case, and the reason for the involvement of so many highranking officials, was which of the penalties in Hammurabi's laws applied. The thieves admitted the theft, but supplied details which showed that it took place outside the temple wall. Their evidence, which proved that the crime was not sacrilegious, was accepted, and in consequence the sentence imposed was the lesser one of thirty-fold restitution.

Laws of Lipit-Ishtar,[2] Ur-Nammu and Eshnunna

In the 1940s some new laws were identified which robbed the Hammurabi Code of its chronological priority. These laws, written in Sumerian, had been promulgated by Lipit-Ishtar (1934–1924 BC) of Isin, a city which made itself predominant in south Mesopotamia after the fall of the III Ur empire. There is a prologue which speaks of the gods raising Lipit-Ishtar to power 'to establish justice in the land, ... to bring wellbeing to the people of Sumer and Akkad [south and north Babylonia]'. Lipit-Ishtar then mentions how he achieved this, apparently by releasing citizens from slavery and bringing broken families together, but the passage is broken and obscure. Then come the laws. There are about twenty virtually complete and fully intelligible clauses, which cover rather a limited range of matters, namely: issues related to ownership of land, including theft from or damage to an orchard; runaway slaves; inheritance; betrothal and marriage; and injury to hired animals. The most extensive single group are the inheritance laws; the following extract from these serves to illustrate the form and approach of the whole:

§24: If a woman whom a man took as secondary wife bore him children, the dowry which she brought from her father's house belongs to her children, but the children of the (primary) wife and the children of the second wife shall share equally in the property of their father.

§25: If a man married a wife and she bore him children and those children are living, and a slave-girl also bore children for her master, (even if) the father granted freedom to the slave-girl and her children, the slave-girl's children shall not share the estate with the children of their master.

§26: If the wife died, and after her death the man took his slave-girl as wife, the children of the (first) wife are (still) the heirs. The children which the slave-girl bore to her master shall . . . (The end of the law is broken).

§27: If a man's wife has not borne him children, but a prostitute from the streets has borne him children, he shall provide grain, oil and clothing for that prostitute. The children which the prostitute has borne him shall be his heirs, but as long as his wife lives the prostitute shall not live in the house with his wife.

§28: If a man has turned his face away from his wife, . . . but she has not gone away, . . . and he married a woman as a secondary wife, he shall continue to support his wife.

Limited though they are, the Lipit-Ishtar laws show several features of the society of the time. There was a clear distinction of rights between slave and free; a man could emancipate and marry a slave-girl; a wife had definite rights at law, and in particular enjoyed the security that her husband could not arbitrarily divorce her and throw her out of the house in favour of another woman. Land ownership brought privileges but also responsibilities, as the following section of the laws shows:

§11: If next to a man's estate, another man's uncultivated land lies waste and the houseowner has told the owner of the uncultivated land, 'Because your land lies waste someone may break into my estate; safeguard your estate', and this agreement is confirmed by him, the owner of the uncultivated ground shall make good to the owner of the estate any of his property that is lost.

Still earlier laws were to appear. In the 1950s and 1960s there were found two duplicate tablets, neither complete, of Sumerian laws deriving from Ur-Nammu,[3] who founded the Third Dynasty of Ur at about 2100 BC. The extant text, after a broken account of Ur-Nammu's rise to power, goes on to mention dealing with abuses in taxation and setting up standard weights and measures. Then comes a significant statement of the principle Ur-Nammu adopted to prevent the exploitation of the economically weak by the strong:

> *The orphan was not given over to the rich man; the widow not given over to the powerful man; the man of one shekel was not given over to the man of one mina.*

The extant laws follow; those which are completely preserved or nearly so concern the following topics:

> *§4: A wife who chases and seduces a man shall be put to death, but the man shall go free.*
>
> *§5: Penalty for raping someone's virgin slave-girl.*
>
> *§§6–8: Payments to divorced wife. ['If a man divorces his chief wife, he shall pay her one mina of silver. If it is a former widow whom he divorces, he shall pay her half a mina of silver. If the man cohabited with the widow without a marriage contract, he need not pay her any silver.']*
>
> *§§10–11: Payment for false accusation.*
>
> *§12: Compensation by prospective father-in-law to son-in-law for broken betrothal contract.*
>
> *§14: Payment for return of runaway slave.*
>
> *§§15–19: Penalties for inflicting bodily injury. ['If a man has broken the limb of another man with a weapon in a fight, he shall pay one mina of silver. If a man severed the nose of another man . . . he shall pay two-thirds of a mina of silver.']*
>
> *§§22–23: Penalties for insolence by a slave-girl to her mistress.*
>
> *§§25–26: Penalty for perjury or refusal to testify in a lawsuit.*
>
> *§§27–29: Agricultural laws: (27) A man who wrongfully ploughs another man's field cannot claim his expenses; (28) Rate of damages to be paid by a man who floods another man's field; (29) Damages payable by man who does not cultivate a field he has leased.*

The text when complete probably contained nearly twice this number of laws. Their rather miscellaneous subject-matter strongly suggests that they were records of decisions by Ur-Nammu in actual cases. There is no indication of any general attempt to draw up a set of regulations to deal with problems of the society of the time.

Perhaps the most significant aspect of the Ur-Nammu laws—the earliest we yet have—is that, unlike the laws of Hammurabi and the Bible, they do not envisage the barbarism of the lex talionis—the principle of an eye for an eye and a tooth for a tooth—as a penalty for causing bodily injury.

There is one further major collection of laws to be mentioned from ancient south Mesopotamia—the laws of Eshnunna.[4] Eshnunna was an Old Babylonian kingdom lying along the Diyala and stretching as far south as the Tigris. In excavations in 1945 and 1947 at Tell Harmal, then just outside Baghdad, now engulfed in the rapidly growing city, there were found two almost duplicate tablets containing laws from that kingdom. They are of particular interest to assyriologists and jurists, because substantial parts of them are similar in substance to the Laws of Hammurabi, but about a century older, and this gives some hints as to how collections of laws developed.

The text begins with a dating, now broken. Then come two lists of prices: one of these states how much barley, oil, wool, salt, natron, or copper could be bought for one shekel of silver, and the other gives the amount of barley which might be bought for one unit of various kinds of oil. This is followed by rates of hire: items mentioned are a wagon with its oxen and driver, a boat with a boatman, a donkey with its driver, and various hired workers. This official tariff of prices and rates of hire strongly suggests that the Eshnunna laws developed out of an economic edict.

How, if this was the case, did it come about? How could laws grow out of economic measures? When we examine the text further, the answer looks fairly transparent. Two sections about rates of hire are followed by specific legal decisions. The first group of clauses reads:

§4: *The hire of a boat is two qa (of barley) per gur of capacity, and the hire of a boatman is 11 qa of barley; (for that) he shall operate it all day.*
§5: *If a boatman was negligent and allowed the boat to sink, he shall pay in full the value of as much as he caused to sink.*
§6: *If a man has seized by fraud a boat which is not his, he shall weigh out ten shekels of silver.*

The second group is as follows:

§7: *The hire of a harvester is 20 qa of barley. If (payment is in) silver, his hire is one-fifteenth of a shekel.*
§8: *The hire of a winnower is 10 qa of barley.*
§9: *If a man gave a hired man one shekel of silver for harvesting, if (the person contracting) did not hold to his obligation and did not do his harvesting at all, he shall weight out ten shekels of silver.*

We see here how easily an economic decree can serve as a stimulus to the rise of written laws. The original tariff list prescribed rates of hire for a boat and a boatman. But various things can happen in using a boat: the hirer may be aggrieved because the boat sinks and he loses his goods, or the boat's owner may suffer loss because someone uses it without authorization. Issues of this kind must have arisen for decision. It would be natural to link the decisions to the context in which the problem arose, and to enter them in the records immediately after the section of the decree dealing with the rate of hire of boats and boatmen. Similarly, with rates of hire prescribed for harvesters, sooner or later someone would default after contracting to undertake the harvesting; it would be appropriate to insert the official decision on the breach of contract immediately after the statement on rate of hire.

Once the original economic tariff had begun to incorporate decisions on matters arising out of the tariff, it was only a step to adding decisions on other economic and social issues, until the tariff element was completely submerged in other material. We find this development in the laws of Hammurabi, which still retain some tariffs for rates of hire and wage rates, but modestly near the end, and in the Hittite laws.

The concerns of the Eshnunna laws were basically economic and social: essentially they legislated for matters which were potentially disruptive of society. The primary concerns of the time were property rights, marriage rights and the rights of parents over unmarried women, and the protection of the person of the free citizen. Accordingly, the laws deal predominantly with theft and related offences; marriage, divorce and sexual offences; assault, bodily injuries, and death from negligence; contracts and sale of property; and rights over slaves.

This collection of laws seems to have grown up piecemeal; they show little evidence of attempt at logical arrangement. For instance, problems concerning marriage and divorce recur in three separate sections.

The following group illustrates some of the concerns of the laws and also shows their lack of systematic arrangement:

§30: If a man hated his town and his lord and fled, and another man thereupon took his wife, if he returns he shall have no claim to his wife.

§31: If a man slept with a(nother) man's slave-girl, he shall weigh out one-third of a shekel of silver, and the slave-girl is (still the property) of her owner.

§32: If a man put his son out for suckling and rearing but for the three years (up to weaning) did not give provisions, toilet oil and clothing, he shall weigh out ten minas of silver for the rearing of his son, and then take his son back.

§33: If a slave-girl deceitfully handed over her son to a free woman, if his master traces him, (even) after he has grown up, he may seize him and take him back.

Laws concerned with assault present an obvious point of comparison with other ancient legislation:

§42: If a man bit a man's nose and severed it, he shall weigh out one mina of silver.

(For damage to) an eye, one mina; a tooth, half a mina; an ear, half a mina; for a blow on the cheek, he shall weigh out ten shekels of silver.

§43: If a man severed a man's finger, he shall weigh out two-thirds of a mina of silver.

§44: If a man knocked a man down in the dark and broke his hand, he shall weigh out half a mina of silver.

§45: If he broke his foot, he shall weigh out half a mina of silver.

Here the principle of talion—an eye for an eye and a tooth for a tooth—so marked in the Bible and also in the laws of Hammurabi, is completely absent. In view of what we know of untamed human nature and the whole history of man, it would seem self-evident that direct revenge for an injury is more primitive than acceptance of a pecuniary recompense. Moreover, this is directly confirmed by the Hittite laws, which state that formerly theft of beehives was punished by exposure to bee sting, but later by a fine, and similarly that another type of theft was formerly a capital crime but was now punished by a fine. Curiously, some scholars attempt to argue that pecuniary recompense for personal injury was more primitive than talion, on the ground that the laws of Ur-Nammu and the laws of Eshnunna prescribe compensation, whereas the laws of Hammurabi and the Bible, both of them later than the other two, prescribe revenge. But this proves nothing: Ur-Nammu's kingdom was based on one of the ancient Sumerian city-states, with a thousand years of city life behind it, and the kingdom of Eshnunna shared in a similar background to a lesser extent. By contrast, Hammurabi's background was that of Amorite nomads only a century or so removed from the tribal society of the desert, and the background of the Old Testament laws was socially even more primitive.

Not only do the laws of Eshnunna not set out to be a comprehensive legal code, but there are major areas of human behaviour in which problems must have arisen, which they do not even hint at. Murder and incest are two glaring examples. Probably the procedure in such matters was so rigidly established by longstanding custom that the need to prescribe particular solutions never arose.

Hittite laws[5]

At Boghazkoi (site of the ancient Hittite capital, Hattusha, 90–100 miles east of Ankara), excavators found clay tablets inscribed with laws; these lacked the prologue and epilogue which shows the laws on the stele of Hammurabi to be an official compilation, and were evidently collections for the use of jurists. The laws, which are mainly later copies of laws probably first drafted at about 1650 BC, represent not only a codification but also a revision of more ancient Hittite law, showing this by explicit mention of former legal practices now changed. The extant laws, mainly on two tablets, one largely complete, the other with gaps, comprise two hundred clauses.

The most common form of the Hittite laws is

If a man [does such-and-such], he shall [be subject to such-and-such penalty].

The contents cover aspects of life ranging from land tenure to black magic to permitted and forbidden forms of sexual relations. The following summary covers the great majority of the laws; a few obscure and broken ones are omitted:

§§1–8: Causing death or bodily injury.

§§19–21: Kidnapping.

§§22–24: Runaway slaves.

§§25: Damage to property.

§§26–36: Divorce, dowries, betrothal, marriage.

§§37–38: Deaths from feud resultant upon an elopement or lawsuit.

§§39–43: Land tenure and feudal service.

§§45: Theft by retaining lost property. A later modification prescribes that it is only theft if the finder has not secured witnesses that he attempted to trace the owner.

§§46–56: Land tenure and feudal service.

§§57–78: Theft, death or injury of agricultural animals.

§79: Straying oxen.

§§81–86: Theft of or injury to a pig.

§§87–90: Killing a dog.

§§91–92: Theft of bees.

§§93–133: Burglary, arson and various types of theft.

§§142–144: Damage to or loss of another person's property.

§145: Payment to builder and penalty for default.

§§146–148: Penalties for gazumping.

§§150–161: Wage rates.

§162: Penalty for diverting an irrigation ditch.

§164: Penalty for a ritual offence.

§§166–167: Penalty for over-sowing another man's sown field; formerly a ritual death, now a fine.

§§168–169: Boundary violations.

§170: Practice of black magic.

§171: Disinheritance and reinstatement of son by mother.

§172: Payment for saving a person from death by famine.

§173: Penalties for rejection of legitimate authority.

§174: Fine for causing death in a fight.

§175: Status of free woman who marries a slave.

§§176–186: Price tariff.

§§187–189: Sexual offences: bestiality, incest.

§§192–195: Permitted sexual behaviour: a man may marry deceased wife's sister; Levirate marriage is prescribed; a man may in some circumstances have sexual relations with sisters and their mother, and several kinsmen may have sexual relations with the same woman.

§195: Adultery of a man with his brother's wife or with the daughter or mother or sister of his own wife is a capital offence.

§§197–198: Rape and adultery.

§§199–200: Bestiality.

Obviously, there is here some degree of organization by subject matter, although the contents are far from being fully systematic. Thus, there are two separate groups of laws concerned with land tenure and feudal service, and the laws deal twice with bestiality and twice (§§31–36 and 175) with marriage between a free and an unfree person.

One of the interesting features in the Hittite laws, rare in other ancient Near Eastern legislation, is a tendency to include statements of what is, as well as what is not, permitted. For example, part of the collection of laws on sexual behaviour near the end reads:

§190: If a man has sexual relations with his stepmother, it is no offence. But if his father is still alive, it is a criminal abomination.

§193: If a man has a wife and the man dies, his brother shall take his wife, then his father shall take her. If in the second place his father dies, and his brother [variant 'the son of his brother'] takes the wife whom he had, it is not an offence.

§194: If a free man has sexual relations with unfree girls and their mother, it is not an offence. If men in the relationship of brothers sleep with (the same) free woman, there is no offence.

The lex talionis was not applied in the Hittite laws:

§7: If someone blinds a free man or knocks out his teeth, formerly he would give one mina of silver, now he gives 20 shekels of silver and pledges his estate as security.

§8: If someone blinds a male or female slave or knocks out his or her teeth, he shall give 10 shekels of silver and pledge his house as security.

§7 illustrates another feature of the Hittite laws—their reforming nature: it notes an earlier penalty and then states the revised one. The laws as a whole contain a number of references to former provisions, subsequently modified, generally in the direction of greater clemency. The most striking example is related to the illicit second sowing of a field which had already been sown. At the earliest period, the Hittites treated this as a matter of the greatest gravity, presumably because it broke religious taboos and was an offence against the supernatural powers controlling the soil and the corn. It was so grave a matter that the offender had to suffer the ritual death of being torn to pieces between two teams of oxen:

> *§166: If someone sows seed upon seed, his neck shall be put to a plough, and they shall harness a pair of oxen. One shall face one way, and the other shall face the other way; the man shall be killed and the oxen shall also be killed. He who sowed the field first, shall take it for himself. Formerly they proceeded so.*

But by the time the final form of the laws was promulgated, the procedure had been modified, and the punishment was effected symbolically:

> *§167: But now a sheep serves in place of the man, and two sheep serve in place of the oxen. He shall give 30 loaves of bread (and) 3 vessels of strong beer and shall reconsecrate the field. He who sowed the field first, shall reap it for himself.*

The Hittite laws contained a provision to deal with a problem which is still found in advanced societies—the bidding up of prices of property, by the procedure commonly called gazumping:

> *§146: If someone buys a house or . . . a garden or a pasture and another person goes and . . . offers a price above the (first) price, it is an offence, and he shall give as compensation one mina of silver. (The purchaser) will pay only the first price.*

The following two clauses extend the principle to buying a slave, a horse, a mule or an ass.

These laws pay little attention to divorce, but such as there is shows an approach which is not wholly male-orientated:

> *§31: If a free man and an unfree woman live together, and he takes her as his wife and they form a family and have children, if afterwards . . . they break up, the man shall take the children, but the woman shall take one child.*
>
> *§32: If an unfree man married a free woman, their legal situation is the same.*
>
> *§33: If an unfree man marries an unfree woman, their legal situation is the same.*

The occurrence of legislation upon marriage between free citizens and unfree persons suggests that this was not uncommon. The laws decree that if an unfree man paid the bride-price for a free woman, she retained her free status, otherwise she took her husband's status for three years. Clearly, since an unfree man might be in the position to pay a bride-price, it was possible for his class to own property, for which reason we mostly avoid the term 'slave' for such people.

Several of the Hittite laws make it clear that in some cases the king in person might give the decision in a case.

Assyrian laws[6]

Ashur, the ancient capital of Assyria, was excavated by a German team between 1903 and 1914. It yielded a large number of cuneiform tablets, amongst them two groups of laws. These proved to be copies from about 1100 BC of material originally compiled two centuries or so earlier. The subject matter falls into two main areas, land tenure and law dealing with women. The form and content of these laws show that, unlike those of Hammurabi and earlier rulers, they were not based on royal decrees in actual cases. Rather, they were, like the Hittite laws, a compilation by jurists of traditional legal practice. They contain no novelties of principle. The laws on land tenure are of specialized interest, and the main feature of those about women is their harshness: women in traditional Assyrian society, at least as reflected in these laws, were very much the chattels of men. The last paragraph specifically lays down that, short of murder, a man might do what he pleased to his wife:

> *Apart from the penalties for a married woman which are written on the tablet, a man may flog his wife, he may pull out her hair, he may damage and split her ears. There is nothing wrong in this.*

What is meant by the 'other penalties' to which an erring wife was liable is illustrated by the following:

> *If either a slave or a slave-girl has received anything from the hand of a man's wife, they shall cut off the nose and ears of the slave or slave-girl and they shall repay the stolen property. The man shall cut off his wife's ears. But if the man has released his wife and not cut off her ears, they shall not cut off those of the slave or slave-girl and they shall not repay the stolen property.*

Obviously, Assyrian society held that a wife who had embezzled her husband's property had committed an offence not only against him but against the proper order of things. The husband was not allowed to overlook his wife's part in the offence and could only spare her mutilation by dropping the case altogether.

Law in Egypt

Some classical authors, amongst them Cicero, much admired the judicial system of Egypt, and Diodorus Siculus gave a detailed account of how the system worked, claiming it as based on eight volumes of written law.[7] However, the manner in which Diodorus sets out his account, attributing to the Egyptians the deliberate exclusion of abuses characteristic of Greek courts, suggests that he was helping out such definite information as he had with a good deal of theory, and his positive assertion about written Egyptian law could have been part of the theory.

Ancient Egypt undoubtedly had an effective judicial system, since we have records of lawsuits, but a judicial system does not necessarily imply written law. No law codes have yet been found in Egypt earlier than the third century BC, when Egyptian institutions were changing under strong Hellenistic influence, and some egyptologists conclude that there were no native law codes. Others, however, treat the absence of Egyptian law codes as an accident of archaeology, and attempt to prove the existence of written law from statements, often ambiguous, in ancient Egyptian literature.[8] But if written law did exist in ancient Egypt, we know nothing of its contents.

Administration of justice

The manner in which justice was administered differed considerably from place to place and period to period, but there were some governing principles which applied everywhere.

Because the gods had established the existing order, any interference with that order was an offence against the gods. Law was a means of controlling such interference, and everywhere was attributed to the gods. Since the ruler was the representative of the gods on earth, he was directly responsible for giving justice on their behalf. In practice he could delegate this duty. We find, for example, the Egyptian king authorizing his vizier to act for him. The Hammurabi Code specifically mentions judges, and envisages circumstances in which they could be disqualified from acting, suggesting that in this case they were professionals: there is evidence that such judges sometimes received a fee. There were, however, other circumstances in which the people who constituted a court were definitely non-professional and simply the chief citizens of the district. The Hammurabi Code assumes the judges to be sitting in a body in the assembly of citizens, but in actual records of court cases we sometimes find them sitting in the local temples, or in the gate of a temple, particularly the temple of Shamash, god of justice. In Israel the gate of the city was the place where judges normally sat (Deuteronomy 21:19; 22:15). In Egypt a high official deputed by the king to act as judge might sit in his own audience hall, as we know the vizier Rekhmire[c] did in the fifteenth century BC (p. 29).

But, despite the king normally delegating this duty, he always retained ultimate responsibility for the giving of justice, and even in the most complex societies of the ancient Near East he frequently played a direct personal role in deciding actual lawsuits. Hammurabi's Code makes it clear that its laws were based on actual decisions by the king, and we have letters showing Hammurabi directly giving judgement. Similar direct royal participation is shown in the Hittite laws, where certain cases, particularly those involving sorcery or breach of taboos, were reserved for the king's court; for example:

§188: If a man sins [i.e. commits bestiality] with a sheep, it is a criminal abomination and he should be killed. They shall bring him to the king's court. The king may kill him or the king may let him live. He must not enter into the king's presence.

Some scholars take the last clause to mean 'he must not appeal to the king', but this hardly makes sense, since the king was considering the matter already. The point was that the king had to be ritually protected from contact with any breach of taboo, which the culprit represented.

Because of the divine background, the basic principle in legal judgements was that any upsetting of the established order deserved punishment, and any injustice deserved redress. To redress wrongs, penalties could affect individuals other than those who has actually offended. Thus, in Hammurabi's laws (§23), if a man were robbed and the robber not caught, the local authorities had to make good the loss; in the Bible, Deuteronomy 21:1–9 makes the elders of the nearest town responsible in the event of an unsolved murder. At the Hittite royal court, the misdeeds of a bad servant brought punishment upon his whole family, on the supposed analogy of the behaviour of a god, who, when angered by someone, took revenge not only on the offender but also on all his family and possessions. Israelite thinking fully accepted this religio-legal principle, for Numbers 16:1–33 gives a story of how, when three men challenged Moses, not only the three men and their followers but also all their household were swallowed up by the ground.

Interferences with the established order most frequently involved sacral offences, offences against the state, or moral offences such as adultery; injustices to be righted were predominantly economic. This often gave a division which superficially corresponds to the modern distinction between civil and criminal law. But a distinction in those specific terms was not reflected in the drafting of ancient laws. For example, the laws of Eshnunna sandwich a law on rape, which was undoubtedly (in our terminology) a criminal matter for which the punishment was death, between two laws on marriage contracts, which we would regard as matters of civil law. In the laws of Hammurabi, to assist a slave to escape, which in modern thinking would be a civil offence against the owner of the slave, was punishable by death, indicating that ancient Babylonians saw it not primarily as a source of loss to the owner but rather as interference with the social fabric.

In the righting of injustices to individuals, abstract theories of law played no part: the basic object was to settle the dispute to the satisfaction of all parties. Thus, in Mesopotamia, the two sides were often required to swear that they were satisfied, and there was usually a clause forbidding re-opening the case, on threat of heavy penalties. In some Egyptian maxims of the third millennium, presented as advice by the vizier Ptahhotep to his son, it is stressed that a litigant is more interested in receiving a fair hearing than in actually winning his case:

> *Do not dismiss him before he has relieved his mind by saying what he came to tell. A suppliant wants attention paid to his words more than he wants to win his suit. . . .*

Egyptians accepted it as one of the basic duties of an official that he should hear cases and render justice. We have already seen (p. 29) the importance the fifteenth-century vizier Rekhmire^c attached to this, and how he daily gave judgement in his audience hall.

The pre-classical world provides numerous records of actual lawsuits. Amongst such records from Mesopotamia is the earliest report of a murder trial. This took place in the kingdom of Isin at the beginning of the second millennium. When the charge was made, the case was first brought to the king, who, after establishing that three men had killed another, remitted it to the Assembly of the city of Nippur to discuss whether or not the murdered man's wife shared in the guilt, because the murderers had afterwards told her what they had done. The record from this point reads:

> *[Nine named men] spoke up and said: 'Those who have killed a man are not fit to live. Those three men and that woman should be killed. . . .'*
> *[Two named men] addressed the Assembly, saying: 'Did [the wife] kill her husband, that that woman should be put to death?'*

The Assembly then discussed the question and decided that, as the wife had not been a party to the killing, the fact that she was friendly with her husband's enemies and learnt of the murder subsequently did not make her guilty of murder. The Nippur Assembly handed the three men over for execution.

There was no advocacy in pre-classical courts, and there is no proof of any cross-examination, although at least in Egypt a good beating might be administered in an attempt to extort a confession. The basic procedure everywhere was for the court to examine any relevant documents and then hear statements by the accuser, the accused and any witnesses. In

Mesopotamia and Egypt, and probably everywhere, all those testifying had to take an oath by the gods. In Mesopotamia, if there proved to be conflict of evidence, the contestants would be sent to the ordeal—that is, they would be required to jump into the river—when fear of divine wrath against anyone committing perjury under oath would be likely to result in the lying party confessing. The ordeal was found in a different form in Israelite law, where a woman denying an accusation of adultery was required to take an oath and then drink water polluted with dust from the floor, her guilt or innocence being proved by the chance of whether or not the dust contained the germs of typhoid fever (Numbers 5:11–27).

Egyptian and Hittite lawsuits

The record of a lawsuit of the thirteenth century gives some picture of court procedure. A woman, Iri-nofret, had bought a young Syrian slave-girl from a merchant and paid a price calculated in silver but actually rendered in the form of linen, bronze vessels, copper and honey. A soldier subsequently claimed that some of the payment consisted of goods which belonged to another woman. In the court proceedings, after Iri-nofret had given details of the original transaction, the judges commanded her to take an oath that none of the goods comprising the payment belonged to the other woman, under pain of one hundred lashes and forfeiture of the slave-girl. She did so and the oath was recorded. The soldier was then asked to produce witnesses in support of his claim. He produced three men and two women, who duly took an oath before the tribunal to speak the truth. The outcome of the case is lost. This case, and others like it, show that women had equality with men in Egyptian courts.

From the twelfth century BC we have the record of a trial for conspiracy in a plot to supplant Ramesses III by one of his sons.[9] A dozen palace officials, all identified in the records by their names and titles, were appointed to act as a court, but two of them apparently took no part. The other ten sat as two separate tribunals of six and four, dealing with different groups of prisoners. The various accused—the majordomo of the palace, the royal prince who was to have seized the throne, and such people as butlers and other palace personnel, military commanders, scribes, priests, and the unnamed wives of guards—were brought in in turn and examined. In each case there is a very brief statement of what the accused was alleged to have done. The case against one military commander was that his sister had written to him urging him to return to lead a rebellion, although no evidence is given that he actually did so. The offence alleged against one of the butlers was that he failed to report the conspiracy when he heard of it amongst the harem women. The prince had colluded in the plot with his mother, a secondary wife of Ramesses III. Nothing more is said of the court procedure than that the judges examined the accused and in all cases found them guilty. This might look as though the proceedings were a mere formality to give legality to a condemnation already decided upon, but there are grounds for doubting this. In particular, there must have been a very thorough sifting of evidence, for at the end of the document, where the verdicts are given on the accused, we find that two of the original twelve judges were also condemned, and a third was severely reprimanded for having been associated with the guilty persons. Obviously, no suspicions can have been held against these judges when they were originally appointed, and their implication in the conspiracy can only have come to light as a consequence of a thorough investigation.

The penalties imposed are not stated in all cases, but we know that some of the less serious offenders were punished by cropping their noses and ears. The guilty prince and at least some of the others found guilty and condemned to death were allowed to commit suicide. This avoidance of direct imposition of the death penalty was apparently ancient: Diodorus Siculus states that the Ethiopians—to whom he attributes the beginning of Egyptian civilization—had the custom that the king did not put a condemned man to death but sent him a token of death, whereupon the guilty person immediately took his own life.[10]

We have the record of a suit for royal divorce at about 1250 BC, heard by the Hittite Great King Tudhaliya IV. The situation is concisely set out in the document; it is to be noticed that the lady is never referred to by her name, perhaps indicating that the rift was more dynastic than personal.

> *Before the Sun-god, Tudhaliya, the Great King, King of Hatti.*
>
> *Amistamru, king of Ugarit, took as his wife the daughter of Bente-shina, king of Amurru [a neighbouring state in Syria]. She sought to do harm [literally 'the ill of his head'] against Amistamru. Amistamru, king of Ugarit, therefore left the daughter of Bente-shina for ever.*
>
> *Everything that the daughter of Bente-shina brought into the house of Amistamru, let her take and let her go away from the house of Amistamru. Anything (of hers) that Amistamru has been appropriating, let the people of Amurru take an oath (that it is hers) and let Amistamru repay it in full.*
>
> *Utri-sharruma is the Crown Prince in Ugarit. If Utri-sharruma says, 'I will go after my mother', let him deposit his regalia upon the stool and let him go. Amistamru, king of Ugarit, will appoint another son of his to the Crown Princeship in Ugarit. If Utri-sharruma intends to take his mother and return her to Ugarit to act as queen after Amistamru has gone to his fate [i.e. died], let Utri-*

sharruma deposit his regalia upon the stool, and let him go anywhere he likes, and the Sun-god will appoint another son of Amistamru to the kingship.

In after days, the daughter of Bente-shina shall not lay claim to her sons, her daughters, or her sons-in-law; they belong to Amistamru, king of Ugarit. If she makes a claim, this tablet will prevail against her.[11]

9

The Brotherhood of Nations

Ovid gives a picture of a primeval golden age, free of aggression and greed:

With no one to impose punishment, without any laws, men kept faith and did what was right. . . . The peoples passed their lives in security and peace, without need for armies.[1]

Ovid's golden age belonged to the fantasy world of never-never. Man's inhumanity to man is already all too evident in our earliest sources. From when we first meet them, the Sumerian plain-dwellers had no compunction in raiding the mountain peoples to kill, loot and enslave: this is put beyond doubt by the ideogram for 'slave-girl', which is compounded of 'woman' and 'mountain', and that for 'slave', which is 'male' and 'mountain'. In Egypt, the earliest records are carved slate palettes from about 3000 BC, showing kings proudly destroying enemies (plate 12). The Bible, with a keener perception than Ovid's of the brutality of human nature in the raw, has Cain kill his brother in the first generation after Creation.

But during the third millennium a public conscience began to develop against unbridled aggression. In Mesopotamia we see it in the form of criticism of unprovoked destruction of one city-state by another, expressed theologically as a decree of condemnation by the great gods. This comes out most sharply in comment on the fate of Agade, the capital of the first empire, created by Sargon early in the twenty-fourth century.

It was Enlil, the great god of Sumer, who had given dominance in the land to Agade, and there the great goddess Inanna had made her seat. And so it became rich and powerful:

Ships brought the wealth of Sumer up (to Agade),
The Amorites of the wild lands, people who knew not grain,
Came in with rampaging bulls and goats.

Meluhhans [Indus valley people], people of the black wild lands,
Brought along (their) exotic wares.

But Sargon's principal successor, Naram-Sin, attacked and looted Enlil's city, Nippur, and even desecrated his great temple there, known as Ekur. Enraged, Enlil brought down upon the whole land of Sumer a barbarous people,

> *Gutium, a people who know no restraint,*
> *In the likeness of mankind, with the mind of a dog, and the face of an ape,*
> *Enlil brought them forth from the wild lands.*
> *Like locust swarms they covered the land.*[2]

At this point the poet faced the problem which has recurred so often since. He had to resolve a conflict between facts and theology. In historical fact, the invasion by the Gutians brought devastation throughout the whole land, to Enlil's own city Nippur no less than to other centres. But the major long-term consequence was the downfall of Agade, by the damage done to its economic and political infrastructure. The poem therefore represents events in two stages. First it tells of Enlil in his rage allowing the Gutians to devastate the whole land unchecked. But then it brings in reason to modify the instinct of vengeful indiscriminate destruction. It depicts other more reasonable gods intervening to calm Enlil's anger, and to urge him to limit the Gutian attack solely to the destruction of Agade for its desecration of Ekur. This represents a theological adjustment of history, and in its attitudes we see reflected the growth of a constraint by public opinion upon the arbitrary destruction by conquerors of other Sumerian cities.

But the constraint operated only in relation to military action between Sumerian city-states. Outside that context, Mesopotamian warfare in the third millennium remained total war. Contemporary texts glorify the Sumerian king Shulgi for the merciless way in which he hammered the Gutians. He was not content merely to inflict a military defeat: he went on to destroy the Gutians' fields of barley, leaving nothing but weeds growing; he cut down trees and uprooted palms; he destroyed fig-gardens and robbed and devastated cities; he took all the cattle and sheep as loot, and scattered the Gutians over the face of the earth.[3] Egyptian kings of the time were no less ruthless.

Treaties, overlords and vassals

Already well before the end of the third millennium, international relationships were being formalized by treaties. Naram-Sin, one of the two greatest kings of the world's first major empire, in the twenty-third century made an alliance with a king of Elam (south-west Iran), in which the Elamite king stated his allegiance in the terms: 'The enemy of Naram-Sin is my enemy; the friend of Naram-Sin is my friend.' In Mesopotamia and Syria, in the century from 1900 BC, petty states were joining in shifting coalitions, a situation described in a contemporary letter:

> *No king is powerful by himself. Ten or fifteen kings follow Hammurabi of Babylon, the same number follow Rim-Sin of Larsa, the same number follow (the king of) Eshnunna; twenty kings follow (the king of) Yamhad.*

One of the features of such groupings was that rulers would lend each other troops on a reciprocal basis, a situation explicitly stated in a letter:

> *Send me troops so that I may achieve this objective. Then I will send contingents to you with your troops. So achieve what you want.*

By the second half of the second millennium it was common for rulers to make written treaties governing the relations between them. About two dozen such treaties are known from the archives of the Hittite empire at Boghazkoi, and lesser numbers from Ugarit (in north Syria) and Assyria. The language used was generally Akkadian, written in cuneiform on clay tablets, even when it was the mother tongue of neither contracting party; but some treaties between the Hittites and kings in Asia Minor were in the Hittite language, and in the first millennium Aramaic began to come into use for international relations. Most known examples of international treaties were between an overlord and a vassal, but this is probably only because there were many more vassals than major powers. An example of a treaty between major powers is one made at about 1280 BC between Ramesses II of Egypt and the Hittite king Hattushilish. It exists in an Egyptian version carved on the walls of two Egyptian buildings, and a version in Akkadian on cuneiform texts from Boghazkoi in eastern Turkey.[4] The two versions agree closely in their stipulations, but differ in the introduction, which in the Egyptian version has obviously been edited to the glory of the pharaoh. The texts recorded a treaty of peace for ever between the two rulers and their lands. They prescribed that the ruler of Hatti (Hittite-land) should not transgress the boundaries of Egypt nor the ruler of Egypt the borders of the land of Hatti. If Hatti were attacked from outside and called upon Egypt for help, the king of Egypt was to send infantry and chariotry against the enemy, and correspondingly if an external enemy attacked Egypt. Similarly, if there were a rebellion against one ruler, the other was to assist in destroying the rebels. There were also extradition clauses. A person who fled from Egypt to Hatti, whether a nobleman who went to the court or a lesser man who entered the service of some citizen, should not be allowed to settle in the land of Hatti but should be returned to the Egyptian ruler, and correspondingly for refugees from Hatti. But the treaty provided that in the event of such extraditions the person extradited should not be punished: 'The great prince of Hatti shall not . . . harm his ears; . . . he shall not charge him with any crime.' The version preserved (in Akkadian cuneiform) at the Hittite capital provided that at the death of the current Hittite ruler, the Egyptian king should support the succession of his son, sending military forces if necessary. There was probably a corresponding provision, now lost, to secure the Egyptian succession.

A minor kingdom would normally become a vassal of a major one either in recognition of the political reality that represented its only chance of survival, or from expectation of economic advantage. The overlord would bind his vassal to him by formal procedures backed by religious sanctions. Thus, the suzerain would formally institute his vassal by anointing his head with oil, in the same way that Israelite kings were anointed as representatives of Yahweh. He would also promulgate treaty terms, which both parties accepted under oath by the gods. Such terms always limited the vassal's right to an independent foreign policy, and sometimes also his economic activities. Thus, a Hittite king required one of his vassals, the state of Amurru in Syria, to take part in a trade embargo: 'No merchant of yours shall go to Assyria, and you shall allow no merchant of theirs into your land.' Treaties also made provision for military aid: the vassal had to render his suzerain assistance in the event of war or revolt, but had the guarantee of defence by his suzerain if his own security came under threat. We see this latter provision in operation in the middle of the fourteenth century, with the Hittite Great King Shuppiluliuma writing to his vassal, the king of the north Syrian state of Ugarit, to record his support in the face of an attack:

Niqmaddu, king of Ugarit, sent a message to Shuppiluliuma, the Great King, thus: 'May the Sun-god, the Great King, my lord, save me from the hand of the enemy. I am a servant of the Sun-god, the Great King, my lord. I am at enmity with the enemy of my lord and I am friendly with the friend of my lord. Some kings are threatening me.'

The Great King heard the utterance of Niqmaddu, and so Shuppiluliuma the Great King sent sons of the King and noblemen with soldiers and chariots to Ugarit, and they forcibly removed the enemy from Ugarit, and all the booty that they took they donated to Niqmaddu.

A few centuries earlier we find a minor ruler, anxious to receive protection, actually asking to become a vassal of a major king. The minor ruler, named Abi-samar, first wrote to say that his cities were under threat, and, as that apparently produced no response, in a second letter urged:

If you abandon Abi-samar, you abandon your own cities. . . . Perhaps you say 'Abi-samar is not my son and my estate is not his estate'. But indeed my estate is your estate and Abi-samar is your son.

We find a similar situation in the Bible in the eighth century, when king Ahaz of Judah, under attack from Israel and Syria,

sent messengers to Tiglath-pileser king of Assyria, saying, I am thy servant and thy son [i.e. I am your vassal]: come up and save me out of the hand of the king of Syria, and out of the hand of the king of Israel. (2 Kings 16:7)

Tiglath-pileser did as Ahaz asked.

Vassals had to pay an annual tribute, and default was tantamount to rebellion. But in return a suzerain both defined and defended the boundaries of his vassals, as we see in the following extract from a letter from the second half of the thirteenth century:

Thus says the king of Carchemish [the overlord] to the king of Ugarit [the vassal]; Greetings to you!

About your frontiers of which you wrote to me, whatever boundaries of yours Armaziti has fixed for you, their position is settled. No one shall change them. And now I have sent Ebina'e and Kurkalli and they shall set up those boundaries for you.[5]

From a century earlier we have the Hittite king Murshilish II, at that time the suzerain of Ugarit, giving a detailed list of towns and mountains which marked Ugarit's frontiers.

If a vassal were in such favourable circumstances that his support was of particular value to the suzerain, he might receive exceptional privileges by treaty. Shunashura, the king of Kizzuwatna in south-east Asia Minor, provides an instance of this; although not powerful enough to maintain independence, he was in an area of such strategical importance that he could affect the balance of power between the Hittites and their Hurrian neighbours to the south-east. The Hittite king therefore gave him special consideration, reflected in a treaty prescribing that when he made a visit he was to be treated with special honour: 'When Shunashura comes before the Sun-god [i.e. the Hittite king], the noblemen of the Sun-god shall rise from their seats for him; no one shall remain seated.'[6]

Extradition clauses, of the kind already noticed, were common in all international treaties, and, far from being a formality, were frequently acted upon. For example, once in the eighteenth century BC a military contingent of the state of Yamhad in north Syria deserted. The ruler, suspecting that they were making for Mari on the middle Euphrates, informed the king of Mari, with a request for their arrest and extradition. This was promptly attended to, and the deserters returned to Yamhad. So compelling was the obligation to extradite nationals at the application of the ruler of their country, that in the late second millennium the Hittite king made it a ground for declaration of war that another ruler had failed to extradite citizens of his on request. It was so binding that the seventh century Assyrian king Ashurbanipal, although the most powerful ruler in the world, felt it necessary to offer a justification when he refused a request from the king of Elam to return some Elamite fugitives.

Rulers often sealed alliances by linking their families in marriage. A nineteenth-century letter illustrates this:

Ishme-dagan [son of the king of Assyria and himself a sub-king] has made peace with the Turukkians [a people in the foothills of the Zagros]. He is taking the daughter of Zaziya [king of the Turukkians] for his son . . . (and) has sent Zaziya gold and silver as a bridal-gift.

Dynastic marriages were a particular feature of international relations during the second half of the second millennium, so that ruling families everywhere became inter-related. The Hittite king Shuppiluliuma took as his queen a Babylonian princess, who received a Hittite name. The same ruler just missed the chance of controlling Egypt: after the death at about 1350 BC of Tutankhamun, last king of the Eighteenth Dynasty, his widow, wishing to maintain the reins of power but reluctant to link herself with an Egyptian commoner, wrote to Shuppiluliuma to request one of his sons as a royal husband. From the Egyptian point of view, there was nothing irregular about marriage with foreign royalty, since during the Eighteenth Dynasty Egyptian princes had married Mitannian princesses during at least three generations. But Shuppiluliuma was suspicious, and sent an official to Egypt to investigate. Before the official returned to report that it was perfectly genuine, the queen had impatiently sent a second letter to reiterate her request. Shuppiluliuma's delay proved unfortunate: it had given the Egyptian opposition to Tutankhamun's widow time to organize, and when a Hittite prince was eventually sent, he was murdered on the way.

Another important dynastic marriage in the same half-century made the daughter of Ashur-uballit of Assyria the wife of the king of Babylonia. Ashur-uballit took the dynastic link so seriously that when a rebellion broke out in Babylonia, in which his daughter's son, the new king, was killed, he intervened militarily to control the succession.

Communications between rulers

Rulers frequently corresponded by letter. This was probably always the most common mechanism of international relationships at all times from the early second millennium onwards, but the accidents of archaeological discovery happen to attest it particularly at two periods, near the beginning and towards the end of the second millennium. The evidence for the earlier period comes from the city of Mari on the middle Euphrates, where excavation yielded over twenty thousand clay tablets inscribed in Akkadian cuneiform from the century after 1850 BC, amongst which were many letters between rulers of states across the whole region from Syria to south Babylonia.

The richest relevant archive from later in the second millennium was also in cuneiform on clay tablets but surprisingly was found in Egypt, a country one does not normally associate with this kind of writing. The pharaoh Amenophis IV (1365–1349 BC), also known as Akhenaten, initiated unpopular revolutionary religious reforms, in the course of which he built a new capital at a site now known as El Amarna in middle Egypt. The reforms did not survive Akhenaten's lifetime and at his death his capital was deserted. In consequence all his diplomatic archives, and some of his father's, remained undisturbed in the ground at El Amarna until re-discovered in the nineteenth century AD. They proved to contain well over 300 letters in two main sub-divisions, those from major kings (such as those of the Hittites, Babylonia, Assyria and Mittanni), and those from Egyptian vassals in Syria and Palestine. The considerable information which these give on international relationships was later supplemented by other cuneiform tablets, of the fourteenth and thirteenth centuries, found at Ras Shamra, the ancient port of Ugarit, in north Syria. The Mari, El Amarna and Ugaritic archives are the principal sources for the material which follows.

The language most commonly used, even between rulers for neither of whom it was the mother tongue, was Akkadian, but there were occasional exceptions. The El Amarna correspondence contains a few letters in Hittite cuneiform, and a few of the international letters found at Ugarit were written in the West Semitic Ugaritic language in the local alphabetic script. In each of the archives mentioned there were occasional documents in the Hurrian language.

Kings conventionally addressed each other in family terms, as either 'father', 'son' or 'brother'. To call anothe ruler 'my father' implied acceptance of his seniority; to address one as 'my brother' was a claim of equality. Some rulers were very sensitive to relative status, and might resent what they considered an inappropriate form of address. We find an instance of this at the beginning of Assyria's rise to international power early in the thirteenth century. Adad-nerari I (1307–1275 BC) addressed the great Hittite king in terms of brotherhood, only to receive the rebuff: 'Why should I write to you about brotherhood? Were you and I born of the same mother?'

Alongside written communications for international diplomacy, kings used messengers (sometimes more than one) to maintain contacts, either resident at each other's courts or sent on particular occasions. Such messengers may be seen as in a sense forerunners of today's ambassadors, if we do not press the parallel too closely. Normally it was assumed that these ambassadors would return home soon after completing the specific negotiations for which they were sent, but on occasions the foreign ruler might detain them at his court, sometimes for several years. This did not represent personal detention of the ambassadors, but rather a problem arising from relations between the two kings. When an ambassador returned home, protocol demanded that a substantial present to his master from the foreign king should accompany him, and the foreign king might delay the return of the ambassador because he was not in a position to send, or was unwilling to send, a suitably lavish gift. Thus the king of Alashiya (Cyprus) writes to the king of Egypt, in a letter which presumably went by the hand of the messenger mentioned as having been detained:

> My brother, do not take it to your heart that your messenger has dwelt for three years in my land; (it is) because the hand of Nergal [a plague epidemic] is present in my land and in my house; my wife had a son who has died. Now, my brother, send your messenger off with my messenger safely and quickly, and then I will send back the present due to my brother.[7]

Sometimes the failure to send back the ambassador with a present was a deliberate snub, the equivalent of breaking off diplomatic relations. When Akhenaten had detained the messengers of Tushratta, king of the Hurrian state of Mittanni, the latter took it as a deliberate breach, and pleaded in a letter: 'Let my brother be on friendly terms with me.'

Presents between rulers were generally exchanged value for value as a disguised form of trade and as a means of keeping existing friendships in good repair. But sometimes one king sent gifts to another, with whom he had had no previous direct communication, as an indication of a desire to establish friendly relations. A rising power was particularly liable to be courted in this way. For instance, after Tuthmosis III (1490–1439 BC) had conquered Megiddo, showing Egypt to be a major power in the Levant, Assyria sent gifts of lapis lazuli and ornamental wood, which the Egyptians chose to describe as tribute, and after further campaigns

Babylonia sent presents of lapis lazuli, and the Hittites silver and precious stones.

On appropriate occasions, such as accession or illness, it was expected that other rulers, particularly vassals, would send congratulations to the king concerned, or enquiries about his wellbeing. For a vassal to fail to visit his suzerain, or at least to send a message on such an occasion, was a grave discourtesy. We see a typical reaction in a letter which a son of the Hittite king wrote to the vassal king of Ugarit to rebuke him for his dereliction of duty:

> Thus speaks Pihawalwi, son of the king, to Ibirana my son. Here all is well with the Sun-king.
> Why have you not come before the Sun-king since you took over the kingship of Ugarit, or why have you not regularly sent your ambassadors? Now here the Sun-king is very annoyed about this affair. Now send your ambassadors before the king as a matter of urgency, and send presents to the king together with presents for me.[8]

We also find the king of Alashiya (Cyprus) apologizing to the king of Egypt for a similar omission:

> You wrote to me saying, 'Why did you not send your messenger to me?' . . . I did not hear when you were performing the ceremonial. You should not take it to heart, for now that I have heard I am sending my messenger to you.

An ambassador at a foreign court might have to conduct negotiations on behalf of his king, but he was not a plenipotentiary. His king knew that he might come under pressure for compromise, and so sometimes gave him detailed written instructions for his negotiations. A clause in a treaty between the Hittite great king Muwatallish and the important vassal Shunashura, king of Kizzuwatna (p. 180), brings out very clearly the limited scope for an ambassador's initiative. The treaty, written in Akkadian (the mother tongue of neither party), contains the stipulation:

> If I, the Sun-god [i.e. the Hittite king], have had a tablet sent to you in which words are set down, and my emissary elaborates it in his own words, if the words of my emissary agree with the words of my tablet, trust that emissary. But if the words of the mouth of the emissary do not agree with the words of the tablet, you should certainly not trust that emissary.[9]

Ambassadors had certain privileges; their property was protected, and they were sometimes granted exemption from customs duties. It was not unknown for them to engage in activities which made their presence unwelcome, and a ruler might declare a particular ambassador *persona non grata* and ask his master to remove him. But however unpopular an ambassador, or the king he represented, might be, normally his person was sacrosanct. But occasionally some of the backwoodsmen of the ancient world ignored the conventions of civilized behaviour and succumbed to the temptation of venting their spleen on the ambassadors of rival rulers. The Bible offers one of the rare examples of this. When king David of Israel sent an embassy to a new ruler of the Ammonites in Transjordan, the Ammonites deliberately insulted David by disfiguring the beards of his men and docking their cloaks to make them a laughingstock (2 Samuel 10:1–11:1). Such an insult could only be expunged by war.

A vassal had no right to send ambassadors independently of his overlord; when Egypt in the fourteenth century received an embassy from Assyria, the king of Babylonia entered a protest, claiming (but contrary to the *de facto* situation) that Assyria was a Babylonian vassal.

Imperialism and warfare

The Old Testament presents believers with a dilemma. On the one hand it is in some sense the word of God, and on the other it attributes some of the worst atrocities of the ancient world to the direct command of the Israelite national god Yahweh. Some Old Testament theologians have attempted to veil this dilemma by hallowing the atrocities with the euphemistic description 'Holy War'.

The dilemma disappears when we recognize that the Israelite attitude to war differed no whit from that of any other people of the ancient Near East. Everywhere the divine will was the formal justification for war. If the wholesale slaughter occasionally perpetrated by ancient Israel in the name of Yahweh is to be whitewashed by talk of 'Holy War', the military exploits of every other state of the ancient Near East deserve the same mitigation.

All ancient peoples acted, by war when necessary, to protect their national and territorial and often their economic interests, and all ancient peoples came to attribute their military response to the will of their national god or gods.

Consider the Assyrians from the second half of the second millennium onwards. Their territory, along the Tigris southwards from Nineveh (Mosul), contained some of the richest farmlands in the Near East. But from about 1500 BC they had been overrun by the Mittannians to their west, and always they were subject to raids from the peoples in the mountains to their east and north. By 1400 BC they had regained independence, and were in no mood to sit passively and await future depredations. Once harvest was in, in early summer, the sturdy Assyrian farmers were for the time being free, and the mountains were clear of snow. The Assyrians therefore developed the practice of marching through the mountains in summer to beat up tribesmen who had threatened their lands in winter and spring. This brought the nearer regions under their control, but always there were further troublesome tribesmen beyond. And so it became accepted that the Assyrians would bring their rule over other peoples and would continuously expand their boundaries. In time, this purely human response to circumstances became enshrined in a theological doctrine: it was now held, with all the force of religious dogma, that the national god Ashur had decreed that Assyria should rule all peoples and should expand its borders to the glory of the god.

The situation of the Israelites differed in degree and details, but in no way in principle. As the tribes attempted to settle in Palestine, they encountered many difficulties, to which they responded in certain ways. The Amalekites offer a good example of how customary war came to be presented in theological expression. These people were nomadic border raiders rather like the Beduin Arabs of much later times, who constantly made hit-and-run attacks upon Israelites settlements. It was impossible to make political terms with these people, as they had no permanent territorial base, and the only possible Israelite response in self-defence was to hit Amalekite raiders as hard as possible whenever they caught them, with no quarter given. In course of time this received theological expression. It was held that Yahweh had said:

I will utterly put out the remembrance of Amalek from under heaven. . . . Yahweh will have war with Amalek from generation to generation (Exodus 17:14, 16),

and by the beginning of the monarchy the idea of God's dislike of the Amalekites had become so deeprooted that some Israelites believed that God wanted everything of the Amalekites destroyed, down to the last baby and animal. Samuel ordered Saul in Yahweh's name:

Go and smite Amalek, and utterly destroy all that they have, and spare them not; but slay both man and woman, infant and suckling, ox and sheep, camel and ass (1 Samuel 15:3).

But not all Israelites were lacking in humanity, and king Saul, having defeated the Amalekites, attempted to moderate the lust for revenge, beginning by sparing the Amalekite king. But harsh ancient custom had by now acquired all the force of divine command, and the ruthless prophet Samuel denounced Saul in the name of Yahweh, and himself hacked the enemy king to pieces at Yahweh's shrine in Gilgal (1 Samuel 15:33).

But this was an exceptional case. Most of Israel's neighbours were

Palestinian-Syrian states, and the divine command for total extermination of enemies only applied to raiding nomads such as the Amalekites. Deuteronomy 20:16 might seem to invalidate this distinction, since it specifically includes the cities of Palestine in Yahweh's command for genocide:

> *Of the cities of these people, which Yahweh thy God doth give thee for an inheritance, thou shalt save alive nothing that breatheth.*

But, despite fundamentalist tradition, the Book of Deuteronomy as we have it comes from the first millennium, long after Moses and Joshua, and by that time there were no Palestinian cities to which these genocidal laws were relevant. The passage quoted does not reflect the actual practice of the Israelites fighting against Palestinian cities at the time of the Settlement, but merely represents what fanatical Yahwists of the first millennium held ought to have been done during the Settlement period to preserve Israel from the taint of Canaanite religious ideas.

The effective Israelite laws of war were that if a city surrendered, its people should become vassals, and if it did not and was conquered, its men should be killed and its women and children reduced to slavery. (Deuteronomy 20:10–14). Although milder than Deuteronomy 20:16, this was still considerably harsher than the practice of any of the major first millennium powers. But even in Israel actual military practice had generally become more humane before the end of the ninth century, so that this harsh religious edict was not applied in practice. 2 Kings 6:8–23 has a story about war between Syria and Israel. It has some odd semi-magical elements, but the significant final point is that when prisoners were taken, and the king of Israel asked if he should kill them, Elisha showed the triumph of humanity over barbarism, and ordered him to feed them and let them go.

Although the representation of war as the will of the gods arose from human reaction to political and geographical circumstances, it developed a force of its own. Conventions developed for the conduct of war, enforced by religious sanctions. Warfare might be harsh and brutal, but it became subject to accepted codes. Because war was waged on behalf of the gods, it could not be undertaken arbitrarily: to avoid the censure of the gods, it needed formal justification and divine approval. Before going to war, kings took omens, and it was a rash king who went to war if these proved adverse. A legend about Naram-Sin, the third and greatest successor of the first Sargon, founder of the third-millennium Dynasty of Agade, offered a dreadful warning of the consequences of such impiety. Naram-Sin, the legend tells, sought by omens the permission of the gods to attack invading hordes in Asia Minor. It was not granted, but Naram-Sin attacked notwithstanding, only to see the annihilation of his armies, amounting to over a quarter of a million men.

From much later, in the first millennium, we have a series of applications to the Sun-god, written on clay tablets, seeking answers, through signs on the internal organs of sacrificial animals, to questions as to whether or not Assyria should make war on such and such peoples. When Sargon II in 714 BC made a major attack on his northern neighbour Urartu (Ararat), which we know from letters had in fact been planned for some years, he made a great point in his report to the national god, which was probably publicly read at the New Year Festival, of justifying his invasion and claiming divine approval:

I approached Uishdish, a province of the land of the Mannaeans, which Ursa [king of Urartu] had seized. Before my arrival, Ursa the Urartian, who does not respect the word of the gods Ashur and Marduk and does not fear the oath by the lord of lords, . . . who does not respect the mighty word of Shamash supreme judge of the gods, and who yearly without ceasing keeps transgressing his bounds, after his earlier sins had committed the great crime of destroying this land and overthrowing its people. . . .

I, Sargon, king of the four quarters, shepherd of Assyria, who respects the oath of Enlil and Marduk, . . . the true king, who speaks only good things, to whom lies are abhorrent, . . . because I had never transgressed the borders of Ursa the Urartian, the wide bounds of his land, nor poured out on the battlefield the blood of his warriors, I raised my hands [to the god Ashur praying him] to bring about his overthrow in battle, to turn back the insolence of his mouth upon himself, and to make him bear his sin.

Ashur my lord heard my words of righteousness. They pleased him. He inclined to my just prayer. He agreed to my request.

Divine sanctions applied equally to peace treaties. If a peace treaty were made, both parties swore by the gods to observe it, and for one side subsequently to attack the other was an offence against the divine powers, destined to bring down the severest punishment upon the offending nation. For example, in the second half of the second millennium the Egyptians and Hittites had made a peace settlement after a dispute over territories in Syria, and had finalized it by an oath by the gods. But the Hittites broke the oath and attacked Egyptian-held territory. Plague broke out amongst Egyptian prisoners and, spreading to the Hittites, swept devastatingly through their land; the son and successor of the Hittite king responsible for the breach of treaty later accepted that this was a punishment imposed by the Storm-god, the head of the pantheon of his own country, for breach of the treaty oath.[10]

Major powers sometimes displayed a sense of international responsibility which went beyond formal treaty terms. This could include economic aid in times of national disaster. Thus, we find the Assyrian king Ashurbanipal (668–626 BC) describing how he acted towards Elam (southwest Iran) near the beginning of his reign:

> *When there was famine in Elam and a food shortage developed, I had corn sent to him to keep his people alive. . . . People of his who had fled before the famine and taken up residence within Assyria until the rains came to his land and a harvest followed, these people, who had been able to stay alive in my land, I sent back to him.*

He mentioned this only because at a later stage relations so far deteriorated that he felt compelled to invade Elam; this proof of his earlier goodwill defended him from international or divine censure.

Towards the end of the seventh century Egypt showed its sense of international responsibility when it intervened in an attempt (which in the event failed) to save its old enemy, the Assyrian empire; a coalition of lesser powers had attacked Assyria, and it seemed that their success would lead to international chaos.[11]

All nations developed conventions which curbed the savagery of war, but they were not necessarily identical conventions; on occasion this could give one army an advantage over the other, or lead to mutual accusations of ill faith. The Egyptians, for example, had a prohibition against surprise attacks, and would even postpone a battle until the enemy was ready. But to the Hittites surprise was a legitimate military tactic, as we know from an occasion when they used it in an attack against the headquarters of the Egyptian king.

Some of the manifestations of ancient (as of modern) warfare were distinctly nasty. The Assyrians have gained a particularly bad name for atrocities in warfare, from a combination of biblical notoriety and their own striking war reliefs in the British Museum. But in fact they were in no way worse than their contemporaries. The Egyptians on occasion were not above massacring defeated enemies. Amenophis II (1439–1413 BC) records that on reaching Ugarit on a campaign, he summoned all those who had opposed him and slew the lot. They also had a gruesome custom of mutilating defeated enemies for trophies. As a typical statement we find an official under the Eighteenth Dynasty twice recording, of battles at Avaris, in which the Hyksos were expelled, 'I fought hand to hand; I brought away a hand'. In the early fifteenth century BC the Egyptians won a battle at Megiddo and the account of the spoil includes eighty-three hands, another instance of the unpleasant custom. However, as this detail is mentioned alongside 340 living prisoners and over 900 chariots, it is at the same time an indication that deaths inflicted in the battle were surprisingly light, that prisoners were not always massacred, and that many more Canaanite participants in the battle escaped than were killed or taken prisoner. But on some occasions the slaughter was proportionately much greater: on the wall of a temple at Medinet Habu, Ramesses III (1193–1162 BC) left a pictorial record of a victory he gained over Libyan invaders, and prominent among the spoil depicted are great heaps of phalli of slaughtered Libyans and hands of their allies.

In the league of the smaller and more backward nations with whom the Israelites mainly fought, it was accepted as a regular feature of warfare that the victors would 'dash the children [of the defeated], and rip up their women with child' (2 Kings 8:12). The Israelites themselves were no exception in meting out this treatment, for it is specifically recorded of king Menahem of Israel that, when he conquered a certain area, 'all the women therein that were with child he ripped up' (2 Kings 15:16).

It was quite usual for victors to enslave those taken prisoner in war, and this could include not only combatants but also women. Thus an Egyptian official under the Eighteenth Dynasty records at the capture of Avaris: 'I took captive one man and three women; ... His majesty granted them to me as slaves.' But this was minuscule compared with the 89,600 prisoners whom Amenophis took back from Syria to Memphis as prisoners.[12] He does not state that they were formally enslaved, but they were certainly deprived of their liberty and settled in Egypt. Later, the Assyrians followed the Egyptian example and developed the practice of deporting and resettling substantial segments of conquered populations. Although initially traumatic for the victims, this was not actual enslavement, and in time the population groups concerned received all the economic and social rights of native Assyrians.

From the second millennium onwards, warfare did not invariably involve indiscriminate destruction. When a city came under siege, the besiegers normally invited surrender first, offering the defenders favourable terms: we see an instance of this in the Bible, at the Assyrian siege of Jerusalem in 701 BC (2 Kings 18:31–32). There were, certainly, exceptions to such mildness, but these always received a specific theological justification: a case in point was Sennacherib's sack and devastation of Babylon in 689 BC. The city had been a thorn in Sennacherib's side throughout his reign, but his actual destruction of it was formally justified by the claim that Babylon's god, Marduk, had deserted his city and the gods had put a curse on it for 70 years. Another instance was the havoc wreaked by Sargon II when he invaded Urartu in 714 BC and effected a systematic destruction involving the smashing of the country's irrigation system, the felling of its orchards and ornamental trees, and the devastation of its cultivated fields; he claimed that he was punishing Urartu on behalf of the gods for the impiety of its king.

Occasional destruction of an enemy's economic resources was not limited to the Assyrians; instances can be found amongst Hittites and Egyptians. Some Egyptian kings, for example, mentioned destroying crops or trees in conquered areas. Sesostris I (early second millennium BC), in attacking people south of Egypt, recorded that he seized all their women and set fire to all their corn. Tuthmosis III (1490–1439 BC) boasted of a campaign in Syria that he took all the food supplies and destroyed the growing corn, felled all plantations and fruit trees, and left only bare scorched earth.

But some people in the ancient Near East recognized the destruction of food-producing trees as evil. Deuteronomy 20:19–20 decrees:

> *When thou shalt besiege a city a long time, in making war against it to take it, thou shalt not destroy the trees thereof by forcing an axe against them: for thou mayest eat of them, and thou shalt not cut them down . . . Only the trees which thou knowest that they be not trees for meat, thou shalt destroy and cut them down.*

Unfortunately, such prohibitions tended to be disregarded in practice, even in Israel: 2 Kings 3:25 records that the Israelites, at war with the Moabites, not only cut down 'good trees' (i.e. food-producing trees), but also stopped up wells and did their best to make good land unproductive.

Clashes of armies in the battlefield were likely to be more bloody affairs than sieges, but normally the victors did not set out to massacre the defeated, and sometimes did not even seek to take them prisoner. When king Sargon of Assyria eventually defeated the Urartian army and its allies in his campaign of 714 BC, he was content to allow the survivors to flee, recognizing the enormous propaganda value of the reports they would spread of the might of the Assyrian army. But at the other extreme, some of the earlier Assyrian kings had put out the eyes of thousands of prisoners-of-war, to make them more controllable as labour gangs.

From the second half of the third millennium onwards there are indications that certain rulers maintained the nucleus of a standing army of several thousand men. Such a force could in case of national need be considerably enlarged by conscription of males of military age. Well before the end of the third millennium, Egypt had armies running into tens of thousands, for action against the nomads of Sinai, and by the first millennium there were rulers who spoke of armies of hundreds of thousands.

One of the problems with large armies is to prevent them from terrorizing the civil population, and in Egypt it was a point of pride of an efficient commander that he prevented his troops from robbing travellers or looting towns.[13] With the Assyrian army, except when a besieged city was actually taken there is no indication of any interference with civil populations; when on the move inside Assyrian territory, the troops were normally provisioned by the administrative officers of the province, and in enemy territory tight discipline was necessary for security on the march. But at the taking of a city, it was usual for the commander to give his army licence to loot.

Foreigners abroad

A distinguished foreigner travelling abroad might take with him a letter of introduction to the king, which would secure privileged treatment. Thus, when a certain Hittite prince went to Ugarit, he had the benefit of the following letter from the Hittite king:

> *Thus says the king to Ibirani king of Ugarit: Greetings to you!*
>
> *Now Misramuwa has come to live there with Ahi-sharruma. You are to treat him kindly and according to his rank. . . . If you do not know him, he is brother of Upparmuwa and son of the king.*[14]

Kings sometimes permitted foreigners, presumably those who had made themselves valuable as administrators, commercial agents or advisors, to settle permanently in their land, granting them estates. Thus from Ugarit in the early thirteenth century BC we have the following record of a grant to an Egyptian:

> *From this day Ammistamri, son of Niqmepa, king of Ugarit, has given to Pa'ahi the Egyptian the house of Abdi-ba'al son-in-law of Kunabilu, and the field of Sahteya and three iku [just over 2½ acres] of field from the field of Ilim-masiru. And no one shall take it from the hand of Pa'ahi or from the hand of his son or the son of his sons. This gift is given for ever.*[15]

But this was a privilege granted to few. Most of those who travelled in a foreign country were merchants, and they always ran the risk of being robbed and murdered for the goods they carried. Rulers therefore made treaties to secure protection for their citizens in such circumstances. We see several thirteenth-century instances of this in documents of Inu-Teshub, great-grandson of the great fourteenth century Hittite king Shuppiluliuma, who, by virtue of his descent, had been appointed king of Carchemish and Hittite viceroy in north Syria. One document, written on a clay tablet in Akkadian cuneiform, reads:

> *Ini-Teshub king of Carchemish has made this treaty with the men of Ugarit. If a man of Carchemish is killed within Ugarit, if those who killed him are arrested, they shall pay three-fold for the man and they shall pay three-fold for the goods that*

disappeared with him. But if those who killed him are not found, they [the people of Ugarit] shall pay three-fold for the life and as to the goods that disappeared with him, they shall pay the capital value of so much as disappeared. And if a man of Ugarit is killed in Carchemish, compensation arrangements are the same.

In other documents Ini-Teshub actually gives judgement in cases of the type envisaged; in one instance a group of merchants of Carchemish had been murdered in Ugarit, and in another Ini-Teshub was arbitrator when a merchant of a third vassal state had been killed in Ugarit.

It was accepted that kings had responsibilities for the property and personal safety of foreigners in their land and for the safe and convenient passage of merchant caravans through their territory. In a letter from about 1800 BC, Shamshi-Adad, the king of Assyria, rebukes his son Yasmah-Adad, sub-king of Mari on the middle Euphrates, because some travellers from north Syria had been unable to cross the Euphrates in Yasmah-Adad's territory because there were no boats. In future, ordered Shamshi-Adad, boats must always be available so that whoever came along might cross the river without delay.

A king's accepted responsibility towards a foreign resident in his land is illustrated in a fourteenth-century letter from the king of Alashiya (Cyprus) to the king of Egypt:

A man [of Alashiya] has died in Egypt and his property is in your land but his son and his wife are with me. Now, my brother, bring forth the property of the man of Alashiya and give it into the hand of my messenger.[16]

Obligations arising from the passage of one king's subjects through the territory of another were reciprocal, so that every ruler was held responsible for any criminal offences by his subjects abroad.

Indoctrination

Major powers recognized the value of securing acceptance of their institutions, and made conscious efforts to this end. One of the most effective ways of extending their influence was to indoctrinate potential rulers; major powers did this by taking the sons of vassal rulers to be educated at the court of the overlord. Thus, Tuthmosis III took the children and brothers of chiefs of places in Palestine, to be brought up in Egypt so that when a chief died, his sons, reared in the Egyptian cultural tradition, would replace him. The Assyrians acted similarly with their vassals. This practice had a secondary value to the overlord, in that the vassal princes also served as hostages for the good behaviour of the vassal sub-king, whose sons they were.

It was quite usual to resettle prisoners of war in the land of the victor: there was no racial prejudice against them and in time they or their descendants might acquire full citizen rights and positions of responsibility. The major power not only accepted the assimilation of such peoples, but took active steps to promote it. Thus, when 2000 Libyans were taken prisoner by Egypt in the twelfth century, there were deliberate attempts to Egyptianize them by forcing them to speak Egyptian. Sargon II of Assyria in the late eighth century BC made similar efforts to assimilate deportees. He built a new capital called Dur-sharrukin (Fort Sargon) and then populated it with subject 'peoples of the four quarters, of strange tongues and different speech'. In order to make them good Assyrians, he tells us,

> *I sent natives of Assyria, competent in everything, . . . to instruct them in custom and to serve the gods and the king.*

The extensive commercial intercourse in the ancient world had the consequence that there were few places where a traveller from one of the major states would not find someone who understood his language. There was a famous Egyptian story about a courtier, Sinuhe, of the twentieth century BC, who, fearing he might be implicated in political intrigue at the death of a king, fled to Palestine.[17] There he met a sheikh who had been in Egypt, and who assured him that he would find other Egyptian speakers in north Palestine. Near the end of the same millennium, just after 1100 BC, another Egyptian, Wen-amon, in the course of a mission to the Lebanon to obtain timber, took shelter in Cyprus from pirates. After making his way to the house of the town's ruler, he asked: 'Is there anyone here who understands Egyptian?' There was.[18]

10

Natural Resources

Civilization depends upon the practical application of creative ideas, either to shape human society or to control the environment in which humans live. In large part, human progress rests upon technology.

Man's earliest technological advance was his use of fire, but this began so far back in prehistory as to leave no trace of its discovery in the mythology of either the Sumerians or the Egyptians. It is, however, reflected in the mythology of some other peoples; an obvious instance is the Greeks, with their myth of Prometheus stealing fire from the gods. Such myths may indicate that the ancestors of the peoples concerned first acquired fire technology so recently that it still remained in their folk memory. Pliny mentions that as late as the second century BC there were still tribes in Africa who did not know the use of fire.[1]

Pottery

A second major step in technology was the application of fire to clay to make pottery. Quite a number of archaeological sites have in their brief day of glory been heralded as revealing the earliest pottery of all, only to be displaced by some later find. At the time of writing, the earliest evidence of pottery-making consists of what are described as five lightly fired clay vessels, found at Mureybet on the Euphrates in north Syria, not far from the foothills of the Taurus. They were in a stratum provisionally dated by radiocarbon analysis to about 8000 BC. But this seems to have been a false start: no further pottery vessels were found in later levels of the site. Possibly inadequate firing left such vessels so easily broken that they proved of little practical use, or perhaps the five vessels found were all that remained from a much larger range, most of which were so inadequately fired that they failed to resist the ravages of water, or were so soft that they disintegrated as salts crystallized out.

The beginning of an enduring pottery technology had to wait (if the chronologies offered by the archaeologists are valid) for another thousand years. Then, at around 7000 BC, we meet pottery at Gangdareh, a site in western Iran in the central Zagros. This time it was a successful development, and many other sites (such as Tepe Guran in Luristan at about 6500 BC, Ali Kosh in southwest Iran at about 6000 BC, Jarmo in Iraqi Kurdistan somewhere within the same time range, and Çatal Hüyük near Konya and Beldibi near Antalya, both in Asia Minor at about 6200 BC) trace the spread of pottery technology throughout the Near East.

Early pots were built up from coils of clay, which were shaped, dried and then baked. We have no information upon how pottery came to be invented, but one can imagine people using clay containers for cooking food over an open fire, and, on subsequently finding that they had become hard and waterproof, recognizing their usefulness. Early production over an open fire must have been hit-or-miss (perhaps explaining why the experiment was not persisted with at Mureybet), but a time must have come when someone thought of enclosing the clay vessels for baking in a container fixed above a firepit, to give better management of the process. One can see how such a system could eventually develop into a kiln, in which the potters had close control over burning conditions, and could achieve very high temperatures. With increasing control, it became possible to produce vessels in many sizes and types, and by 5000 BC pottery, some of it beautifully decorated, was being made everywhere from Egypt through Palestine to Anatolia and Iran. Before 3000 BC the potter's wheel was in use in Mesopotamia, greatly increasing the ease and efficiency of pottery making, and establishing the potter as a specialist craftsman.

Metallurgy

Man's discovery, that applying heat under controlled conditions could alter the nature of materials, proved of importance for other processes than pottery making: it eventually led to the development of metallurgy. Gold is likely to have been the first metal known to man, since it occurs naturally in pure form and is very conspicuous and beautiful. But it is too soft to be of practical value for making tools. Lead, which is very easily produced simply by roasting its sulphide ore, galena, in an ordinary wood fire, has the same drawback without the beauty. It was smelted very early, but it never became of major importance to the early civilizations, although it found employment for such purposes as figurines, vessels, blocks to take cuneiform inscriptions, and other uses appropriate to a soft metal. The first metal to be used for a wide spectrum of practical purposes and (including its alloys) the only one in general use until just before the first millennium, was copper. This is of widespread occurrence in the form of oxide, carbonate and sulphide ores, and is occasionally found as nuggets of a native metal.

It hardly needs stressing that the use of copper can only have begun where native copper was found. The date when it began remains in dispute. An oval-shaped pendant found in a cave in northeast Iraq, dated to the early ninth millennium, has been claimed to represent man's earliest use of metallic copper, but the object is so corroded that it is not provable that it was ever in metallic form: it may simply have been a piece of malachite (an attractive green crystalline form of copper carbonate), used as an ornament or amulet.

The earliest objects which were certainly of copper were a pin and a bodkin dated to between 7500 and 7000 BC, from southeast Turkey. Analysis showed them to consist of native copper shaped by hammering. The site at which they were found was within twelve miles of Ergani (north-west of Diyarbekr), which has always been a major source of copper. Another find of early date came from southwest Iran, in the form of a bead of native copper found in Ali Kosh in a level of about 6500 BC. South Syria yielded a pendant of native copper of the same date, and there are copper objects of the same period from Anatolia, although whether they are of native or smelted copper is not yet settled. From north Iraq there are finds of beads and a small knife, probably of native copper, dating from shortly before 5500 BC; and Sialk, near Kashan, provides evidence for the use of copper in the same period in north Iran. By 4000 BC copper was being smelted from its ores at Sialk and many other Near Eastern sites. Since the use of copper did not begin in Europe until about 4000 BC, this evidence puts it beyond question that copper technology began in western Asia.

Evidence on the invention of the smelting process to extract copper is sparse, but a find at Çatal Hüyük, near Konya in Anatolia, seems to place it not later than 5500 BC; a level of that date produced what seemed to be a lump of slag; and slag is a by-product of smelting. A site in north Mesopotamia, Yarim Tepe, seems to support this dating, for in a mid-sixth-millennium stratum archaeologists found not only a copper bead but also lumps of copper ore, presumed to be raw material from which it was intended to extract copper.

Anatolia is undoubtedly the most important region for finds of early copper, not surprisingly, since it has the richest copper ore deposits in the whole Near East. Small amounts of copper are also found in fifth-millennium levels in both Mesopotamia and Egypt.

Copper technology involves two main processes, melting and smelting. As the similarity of these two terms can be confusing to those without a scientific background, definitions may be helpful. Melting in this context means heating copper in its form of a yellow metal until, at a temperature of 1083°C, it becomes a liquid which can be poured and cast. Smelting means heating copper ores (rocks typically blue or green in colour, which are chemically oxides, carbonates or sulphides) with charcoal to a temperature sufficient to bring about a process called reduction, in which the oxide, carbonate or sulphide components are removed, leaving metallic copper. This reaction begins at temperatures above 700°C.

Examination under the microscope can reveal whether a specimen of copper is of native metal which has never been subject to high temperatures, or of metal which has at some time been melted. Many specimens from the fifth millennium onwards had in fact been melted. This does not in itself prove the practice of smelting, since a piece of melted copper could have begun as native metal, but it does prove the technical ability to reach the melting point of copper (1083°C), which is several hundred degrees higher than the temperature needed to smelt copper ores (700–800°C).

One wonders how early man discovered that, unlike ordinary stone, native copper could, when heated sufficiently, be melted and poured. The knowledge may have been an offshoot from the technique of annealing copper. Copper can be both shaped and hardened by hammering, but repeated hammering gradually makes it more brittle, and eventually it refuses to respond to further hammering except by cracking. If hammered copper is then heated, its malleability is restored, making possible further modification of its shape by hammering. It is likely that early man, in an attempt to increase the malleability of his copper, would apply higher and higher temperatures, by putting the piece of metal into a kiln, until he finally found that the whole lump had melted and afterwards set in the shape of its container. Casting in open moulds would be the obvious next step. This of course would require suitable crucibles, and a number of prehistoric crucibles have been found.

The widespread use of copper could not come about so long as the only source was the native metal, which is rare. Further development had to await the invention of smelting.

The actual circumstances of the discovery of the process have been the subject of many theories, the best-known being the camp-fire hypothesis. This suggested that early man happened to light a camp-fire over an out-crop of copper ore, and was agreeably surprised to find a lump of copper there in the morning. Metallurgists points out that it is highly improbable that the correct conditions for the reduction of copper ores would ever be achieved in such circumstances, since the temperature of a wood fire does not exceed 600–700°C, whilst the temperature required for the reduction of oxide or carbonate ores of copper is 700–800°C.

Some metallurgists have proposed a more convincing theory. Early man would seek for native copper, and would often find it embedded in lumps of copper ore. Once he had learnt that copper could be melted, he would put the whole lot into his kiln, expecting the copper to melt and run off from the impurities. (The kiln need have been no more than an enclosed fire-pit in the ground, with means of applying a forced draught either by bellows, fanning, or catching the wind on a hill-top.) If there were reducing conditions in the kiln, the ore adhering to the metal would be *smelted* at the same time as the native copper was *melted*. Early man would not fail to notice that he had taken substantially more copper out of his kiln than he had put in, and he would draw the conclusion that he had cooked some of it out of the coloured stones mixed up with the native copper. From this there would follow deliberate smelting operations.

By the fourth millennium, the two processes of copper smelting and casting were being widely practised from Iran to Greece. For casting, it was necessary to melt in a crucible the copper already produced by smelting; a site near Beer-sheba, not later than 3000 BC, contained the remains of a furnace suitable for casting. Casting processes used from the fourth millennium onwards included the quite sophisticated 'lost wax' (cire perdue) method: in this, the shape required was first sculpted in wax, and then enclosed in a clay mould; by melting the wax out, the artificer could produce a hollow mould ready to receive the molten metal. By the middle of the third millennium there was a flourishing industry in copper smelting as far south as the southernmost extremity of Egypt, as we know from the finding of a copper-producing installation at Buhen, datable to the Fourth and Fifth Dynasties. The remains included rough stone mortars for pounding up the ore, fragments of pottery crucibles, moulds for casting the ingots, pieces of charcoal for the reduction process, copper slag, and driblets of copper which had spilt from the crucibles.

Bronze

Prehistoric man has the credit for the beginning of copper technology, but its most important extension, the invention and spread of tin-bronze, took place within historical times.

Copper by itself is a most useful metal: it is easier to shape than stone, and by hammering can be made harder than mild steel. It becomes still more versatile when alloyed with other elements; an alloy of copper containing a small proportion of either arsenic or tin is stronger than pure copper, easier to cast and less subject to corrosion. Any such alloys may be called bronze, but if not otherwise qualified the term is usually understood to mean the alloy of copper and tin.

Archaeologists now and again claim to have found bronze objects from as early as the fifth millennium, but most such claims prove on examination to be based on either erroneous identification of the metal or confusion about its stratification level. The only examples which seems to stand up to scrutiny are copper-arsenic alloys from Tepe Yahya in south Iran, from a level dated to 4500–4000 BC. But the copper ores in that region include copper arsenides (Cu_3As and Cu_5As); and these early alloys could have arisen, adventitiously and unrecognized, from the use of such ores. After the Tepe Yahya finds, the next examples of bronze known, also arsenical, are from the late fourth millennium, from Palestine and the Caucasus region.

Although the earliest arsenical bronze could have derived accidentally from the smelting of copper ores containing arsenic, the composition of some later examples shows that arsenic was added deliberately. Such bronze was almost certainly made by smelting a mixture of ores. Although native arsenic does occur, to make an alloy by adding this to melted copper was hardly practicable, since if there were oxidizing conditions at any stage, the arsenic would become an oxide which would vaporize and be lost.

The use of arsenical ores must have exposed the prehistoric smiths to serious health hazards and this may explain a theme which is widespread in mythology, the representation of the smith-god as a cripple. Every reader of the classics knows that the Greek smith-god Hephaestus and his Roman counterpart Vulcan were always represented as lame, but, as Robert Graves pointed out, they were not alone; smith-gods from Scandinavia to West Africa shared the same characteristics.[2] Graves suggested that underlying this was a primitive custom of laming smiths to prevent them running off to join enemy tribes, but this seems far-fetched. One does not see why a smith should be more liable to decamp than a merchant, whose departure would have been of equal economic importance, or a witch-doctor, whose defection would (in terms of primitive thought) have constituted a much greater loss to the tribe. But the tradition is easily explained from the arsenic in the bronze wrought by prehistoric smiths: sooner or later their health would be ruined by chronic arsenic poisoning, leaving them wrecks of men. Some modern metallurgists have discounted this theory, on the grounds that the loss of arsenic into the atmosphere would not have been sufficient to poison the early smiths;[3] but they are confusing acute arsenic poisoning, to which their consideration would apply, with chronic arsenic poisoning, which involves the absorption of very small quantities of arsenic over a long period, with symptoms which include muscular atrophy and loss of reflexes, and thus lameness.

Arsenical bronze continued in use in many places from Crete and Anatolia to Egypt and Mesopotamia throughout much of the third millennium, but tin-bronze appeared at the beginning of that millennium and gradually spread, until by 1900 BC it had almost completely replaced the older alloy. Ur had good tin-bronze in the first half of the third millennium and there are examples of the same period from both Crete and Syria. Two bronze objects, containing respectively 5 per cent and 10 per cent of tin, were found at Alishar in Anatolia, in a level dated to about 2600 BC; and Cyprus and the Cyclades demonstrate tin-bronze metallurgy from the middle of the third millennium, stylistically linked to Anatolia. Striking bronze work, pointing to an advanced bronze metallurgy, comes from Luristan (in the Zagros between Iran and Iraq) from the same date, and as far away as the Indus valley there are bronze figurines from the second half of the third millennium, made by the cire perdue process. A Sumerian text of not later than 2500 BC mentions bronze alongside copper and tin, and from about a century later we have a text which gives the actual proportions in which copper and tin were mixed and melted to make bronze. After a line mentioning bronze, the text specifies '$1\frac{1}{3}$ minas of copper with $13\frac{1}{3}$ shekels of tin'. Since one mina equals sixty shekels, this gives a ratio of exactly 6:1.

There is much we do not know about the making of bronze in the third millennium. A major problem is where the bronze-makers obtained their tin. The only known source of tin close to any early centre of ancient Near Eastern civilization is the eastern desert of Egypt, but this was certainly not worked in antiquity, since Egypt was the latest major region in the ancient Near East to take up tin-bronze, not adopting it until well into the second millennium. If there are any tin ores in Anatolia (Asiatic Turkey), they were certainly not known in antiquity, since at around 1900 BC tin was being imported there from Assyria. But Assyria itself certainly had no tin deposits, and nor did Babylonia to its south. This leaves, as the only reasonable candidates as a source of tin for ancient bronze manufacture, either the Zagros or Iran. There is now evidence for a source of tin in eastern Iran, which one may guess as the most probable source for the most ancient civilizations.

The relevance of the source of tin to the invention of tin-bronze is obvious: the technology can only have begun where tin ore was available for mixing with copper ore, first probably accidentally, then, when the properties of the new alloy became apparent, by design. This points to tin-bronze technology beginning in the Zagros or Iran.

Strong trading and cultural links already existed between those regions and adjacent south Mesopotamia before the beginning of the third millennium. Since south Mesopotamia already made substantial use of copper and imported copper ores, there is every probability that knowledge of tin-bronze reached that area soon after its introduction further east, by way of trade. From Mesopotamia it would have spread to other parts of the Near East, although it was not significantly taken up in Egypt until the second millennium. The lateness of the Egyptian adoption of tin-bronze does not necessarily indicate backwardness. Arsenic in a copper alloy can segregate on the surface of the metal, forming a pleasing silvery surface which can be polished to produce a very effective mirror, and the Egyptians knew and used this process. They may have exercised a deliberate preference for arsenical bronze down to the second millennium, when they finally adopted tin-bronze.

The manner in which the Egyptians produced their tin-bronze is clearly depicted in a painting on a tomb at Thebes showing a metal-working scene; it includes a copper ingot and a tin ingot, clearly represented in different colours and shapes. Obviously at that time and place bronze was made by fusing together metallic copper and tin, not by smelting a mixture of their ores.

Copper and bronze technology gradually spread to the furthest extremities of the Euro-Asian landmass but did not reach China until 2000 BC at the earliest; a date for bronze as early as 3500 BC has been claimed for Thailand, but this cannot be taken seriously, as the stratification of the sites is confused, and radiocarbon determinations date the finds no earlier than the first millennium.

In the first millennium Cornwall was the major source of tin for the Mediterranean area, and it has been suggested, although without any evidence other than probability, that the link already existed by 1400 BC, when there was flourishing bronze production in the Aegean region.

Iron

Iron is the dominant element in the earth's core and its ores are very widespread in the earth's crust. Metallic iron of terrestrial origin is found occasionally, but not in the Near East. But native iron of meteoric origin can occur anywhere in the world. Almost all meteorites contain some native iron, and some are an almost pure alloy of iron with some nickel, usually between 7 per cent and 15 per cent, with a characteristic structure. The presence of nickel within this range in a specimen of iron points to meteoric origin, which is clinched if it shows the characteristic structure.

Under the right conditions, iron ores are reduced to metallic iron at about 1200°C, the metal being left as a spongy mass in which the iron is mixed with impurities. To make this of practical use, it must either be melted and cast by heating it above the melting point of iron (which was impossible in ancient times, since that temperature is 1528°C, and early furnaces could at the most reach 1300–1400°C), or repeatedly hammered when hot, to compact the metallic iron and remove residual slag; this last process is known as forging.

Iron did not come into general use until the beginning of the first millennium BC, but there are rare examples of it from preceding millennia. The oldest iron object is a small piece of some implement from Samarra in Iraq, dated to about 5000 BC. Analysis shows the iron to have been smelted, but is unable to tell us whether the smelting was accidental (as a by-product of copper smelting) or deliberate; however, the fact that this iron smelting stands alone for two thousand years makes it virtually certain that it was a lucky accident. The next finds of iron are three balls from a level at Sialk in Iran dated to the first half of the fifth millennium: their nickel content indicates that they are of meteoric origin, and since meteorites are frequently spherical, they may simply be in the form in which they were picked up after dropping from the sky. The only other finds of iron certainly from before 3000 BC are nine beads and a ring from graves in Egypt, dated to the second half of the fourth millennium: one of the beads is of meteoric origin, but the others and the ring have not been analysed.

The third millennium provides rather more iron objects, but even so the total finds from Mesopotamia, Anatolia and Egypt together do not reach 25—less than one every 40 years—and some of these are mere heaps of rust. Some specimens from each country are of meteoric origin, others smelted. All are so badly corroded that modern metallurgists are unable to tell whether the smelted iron was produced deliberately or accidentally, how well the iron was worked, or whether it had been carburized (p. 206). The only identifiable objects are a crescent-shaped plaque, an amulet, some pins, and blades of weapons or tools. Almost all come from rich graves, temples or treasure hoards, indicating that they were particularly precious objects; clearly, during the third millennium iron was still a commodity of exceptional rarity and value.

From the first half of the second millennium there is a decrease, rather than an increase, in reported finds of iron. This is odd, and may reflect archaeological practices rather than changing circumstances in the ancient world. Sites of this period in Mesopotamia, from which no iron at all has been reported, tend to be particularly rich in cuneiform tablets, and an archaeologist busy with important new archives may not have the resources to attend to finds consisting only of shapeless lumps of apparent rust. That there was not a real regression in the use of iron is shown by contemporary texts. In Cappadocia (north-central Anatolia) at about 1900 BC, there was an Assyrian merchant colony trading in tin and textiles (pp. 143ff.). The tin was bought by Anatolian metallurgists who were mining and smelting copper and needed it to make bronze. The archives of this colony tell us of a wide range of transactions involving its members, and amongst them are recurrent mentions of a commodity called *amutu*. This was available to the merchants in only very small quantities; the largest amount we hear of is one mina (about a pound), and on one occasion it took three months to collect less than an ounce of it. It was something which could be refined, sometimes losing weight in the process, and it was so valuable that one correspondent considered it underpriced at eight times its weight in gold. This can only have been iron. Another term mentioned alongside *amutu*, and sometimes apparently alternating with it, was *asi'u*. This was controlled by the royal authority, which could forbid its export, and it was valuable enough to be sent as a present for a ruler. It differed from *amutu* in never having a price put to it in extant documents. *Asi'u* may have been iron in the spongy form it takes when first smelted, and *amutu* the same iron after forging.

The evidence of the tin imports shows that the Anatolians had a thriving metal industry in copper and bronze. The texts about *amutu* suggest that they were now beginning the production of iron, in small and uncertain amounts. Possibly rather more iron was produced than one might suppose from the texts: the controls exercised over the distribution of *asi'u* suggest that the Anatolians would not readily have made iron available to foreigners, and in order to get round an embargo, the Assyrians may well have had to pay exceptionally high prices for very small amounts.

From the first half of the second millennium there are also a few mentions of iron from other sites, as a prestige material for decorative and ceremonial use; the sites in question range from Syria through Mari on the middle Euphrates to Iran.

Texts show a significant increase in the use of iron in the second half of the second millennium. There are also archaeological finds, of which one of the most impressive was an axe at Ugarit with an iron blade, dating to about 1400 BC; but the nickel content of the iron suggests that it was of meteoric origin, so that it is not relevant to developments in iron smelting. This particular axe was only for ceremonial purposes, but possible practical applications for iron were already beginning to be recognized by 1400 BC, as we learn from a text of about that date from Nuzi in eastern Assyria, which refers to 'a coat of mail for a horse, of which the breastplate and the limb-coverings are iron'. A few utilitarian objects of iron, such as small tools and arrow-heads, have been found from between 1400 and 1200 BC.

The increased textual mention of iron is particularly marked in documents from Hittite Anatolia, suggesting that we have to look to that area for the developments in iron technology which eventually moved the metal out of the domain of the precious and decorative to become a commodity of the highest practical value for everyday use. By the first half of the thirteenth century the Hittite realm was the recognized source of the best iron, as we find from a letter from a Hittite king, in which he excuses himself for inability to fulfil an order. The letter is written in Akkadian, probably to the king of Assyria:

> *In the matter of the good iron about which you wrote, good iron is not (currently) available in my storehouse in Kizzuwatna. I have already told you that this is a bad time for producing iron. They will be producing good iron, but they won't have finished yet. I shall send it to you when they have finished. At present I am sending you an iron dagger-blade.*

The Hittite evidence offers partial support for the tradition, reflected in some Greek authors, that systematic iron production began in Anatolia, although the Greeks put it further north than Kizzuwatna, which was in the southern half. Finds from a number of sites in northern Anatolia prove that copper and bronze production and casting began there early—we have already mentioned the evidence of copper mining there by 2800 BC—and had reached a high standard by the beginning of the second millennium. The Cappadocian archives tie in with this. Geology points in the same direction, for the area contains abundant supplies of ores of copper, lead and iron.

The reduction of copper ores in the smelting process produces fine globules of copper mixed in with the unwanted mineral material, which is technically called gangue. There is the problem of separating the desired metal from the waste. If the gangue remains solid, this is difficult, but the process can be facilitated by adding other substances as a flux to reduce the melting point of the gangue, so that the whole mass liquifies, allowing the heavier copper to separate out from the gangue (called slag in the final stage) and run down to the bottom. This was perfectly practicable in ancient times: early furnaces could reach a temperature of up to 1400°C, and the melting point of copper is 1083°C and slag melts in the temperature range 1150–1250°C. One of the commonest of the materials added as a flux was haematite (iron oxide, $Fe_2 O_3$). In some conditions iron is produced from the flux in the course of copper smelting. An ancient instance in which this happened is known from the fifteenth-century site

Atshana (ancient Alalakh) on the Orontes in north Syria (now politically part of Turkey), where Sir Leonard Woolley found lumps of copper and iron melted together. It is therefore technically possible that iron smelting began as a by-product of copper smelting. The requirements for it to happen accidentally were that fluxes should be used in smelting and that there should be high grade iron ores in the area from which the copper ores were obtained. But even if the accidental production of iron occurred, not every metalworker would notice its significance, and the people most likely to do so would be metallurgists who were already practising an advanced metal technology. All these conditions were met in northern Anatolia at the beginning of the second millennium.

Iron technology is more complex than the processes for smelting copper and making bronze. Not only is the melting point of iron much higher than those of copper and bronze, but there is the complication that the physical properties of iron are considerably affected by the proportion of carbon it contains. As already noted, iron as first produced in an early smelting furnace would be a spongy mass which would require forging. Sufficient forging could produce wrought iron, which is almost free of carbon; this has the characteristic of being malleable, but it is not very hard. Wrought iron can be made to absorb more carbon by reheating it in a furnace in contact with carboniferous materials: this process is known as carburizing. However, in order to give the resultant metal its maximum hardness, it has to be suddenly cooled by quenching in water or oil; it is then known as steel. Iron could not come into widespread use until the iron metallurgists had mastered these processes. We have evidence, from a knife found in Cyprus, that steel was being made there by carburizing and hardening by quenching before 1000 BC, but earlier stages in this development remain obscure.

We should perhaps mention that claims have been made for the use of iron in Thailand as early as between 1600 and 1200 BC; but such claims are invalidated by confused stratification of the sites concerned, and radiocarbon determinations give no earlier date than 750 BC.

Why and when did iron come into general use? One scholar has linked the beginning of the appearance of iron in the Aegean, as a serious functional (as distinct from ornamental) material, to a supposed shortage of tin, and hence of bronze, in the eleventh century. This seems to be valid for the limited period and region for which he argues, but some other scholars have expanded this into a more far-reaching hypothesis which purports to explain the coming of iron over the whole of the eastern Mediterranean and Near East from a shortage of bronze. Thus one authority argues that at around 1200 BC, the period which saw the collapse of the Hittite empire, 'men were being forced towards the new metal [iron] by the disruption of the trade in copper and tin in a moment of social chaos in the Eastern Mediterranean', and 'in such places as Cyprus, the demand for bronze must have been undergoing great expansion, prompting attention to the production of iron and steel well before the disasters of the Sea Peoples swept over the Eastern Mediterranean'.[4] I venture to suggest that this hypothesis in its wider form is not well founded.

The only textual evidence I have come across, which is supposed to prove a shortage of bronze in the period concerned, lies in Minoan Linear B archives, dated to just before 1200 BC, from Pylos (Pilos), a Mycenaean city on the southwestern coast of the Greek Peloponnesus. It will be remembered (pp. 94f.) that Minoan Linear B was a form of syllabic writing on clay tablets, adapted for records in Greek from an older system invented in Crete for some other language. Because its signs were based on the needs of the phonology of a language of quite a different type, it was not a very efficient way of writing Greek: thus the Greek word *chalkos*, meaning 'bronze' or 'copper', had to be written with the signs *ka-ko*, and *khalkewes*, 'bronzesmiths' or 'coppersmiths', is *ka-ke-we*. The system did not represent *l* at all, and either omitted it or rendered it with a syllable containing *r*.

There is a group of tablets in the Pylos archives which altogether name 274 smiths, in groups of up to 26. The tablets contain entries of the following kind:[5]

[Place name] *ka-ke-we ta-ra-si-ia e-ko-to*

followed by several lines on the pattern

[Personal name] [symbol for bronze] [number]

followed by

to-so-de a-ta-ra-si-io ka-ke-we

followed by several more personal names. *ta-ra-si-ia* is ultimately connected with the word 'talent', which originally meant 'weight' and in this context the Linear B word is assumed to mean 'allocation'. *e-ko-to* is recognizable as the Greek *ekhontes*, meaning 'having'. In the other line of Linear B quoted, *a-ta-ra-si-io* is apparently a form of *ta-ra-si-ia* with the Greek negative particle *a* prefixed, and so is taken to mean 'non-allocation'. *to-so-de* is taken as Greek *tossoide*, meaning 'so many'. The whole document is then interpreted in the sense

Bronzesmiths having an allocation, specified by name and amount; so many bronzesmiths without allocation, specified by name.

These documents are then taken to indicate that there was not sufficient bronze to go round, proving a shortage.

There are several flaws in this argument. If the text really does refer to deliveries of bronze to bronzesmiths, the fact that some are said to have received none does not prove there was a shortage. The inclusion of nil deliveries may have been based on some administrative procedure we do not know: if it was merely a matter of there not being enough bronze to go round, why bother to name those who did not receive any? There is another text which does not name smiths but simply gives a total for the amount of bronze, which is just over a ton. Now a wrecked ship of this period was found at Cape Gelidonya off south Turkey, carrying a cargo of ingots, and the estimated weight of this cargo was just over a ton.[6] It is possible, then, that the Pylos archives prove not a bronze shortage, but that consignments of bronze came in by sea and were distributed in an orderly manner: there is no reason to think that we have more than a small fraction of the original records for such transactions.

There is another text amongst the Pylos documents which has been called in aid to support the theory of a bronze shortage.[7] It begins with terms which may denote officials, and says that they will contribute

ka-ko na-wi-io pa-ta-io-i-qe e-ke-si-qe ai-ka-sa-ma.

ka-ko is 'bronze' or 'copper', and the three final words quoted are reasonably taken as 'points [i.e. sharp metal heads] for arrows and spears'. *na-wi-io* is not otherwise known, but one school of thought suggests that it is related to Greek *naos*, 'temple', and that the reference is to stripping the temples of bronze to make weapons in a national emergency, which would imply a desperate shortage of the metal. But the meaning 'temple' is a mere guess, and *na-wi-io* could equally well be related to Doric Greek *naios*, 'belonging to a ship'; this would agree with the interpretation of the other texts as the distribution of a ship's cargo, and would not lead to any conclusion about shortages. Even if *na-wi-io* is related to the word for 'temple', it could refer to a consignment of metal being received for the benefit of the temple rather than being stripped from it.

It appears that a far-reaching theory has been built on very flimsy evidence. It is difficult to see why circumstances at around 1200 BC should have driven people in the Levant and Near East as a whole to the use of iron. Tin supplies might well be affected, making bronze difficult to obtain, but copper had continued in use for many purposes for a full millennium after bronze became generally available, and in the absence of tin could be employed for anything for which bronze was more usual. And sources of copper ore were available within reasonable distance in every region—in the Zagros (as a source for Mesopotamia), in many parts of Anatolia, in Palestine, in Sinai, in Cyprus. It might be argued that even although copper ores were available everywhere, metallurgists able to smelt them were not. But areas which lacked local metallurgists able to produce copper, certainly could not operate the more difficult metallurgy of producing iron; and any trading problems which prevented the import of finished copper or bronze would operate equally against the import of finished iron.

We do not have to depend upon *a priori* argument. There is good textual evidence that copper and bronze were still common in the century before 1200 BC and remained common afterwards. James D. Muhly points out that 'thirteenth-century texts at Ugarit [in north Syria] give no indication of a shortage of copper'.[8] Assyria was still trading in tin in the reign of Shalmaneser I (1274–1245 BC), and the troops of his successor Tukulti-Ninurta I (1244–1208 BC) used copper picks for road clearance as a matter of course. A century later the army of Tiglath-Pileser I (1114–1076 BC) were still using copper picks in just the same way, and that king took bronze, copper and copper ore as war spoil and tribute, and used bronze for decoration. It is true that this king does make a mention of iron arrow heads, but not as something in general use by his army; they were a de luxe weapon which he himself used when demonstrating his prowess.[9] Thus, there was no general shortage of copper or tin in the Near East just before 1200 BC, and there was still plenty of copper and bronze just before 1100 BC, with copper common enough to be used by ordinary soldiers, but iron still so rare that it was restricted in military use to royal circles. Ashurd-bel-kala (1073–1056 BC) was still using bronze bands on the doors of his city gates and Ashur-dan II (934–912 BC) mentions bronze and tin as plunder from the southern fringe of Anatolia, but says nothing of iron. It is not until the early ninth century that we find an Assyrian king, Tukulti-ninurta II (890–884 BC), recording iron along with bronze and tin as plunder or tribute.[10] Obviously, amongst Assyria and its neighbours, iron had not begun to replace bronze as the commonest metal before the beginning of the ninth century.

Palestine gives the same picture. Samson, when caught by the Philistines in the early eleventh century, was bound in bronze (not iron) fetters (Judges 16:21). When king David at around 1000 BC made a northward expansion, he conquered the Aramaean state of Zobah up in Syria and 'took very much bronze' (2 Samuel 8:8). Not iron, one notes. Just after 1000 BC, Solomon enlisted from Tyre a skilled craftsman, Hiram, who is described in 1 Kings 7:14 as 'a worker in bronze'. 2 Chronicles 2:14 contains a retelling of the same narrative from a much later period, and says that Hiram was a worker in iron as well as bronze:

clearly the difference is because when 2 Chronicles was written it was taken for granted that a metal craftsman would be competent in both bronzework and ironwork, whereas when the event happened, it was only bronze, and not iron, that came into consideration as a material in common use.

Archaeological finds confirm that iron did not suddenly replace bronze everywhere just after 1200 BC. There are a few iron knives known from the twelfth century, but they amount only to about nine, spread over Palestine, Syria, Cyprus and the Aegean. But by the eleventh century iron knives—some of them of hard steel—outnumber those of bronze in Cyprus and Syria, and are about equal in eastern Greece. Agricultural implements in iron do not occur until the eleventh century, and remain far less common than those in bronze until the tenth; a similar picture applies to weapons; and even in the tenth century finds of iron weapons outnumber those of bronze only in Palestine, Cyprus, eastern Greece and Crete: from western Greece and beyond there are no significant finds of iron from before 900 BC. By that date Egypt had axes and other implements of iron carburized and quenched to produce steel. Further east, in Mesopotamia and neighbouring areas, iron seems to have come into general use by 900 BC, although without in any way displacing bronze, which continues to be attested in large amounts both in texts and in archaeological finds.

Technology

Whole books could be written, and indeed have been written, about the many materials which the pre-classical civilizations utilized and the technologies they devised to exploit them. Amongst the more impressive and enduring achievements were the invention of glass, probably in Mesopotamia in the third millennium, with widespread use in Egypt by the Eighteenth Dynasty; many aspects of chemical technology, such as (probably) the production of artificial lapis lazuli in Sumer as early as the first half of the third millennium;[11] the preparation of cosmetics and perfumes, in both Mesopotamia and Egypt; dyeing technology; shipbuilding; the control of watercourses by weirs and dams; and the extraction, shaping and transportation of large blocks of stone. A summary of all this within the space available would not be practicable; the reader desiring a detailed treatment of the data for the two primary regions, Egypt and Mesopotamia, will find helpful accounts of most of these points and many others in A. Lucas, *Ancient Egyptian Materials and Industries*, London, 1962 and P. R. S. Moorey, *Materials and Manufacture in Ancient Mesopotamia*, Oxford, 1985.

One point that deserves emphasis is the Egyptian mastery in the manipulation of stone. Although all the ancient civilizations used stone, none approached the Egyptians in the extent of their use and expertise. The actual manipulation of stone is clear to see in the pyramids, where the great cubic blocks are so tight fitting that one cannot put a knife blade between them (plate 14). Types of stone used by the Egyptians ranged from soft, such as alabaster, limestone and sandstone, to very hard, such as basalt and granite. The limestone presented no logistic difficulties, as there were quarries available close to Cairo. A more distant source of stone was Wadi Hammamat in the eastern desert northeast of Luxor, for which as many as 19,000 men were engaged in one expedition near the beginning of the second millennium. Granite demanded expeditions even further afield, to Aswan in the south. Precisely how the blocks of granite were extracted is still a matter of some controversy. Part of the work was certainly done by pounding with natural balls of dolerite weighing an average of about twelve pounds, possibly fixed to a haft to be used as giant pestles, but the experts differ as to whether the Egyptians had copper alloys hard enough to be effective as chisels on granite; another suggestion is that part of the cutting out of granite blocks was by vertical drilling using copper tubing rotated by bowdrills with sand as an abrasive, followed by the hammering in of wedges. The sheer size of some of the granite obelisks extracted makes their transportation and eventual erection a stupendous achievement; some of them were a hundred or more feet long and weighed up to 455 tons. Despite this, most of them were successfully moved several hundred miles down the Nile on giant barges, or barge-shaped rafts, built for the purpose. There was one notable failure: the biggest of all, which was 137 feet long and would have weighed over 1100 tons if extracted, developed fissures in a late state of the cutting out, and had to be abandoned, to remain in situ to the present day.

Animal Resources

The domestication of the principal large mammals used for food—goat, sheep, cow, pig—was an achievement of Neolithic peoples, in which the early civilizations played no part. In this respect the early civilizations served only as transmitters of dietary custom both positively and negatively. Negatively, mammals which were not domesticated and widely eaten by Neolithic peoples, for example, the dog, cat, horse, donkey, camel, never came into general use as food in either the early civilizations or the civilizations of Greece, Rome and the western world eventually descended from them. It is true that each of these animals has been eaten, or is eaten, in limited geographical contexts, but this is chiefly by peoples (such as the Chinese who eat dogs or Beduin Arabs who eat camels) not in the mainstream of descent from the early civilizations.

The principal achievement of the early civilizations in the exploitations of large mammals was related to their value as a source of power. Occasionally this has been questioned, as by a scholar who asserts that cattle 'were probably . . . first tamed for the sake of their traction-power, and only secondarily on account of their milk and meat'. But this does not fit with the actual evidence. Cattle were certainly domesticated by 6200 BC (a radiocarbon dating) in south-eastern Europe, and at that date the people of south-eastern Europe had no implements which could be used with a draught animal; there is no evidence anywhere for either ploughs or wheeled vehicles or even sledges before the fourth millennium. Also, it is impossible that, before cattle were domesticated as a source of meat, people who only knew cattle as dangerous wild animals, which, when an attempt is made to catch them in the herd, stampede, and when an individual beast is cornered lowers its horns and charges, could envisage that they could be tamed and trained to drag a load. These considerations are not theoretical only; the third-millennium Sumerians (and presumably other ancient peoples) were so well aware of the impossibility of taking cattle direct from the wild and hoping to use them for draught purposes that they incorporated the matter in proverbs: 'the wild ox is taboo for the plough', or 'the wild ox is for ever free from the plough'.

Prehistoric peoples from the Old Stone Age onwards undoubtedly hunted wild cattle as a source of meat (a bone of a wild cow or bull with an arrow wound has been found), and it must have been solely as a source of meat that the Neolithic peoples domesticated them. Their use as draught animals and a source of milk came later, almost certainly in the Near East.

Domesticated cattle had reached north Iraq by 5000 BC. There is no archaeological evidence for ploughs before the fourth millennium, but they had certainly been invented before 3000 BC, as the representation of a plough occurs amongst the earliest pictograms. What is more, it must have been invented by the Sumerians, since the name of the plough was Sumerian, not a loanword, as it would have been if the implement (and the name with it) had been introduced from abroad.

The Sumerians were using oxen for dragging both ploughs and carts from at least the early third millennium. Many varieties of plough developed, perhaps the most ingenious, certainly invented by the Sumerians, being the seeder-plough, which enabled ploughing and seeding to be performed in one operation. Ploughs for really heavy work needed more than one draught beast, and some are described as yoked with two, three, four, six or even eight oxen. The Sumerians also developed forms of wagons and carts to be drawn by oxen. In Egypt, however, wheeled vehicles did not come into use until the second millennium. This was not an indication of technological backwardness: the Nile was so convenient for transport throughout the length of the land that land vehicles were not essential, and when it was necessary to drag loads to the nearest point of the river for shipment there was always abundant organized manpower for the task. Oxen, most usually in pairs, were, however, in common use in Egypt for drawing ploughs as early as the Old Kingdom period, and in Cyprus from the end of the third millennium. A further use of ox-power was as a means of threshing corn, firstly simply by repeatedly walking over it, later by dragging a form of sledge studded with flints: the Sumerians introduced ox-drawn threshing-sledges of this kind during the third millennium, and this quickly spread to other parts of the Near East.

There was a species of wild ass in the Near East, which survived in Iraq until the early twentieth century AD, but this was notoriously impossible to tame: the Bible calls Ishmael, the supposed ancestor of the Beduin Arabs, 'a wild ass of a man, his hand against every man and every man's hand against him' (Genesis 16:12 RSV). The domestic donkey derives from an African species of ass, of which one subspecies was not entirely extinct in the wild in Egypt as late as the second millennium. It was domesticated by the Egyptians before the end of the fourth millennium, and reached Palestine by 3000 BC and other parts of the Near East soon afterwards. Like other large mammals, it was probably originally domesticated as a source of meat, but it proved so valuable as a pack-animal, in view of its ability to negotiate almost any terrain, and so tractable and patient, that load-carrying quickly became its primary use. During the third millennium the people of south Mesopotamia began to ride it, and also brought it into use for drawing carts, and sometimes ploughs, as well as for a primitive form of war-chariot. In view of the donkey's lack of speed under a load, the donkey-drawn chariot was no more than a mobile platform on which an archer was moved into battle. More effective use of chariotry had to await the domestication of the horse.

The earliest evidence of the domestication of the horse is from south Ukraine, in the second half of the fourth millennium. There may have been other centres of domestication, in central Europe and central Asia. Possession of the domesticated horse spread southwards, and had reached Iran by 3000 BC, where it is represented on pictographic tablets (see illustration, p. 90). From Iran it came to Mesopotamia during the third millennium, across passes of the Zagros. The Sumerians consequently knew it as ANŠE.KUR.RA, which meant 'donkey of the KUR', KUR denoting the Zagros range between south Mesopotamia and Iran. It did not come into common use in Mesopotamia until the second millennium; it is attested for Greece by 1900 BC, but did not reach Egypt until about 1600 BC.

The delay in exploiting the horse in south Mesopotamia was probably because the Sumerians thought of it, as their name for it suggests, as a kind of donkey, more nervous and less tractable than the standard sort. The sentiments horses evoked are suggested by a description of demons, which were troublesome and unpredictable, as 'horses that grew up in the mountains'. The earliest specific use of horses which we meet is as pack-animals alongside donkeys, at the beginning of the second millennium. At about the same time, they were beginning to be ridden, but this was considered a rather unworthy means of transport, and we have a letter recommending a king against it, as a chariot drawn by mules was more prestigious. However, this indicates one use of the horse which the Sumerians had developed—the breeding of mules, a means of combining the strength of a horse with the surefootedness and (except for occasional stubbornness) the docility of the ass. Horses were also beginning to be used at this time as draught animals for wagons, and there is one mention of them in connection with a chariot, but in the context this was probably no more than a ceremonial wagon.

The horse did not really come into its own until the development of an efficient horse-drawn chariot. This was an achievement which reached both Mesopotamia and Egypt at about 1600 BC, in the case of Mesopotamia through the Mittannians, a Hurrian-based kingdom to the north-west, and in the case of Egypt through the invasion of the Hyksos, an ethnically mixed group with Hurrian elements. The first Egyptian chariots were imported, but they were being made in Egypt during the Eighteenth Dynasty (1553–1305 BC). Amenophis II (1439–1413 BC) was fascinated with chariot horses and boasted of his skill as a trainer and charioteer. He reared, so he claimed, horses of unrivalled mettle, which he could drive at a gallop in his chariot without bringing them out in a sweat.

It is difficult to fix the date when horses were first ridden. Archaeologists attempt to settle it by the date at which appropriate harness is first found, but this makes the false assumption that horses can only be ridden if equipped with a mouth-bit or the like. I was once given a horse to ride in south Iraq which had only a single light rein attached to the left side of its face. The horse docilely moved right when the rein was laid (not pulled) on the upper side of its neck, and left for the lower side. I was told that such animals were never broken, but were simply ridden bareback by small children almost from birth. Early man may well have trained horses for bareback riding in the same way, and no trace of harness would have been left for archaeologists to discover.

The riding of horses was certainly becoming widespread in the Near East by 1400 BC, the Mittannians (Hurrians) being the leaders in this. Amenophis II mentions that when he took Mittannian prisoners, one of them, a member of the nobility, rode with him on horseback. Such riding eventually led to the military use of cavalry. The Bible repeatedly refers to horseriders (Hebrew *parashim*) alongside chariotry in the Egyptian forces at and before the Israelite exodus from Egypt (Genesis 50:9; Exodus 14:9,17,18,23,26,28;15:19,21), and unless these are all taken as anachronisms, which is unlikely since Exodus 15 contains some of the earliest literary material in the Bible, it shows that Egypt had already developed cavalry by 1300 BC, which is very probable, in view of the interest of Amenophis II in the Mittannian rider. But as late as 1000 BC there were still parts of the Near East where horses were little valued: king David of Israel, for example, on capturing a thousand chariot teams, had so little conception of how to use them that he hamstrung all the horses except enough for a hundred chariots (2 Samuel 8:4).

Although Mittanni appears to have initiated the use of cavalry, followed by Egypt, it was Assyria which developed it as a major war weapon, from the end of the second millennium. Efficient cavalry requires well-trained horses ridden by men capable of operating as a cohesive fighting unit. The peoples of Anatolia and northwest Iran, the main horsebreeding regions from at least the end of the second millennium, had the trained horses but no military tradition to enable them to operate as efficient cavalry. The Assyrians used their armies to obtain horses as tribute from those areas and with them developed highly disciplined cavalry units capable of breaking any infantry by their terrifying charge.

Beekeeping

Prehistoric man hunted wild honey from 8000 BC onwards, as rock paintings in Spain show, and probably earlier. The earliest certain evidence of beekeeping, as distinct from honey-collecting, comes from Egypt at about 2400 BC, in the form of a stone bas-relief showing a battery of hives placed horizontally in several columns of nine superimposed layers. The beekeeper is kneeling in front of one hive, collecting comb in a pottery dish with a fitting lid. Two other men are standing nearby, one apparently dropping pieces of broken comb into a large pot and the other straining honey from a basin into a tall jar.

The Hittite laws show that the Hittites practised beekeeping from early in the second millennium, for there are laws concerning the theft of hives, and one mentions penalties that apply in older times. Beekeepers are also said to be mentioned in Mycenaean documents of the late second millennium from Pylos.

From eighth-century Assyria we have an actual record of the introduction of beekeeping. A governor on the middle Euphrates set up an inscription in which he recorded

I am Shamash-resh-usur, Governor of Suhu and Mari. Bees which gather honey, which no one among my predecessors had seen nor brought down to the land of Suhu, I brought down from the mountains of [eastern Turkey] and established in [my town]. They collect honey and wax. I understand how to do the extraction of the honey and wax, and the gardeners also understand it. Let any person who comes along subsequently ask the old men of the country whether it is true that Shamash-resh-usur the Governor of Suhu introduced bees.

Plant Resources

The supremely important food plants wheat and barley were themselves basic to the Neolithic Revolution, and their exploitation by the early civilizations was limited to adapting cultivation techniques to reliance upon irrigation instead of rainfall. The major problem here was that faulty irrigation techniques could increase the salinity of the soil to a point at which it would no longer grow cereal crops; this may explain the abandoning of some early settlements in south Mesopotamia, and certainly explains the way in which barley, which is more tolerant of salinity than wheat, gradually increased its relative importance.

Almost equalling wheat and barley as a source of human food in south Mesopotamia was the date-palm, which has the advantage of being much more tolerant of salinity than cereal crops. The date-palm does not fruit in the regions of the Taurus and Zagros foothills where the Neolithic Revolution began, and its cultivation must have originated with the earliest settlers in south Mesopotamia, where it is native. But the date-palm in the wild form does not fruit heavily; there are separate male and female plants and artificial fertilization is necessary to achieve maximum cropping. Moreover, left to itself it makes squat trees with an impenetrable jungle of sword-like leaves (plate 17). It was one of the achievements of the Sumerians of the late fourth or early third millennium that they learnt to trim side-growth to produce tall trees suitable for orchard cultivation (plate 18), and devised methods of artificial pollination which made the date-palm a major source of food. The Code of Hammurabi contains laws dealing with artificial pollination.

The ancients appreciated trees: in Egypt the ideal house, as shown in tomb paintings, was in a clearing surrounded by trees, with birds and a pool where lotus flowers grew. Assyrian kings were susceptible to natural beauty, as we know from descriptions they left of scenery. They even attempted sometimes to reproduce it in their own capitals. Classical tradition makes the Hanging Gardens of Babylon a royal attempt to simulate the forested mountains of Media, and although the tradition probably has the details wrong, it correctly reflects attitudes of some Mesopotamian rulers. Several kings, both in Egypt and Mesopotamia, brought back trees and other plants from abroad and attempted to establish them in their own lands; Tuthmosis III, for example, in the middle of the second millennium brought back specimens of flowering plants that grew in Syria, and considered this so significant that he represented them in reliefs on a temple. His immediate predecessor Queen Hatshepsut had done something even more ambitious; she had brought back incense trees, which in nature grow only in the regions both sides of the southern end of the Red Sea, and attempted to establish a plantation in Egypt (see plate 4). Some Assyrian kings were equally enterprising: in the first millennium both Ashurnasirpal III and Sennacherib planted foreign trees around their capitals, respectively Calah and Nineveh. Sennacherib, in his efforts to beautify Nineveh, created a great park where he introduced what he described as 'every kind of plant and tree, brought from the mountains and Chaldea'; this included aromatic plants and various fruits and timber trees. Perhaps his most important introduction was cotton, which he described as 'trees bearing wool', which people wove into garments. Sennacherib is not more specific about the source of the cotton plants, but they must have come ultimately from the Indus valley, since cotton was one of the products we owe to the Harappans, who were already using cotton fibres in the third millennium.

Another plant of the highest importance, which the Harappans were probably the first to domesticate, is rice; there is evidence for its use in late Harappan settlements. It was not introduced into Mesopotamia until after 500 BC, probably because it could not compete with barley, and its cultivation was not taken up in Egypt until after the Arab conquest in the first millennium AD.

The cultivation of the valuable oil-plant sesame also probably began in the Harappan civilization, where it has been found. The actual word 'sesame' is ultimately of Akkadian origin, from a term *šamaššammu* meaning literally 'oil-plant'. This has misled assyriologists into thinking that the early use of the term *šamaššammu* proved that sesame was cultivated in Mesopotamia very early; in fact, the name *šamaššammu*

217

probably originally referred to linseed, and was transferred to sesame when, late in the first millennium BC, that was introduced to Mesopotamia and replaced linseed as the most important oil-plant.

Flax, the fibres of the plant which produces linseed oil, was used in Egypt for linen fabrics since Neolithic times. The earliest evidence for linen in Mesopotamia is the third millennium, which suggests that knowledge of the technology for making linen from flax diffused from Egypt.

All ancient peoples used oils for anointing, and in view of the use of flax for linen, it is probable that linseed oil was Egypt's predominant native oil from earliest times, as it certainly was in Mesopotamia. However, from earliest times the Egyptians imported olive oil from Palestine and Syria. The olive tree itself, which was a native of Syria and Asia Minor, does not grow naturally either in south Mesopotamia or in Egypt, and although the Egyptians made occasional attempts to introduce it from as early as the third millennium, it does not appear to have become established in Egypt before the first millennium. Olive orchards are often mentioned in texts in the Akkadian language, but these are mainly texts from Syria, where the trees grew naturally. Olive trees will, however, grow well in Assyria, although not in Babylonia, and in the first millennium both Ashurnasirpal III in the ninth century and Sennacherib in the early seventh included olive trees in the plantations they established in their parks; there are still large stands of olive trees, presumably descendants of the introductions of the first millennium BC, in and near Nineveh and Calah.

In addition to actual importations of foreign trees of economic value, the ancient peoples of the Near East must have been the first to devise, by trial and error, many of the techniques subsequently used for their better exploitation. We have mentioned the obvious case of the efficient cultivation of date-palms. But scribes everywhere were normally interested only in recording what was done traditionally, and it was only when a progressive king took an interest in technology that any advance would ever be mentioned: Sennacherib, for example, recorded the invention of a new metal-casting process and prospecting for new sources of minerals. But this situation made it most unlikely that slow and unspectacular but extremely important advances in plant exploit-ation would ever be recorded, and at most points there is no way in which archaeology could demonstrate them. We are therefore only likely to hear about them by accident. One instance of this comes from a report by Pliny:

Now about leaves of palms being planted by the Babylonians so as to produce a tree, I am surprised that Trogus gave it credence.[12]

Obviously the Babylonians had discovered that some trees, amongst them date-palms, can be grown from leaf cuttings. That Pliny doubted the possibility, serves only to show that it was a genuine tradition, untouched by his imagination.

11

Mathematics and Astronomy

Mathematics

Widespread classical tradition held that Greek mathematics and astronomy both owed much to the Egyptians and Babylonians, and some authors mention specific borrowings in these areas. Strabo, for example, says that the Greeks learnt the exact length of the year through Plato and Eudoxos, who allegedly lived in Heliopolis for thirteen years in the fourth century BC.[1] However, such claims are not necessarily to be accepted at their face value, and the actual achievements of the two main cultural areas of the pre-Greek world deserve examination on the basis of their own records.

Mathematics was an area where the peoples of Mesopotamia and Egypt differed considerably in their achievements. In Mesopotamia there was a considerable achievement, extending to the use of algebraic processes. But Egyptian activity in this area never went beyond elementary arithmetic, and rather clumsy arithmetic at that. Some people might contest this statement, on the grounds that the Egyptians made use of geometry for land measurement and building purposes, but such procedures, as operated by the Egyptians, were no more than the application of elementary arithmetic.

Egyptian fractions also were very clumsy; with the exception of $\frac{2}{3}$, the only fractions used were unitary ones, that is, fractions in the form of $\frac{1}{n}$. If a single term did not give the fractional number required, the fraction required was represented by two or more terms, each in the form $\frac{1}{n}$. Thus $\frac{5}{6}$ would have been represented in the form $\frac{1}{2} (+) \frac{1}{3}$.

Egyptians used only one arithmetical procedure—addition—although they manipulated this to achieve both multiplication and division. Some examples will illustrate this.

Suppose an Egyptian scribe wished to multiply one number by another number greater than 2, say, 19 multiplied by 23. He would first multiply

19 by 2, by adding 19 to itself, giving 38. Then he would multiply 19 by 4, by adding 38 to 38, giving 76. Then he would multiply 19 by 8 by adding 76 to 76, giving 152. Finally he would multiply 19 by 16 by adding 152 to 152, giving 304.

The scribe would set out his results in this manner:

1	19
2	38
4	76
8	152
16	304

He would then see which of the multipliers added up to 23. In this case it was 1, 2, 4, 16. He would then add up the numbers in the right-hand column which corresponded to those multipliers in the left-hand. I.e., he would add 19 + 38 + 76 + 304, giving the result 437. The procedure is not elegant but gives the right answer.

For division the scribe would use the inverse of this procedure. Suppose the problem were to divide 437 by 19. Then the scribe would set out his numbers, until those in the right hand column were sufficient to add up to more than 437. The numbers would be precisely as in the preceding table, set out in the same way. The scribe would inspect the numbers on the right, to see if there was a set of numbers which added up to exactly 437; he would find that 304 + 76 + 38 + 19 did so. Adding the corresponding numbers in the left-hand column, i.e., 16 + 4 + 2 + 1, would give the answer, namely 23.

Sometimes a division sum would be one in which the answer was not a whole number. This would require the introduction of fractions into the procedure. Take, for example, the problem of dividing 25 by 8. The scribe would write down

1	8*
2	16*
$\frac{1}{2}$	4
$\frac{1}{4}$	2
$\frac{1}{8}$	1*

The numbers in the right-hand column required to make up 25 are those marked with an asterisk. The answer to the problem is therefore the sum of the corresponding numbers in the left-hand column = $1 + 2 + \frac{1}{8} = 3\frac{1}{8}$.

The failure of the Egyptians to develop convenient mathematical procedures is surprising, as their intelligence and inventiveness are beyond question. But they were very conservative, and it may be that their very primitive and clumsy mathematical procedures are a legacy from a very early development which became fossilized.

Egyptian and Sumerian numeration

The Egyptians used only a decimal system. The following examples illustrate their numerals:

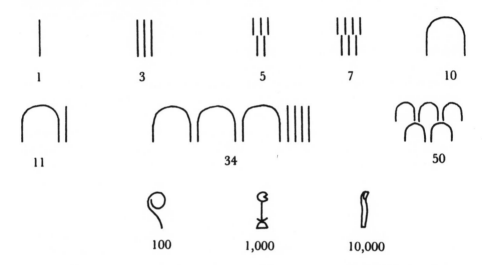

The Sumerians invented two different systems of numeration; one was decimal (based on powers of ten, 1–10–100–1000, like the system we commonly use), and the other sexagesimal. The latter, based on powers of 60 (1–60–3600), is not wholly unfamiliar to us, since we still use it for the division of hours and minutes, and in part for the degrees in a circle. In ancient Babylonia, administration and business mainly used the decimal system, although the influence of the sexagesimal could be seen in writing numbers larger than 60, or in weights, where the mina was divided into sixty shekels. The main contexts in which sexagesimal numeration predominated were mathematical and astronomical calculations.

Numerals were mainly written with particular signs, corresponding to our figures. These signs were basically simple, formed mainly by combination of strokes denoting 1 and, according to whether the decimal or sexagesimal system was employed, 10 or 60. In the earliest stage, at about 3000 BC, there were two basic numeral strokes, formed by pressing a round reed into the clay, either obliquely or at right angles. The oblique stroke produced a kind of modified oval which was flat at the deep end and rounded at the other, and the stroke at right angles gave an impressed circle. The oval served as 1 or, originally in larger form, as the higher power, 60, in the sexagesimal system. The circle represented 10, and, (according to the system being used), a larger form of it could denote either 100 (= 10 × 10) or 3600 (= 60 × 60).

As the pictograms of the earliest writing evolved into signs composed of wedge-shaped impressions, the numeral signs were correspondingly modified. The symbol for 1 became a single vertical wedge and that for 10 a broad oblique wedge. The single vertical wedge continued to be used for 60, the next power up in the sexagesimal system, but the difference in size soon disappeared. This caused less confusion than might be supposed, because the sexagesimal system used a place-value notation. That is to say, as in our own system (which ultimately derives from ancient Mesopotamia) the power of a symbol depended upon its position in a sequence. With us, the symbol 8 in 78 denotes 'eight', but in 87 the same symbol denotes 'eighty'; in the same way, in the Babylonian system, in ⟨𝅘 the vertical wedge denotes 1 (making the number 11), but in 𝅘 it denotes 60 (making the number 70). This has advantages, especially when doing multiplication, over the non-place-value Roman system, which had to use long groups of combinations of I, V, X, C, L, D and M.

The sexagesimal system had its influence on the decimal system in numbers over 60. 100 could be written in various ways; we have already mentioned one, used in the early period. Later it was commonly written by a sign which represented ME, approximately the pronunciation of the Semitic word for 100. Alternatively, under the influence of the sexagesimal system, it could be written by a combination of one vertical wedge (representing 60) plus four large oblique wedges, each representing 10. The decimal system sign for 1000 was a combination of the broad oblique wedge for 10 and the ME sign for 100.

In the sexagesimal system, there was a special sign for the largest number, 3600. This was originally a very large form of the impressed circle, which with cuneiform writing developed into a group of wedge-shaped strokes.

Other refinements included the occasional incorporation of a minus sign to denote a number just less than an exact group of tens.

The following are examples of numerals in their developed form:

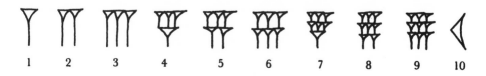

1	2	3	4	5	6	7	8	9	10

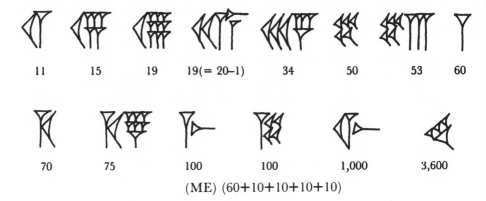

11	15	19	19(= 20–1)	34	50	53	60

70	75	100	100	1,000	3,600
			(ME) (60+10+10+10+10)		

One of the most important of all developments was a means of indicating zero, used with numerals written in the sexagesimal system. Suppose one wished to write the numeral 3727, which is 3600 + 2 × 60 + 7. This could be written

and it would be clear that the first element represented a multiple of 60^2, the second a multiple of 60 and the third a multiple of 1. But consider the problem of writing 3607. If the scribe wrote

it could be clear from the context that the first element represented 60^2, but the second element could be taken as 7 × 60 (= 420), instead of the intended 7 × 1. To preclude such confusions, scribes in the Old Babylonian period would often (not invariably) write a number of this kind widely spaced in the form

indicating that the number contained no element which was a multiple of

60. But the utility of this method depended upon maintaining accurate spacing, and confusion could still arise. Eventually the Babylonians overcame this by inventing a special sign for zero. This was definitely in use, in the form ✦ , by 300 BC, and may have been invented as early as 700 BC. Using this symbol, 3607 could then be written unambiguously in the sexagesimal system as

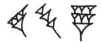

Mathematical calculations

No one with any feeling for mathematics can fail to be impressed by the achievements of the Babylonians. It is true that many of their mathematical procedures were a matter of consulting tables, but those tables must have been devised by people with very high mathematical skills. The mathematical expertise of some Babylonians of about 1800 BC, or perhaps their predecessors, exceeded that of most people today other than those with a degree in Mathematics. For example, they had calculated the square root of 2 correct to 1 in two million. They also compiled lists of sexagesimal reciprocals, which, when expressed in our decimal numeration, prove to be correct to three or four places of decimals. (A sexesimal reciprocal of a number is the result when the sexagesimal unit 60 is divided by that number. Thus the sexagesimal reciprocal of 2 is 30.) Here is an extract from a table of sexagesimal reciprocals of about 1800 BC, with decimal equivalents:

Sexagesimal number	Sexagesimal reciprocal	Decimal value of sexagesimal number	Decimal value of ancient calculation of sexagesimal reciprocal	Correct decimal value of sexagesimal reciprocal	% error
1;10	51;25;42	1.1667	51.4284	51.4286	.0004
1;11	50;42;15	1.1833	50.7042	50.7042	nil
1;12	50	1.2	50	50	nil
1;13	49;18;55	1.2167	49.3153	49.3151	.0004
1;14	48;38;55	1.2333	48.6486	48.6486	nil
1;15	48	1.25	48	48	nil
1;16	47;22;6	1.2667	47.3683	47.3684	.00025

Also, twelve hundred years before Pythagoras was born, the Babylonians were familiar with the facts with which the Theorem of Pythagoras deals—that in any right-angled triangle, the square of the hypotenuse is equal to the sum of the squares of the other two sides. There are tables of calculations—again correct to three or four places of decimals when converted to our terminology—listing numbers linking the length of one side to given lengths for the other two sides. The early-second-millennium mathematicians had also calculated the value of the mathematical constant π as $3\frac{1}{8}$, which is within about $\frac{1}{2}$ per cent of the correct value.

Already by the Old Babylonian period, about 1800 BC, the Babylonians could solve problems for which we would use algebra. The following is an example. I give a literal translation, followed by an explanation using modern terminology to show the steps in the Babylonian scholar's procedure. Line numbers are provided for ease of reference.

> *1. I have added the area [literally, 'surface'] of my two squares: 28;20.*
>
> *2. (The side of) one square is a quarter (the side of) the (other) square.*
>
> *3. You put down 4 and 1.*
>
> *4. You multiply 4 by 4: 16.*
>
> *5. You multiply 1 by 1: 1.*
>
> *6. You add 1 and 16: 17.*
>
> *7. The reciprocal of 17 cannot be solved. [i.e. the sexagesimal unit 60 cannot be divided by 17 to give a whole number].*
>
> *8. What must I put to 17 [i.e., multiply it by] which will give me 28;20? 1;40.*
>
> *9. This is the square of 10.*
>
> *10. You multiply 10 by 4 and 40 is (the side of) one square.*
>
> *11. You multiply 10 by 1 and 10 is (the side of) the second square.*

The numerals are in the sexagesimal system. Therefore, in terms of our decimal system, 28;20 represents $(28 \times 60) + 20 = 1680 + 20 = 1700$.

The area of a square is the square of its sides. Call the sides of the two square x and y. Then

> *1.* $x^2 + y^2 = 1700$.
>
> *2.* $x = 4y$.
>
> *3. Assume the sides of the two square are 4 and 1.*
>
> *4. In that case, area of larger square would be $4 \times 4 = 16$, and*
>
> *5. Area of smaller square would be $1 \times 1 = 1$.*
>
> *6. Then total area would be 17.*
>
> *7. This does not give the right answer.*
>
> *8. By what has 17 to be multiplied to give the real total area of 1700? Answer: 100.*
>
> *9. 100 is the square of 10.*
>
> *10. Therefore multiply 4 by 10, giving 40 as the side of the larger square [= x].*
>
> *11. Multiply 1 by 10, giving 10 as the side of the smaller square [= y].*

As early as about 1800 BC, Babylonian mathematical expertise extended to calculating cube roots. The following is an example:

1. Procedure [literally, 'the tying up'] for a cube root.

2. The cube root of 3;22;30—what is it?

3. In the matter of 3;22;30 they have not given you the cube root.

4. They do give you a cube root for 7;30.

5. Put it down beneath 3;22;30.

6. Thus: 3;22;30 . . . 7;30.

7. The cube root of 7;30—what is it? 30.

8. Solve the (sexagesimal) reciprocal of 7;30 and (you get) 8.

9. Multiply 8 by 3;22;30. This gives 27.

10. The cube root of 27, what is it? 3.

11. Multiply 3, the cube root, by 30, the other cube root.

12. (It makes) 1;30.

13. The cube root of 3;22;30 is 1;30.

To understand the procedure used in this calculation, it is helpful to know what the numbers given in sexagesimal form mean in decimal terms. In second millennium Babylonian mathematics, the scribes did not consistently make clear in what powers they were operating. Thus a sexagesimal writing 7;30 could mean

either	$(7 \times 60 \times 60) + (30 \times 60)$	= (in decimal numeration) 27,000
or	$(7 \times 60) + (30 \times 1)$	= (in decimal numeration) 450
or	$(7 \times 1) + (30 \times \frac{1}{60}$	= (in decimal numeration) 7.5

But although any of these numbers could be written as the cuneiform equivalent of 7;30, their cube roots would not have the same figures. In decimal form, the cube root of the first is 30, of the second approximately 7.6631 and of the third approximately 1.9574.

Line 7 gives the cube root of sexagesimal 7;30 as 30. Since 30 cubed equals decimal 27,000, sexagesimal 7;30 must represent $(7 \times 60 \times 60) + (30 \times 60)$, which has this value.

We therefore conclude that, correspondingly, in the sexagesimal number 3;22;30 the last element represents the power of 60, so that the number as a whole represents $(3 \times 60 \times 60 \times 60) + (22 \times 60 \times 60) + (30 \times 60) =$ decimal 729,000.

In modern terminology and decimal notation, the steps the Babylonian mathematician took were as follows:

2. What is the cube root of 729,000?

3. The answer is not given in existing tables of cube roots.

4. The tables do give a value for the cube root of 27,000.

7. The value the tables give for the cube root of 27,000 is 30.

The scribe now shows that he is aware of a relationship between numbers which we would express algebraically as

$$\sqrt[3]{N} = \sqrt[3]{M} \times \sqrt[3]{\frac{N}{M}}$$

For convenience, we will refer to the sexagesimal number 3;22;30 as N and the smaller number 7;30 as M. The Babylonian chose M because it was a number of which the cube root was given in tables. He now wished to calculate N in terms of a multiple of M, *i.e.* to find the value of $\frac{N}{M}$. To do this most conveniently, he used a principle relating to ratios between numbers.

In the decimal system, if we wish to find the ratio between two numbers, such as 1200 and 8400, the answer is the same regardless of the power of numbers at which we work. I.e. we get the same answer whether we treat the numbers as 120 and 840, or 12 and 84, or 1.2 and 8.4. The Babylonian used this principle to simplify things; for his next step he treated M and N not as

(7 × 60 × 60) + (30 × 60) and
(3 × 60 × 60 × 60) + (22 × 60 × 60) + (30 × 60)
but as (7 × 1) + (30 × $\frac{1}{60}$) [= (in decimal numeration) 7.5]
and (3 × 60) + (22 × 1) + (30 × $\frac{1}{60}$) [= (in decimal numeration) 202.5].

The scribe saw that he could calculate the ratio between M and N by multiplying both numbers by such a number that the answer in the case of M came to 1; N multiplied by that number would give the ratio of N to M.

By definition, the value 1 is obtained by multiplying a number by its reciprocal. Therefore, by multiplying N by the reciprocal of M, the ratio between the numbers (algebraically the value $\frac{N}{M}$), would be obtained. The Babylonian scholar could obtain the reciprocal from tables, in which the sexagesimal base number 60 was taken as the unit.

8. The tables gives the sexagesimal reciprocal of 7;30 as 8. [I.e., 60 divided by (in decimal numeration) 7.5 = 8]

9. Multiply sexagesimal 3;22;30 [i.e. (3 × 60) + (22 × 1)] + (30 × $\frac{21}{60}$)] by 8. This gives 27 units of 60.

10. The cube root of 27 is 3.

11. Multiply the two cube roots 3 and 30.

12. The result is (in decimal numeration) 90, which is sexagesimal 1;30 [(1 × 60) + 30 × 1)].

13. The cube root of sexagesimal 3;22;30 [in decimal numeration 729,000] is sexagesimal 1;30 [in decimal numeration 90].

Astronomy

In view of the low level of their mathematics, it is not surprising to find that the Egyptians made very little contribution to theoretical mathematical astronomy; as far as current evidence goes, they produced no texts which deserve this description until the final centuries before the Christian era, after they had become open to Babylonian and Hellenistic influences. Although the Egyptians recognized many constellations, stars and planets, and identified some of them with their deities, they did not theorize upon astronomical phenomena, and paid little attention to recording them, except insofar as they had a practical application in producing calendars to serve the needs of agriculture and administration. None the less, by imaginative applications of observed astronomical phenomena, the Egyptians arrived at procedures for time measurement which have had the highest subsequent importance.

The moon's regular sequence from new to full to waning and disappearance constitutes an astronomical time-marker which no human community can fail to observe. The sun equally has a seasonal pattern, although this may not be readily apparent to nomadic peoples, whose physical environment may constantly change, leaving them no permanent points of reference on the horizon. However, settled peoples will certainly observe that the sun rises and sets upon slightly different points of the horizon each day until it reaches extremes from which it then moves back, and will become aware that the sun's extreme positions on the horizon coincide with its highest and lowest courses across the sky. Nature also marks off certain regular time-spans, for example, those between successive germinations, flowering or ripening of particular plants; and it soon becomes obvious that these natural time-spans are linked to the sequences of the sun.

A purely lunar calendar may be adequate for peoples who are still in a nomadic pre-agricultural stage, and almost all primitive peoples began with a lunar calendar, which is sometimes tenaciously retained even when changing conditions make it no longer appropriate: Muslims still use such a calendar unmodified, whilst Judaism retains lunar months in its otherwise solar year. Christianity uses, alongside the solar calendar by which Christmas is fixed, an old lunar calendar for calculating the date of Easter and the linked festivals from Septuagesima to Trinity. This lunar element in the three great monotheistic religions reflects the nomadic background of their earliest source, Israelite religion.

A purely lunar calendar is inadequate for an agricultural society, since agriculture depends upon the sun, and agricultural operations must be timed in relation to the sun. The average length of a lunar month is approximately 29½ days, so that twelve lunar months amount to 354 days. Thus a year of twelve lunar months gets out of step with the solar year of 365¼ days, or the year of nature, by a full eleven days a year.

Efficient agriculture (and animal husbandry in non-nomadic communities) require forward planning: the herdsman, eking out his store of cattle-feed during the lean season, needs to know how long before he may expect the new growth of pasture; the farmer must clear his ground and sow at the time most favourable for utilizing his water supply and the growing season. Therefore, either a solar calendar must be adopted, or, if a lunar calendar continues in use, means must be found to keep it in step with the solar and natural year.

The earliest calendars of both Mesopotamians and Egyptians, as of all other ancient peoples, were lunar, going back into prehistoric times. Not later than the early third millennium, steps were taken in both civilizations to keep the lunar calendar in alignment with the solar year. But differing physical environments led to very different solutions.

Throughout its history, Egypt used several different calendars. All were linked in some way to the original lunar calendar, and in none of them, except the civil calendar which we shall discuss later, was anything other than observation ever used to fix the beginning of the months. It is true that one Egyptian text, Papyrus Carlsberg, gives a mathematical scheme for determining the beginning of lunar months over a 25-year cycle, but this was not written until AD 144 or later, and it has been proved that the cyclic lunar calendar with which it deals was not introduced until the fourth century BC.

However, because of Egypt's dependence upon agriculture, the original purely lunar calendar must have been linked to the solar or natural year very much earlier than the fourth century BC. This came about because of a geographical feature peculiar to Egypt— the behaviour of the Nile. The Nile rises and floods the land in a very uniform and predictable pattern, so that in ancient times it became thought of as dividing the Egyptian agricultural year into three seasons. The first season was the time of inundation, from when the river began to rise until it had fallen sufficiently to permit sowing. The second season was the time from sowing to harvest, and the third was the period of low water between harvest and the beginning of the next inundation. Experience showed that each of these seasons lasted about four lunar months.

The importance of the inundation to Egyptian agriculture led to the concept that the beginning of the year was linked to it. The year became thought of as beginning with the lunar month immediately after the Nile began to rise. But in terms of the solar year the beginning of the Nile's rise is variable, commonly by up to a fortnight across the end of May and the beginning of June, in exceptional years by over two months. This means that a year linked to the rise of the Nile might have anything between eleven and fourteen lunar months. By the beginning of the third millennium at latest, the Egyptians had found a more accurate basis for fixing the year length. This was based on the rising of the brightest of the stars, Sirius, which the Egyptians knew by a name written as Spdt, which has been transmitted to us in the Greek form Sothis.

Because of the rotation of the earth, all stars, except those apparently near the earth's axis, appear to rise in the east and set in the west. Because the earth revolves around the sun, the sun appears to move in a complete circle among the stars once a year. When the earth, the sun and Sirius are in line, and for some time before and after this, Sirius will be invisible, the actual period of invisibility being seventy days a year. After the period of invisibility the relative motions of earth and sun are such that Sirius becomes briefly visible just above the eastern horizon immediately before the sun rises; as soon as the sun rises, of course, it renders Sirius invisible again. This is called the heliacal rising of Sirius; within any person's lifetime it occurs on the same solar date each year, although over a longer period there is a gradual retardation amounting to one day every 120 years. We know that already by the beginning of the third millennium, the Egyptians had linked the heliacal rising of Sirius both to the beginning of the year and to the rise of the Nile; this conclusion is based on an ivory tablet from that time which—assuming the correctness of a translation which has sometimes been challenged—identifies Sothis as 'the opener of the year; the inundation'. To be the harbinger of the new year, the heliacal rising of Sirius had to fall within the last month of the old year. This required manipulation. Let us imagine a year in which the heliacal rising occurred in the middle of the 12th month, i.e. during the 15th night. The next heliacal rising would be 365 days later, i.e. 12 lunar months (354 days) plus 11 days later, and thus would fall during the 26th night of the last month of the year. The following year the heliacal rising would, if nothing were done, be 11 days later than the 26th night of the 12th month, and so right outside its proper month. To ensure that the heliacal rising of Sirius took place within the last month of the year, it was necessary to intercalate a 13th month. This applied whenever the heliacal rising in the previous year was less than 11 days (365–354) from the end of the 12th lunar month.

The Sirius-controlled lunar calendar gave a year in which the number of months could be either twelve or thirteen. Not only did the number of months in the year vary, but also the number of days in a lunar month. The actual length of a lunar month (the period from new moon to new moon or invisibility to invisibility) is 29½ days, but for practical calendary purposes the month must always be regarded as starting at the same point in the day (whether morning or evening). This made it impossible to take account of the odd half days month by month, and so the effective length of a month had to be treated as either 29 or 30 days.

The irregularity in a calendar based on observation of the moon creates inconveniences. Even in the modern world, the variable lunar-based date of Easter can cause problems, for example, in producing an unduly long school term between Christmas and Easter. Likewise, in a highly bureaucratic country such as ancient Egypt became soon after 3000 BC, a purely lunar calendar could and did occasion considerable administrative inconvenience. To overcome these disadvantages, the Egyptians in the early third millennium devised a schematic lunar year; they did this by calculating the average number of days in a year and dividing them into a standard number of months of regular length. We do not for certain know how they arrived at their figure for the length of a year, but two methods were available to them. The simplest was to count the days between successive heliacal risings of Sirius, although, as weather conditions could affect the date of the first heliacal sighting of Sirius, this would have to be averaged over several years. The other possible method was to average the total days in a series of lunar years. Despite the fact that the number of days in any given lunar year may range from 354 (12 months) to 384 (13 months), the average after ten years will always come very close to 365. This period of 365 days was then, on the analogy of the true lunar calendar, divided into twelve months, but for regularity each month was given 30 days. This left five extra (technically 'epagomenal') days, which were placed between the end of the old year and the beginning of the new, in the same way as an intercalary month when it was needed in the true lunar calendar.

This civil calendar was used for administrative and fiscal purposes; it did not wholly replace the older lunar calendar, which remained the basis for fixing religious festivals. Because the civil calendar had 365 days, as against the 365¼ of the solar year, it would get out of step with solar and sidereal phenomena at the rate of one day in four years or 25 days a century. Thus, a century and a half after its introduction, it would be well over a month out from the religious calendar, which, although lunar, was tied to the solar year by the rising of Sirius. This gave problems, the solutions to which are outside our immediate concern. The point of major importance is that in the third-millennium Egyptian civil calendar we have what one distinguished historian of science, Otto Neugebauer, called 'the only intelligent calendar which ever existed in human history'; it remained in use throughout the Middle Ages, and Copernicus employed it for his calculations. In 46 BC Julius Caesar decided to reform the old Roman lunar-based calendar, and for this purpose sought the advice of an Egyptian astronomer, Sosigenes. The resulting Julian calendar, related to the Egyptian civil calendar through Sosigenes, gained in accuracy by its correction for the length of the year as 365¼ rather than 365 days, but lost the convenience of months of uniform length. A further correction in the sixteenth century gave the Gregorian calendar commonly used today.

There was a further feature of the Egyptian civil year which, although it played no part in the development of later calendars, had important consequences for later systems of time-measurement. Each of the twelve months of the civil calendar was divided into three parts of ten days each, conveniently called decades, using an old sense of that word (not originally restricted to the meaning 'ten years'), and these decades were linked to what used to be called diagonal calendars and are now known as 'star clocks'.

Star Clocks

We have noted the phenomenon known as the heliacal rising of Sirius. Since Sirius, after moving up the sky from its rising one night and then disappearing during the day, reappears the next night in the same position at approximately the same time, the apparent rate of its movement across the sky is as though it passed through a full circle, *i.e.* 360°, in about 24 hours; this gives an apparent movement of 10° in about 40 minutes (the precise time varying with latitude, time of year, and other factors). In fact, because of the earth's revolution around the sun, Sirius, which is seen just above the horizon at dawn on the night of its heliacal rising, reaches a position a little higher in the sky each successive dawn, which means that it rises a constantly increasing time before dawn. Thus every ten days Sirius will rise forty or so minutes earlier.

Many other stars besides Sirius can be observed to rise heliacally. The Egyptians used this fact to draw up star-clock charts. We have seen how in the third millennium they devised a civil calendar with twelve months of 30 days each, which gave 36 decades, plus the five epagomenal days. They then selected suitable stars or constellations so that for each of the 36 decades there was one which rose heliacally on its first day; additional provision was made for the epagomenal days. Using a Greek term, we refer to the stars or constellations so chosen as the decans. Charts of these decans were then drawn up to serve as means of telling the time during the night. The reason the Egyptians wanted to know the time at night was probably to ensure that nocturnal religious rites were celebrated at the proper time.

The Star Clock charts actually preserved were not the real thing; they were never used for telling the time at night. They are, in fact, painted inside late-third-millennium coffins, where they had a magical application for the use of the dead. But these magical copies must go back to real Star Clock charts actually used for telling the time at night earlier during the third millennium.

The Star-Clock charts are divided into 36 columns, plus a section for the epagomenal days. They are read from right to left, with headings relating them to the 36 decades. In the columns are twelve rows of names of decans. The manner in which they are set out may be represented schematically as below; to simplify it, only 13 columns are given:

13	*12*	*11*	*10*	*9*	*8*	*7*	*6*	*5*	*4*	*3*	*2*	*1*
M	L	K	J	I	H	G	F	E	D	C	B	A
N	M	L	K	J	I	H	G	F	E	D	C	B
O	N	M	L	K	J	I	H	G	F	E	D	C
P	O	N	M	L	K	J	I	H	G	F	E	D
Q	P	O	N	M	L	K	J	I	H	G	F	E
R	Q	P	O	N	M	L	K	J	I	H	G	F
S	R	Q	P	O	N	M	L	K	J	I	H	G
T	S	R	Q	P	O	N	M	L	K	J	I	H
U	T	S	R	Q	P	O	N	M	L	K	J	I
V	U	T	S	R	Q	P	O	N	M	L	K	J
W	V	U	T	S	R	Q	P	O	N	M	L	K
X	W	V	U	T	S	R	Q	P	O	N	M	L

Quite simple (although ingenious) principles underlie such a chart. At the beginning of the year, the star or constellation *L* rises heliacally, i.e. it is seen at the end of the night, moments before the impending rise of the sun makes the last of the stars disappear. Ten days later, at the beginning of Decade 2, *L* is rising 40 minutes or so earlier, and it is then *M* which is rising heliacally. After twenty days, as Decade 3 begins, it will be star or constellation *N* which is rising heliacally, and M will have risen 40 or so minutes earlier and *L* 80 or so minutes earlier. After 120 days, L will rise just after nightfall, and *M, N, O, P, Q, R, S, T, U, V*, in sequence throughout the night, with finally *W* shortly before daybreak.

By looking at the night sky to see how many of the decans in the sequence appropriate for the current decade had already risen, and then consulting the chart, an observer could know what proportion of the night had passed. Suppose, for example, it was the beginning of the third month, so that sixty days (six decades of days) had passed and the seventh decade had begun. An observer looked at the night sky and could see the stars or constellations *G, H, I, J, K, L*, but not *M, N, O, P. Q, R*. He thereby knew that six-twelfths of the night had passed. The decans thus served to divide the night into 12 time-divisions.

Why twelve time-divisions? The whole table of decans covers a complete year of apparent stellar motion, which is a complete circle of 360°. The maximum amount of sky visible is however only a semi-circle (180°) from the eastern to the western horizon. To cover this, only half the decans *i.e.* 18 (since the appropriate pro-rata allowance for the epagomenal days would be negligible) should be required. However, there is a factor which substantially reduces this. It does not become completely dark immediately after sunset or remain completely dark until the moment of sunrise, and during these periods of partial darkness stars, except the brightest, such as Sirius, will not be visible near the horizon. In their charts, therefore, the Egyptians did not include decans to cover the complete 180° of sky from horizon to horizon; they omitted three decans from the beginning of the night and three from the end, leaving only 12 rows of decans instead of the theoretically possible 18. In effect they were concerning themselves only with the period of total darkness, not the full period from sunset to sunrise.

Since the night is longer in midwinter than in midsummer, the 12 time-divisions this system provided were not of uniform length throughout the year. The Egyptians were aware of the disadvantage of this, and had already begun to deal with the problem by the twelfth century. From that period we have a papyrus text giving the hours of daylight and darkness for each month. In this list, the total number of hours always equals 24 but the division between daylight and darkness varies with the time of year. Clearly an attempt was being made to produce hours of equal length. Even though the actual figures indicate that an exact uniformity of hours had at that time not quite been achieved, this was the ultimate basis of the 12-hour and 24-hour time-system still in use.

The division of the hour into minutes and seconds was not an Egyptian achievement but goes back to the Mesopotamian way of counting in sixties.

Star clocks were not the only Egyptian invention for telling the time. Another device was what is known as a shadow clock. Our best information on this comes from a text from the tomb of king Sethos I (1303–1290), which gives instructions for making such a clock. A base with four marks along it supported a crossbar above one end. It was set up facing east, and as the sun moved round to the south and rose higher, so that the shadow of the raised crossbar shortened, the shadow moved across each of the marks in turn, so marking off four time-divisions. At noon the instrument was reversed, and the shadow correspondingly marked off another four time-divisions as the sun went round to the west, sinking lower. The text regards two time-divisions as having passed in the morning before the sun shines on the clock and two more similarly in the evening, so that this system seems to have included the twilight period not taken account of in the star clocks. Clearly, this covered more than half of a complete day and night and the star clocks rather less than half, so that the twelve daylight time-divisions would each be longer than those of nighttime.

By the middle of the second millennium the Egyptians had also invented the water clock. This was, like the earlier star clocks, originally used for telling the time during the period of total darkness. It consisted of a vessel which at the onset of darkness was filled with water, which then trickled out through a small outlet. The instrument is known from three fragmentary specimens, ranging in date from the mid-second millennium to about 600 BC. Calibration on the inside of the vessel showed by the level of the water how many divisions of the night had elapsed. At the time of the invention of the water clock time-measurement was still influenced by the concept, derived from the star clocks, that the night, whatever its length, should be divided into 12 periods. Obviously, in the long winter nights each period was longer than in summer, and the calibration had to allow for this. It did so by providing separate scales for each of the twelve lunar months.

Astronomy in Mesopotamia

The Babylonians and Assyrians kept detailed records of many phenomena, ranging from weather conditions to the behaviour of ants, as a source of omens. Amongst their records were detailed observations of the position and movement of heavenly bodies, which when used in combination with Babylonians mathematical expertise, gave rise to the beginning of true mathematical astronomy.

The earliest relevant text was a series of recordings over 21 years, during the reign of Ammisaduga, a Babylonian king of the first half of the second millennium, of the heliacal risings and settings of Venus. Whether these observations were taken, like many later ones, as a basis for astrological predictions, or (as is not impossible) out of purely scientific curiosity on the part of some observer interested in the motions of the planet Venus, we are unable to determine. The observations were later copied and recopied and incorporated into a major astrological collection with which they had nothing to do originally. Despite some errors of transmission, they proved accurate enough to enable modern astronomers to date the years in which they were taken (or, rather, several alternative series of years, since the motion of Venus repeats after several decades).

The earliest of the next relevant group of documents comes from

Assyria, towards the end of the second millennium. The documents in question are known as astrolabes, the form of which depended upon a combination of mythology with observational astronomy. In terms of mythology it was held that there were three regions of the heavens (that is, the sky), under the control respectively of the three great gods Ea, Anu, and Enlil. This concept provided a useful framework for representing the positions of various major constellations, stars and planets in different months. The data were arranged either in columns or in the form of three concentric circles, divided into 12 sectors, in this way:

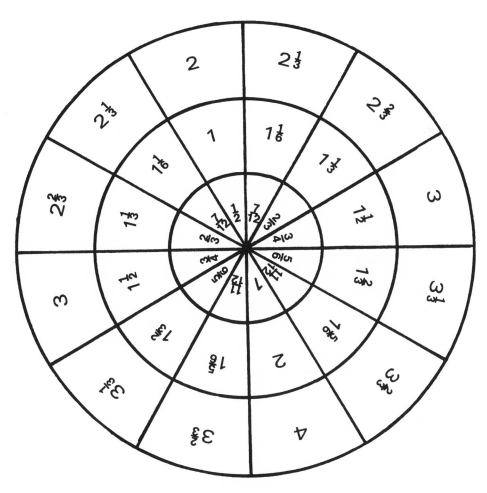

Although we have older copies of the material in tabular than in circular form, there are reasons for thinking that the circular form was the original way of presenting the material. The three concentric circles, or the three columns in the tabular form, represent different parts of the sky; the twelve sectors, or a column in the tabular form, represent the twelve months of the year. The relation between the stars and the months is that, as one of the astrolabes expressly states, the heliacal rising of each star named occurs in the month in which it is placed.

Two of the astrolabes have the stars accompanied by numbers which in the outer ring increase and decrease by arithmetical progression from 2 to 4 and back to 2. In the middle ring a corresponding progression occurs, but with all the numbers halved, and in the innermost ring all the numbers have a quarter of the value of those in the outer ring. These numbers seem to be related to the length of the day, since the highest value, 4, occurs in the month of high summer. We know that the day (and, indeed, also the night) was divided into three watches, and the length of a watch would have varied with the time of year. The middle and inner rings may give figures for the length of half-watches and quarter-watches; if so, the innermost ring would show that the period of daylight was divided into twelve variable-length 'hours'. The actual units of time would have been measured by water clocks, which were used in Mesopotamia as in Egypt.

Despite a superficial resemblance of the circular astrolabes to a zodiacal chart, there was no direct connection. The zodiac, a diagrammatic representation of the movement of the sun and planets relative to certain constellations, was indeed a Babylonian invention, but it did not come about until the fourth century BC.

Observations of lunar and planetary motions were particularly marked in Assyria from the eighth century BC. The basic stimulus was undoubtedly to obtain astrological omens, but this folly had the happy consequence of producing records of lunar and planetary motions over long periods. According to the Greek astronomer Ptolemy, there was a series of records available going back to 747 BC. The records would show that lunar eclipses only occurred at full moon, and also that the period between successive lunar eclipses was very frequently 6, 12 or 18 months. This gave the possibility of predicting lunar eclipses, and Assyrian astronomers began to do so in the seventh century BC. We know this, because we have a report to the king predicting one, followed by a further report recording that it had actually occurred.[2]

These observations probably also played a part in an improvement in the calendar. Whereas in Egypt, an efficient civil calendar had been introduced, based on the solar year, the lunar calendar remained in use for all purposes in Mesopotamia. To bring it into line with the solar year, it required the intercalation of an additional month every three years, sometimes every two. Until the middle of the first millennium this was always done ad hoc, when it became apparent that the lunar year was more than a month out from the solar year. But shortly after 500 BC a 19-year cycle was introduced, with seven intercalations at predetermined intervals.[3] The period was fixed at nineteen years because that period corresponds exactly to 235 lunar months (12 years of 12 lunar months plus 7 years which had an added intercalated month).

But the most important Babylonian material on mathematical astronomy comes from the period from 300 BC to the early decades of the Christian era. It consists of about 300 texts, some of them of the class known as ephemerides, that is, day-to-day or month-to-month positions of heavenly bodies, and the others procedure texts, giving the rules for calculations from the ephemerides. The lunar tables amongst these texts were intended to determine the position of the full moon and new moon and the exact times at which they occurred. Other tables related to calculations of the cardinal points (first and last visibility, beginning and end of retrograde motion) of the planets Venus, Mercury, Saturn, Jupiter and Mars. A detailed explanation of procedures and results would require a highly technical mathematical treatment which is beyond the scope of this book.[4] But it may be said that the Babylonians concerned were employing a sophisticated mathematical astronomy relating to planetary and lunar motion which was not surpassed until the coming of Copernicus.

12

Medicine

In the fifth century BC the Greek traveller Herodotus commented on current medical practice in Egypt

> *The art of healing is with them divided up, so that each physician treats one ailment and no more. [Egypt] is full of physicians, some treating diseases of the eyes, others the head, others the teeth, others the stomach, and others unspecified diseases.*

Contrariwise, according to Herodotus, the Babylonians had no physicians at all:

> *They bring out the sick into the public square, for they feel no need of physicians. Then people approach the sufferer, and, if they have suffered from the same illness or known someone else who has, give advice about the illness.*[1]

Either the situation had changed considerably in both countries by the time Herodotus visited them, or he generalized too widely on the basis of limited observation or hearsay information, since in neither country is what he tells us wholly compatible with the picture we get from ancient texts. However, there certainly were some countries with no doctors at all. A petty ruler from south Palestine, writing to the pharaoh in the fourteenth century, requested the sending of a doctor from the Egyptian court because there was no medical man available in his land.[2]

Physicians in Egypt[3]

Already in the Old Kingdom (2635–2155 BC), we hear of over 50 physicians (Egyptian *swnw*), mainly from their names on tombs. These chance finds by archaeologists are likely to represent only a small proportion of all the doctors who practised in Egypt during the third millennium. From later periods we know rather fewer Egyptian physicians by name—only 20 from the Middle Kingdom and 40 from the New Kingdom.

240

There are large gaps in our knowledge of what Egyptian physicians did, and how they were trained and organized. But it is clear that Herodotus was not wholly in error when he spoke of specialization, for already in the third millennium we meet, for example, 'a physician of the eyes', a physician of the belly', and 'a shepherd of the anus'; the last was probably someone who administered enemas. But the specialization was not as complete as Herodotus would have us believe, since some physicians certainly treated more than one aspect of illness.

The great majority of physicians were men, but the profession was not exclusively a male preserve: the title 'Lady Director of Lady Physicians' proves the existence of a group of women who practised as doctors.

Medicine was one of the literate professions in Egypt. It had to be, since there were Egyptian medical texts which physicians were expected to consult in the course of treatment. Some physicians included the term 'scribe' amongst their titles; some, but by no means all, Egyptian physicians were also priests. The finding of prescriptions written on ostraca (potsherds or fragments of limestone) gives further proof of the literacy of Egyptian medical men.

In view of the strength of the hereditary principle in ancient Egypt, it is not surprising that the profession of doctor often continued from father to son. But the principle did not operate exclusively: alongside families whose menfolk were physicians from generation to generation, there were doctors whose fathers held no medical title.

The medical profession seems, like the administration of ancient Egypt in general, to have been organized hierarchically. At least seven titles occur in which the element *swnw* 'physician' is qualified by another term marking rank or seniority. However, a resounding title may reflect high social standing rather than authority, and these titles may have been less indicators of successive medical grades than marks of social rank. Whether they marked primarily social rank or professional status, we have no knowledge of how a man (or woman) rose from one of these titles to another.

So far as we can judge from titles, the ranking of physicians (whether social or professional) seems to have been as follows. At the top was someone grandly known as the Chief Physician of the South and North, apparently the doctor of highest rank in the whole of the two kingdoms of Upper and Lower Egypt. A title Chief Physician of the North suggests that this doctor came next; analogy suggests a parallel Chief Physician of the South, but that title has not been found. Lesser titles follow: these include Master of Physicians, Director of Physicians, Inspector of Physicians, and Chief Physician, assumed, mainly on the basis of the meaning of the qualifying terms, to be in that order of rank. Then come plain physicians, and, below them, auxiliaries known as Bandagers.

Some physicians served within the palace and royal entourage; we know this from titles of the type 'Physician of the palace', 'Physician of the king', 'Chief Oculist of the palace', 'Inspector of Physicians of the king'. It is not clear whether this implied two parallel medical staffs, one'to treat palace personnel generally and the other specifically attached to the person of the king, or whether the titles qualified by 'palace' or 'king' were alternative designations for the same posts.

But physicians were not restricted to court circles, and some served within particular communities. We find, for instance, a man described as 'Chief of Physicians of the Place of Truth'. 'The Place of Truth' originally meant a site sacred to the dead, such as a royal tomb or a necropolis, but it came to take a wider sense, so that it could cover, for example, the whole community of priests, scribes, administrators, guards, labourers and so on, which had grown up around a royal tomb or a necropolis. And so the 'Chief of Physicians of the Place of Truth' probably held a post in such a community. Elsewhere we find inscriptions in quarries or mines showing the presence of medical men, obviously in charge of the health of the thousands of people toiling in such places, often in unhealthy conditions.

Foreign rulers, even of major states, held Egyptian doctors in high repute, and we know of several instances of them applying to the pharaoh for a physician. The following extract from a thirteenth-century letter shows how Ramesses II dealt with one such request. He is writing to the Hittite king Hattushilish, using not Egyptian but Akkadian, the international language of the time. After courteous greetings to Hattushilish, whom he addresses as 'my brother', he proceeds to business:

About the matter on which my brother sent me a message concerning his sister, saying: 'Let my brother send me a man to prepare drugs to give her so that she bears a child'—in such terms my brother sent me a message.

So I say to my brother: 'See! The king your brother [i.e. I, Ramesses] knows Matanazi your sister. I say this: She is fifty years old—if not sixty—and, see, a lady who has completed fifty years—if not sixty—it is not possible to prepare drugs to give her so that she bears a child.

However, just let the Sun-god and Weather-god give command and anything they do for my brother's sister will be brought into effect. So the king your brother [i.e. I, Ramesses] will send a capable magician with a capable physician and together they shall make for her drugs so that she bears a child.'

Clearly, Ramesses made a sharp distinction between rational medicine, which was limited in what it could do, and magic, which could (the gods willing) achieve the impossible.

In another case the pharaoh had been asked for help in treating the eyes of the Hittite king, and he was sending the requisite drugs through an

Egyptian ambassador: here there is reliance upon the substances themselves, without spells or priests or other hocus pocus, a clear signal that the treatment envisaged was rational in its approach.

Medical problems and medical texts

The examination of mummies, coupled with descriptions in texts and representations in art, shows some of the medical problems of ancient Egyptians.[4] One of the most prevalent was infestation with parasitic worms—guinea worms which result in leg ulceration, roundworms, tapeworms and hookworms. Every mummy examined showed some such infestation and some suffered from several varieties of these parasites. Arthritis was very common, particularly osteoarthritis. Other diseases and disorders included schistosomiasis (bilharzia, caused by a waterborne worm, the human equivalent of liverfluke in sheep), smallpox, tuberculosis, trachoma, arteriosclerosis (hardening of the arteries), gallstones and kidney stones, vaginal prolapse, ulcers, spina bifida, gout, appendicitis, hernia, varicose veins, piles and lung damage (pneumoconiosis) resulting from inhaling sand or smoke from fires or oil lamps in ill-ventilated rooms. A text describes angina pectoris, with the prognosis that death threatens the sufferer. One of the pharaohs suffered from clubfoot, and another, the religious reformer Akhenaten, possibly from a hormone disorder producing acromegaly. A bonus for the ancient Egyptians was that compound fractures were followed by complications from sepsis more rarely than with us, although open fractures were almost invariably fatal. No corresponding catalogue of diseases can be offered for Mesopotamia or other parts of the ancient Near East, as no bodies have been preserved.

One of the worst afflictions of older Egyptians must have been toothache. Up to the mid-twenties most Egyptians had perfect teeth, but later the teeth became severely worn, eventually producing painful gum abscesses. Ramesses II had many teeth worn down to the pulp chambers and his gums were so badly diseased that it is likely to have shortened his life. A major factor in this excessive wear on the teeth was impurities in bread, resulting from contamination by windblown sand during harvesting and storage and possibly the addition of gritty matter during grinding to improve the efficiency of the operation. Dental caries, on the other hand, was much less common than in the modern western world, perhaps from the absence of refined sugar.

There is no evidence for dentists in ancient Egypt. A hieroglyphic group based on the sign which represents an elephant's tusk was formerly translated 'dentist', but there is nothing to support this interpretation beyond the rather improbable assumption that the Egyptians used the picture of an elephant's tusk to mean a human tooth. The examination of mummies seems to produce positive evidence that there were no dentists, since even teeth which were so bad that they were damaging health and could easily have been extracted were never removed by operation. It is true that the Ebers Papyrus (pp. 248–50) contains prescriptions against such conditions as loose teeth, toothache and gumboils, but none of these involved dental surgery; at the best they used disinfectants, astringents or mild analgesics and at the worst were mere magic.

In contrast to Egypt, there is proof of a technique for extracting aching teeth in Mesopotamia. This was wrapped up in a magical rigmarole, but with practical measures at the key point. The whole thing is presented in the framework of a myth:

> *After the god Anu made the heavens, the heavens made the earth, the earth made the rivers, the rivers made the canals, the canals made the mud, the mud made the worm. The worm came weeping . . . before Ea: 'What are you going to give me for food. . . ?' (Said Ea): 'I give you the ripe fig . . .'. (Said the worm): 'What is the ripe fig to me? Let me drink among the teeth, . . . and destroy the marrow of the gums.'*
> Fix the peg *[i.e., forceps]* and grip the root!
> *Because you said this, O worm, may Ea strike you with the might of his fist.*

'Fix the forceps and grip the root!' is clearly an instruction to the operator, and the final sentence must have accompanied a forceful wrench by which he pulled the tooth out.

Some authorities have claimed that a form of restorative dentistry was practised in Old Kingdom Egypt, basing this view on the finding of two natural teeth held together with gold wire through fine drilled holes, taken to be a bridge. But this is suspect. The teeth were found in rubble, not in a human jaw, and the wire would never have held the teeth stable in a wearer's mouth. When we recall John Buchan's mention of a Scottish Presbyterian who saved all his shed teeth against the day of resurrection, we cannot exclude the possibility that some ancient Egyptian was keeping these teeth by him for the afterlife rather than to improve his appearance in this.

According to tradition, Egyptian medical knowledge was committed to writing from a very early date. One group of texts contains the claim that they were found in a chest under the feet of a divine statue during the First Dynasty (beginning of the third millennium) and another collection of prescriptions allegedly descended from the sky into the courtyard of a temple during the reign of Khufu, builder of the Great Pyramid (twenty-sixth century). In some cases, tradition had it, the gods themselves invented prescriptions in the mythic era before history began. Whatever the value of these traditions, there is solid evidence for the existence of medical writings by the Fifth Dynasty (twenty-fifth century). Wesh-Ptah, vizier and chief architect of the Fifth Dynasty king Neferirkare, was proudly showing his royal master round some new buildings when he collapsed unconscious. The pharaoh, clearly a man of action, took charge in this emergency and sent not only for physicians but also for medical books which they might consult: for those medical texts to have had accepted authority amongst living physicians, they must have had a long history behind them.

The nomenclature for the various papyrus scrolls containing Egyptian medical texts is confusing. Some are named after their original modern owners, one after a lady who financed the expedition which acquired it, others after their place of discovery, and the rest after the cities in whose museums they now are. All are copies of older material; the dates given are those of the existing copies, not of the period in which the material originated, which could be a millennium or more earlier. Nine principal Egyptian medical papyri are known, ranging in date from the early second millennium to the Christian period. Basically their contents are diagnoses and prescriptions, sometimes purely medical or surgical, sometimes heavily contaminated with magic. Only those most important for our knowledge of Egyptian medical practice are mentioned here.

The oldest papyrus bearing medical texts is the *Kahun Papyrus*, of the twentieth century BC. The medical part of it (it also contains veterinary and mathematical material) runs to only three pages, the first fairly well preserved but the rest with substantial parts illegible. The contents are gynaecological. The first and second pages contain seventeen case-studies related to women's diseases, all in the form

> *Treatment for a woman [suffering such and such symptoms];*
> *Say with regard to it [diagnosis];*
> *Do for it [prescription].*

Predominantly the substances used were concoctions of beer, milk, oil and various plant and animal substances, which might be administered by mouth, as ointments, by introduction into the vagina, or by fumigation. The following is an example of these case-studies:

> *Treatment for a woman who suffers in her womb in walking.*
> *Say with regard to it: 'What is the smell which you make perceived?'. If she says to you, I am making the smell of roast meat perceived', you shall say of it: 'It is* nemsu-*disease of the womb.'*

245

You shall do this for it. Fumigate her with all those kinds of roast meat, of which she makes the smell perceived.

The first editor, a most distinguished Egyptologist, interpreted 'to make perceived' as 'to emit', and suggested that this referred to a smell associated with cancer of the womb. But if the woman had to be asked about the smell, it was surely something subjective to her, suggesting a psychological disorder. If the trouble was psychological, the treatment might well have had a favourable effect but it would have been useless and mere magic against cancer.

In another case dealt with, the trouble was certainly psychological:

Treatment for a woman who loves bed, so that she does not get up. . . .
Say with regard to it: it is amemu-*trouble of the womb.*
You shall do this for it. Let her drink two measures of [an unidentified substance], let her vomit it out at once.

Taking to bed and refusing to rise is a classic symptom of depression; the Egyptian physician attempted to deal with it by administering an emetic.

Another diagnosis attributes pains in the neck to some trouble in the womb (perhaps prolapse, but Egyptologists are not certain of the meaning of the word): indeed, most of the legible diagnoses attribute the symptoms to some trouble in the womb. It is interesting in this connection to note that the word 'hysteria' is derived from the Greek *hystera*, 'womb', in consequence of an old belief that women with psychological problems were suffering from trouble in the womb. The link which this papyrus makes between the womb and depression, and perhaps other psychological disorders, suggests that the early Egyptians were already thinking on those lines.

The third page of the *Kahun* papyrus, also with seventeen case-studies, concerns sterility and pregnancy. One of the more legible examples reads:

To tell if a woman will conceive or not conceive, you shall . . . [text uncertain].
If you find the muscles of her breast firm(?), you shall say that that woman will conceive.
If you find them soft, you shall say that she will conceive with difficulty. If you find her [text partly uncertain, partly lost, but presumably describing a finding denoting that the woman would not conceive].

Another way of testing for ability to conceive was to introduce garlic into the woman's vagina. If the smell of garlic appeared on her breath the next day, she would conceive. Scientifically unsound as this test was, rational thinking and not magic lay behind it: the Egyptians must have thought that failure to conceive was linked to blocked passages inside the woman's body, which would also prevent the transmission of the scent of garlic.

In another case-study, the practitioner drew a conclusion as to whether or not a woman was capable of bearing by her reflex when he touched some part of her body with his finger. Details are very unclear. Yet another case-study makes a diagnosis from the offensive smell of a woman's urine.[5]

These were tests of female fertility, not pregnancy. The Babylonians went further and attempted actual pregnancy tests. These involved placing in the woman's vagina a tampon impregnated with the juice of various plants in a solution of alum. This was left in position either overnight or for three days. Pregnancy or non-pregnancy was indicated by colour changes between red and green.[6] Evidently the plants were chosen for the ability of their juices to change colour in the manner of litmus according to the pH value (degree of acidity of alkalinity) of the woman's secretions.

There are other papyri, or fragments, rather similar in their contents to the gynaecological part of *Kahun*. The reverse of the *Berlin Papyrus*, a document of about 1250 BC, deals with methods of ascertaining pregnancy and the sex of unborn children. *Ramesseum IV and V* are also similar to *Kahun*, and are of about the same age.

Most of the case notes in *Kahun* and *Ramesseum IV and V* contain sound medical observation mingled with nonsense. Some of the nonsense is the result of nothing worse than inadequate anatomical or physiological knowledge, but most derives from magical thinking. Magic is a system of speciously relating phenomena, which was rife in the ancient world, and is by no means wholly eliminated from the modern. It rests on the assumption that an object with certain qualities, or an action of a certain kind, can be brought into active relationship with other similar objects or actions: if the measures taken are intended to produce a like response, we term it sympathetic magic; if to repel something evil, apotropaic magic. In the case of the fumigation with roast meat, if the woman was actually emitting the smell of roast meat as a symptom of disease, and fumigation with roast meat was intended to drive away the smell and hence the disease associated with it, that was apotropaic magic. But if the woman's problem was psychological and subjective, the treatment was not necessarily magical. Such procedures as tests for fertility, on the basis of examination of the breasts or the smell of garlic being transmitted from the woman's vagina to her breath, are not magical at all. They may perhaps be invalid, if they are based on faulty assumptions about anatomy or physiology, but given the assumptions, the arguments are not (as magic is) irrational.

Magical elements were certainly present in many Egyptian medical texts. For example, more than half of the *London Medical Papyrus*, a text of about 1350 BC, comprises incantations and the like, and the genuinely medical part is limited to twenty-five prescriptions.

The longest of all medical papyri is the *Ebers Papyrus*, running to 108 pages and 877 paragraphs. The existing copy bears a date which shows that it was in existence at 1550 BC. Here the magical dimension of Egyptian medicine is put beyond doubt by the introduction, which claims divine origin for the work, and tells how Re^c had sent the god Thoth to give the physicians skill to heal mankind. It also contains spells to enhance the value of its prescriptions, for example:

> *Incantation (for use) when drinking a remedy. 'Come, remedy! Come, you who expel evil things from my belly and my limbs!' The spell has power over the remedy.*

Then follows the text of the spell, a rigmarole about the gods Horus and Seth in mythic times, and at the end the rubric

> *Spoken when drinking a remedy.*

The religio-magical component of this compilation is emphasized by the claims it makes for its prescriptions, some of which it attributes directly to the gods; one remedy, for example, was 'made by Isis for Re^c himself to expel illness in the head'.

Disease was sometimes seen as imposed by the gods as a punishment, but the more usual Egyptian view, reflected particularly in the *Ebers Papyrus*, seems to have been that it was caused by something evil in the body, whether a worm, foul matter or a devil. The basic object of treatment was to get the foul thing out, and this led to frequent resort to laxatives, often, no doubt, with beneficial effects. Such medicaments included various mineral salts and plant extracts, amongst them some still in use today, such as magnesia, senna pods and figs. These were sometimes administered alone, sometimes with an accompanying magical incantation. Prescriptions might include distinctly disagreeable substances, such as dung or urine, probably on the supposition that their offensiveness would repel evil spirits. Purely magical ideas underlay such procedures as using a pig's eye to cure eye disease.

Typical contents of the *Ebers Papyrus* are prescriptions 'to expel diseases in the belly', 'to open the bowels', 'to empty the belly', 'to treat the belly and to treat the anus', 'for a dislocation in the hind-quarters' [prolapse of the rectum?], and 'for affections of "the mouth of the stomach" '. Other matters dealt with include bites, dandruff, poor hearing, hernia, venereal disease, burns, heart disease, eye disease, dysentery, coughs, abscesses, rheumatism, parasitic worms, and making hair grow: the prescription for the last was allegedly devised for the mother of an early king.

Many of the prescriptions were straightforward instructions for making and administering potions, with no intrusion of magic, such as:

Remedy to open the bowels: milk 25 measures, sycamore-fruit 8 measures, honey 8 measures, are boiled, strained and taken for four days.

In some instances, provision for a clinical examination comes between the naming of the malady and the prescription to treat it. Thus:

Instructions concerning troubles of 'the mouth of the stomach'.

If you examine a man for an obstruction in the 'mouth of his stomach', and he is too troubled to eat, his belly is constricted, and he . . . is like a man suffering from burning in the anus, you shall examine him lying on his back. If you find his belly warm, and something hard in the 'mouth of his stomach', you shall tell him, 'it is a liver case'. You shall prepare the secret herbal remedy which is made by the physician.

Then follows the prescription, a concoction based on dates.

A major element in the treatment in the *Ebers Papyrus* was what we would call herbal medicine, but some of the prescriptions contained an undeniable magical element. Thus, various prescriptions to prevent hair going grey are all concoctions prepared by boiling up substances from creatures which are markedly black. A prescription supposed to make hair grow was compounded of burnt hedgehog quills with oil. The element of sympathetic magic here is unmistakable.

Most medicaments mentioned in the *Ebers Papyrus* were taken by mouth, usually as a liquid, sometimes as pills; other methods of administration included eye drops, rubbing with ointments or plant leaves, bandaging, pouring liquids into the ear, inhalation, suppositories and enemas.

One prescription of particular interest in *Ebers* was a method of contraception:

To make a women not become pregnant for one year, two years or three years, acacia leaves(?) [and other substances] are ground fine with honey, wool(?) is moistened therewith and placed in her vulva.

A treatment for impotence involved bandaging the male member with a concoction of sawdust, fruit juices, fats and salt. Impotence must have been a widespread problem in the ancient world, as there were numerous magical and pseudo-medical treatments for it in Mesopotamia and in the land of the Hittites also.

Following the main body of prescriptions in the *Ebers Papyrus* comes a section of a distinctly different nature. This is a theoretical treatise about the heart and its relation to the rest of the body. Although some of the assumptions are incorrect, it is based on observation and the method is rational. The texts shows that the Egyptian physicians believed that vessels ran from the heart to every limb, although there is no indication that they understood the circulation of the blood. The papyrus also refers to the pulse, which was thought of as the speaking of the heart, and notes the points at which the pulse could be taken. Some sceptics have argued that Egyptian physicians could not have actually timed the pulse in the absence of a device to measure small periods of time, but the same argument would prove that no orchestra conductor can beat time accurately without a metronome at his side.

The *Ebers Papyrus* ends with a group of prescriptions dealing with tumours and swellings.

The *Hearst Papyrus* is similar in content to *Ebers*, and duplicates it at some points. It includes prescriptions for purging the body, for a diseased rectum, broken ribs, boils, tumours, bites, pains in the limbs, heart trouble, retention of urine, parasitic worms, and a festering toe-nail. As with *Ebers*, it is not wholly free of magic, but the magical element is very limited.

Edwin Smith Papyrus

Pride of place amongst Egyptian medical papyri goes to part of the contents of the *Edwin Smith Papyrus*. Scribes at about 1700 BC used this papyrus to copy several old texts bearing upon medical treatment. The papyrus bears 17 columns of writing (377 lines) on the front (recto), and 4½ columns (92 lines) on the back (verso). The first 3½ columns on the verso are mainly incantations against epidemic disease, and the other column, copied in a different hand, deals with extracting the oil of a certain plant to rejuvenate old men; these both have more magic than science in their ancestry.

It is the text of the recto which is of such importance. This is the Egyptian medical document which comes nearest to the modern scientific approach. There are strong indications that it originated about a thousand years earlier than the form in which we have it. It had been copied and re-copied across so many centuries that the original text had become archaic, with parts unintelligible; some later copyist introduced glosses to explain terms and phrases which were no longer current in his time, and the final copyist, who wrote the *Edwin Smith Papyrus* as we have it, incorporated the glosses into the text.

The text constitutes part of a work wholly devoted to surgery, in the form of case-studies, not prescriptions. It is systematically organized, beginning with injuries to the skull and working downwards through the nose, face and upper jaw, region of the temples, ears, lower jaw, lips and chin, throat and neck, collarbone, upper arm, breastbone and ribs, shoulder, and spinal column. Here our information about third millennium surgery comes to an end, since the final copyist abandoned his work, in the middle of a word.

Treatment, where prescribed, is rational and mainly surgical: in the whole of the work as transmitted to us there is only one resort to magic, and this is so grossly at variance with the tone of the rest that one suspects that it was an addition by a later copyist.

The ancient Egyptian surgeon gives one of three verdicts as part of his diagnosis in the cases he describes:

1. An ailment which I will treat.
2. An ailment with which I will contend.
3. An ailment not to be treated.

Verdict 1 is self-explanatory. Verdict 3 meant that the surgeon recognized that no treatment was possible. Verdict 2 indicated that treatment was possible, but the prognosis was doubtful.

The discussion of cases takes a fixed pattern, of which the basic elements are:

1. Title.
2. Examination.
3. Diagnosis.
4. Treatment (unless the case was considered untreatable).
5. Glosses; an explanation of any obscure archaic terms employed in the discussion.

Sometimes the surgeon describes more than one examination, marking stages in the progress of the patient.

Forty-eight cases are discussed, ranging from simple scalp wounds to a compression fracture of a cervical vertebra and a compound fracture of the upper jaw. The nature of the injuries gives scope for speculation upon the circumstances in which this dissertation was compiled. Some of the injuries, such as a deeply pierced throat, or a gaping wound in the eyebrow or shoulder, or a split skull, are of a kind most likely to have occurred in warfare, and some authorities would make the author an army surgeon. But one—a fractured cervical vertebra—is specifically attributed to the victim falling from a height on to his head; in view of the probably date of origin of the work, this might well have been an injury typical of accidents which happened during the building of the Giza pyramids.

Case Ten

[Title]: *Instructions concerning a wound in the top of (a man's) eyebrow.*

[Examintion]: *If you examine a man having a wound in the top of his eyebrow, penetrating to the bone, you should palpate his wound, and draw together his gash for him with stitching.*

[Diagnosis]: *You shall say concerning him: '(A man) having a wound in his eyebrow. An ailment which I will treat.'*

[Treatment]: *After you have stitched it, you should bind fresh meat upon it the first day. If you find that the stitching of the wound has come loose, you should draw it together for him with two strips (of plaster), and you should treat it with grease and honey every day until he recovers.*

[Gloss]: 'two strips'—*this means two bands of linen, which one applies to the two lips of a gaping wound, in order to make one lip join the other.*

Case Thirty-One

[Title]: *Instruction concerning a dislocation in a vertebra of [a man's] neck.*

[Examination]: *If you examine a man having a dislocation in a vertebra of his neck, if you find him paralysed in both arms and both legs because of it, with his phallus erect because of it, and urine drips from his penis without his knowing it; . . . and his eyes are bloodshot; it is a dislocation of a vertebra of his neck extending to his spine which is making him paralysed in both arms and both legs. If the middle vertebra of his neck is dislocated, (this is the cause of the) seminal emission which happens to his phallus.*

[Diagnosis]: *You shall say concerning him: '(He is) a man having a dislocation in a vertebra of his neck, whilst he is paralysed in his two legs and two arms, and his urine dribbles. An ailment which I will not treat.'*

[Glosses]: 'a dislocation (wnh) in a vertebra of his neck'—*he is speaking of a separation of one cervical vertebra from another, the overlying flesh being uninjured; as one says about things which had been joined together, when one has become separated from the other, 'it is* wnh'. 'a seminal emission which happens to his phallus'—*(it means) that his phallus is erect and has a discharge . . .* 'his urine dribbles'—*(it means) that urine drips from his phallus without his control [literally 'and he cannot restrain'].*

Case Thirty-Five

[Title]: *Instructions concerning a fracture in (a man's) collarbone.*

[Examination]: *If you examine a man having a fracture in his collarbone, you will find his collarbone short and separated from the other.*

[Diagnosis]: *You shall say concerning him: 'A man having a fracture in his collarbone. An ailment which I will treat.'*

[Treatment]: *You should place him on his back, with something folded between his two shoulder-blades. You should spread out his two shoulders in order to stretch out his collarbone until the break falls into place. You should make two linen splints for him, and you should apply one of them on the inside and the other on the underside*

252

of his upper arm. You should bind it with [an unidentified substance] and treat it afterwards with honey daily, until he recovers.

Some of the case-studies trace the progress of an injury. One such is case 47, which concerns a gaping wound in the shoulder. At the first examination the surgeon diagnoses the injury as treatable, stitches the wound up, and binds it up with fresh meat. At the second examination he finds that the wound has opened and the stitching has become loose; he now closes the wound with two strips of plaster, and treats it every day with grease, honey and lint. At the third examination the physician finds that things are beginning to go wrong: the wound is inflamed and the patient has a fever. He recognizes that the patient's condition is deteriorating, and he now revises his judgement upon the outcome: he gives the verdict 'an ailment with which I will contend', meaning that he would do his best but could not promise a certain cure. Then comes a further examination, for which there are two possibilities as to what the physician may find:

[Fourth examination; first possibility]: *If you then find that man continuing to have fever, with the wound inflamed,*
[treatment indicated]: *You shall not bind it. You shall moor him at his mooring stakes, until the period of his injury passes by.*
[Fourth examination; alternative possibility]: *If his fever abates and the inflammation in the mouth of his wound goes away entirely,*
[treatment indicated]: *You shall treat him afterwards with grease, honey and lint every day, until he recovers.*

The curious phrase translated 'You shall moor him at his mooring stakes' was archaic Egyptian: a gloss earlier in the papyrus explains it to mean that the patient is to be left on his usual diet with no medication.

The case studies give us a glimpse of some of the techniques and materials available to the Egyptian surgeon. He might stitch up wounds with sutures or close them with linen-based adhesive plaster. Burns were treated with various fatty substances. Lint was used as a surgical dressing, and linen plugs were applied for nasal injuries. There is a representation in art of setting a dislocated shoulder. Bandages were very common. Broken limbs were held in position with splints wrapped in linen: examples of splints to deal with fractures of long bones have been found in graves. Decoctions made from willow or the leaves of acacia, sycamore and other trees served as disinfectants. Some tumours were treated with an instrument called a fire-drill, which presumably means that they were cauterized.

253

Clearly, Egyptian physicians, or at least some of them, knew a good deal about the human body and the injuries it could suffer. Some authorities have seen Egyptian medical science as a by-product of embalming. This has no basis. Certainly embalmers had the opportunity of acquiring considerable knowledge of some aspects of anatomy, since their duties included the removal of certain organs from corpses prior to mummification. But this taught them nothing about the functions of heart, liver, kidneys, lungs, etc. or their possible disorders. Indeed, the whole procedure of embalming shows that the Egyptians at this level were not interested in the function of organs; they were only concerned with giving the dead body a lifelike appearance, and for this purpose sawdust to fill out the cavities was as good as natural functioning organs.

The embalming process gave the Egyptians no significant advantage over the Mesopotamians in anatomical knowledge. Basic knowledge of anatomy was not hard to come by in any early society. Most heads of household would be familiar with animal anatomy from cutting up beasts for food or sacrifice, and it was no big step to see a parallel between animal and human anatomy. Indeed, hieroglyphic writing specifically proves the recognition of such parallels, by the applications to humans of signs originally representing parts of animals. Physicians could learn further details of human anatomy by examining men seriously mutilated by battle injuries, or, indeed, hurt in ordinary accidents. Art shows the kind of accident that could befall a mason; one man shown has had an implement fall on his foot, and another is having something done to an injured eye.

But not all Egyptian surgical knowledge can be explained in this way. The causation of some of the serious injuries described in the *Edwin Smith* case-studies could not have been deduced from analogy with animals, nor, since in some there was no surface damage, recognized from external examination. A case in point is total paralysis resulting from a fall on the head, which the Egyptian surgeon attributed to a crushed vertebra in the neck. He can only have discovered the pathological cause of the symptoms by carrying out a post-mortem dissection of a patient who had died from such injuries. In view of this and other instances, there can be no doubt that at least one third-millennium Egyptian surgeon practised dissection to further his understanding of the human body and the nature of such injuries.

The practice of dissection is not the only indication of the third-millennium surgeon's scientific approach. As the first editor of the *Edwin Smith Papyrus* pointed out, the careful detailed study of cases of the type which the surgeon-author admitted—in the verdict 'an ailment not to be treated'—were beyond his power to assist, shows that he was concerned not only with alleviating suffering but also with an understanding of the underlying nature of the injuries which produced certain symptoms.

This kind of organized fundamental knowledge is a prerequisite for any major advance. One might suppose that the achievements of Egyptian surgery before 2500 BC would have formed a basis for considerable progress later. So far as we know, no further significant progress ever took place in ancient Egypt. The subsequent stagnation after such an impressive start was, paradoxically, probably due to the early medical and surgical texts themselves. In all societies, but especially in ancient ones, there is a tendency for the written word to take on the character of sacred scripture, which then becomes unchallengeable. This is explicit in the *Ebers Papyrus*, which has an introduction explaining that the work was given by the gods themselves: once that attitude develops, further progress is impossible until some upheaval in history smashes the mould. The *Edwin Smith Papyrus* has no introduction claiming divine origin, but it is clear that, before the time of the extant copy, the text of the work had come to be thought of as sacrosanct. We may conclude this from what happened, some centuries later, whenever the scribal copyist came upon an archaic word or phrase: he did not modernize it, but left it as it stood and supplied a gloss. Clearly, by this time there was such a reverence for the old wording, that it was unthinkable to change it.

This canonization of the medical writings began very early. We have already referred to the incident, in the Fifth Dynasty, when the vizier Wesh-Ptah collapsed unconscious in the presence of the king. In this emergency, the king called not only for doctors, but also for the traditional medical writings for them to consult. Since the physicians summoned were attached to the court, they were presumably the most competent practitioners in Egypt at the time, and a competent physician, faced with a man who has collapsed unconscious, has no need to consult a manual of first-aid. But clearly, from the point of view of the king, the medical writings contained an enshrined wisdom greater than that of mere living human physicians. Once this attitude become entrenched in any branch of study, further advance becomes impossible.

Medicine in Mesopotamia

The people of ancient Mesopotamia believed disease to be the consequence of the action of supernatural forces—attacks by demons, gods, and sometimes witchcraft: innumerable cuneiform texts imply this view, and some explicitly state it. For example, a fragment of a myth has one god say to another: 'Let us put diseases in the land with mankind, let us decree death and life.'[7] If diseases were put into the world by supernatural forces, it seemed sensible to use supernatural forces to dispel them. Incantations and magical rituals were the answer to disease. One incantation, preserved in copies from second millennium Babylonia and first millennium Assyria, begins by enumerating ailments that had descended from heaven. Then comes the question: 'Whom am I to send against the daughter of Anu?' The daughter of Anu, the supreme god, was Lamashtu, a terrible she-demon of disease and death. The answer given is: 'The Seven and the Seven, who have golden jugs and pails of pure lapis lazuli'. These two groups of benevolent seven come from a very ancient stratum of the pantheon. And then comes the magical instruction:

> Let them take their golden jugs
> And their pails of pure lapis lazuli;
> Let them draw cleansing water,
> Let them sprinkle it upon the sick man.

But alongside the magical means of treating disease there were also physicians. We first meet the physician (called a.zu in Sumerian and *asu* in Akkadian) in the middle of the third millennium, but most of our data comes from the second or first millennium. The *asu*'s approach to the treatment of illness was relatively rational, with procedures which involved treating the illness itself. But this was not a recommendation to all Babylonians; many of them must have seen the *asu* as a man who treated only symptoms and not the root cause. In the view of such people, when there was illness it was far better to go to the root of the trouble, the supernatural causation, and to effect this there was a different medical functionary, the witch-doctor. With Babylonian society permeated by this attitude, there was little hope for real medical progress in Mesopotamia.

'Witch-doctor' is a translation of the Babylonian term *ashipu*; other possible renderings are 'magician' or 'exorcist'. To many Babylonians in many periods, the *ashipu* was more potent than the *asu* could ever be, for his incantations and rituals had power over everything in heaven and earth: there was nothing, from the demonic forces which brought ill fortune into a house to the powers that caused earthquakes or eclipses, against which he could not act.

We get a picture of the ancient Mesopotamian view of disease, and the part the *ashipu* played in its diagnosis and treatment, from a cuneiform work known under the general title *When an Ashipu goes to the House of a Sick Man*. This work is technically called a 'series', meaning a group of texts on one theme collected in ancient times and edited into a standard form with its own title. The Babylonians divided a series up into sections which they designated 'tablets'. The work we are discussing was put together, probably in the late second millennium, from several earlier series: we know this, because some tablets have a colophon (final brief statement about contents and origin) giving them a double identification, in this way:

> *Third Tablet of* (If), Day One, he is sick; Nature of the Affliction; *Seventeenth Tablet of* When an Ashipu goes to the House of a Sick Man, . . . *135 lines.*

The final form of the work contains four explicitly identified subseries. These are additional to introductory tablets which belonged to the original shorter form of *When an Ashipu goes to the House of a Sick Man.*

The introductory sub-series sticks closely to the theme indicated by the title of the work, taken from its first line. It deals exclusively with what the *ashipu* might encounter on his way to the patient's house or on arrival there. Although the patient has not yet even been seen, the supernatural forces have been busily at work providing all kinds of pointers to his fate; these pointers the skilful witch-doctor was able to interpret, by consulting his texts. For example:

> *If the door of the house, where the sick man lies, gives a cry like a lion, he has infringed a taboo of his god; he will linger on and then die.*
>
> *If he [i.e., the* ashipu*] sees a black pig, that patient will die; (alternatively) it will be difficult that he should recover.*
>
> *If he sees a white pig, that patient will recover; (alternatively) trouble will seize him.*

On and on the list rambles, through other colours of pigs, through colour sequences of oxen and donkeys, and through such chance events as

> *If he sees goat's hair, the hand of a ghost has seized him; his sickness will be long.*
>
> *If he sees a dead man, that patient will recover.*

Further omens are based on either atmospheric phenomena or the behaviour of such chance-seen creatures as birds, snakes or scorpions. Mostly the prognoses are simply either that the patient will die or that he will recover, but sometimes they are a little more detailed. None of these omens had anything to do with the patient himself but all had a great deal to do with the Babylonian belief in magic.

It was in the third tablet that the witch-doctor at last came face to face with the patient's symptoms. This was the first tablet of a sub-series called *When you approach a Sick Man.* Magic continued to reign. The witch-doctor had to begin with an incantation, and then made his diagnosis on the basis

257

of long lists of possible symptoms. The first group is related to the head, and the list then works its way via temples, eyes, nose and lips through all parts of the body down to the feet. Each symptom is followed by a diagnosis, typically in terms of the particular supernatural power which is afflicting the sufferer. Thus:

> *If he is ill in his skull and his ears do not hear, it is the hand of the goddess Ishtar.*
> *If he is affected from the middle of his skull, and his eyebrows, his forehead, his face, his jaw, his neck, his breast, his calves, his ankles hurt him at the same time, and it does not abate in the presence of the witch-doctor, a ghost has seized him.*
> *If he is struck in the head, on the right side; hand of Adad.*
> *If he is struck in the head, on the left side; hand of Shamash; he will die.*
> *If he is struck in the head, and his eyes cloud over; hand of Ningirsu.*
> *If he is struck in the head, and shivering keeps attacking him, and his face is red and yellow, and when his seizure comes upon him, his mind is deranged and he has convulsions; it is a seizure by the demoness Lamashtu; he will go on for a long time [literally 'his days will be long'], but he will die.*

Sometimes the symptom is followed by what at first sight might appear to be a straightforward prognosis without thought of supernatural cause of the trouble, as

> *If (the hair on) the crown of his head goes curly, he will die.*

but this type is no more rational than the others. In its context, such a diagnosis represented not a medical judgement upon a development which might be encountered in some particular disease, but merely a superstitious omen which applied whenever that condition arose in any illness.

The remainder of the work is not significantly more scientific. The third sub-series, *If, Day One, He is Sick; Nature of the Affliction*, takes the witch-doctor through the patient's progress day by day; thus:

> *If he is sick and on day three he gets up; in the evening, remission of the sickness.*
> *If he is sick and on day three he keeps crying 'my belly! my belly', and his belly is inflamed; he will die.*
> *If he is sick and on day four he keeps putting his hands on his belly and his face is overcast with yellow; he will die.*
> *If he is sick and on day four or day five a sweat breaks out on him; remission of the sickness. (Alternatively) if he is (still(?)) suffering from the sickness on day four or day five; hand of the Ahhazu-demon.*
> *If he is sick and on day five or six blood comes out of his mouth, his sickness will remit; it is setu-fever [heatstroke(?)].*
> *If he is sick and on day five or day six, he cries 'Oh! Oh!' again and again without stopping, he will die.*

258

If on day six he becomes critically ill and on day seven he has an abnormal emission (of urine or semen(?)), if when they sprinkle water in his face, he does not open his eyes; he will die. If he blinks [literally 'opens and closes'] his eyes on account of the water they sprinkled on him, he will recover.

Later, the sub-series goes on to symptoms more generally, of the following type:

If, at the onset of his illness, from when it affected him until it ceased, he keeps having first a fever then a shivering, one as much as the other, and after (this) fever and shivering have remitted, his limbs carry a fever and he has (that) fever as much as the former fever, and then it remits and afterwards he has shivering and sweating; this is tihu, erepu, pizu, *or* setu-*fever (heatstroke(?)). On day seven he will have the crisis and recover.*

If, at the onset of his illness, he is bloated; whatever food, beer and fruit he eats, it will not sit on his stomach but he brings it up; he extends his fingers; his eyes stay open; . . . he is in constant pain and his face becomes yellow; (this shows that) the Rabisu-*demon has smitten him. Since he [the demon] touched him, he is fastened to his side; he eats from the food he [the patient] eats and drinks from the water he drinks. That man, by day five or day seven he will recover.*

A fair number of the diagnoses are superficially free of the supernatural aspect, but this is never far below the surface, as we see by reading the following group together:

If during his illness, he keeps calling out; he suffers from a disease of the limbs; he will recover.

If during his illness, he keeps getting up; he suffers from a disease of the limbs; he will recover.

If during his illness, he keeps having a conversation; a ghost, the wraith of a dead person, has seized him; he will recover.

The supernatural causation of disease is clearer still in the two following examples:

If his illness keeps attacking him in the middle watch of the night, he has had sexual intercourse with another man's wife;, hand of the god Ninurta.

If he is ill all day, but well at night; the setu-*disease has made him ill. If he is well all day but ill at night; the* setu-*disease has made him ill, (but if it is) the twenty-seventh day (of the month, it is) the hand of Ninurta.*

Symptoms and observations of the behaviour of patients are often grouped, but not in a way which provides complete diagnostic syndromes. Consider the following:

If the muscles of a man's belly ache, his left temple hurts him, he is always stiff, his speech is impeded, his [lost word] is hot, he has atrophy of his flesh; that man is suffering from a venereal disease [literally 'illness of illicit sex'].

If a man's epigastrium gives him a burning pain and he is hot, he eats food but it does not agree with him, he drinks water but it is not enjoyable for him, and his body is yellow; that man is suffering from a venereal disease.

If a man's penis and epigastrium contain fiery heat, and the bottom of his belly aches, and his belly is in turmoil, his arms and his feet and his belly are hot; that man is suffering from a venereal disease; the hand of the goddess Ishtar.

Neither singly nor in combination would these three clauses serve as an adequate description of any one identifiable disease, venereal or otherwise. That did not trouble the witch-doctor: to describe or identify the disease as a medical fact was not his objective. The final words quoted make evident that the real quest was for the supernatural causation. Indeed, there is no reason to think that the conditions being described were venereal diseases as we understand them: 'illness of illicit sex' may have been no more than a term to cover any disease which included symptoms of discomfort in the urinary-genital region, regarded as punishment by supernatural powers for tabooed sexual behaviour.

On a few occasions, an element of treatment is found within the witch-doctor handbook, as in the following. Symptoms (now lost) have been given of a man's condition and then it is stated

He has a stone in the urethra. If that man drinks beer, that stone will dissolve. If that man does not drink beer but drinks a lot of water, he is destined to die.

Whether or not medically efficacious, this certainly seems to have a rational basis. The same cannot be said of the following prescription, which is strictly magical:

If the hand of a ghost turns for him into epilepsy, that man is suffering from the hand of the god of his city. To deliver him from the hand of the god of his city, (put) . . . the little finger of a dead man, rancid oil, and copper into the skin of a virgin goat; you shall string it on a tendon of a jerbil and put it round his neck, and he will recover.

The irrational in medical treatment

The predominantly irrational element in the Babylonian attitude to illness is further demonstrated by a group of prognoses drawn from a patient's hallucinations:

If, when he was suffering from a long illness, he saw a dog, his illness will return to him; he will die.

If DITTO he saw a pig, his illness will not be removed.
If DITTO he saw a gazelle, that patient will recover.
If DITTO he saw a wild pig, when you have recited an incantation for him, he will recover.

The final sub-series is concerned with pregnancy, childbirth and illnesses of women and children. The initial clauses purport to foretell the sex of unborn children, and whether or not mother and child will do well, from such details as the colour of parts of the pregnant woman's face, the condition of her muscles, the shape of her body and so on. The sex prediction is nonsense, but some of the other clauses may represent reasonable conclusions from experience, as:

If the pregnant woman repeatedly vomits, she will not go full term.
If blood comes from the pregnant woman's mouth, she will not survive childbed.
If the pregnant woman discharges purulent matter from her mouth, she will die together with that which is within her womb.

Superstition makes itself evident again with clauses laying down the dates at which it is favourable or otherwise for a pregnant woman to have sexual intercourse; for example, in a group dealing with the fifth month:

If a woman is pregnant, and in the fifth month on the ninth day someone has sexual relations with her; she will die.
If a woman is pregnant and in the fifth month on the tenth day DITTO; she will live.

If the witch-doctor's manual is to be believed, the exact day of intercourse was literally a matter of life or death. But in practical terms, unless a person had sexual intercourse once only before any pregnancy (and the woman envisaged here obviously had no such inhibitions), it would be impossible to calculate the point of pregnancy correct to a day. But in Babylonian thought the witch-doctor was never wrong, and to justify himself he would start from the conclusion stated in his manual and work back from there to establish the facts. The manual was scripture—copied from originals going back to the holy city of Eridu in archaic times—and could not be mistaken. Therefore if a pregnant woman did die after intercourse, it was plain by the *ashipu*'s twisted logic that she must have had sexual intercourse on a forbidden day.

The work we have been discussing, the longest single composition in cuneiform in the area of medicine, does nothing to enhance the reputation of Babylonia in that field.[8] It shows an approach to illness which was unscientific and shot through and through with superstition.

But this does not give the whole picture, or a just picture. We have already noticed that in Egypt overmuch respect for the written word eventually gave ancient medical texts the status of unchallengeable scripture, to be copied and recopied as authoritative works in their own right, without reference to a mere human practitioner. Something of the same kind occurred in Mesopotamia. Amongst the populations of the third and early second millennia there were some highly creative thinkers. Once their ideas had been committed to writing, the written document acquired a prestige which led to its being carefully copied, edited and preserved. Quickly, and in almost all areas of thought by not later than 1300 BC, it became treasured as sacred scripture, no longer a brave starting point for further advance but something ultimate, unchallengeable, and dead. There was material within the ancient texts used by the *ashipu* which, properly evaluated, could have produced advance. For example, there is the test quoted on p. 259, made on the sixth day. Some acute observer had noticed that when the face of a seriously ill patient was splashed with water, the blinking reflex, or the absence of it, gave a pointer to the outcome of the illness. This should have prompted the search for other significant reflexes, but instead it was treated as a mere omen.

Another reflex, of which someone had once noticed the diagnostic importance, but which had come to be treated as yet another mere omen, is given by the following:

> *If a baby, when you hold it up by its neck, does not wriggle and stretch out its arms, (this means) a seizure by the dust [i.e. the Underworld].*

And so the *ashipu*, who incorporated the force of tradition in the treatment of disease, became the enemy of any kind of progress; he was the fundamentalist of the ancient world, who used excessive reverence for the written word to prevent any kind of further scientific investigation or impartial examination of evidence.

This is where we return to the *asu*, or physician proper. An *ashipu* would frequently work in association with an *asu*, although all the indications are that it was the *ashipu* who held the higher status.

The *asu* himself was not without his hocus pocus; because he belonged to a culture riddled with belief in magic and supernatural causation, he had inevitably absorbed some of those false values. In the first place, he was, like everyone else from the king downwards, subject to taboos, and there were unlucky days on which he should not treat a patient. In general, he was given to reinforcing rational treatment by irrational: for example, we find him very reasonably using a tampon to treat nosebleed, but adding an incantation to be on the safe side. Such mixtures of sense and nonsense were common, and it is quite usual to find a potion which may well have had some genuine therapeutic effect, being administered for an illness defined in supernatural terms, such as 'hand of a ghost'.

But although the physician could not always free himself from the superstitions of his own culture, in great part he used procedures and materials which were rational. Even the witch-doctor was not wholly devoid of rational remedies; we have met in his texts a recipe for attempting to deal with a stone in the urethra by drinking beer. But despite some overlap, the basic approaches were significantly different. The *asu* did not necessarily deny that illnesses were caused by supernatural powers, but he believed the best way of dealing with them was by his medicaments, even though it might be helpful in some cases—perhaps most cases—to supplement their effects by magic. The *ashipu*, on the other hand, believed in the power of magic, as enshrined in his traditional texts, and he worked mainly by incantations and rituals; within that framework, medicaments, if used at all, played only an incidental part.

We learn something of the *asu*'s way of going about his business from a humorous story generally referred to as *The Poor Man of Nippur*, in which a man disguised himself as a physician in order to gain access to a bullying mayor against whom he had a grudge. From this we learn that an *asu* wore a distinctive tonsure, and carried with him as part of his regular equipment a brazier of burning charcoal, presumably for use in preparing his potions. From other sources we know that he took with him a wooden box or a leather bag in which to hold his pharmaceutical materials.

In Mesopotamia, there is no hint of that national hierarchy of physicians of the kind apparently found in Egypt, for the only variations upon the title *asu* are *rab asu* (and its Sumerian equivalent), meaning 'chief physician', and *šanu ša rab asu* 'the chief physician's deputy'. We have not yet found a female physician in the texts, but there probably were some, since one of the goddesses is given an epithet meaning 'chief lady physician', indicating that it was a profession quite proper for women. Although probably commonest at court, where they benefited by royal favour, physicians were certainly well dispersed throughout the community, and normally reckoned on earning their living by fees for their skill. Their general availability, contrary to the statement of Herodotus, is implied by a Babylonian proverb, 'Infection without a doctor is like hunger without food'.

The ingredients of the *asu*'s medicaments reflected his part-rational part-superstitious attitude towards disease. Some ingredients would certainly have alleviated, if not cured, some conditions: this applied to various plant products, aromatics such as cedar resin, oils, sulphur, alum, and various mineral salts. Others, such as the blood of various animals, reptiles or birds, had (at least in the small quantities involved in potions) no such recommendation. Plants were known from which a potion could be extracted to procure abortion, and drugs were available as styptics.

The *asu* had many ways of preparing his medicaments. He might bray the materials by pestle and mortar, cook them in an oven, boil them, dissolve them in beer or oil, or make them into an ointment with fat. Methods of application included bathing with hot infusions, drops into the eye or ear, tampons in the ear or nose, suppositories, poultices, oil-based enemas, inhalation of vapour, use as emetics, blowing liquids through a reed into the nose or ear or up the penis or vagina through a bronze tube, and of course simply by mouth. In the last case, the *asu* would specify whether the medicine was to be taken either with or without food.

Our main source of knowledge of the materials use by the *asu* is what are today called Prescription Texts. The earliest of these, from the late third millennium, is completely rational without the taint of magic which crept into some later counterparts. The following prescription, intended for a poultice, shows the style of presentation:

Having ground up the roots of [various specified plants] with dried river bitumen, and having poured beer over it, and having massaged (the affected area), you shall put (the preparation) on as a poultice.

Prescriptions from later periods are usually arranged according to the part of the body they are intended to treat. In one prescription, for an enema, the procedure was set out as follows:

To remove heat in the stomach, you shall grind up together [seven specified ingredients]. You shall strain, steep in beer, heat in an oven, take out, strain and cool. You shall add [further ingredients]. You shall put this into his anus and he will recover.

For inhalation of vapour, the practitioner was instructed to infuse various plant ingredients in oil and beer and was then told:

you shall prepare a large pot, stop up its sides with wheaten dough, boil the brew (therein) over a fire, and put a reed tube into it. Then let him draw the steam up so that it strikes against his lungs, and he will recover.

The counterpart of this treatment is still used against post-operation congestion in modern hospitals.

The Prescription Texts, originally completely rational, in the course of time gradually became contaminated by such superstitious matters as spells. This was an aspect of the process by which the written form of ancient texts gradually acquired the status of scripture. The second millennium saw the scribes very industriously collecting and editing ancient texts, so that by about 1300 BC most ancient texts had been worked into collections in a standard form. During the process, the scribes were bringing together in their copies all ancient material which they regarded as related; having no medical expertise and little critical judgement, when they came to copy ancient prescriptions against, say, stomach pains, if they happened to know of an ancient incantation against the same problem, they would see it as related material and would add the incantation to the prescription. In the third millennium, prescriptions had been simply a record of the current expertise of the *asu*; by the first millennium, the prescriptions—magical intrusions and all—had developed an authority of their own, and the *asu* was thought of not as an expert in his own right but as a man equipped to apply the ancient prescriptions. We have already seen that a corresponding fossilization of medical progress, after an impressive start, had already begun in Egypt in the third millennium.

Surgery in Mesopotamia

Of the surgical work of the *asu*, we know little; there is nothing corresponding to the *Edwin Smith Papyrus* to indicate the extent of his knowledge of the human body and the injuries to which it was subject. The little we do know of the *asu*'s surgical work comes mainly from the Laws of Hammurabi, which legislate for rates of payment if the *asu*'s surgical treatment proved successful in two types of operation, and penalties if it resulted in the death or blindness of the patient. One of the two operations was called 'making a deep incision', which could result in either a cure or death, and the other was designated 'opening a *nakkaptu*', which might either save an eye or cause blindness.

In the most recent discussion (1982) of the expression 'opened a *nakkaptu*', an ophthalmic surgeon argued that it meant 'operated on a cataract'.[9] However, in other contexts where the word *nakkaptu* occurs, it could not mean 'cataract' but undoubtedly denoted either 'temple' or some area very close to it. The majority of scholars therefore take this as a reference to attempting to treat eye trouble by scarification somewhere near the eye. If they are right (but they can speak only as philologists without expertise in opthalmology), this would put Babylonian surgery on a much lower plane than if the term really did refer to a cataract operation.

The precise meaning of 'making a deep incision in a man' is equally unclear. As it was something which could either kill or cure, and was distinct from treating diseased flesh or mending a broken bone, which are mentioned separately, one wonders if the term might have referred to attempts at excising tumours. The 'physician of an ox or a donkey', that is to say, the veterinary surgeon, might make a corresponding deep incision, on a similar kill or cure basis, in the body of an ox or an ass.

In the early second millennium, it was accepted that where physical injuries were likely to be incurred, it was desirable to have an *asu* at hand; we find a royal officer writing from an exposed fortress to request that an *asu* should be sent in case a slingstone hit one of his men. Physicians must have been strongly represented amongst palace personnel, for in cunei-form correspondence of the time we frequently find requests to the king to send an *asu*. At the Assyrian court, one of the tasks of the physicians was to make a physical examination of other palace personnel, inter alia to ensure that any officials who had access to the harem were properly castrated. Presumably, if the man had not been made safe for women, the *asu* had to attend to the matter.

Equipment used by surgeons must have included splints, since the Laws of Hammurabi refer to the curing of broken bones; and the laws also mention the use of a bronze lancet for the deep incisions already referred to. Much use was also made of what one would call in English, according to whether they were applied wet or dry, poultices or bandages. One instance of this comes in the Assyrian laws, where the *asu* uses a bandage to treat a testicle damaged by a woman in a brawl.

Some cuneiform texts of the early second millennium contain a phrase meaning literally 'extracted from the womb', and some scholars have taken this to refer to birth by caesarian section, which would have an obvious bearing on the expertise of Babylonian surgeons of the time: others explain it as meaning no more than 'newborn baby'. In my view, the former view is not wholly excluded, but it would be rash to base any far-reaching conclusions on such an interpretation.

One point to bear in mind is that surgery and other practical techniques can only be learnt by demonstration, so that there was little reason to commit descriptions of them to writing. Therefore, people of the ancient Near East may have practised certain techniques of treatment without leaving any description. For example, mouth-to-mouth resuscitation of a person who had collapsed was practised from at least the ninth century BC, but we should never have known this but for the accident that it was once used by a biblical holy man. A child had collapsed, probably from sunstroke (2 Kings 4:19), and the prophet Elisha was summoned,

And he went up, and lay upon the child, and put his mouth upon his mouth, and his eyes upon his eyes, and his hands upon his hands: and he stretched himself upon the child; and the flesh of the child waxed warm. Then he returned, and walked in the house to and fro; and went up, and stretched himself upon him: and the child sneezed seven times, and the child opened his eyes (2 Kings 4:34–35).

13

Ancient Religion

This chapter deals primarily not with ancient religions, but with ancient religion; its main objective is to investigate the religious phenomena that united ancient society, rather than details that set them apart. But details cannot be completely ignored, since there are areas where regional differences need to be examined, for the way in which they illustrate the effects of geography and history upon religious developments, and the connection between religion and other aspects of society.

Most major religions of the modern world—Christianity, Judaism, Islam, and Buddhism—and a host of minor ones, have received their imprint from the teaching of a great religious reformer, who, according to believers, brought a direct divine revelation. There is one major exception, Hinduism. Undoubtedly, major reformers have arisen within Hinduism, but in the case of the greatest of them their work has given rise to new religions, such as Buddhism and Jainism. The mainstream of Hinduism has continued without imposed change since prehistoric times, although it has undergone gradual evolutionary modification. All religions of the pre-classical world, except that of later Israel, were unreformed religions, more nearly comparable in their developmental history with Hinduism than with Christianity, Judaism or Islam.

Religious edicts, imposed by divine revelation or a great teacher, can fossilize a religion: certain aspects of behaviour and belief become set in a mandatory pattern, frozen for ever, long after changed circumstances have robbed them of their original relevance. The taboo on pigmeat in Judaism and Islam well illustrates this. The pig, unlike domesticated food animals such as goats, sheep and cows, could not be herded over great distances, and so in prehistoric times was therefore restricted to settled farmers. Tensions between settled agriculturalists and pastoral nomads have always been a fact of life, as the story of the killing of Abel by his brother Cain reflects:

Abel was a keeper of sheep, but Cain was a tiller of the ground (Genesis 4:2).

Because nomadic herdsmen associated the pig with an inferior settled way of life, it became taboo to them. In the case of the Israelites, this taboo was reinforced by the fact that, as the pig was a major source of meat for the Canaanites, who were settled farmers, Canaanite religious rites had grown up around it. Moses (or successors in his name), legislating for a society of nomadic origin which rejected Canaanite social and religious customs, incorporated the pigmeat taboo in the decrees he promulgated in the name of Yahweh, and Muhammad repeated it. And so, because of the divine sanction given by two great religious teachers to a taboo of which the social origin has long since become irrelevant, hundreds of millions of Jews and Muslims still abstain from pigmeat.

Unrevealed religions can still be highly conservative in retaining ancient taboos, as the Hindu taboo upon killing cows illustrates, but the absence of edicts directly imposed in the name of God or a great teacher does allow them to respond rather more easily to changing social circumstances than revealed religions, shackled by ancient teaching, and destructive tensions are less likely to arise.

There is another important difference between pre-classical religions and those underlying western societies today. Western man tends to see religion in terms of doctrines or ethical systems, or even social programmes. Unreformed religions of the ancient world had nothing of this. There were no doctrines in the sense of definitions of required belief, and accepted standards of conduct were not explicitly linked to religion. Good behaviour was more a matter of conforming to age-old custom than of framing one's conduct in the light of a divine decree.

Within limits, religious tolerance characterized ancient peoples. This does not mean that one group could flout another group's religious practices. Far from it. Diodorus Siculus mentions the case of an irate Egyptian mob who lynched a Roman because he killed a sacred cat. But it does mean that if one person were content to accept the religious practices of other people, they would accept his. Accepting a polytheistic view of life, the ancients were under no pressure to deny the existence of the gods of other peoples. The only problem which could arise was the relative rank of their gods, and this commonly reflected political relationships of their worshippers. Difficulties only surfaced when one group assertively denied the very existence of other gods. This was the case with the Jews, who in consequence became the least tolerant of all ancient peoples.

Religious concerns and concepts of early man

It is characteristic of mankind to ask questions about the world in which he lives. The form in which such questions are asked reflects the enquirer's attitude to his world. For example, a question in the form 'Who made the stars?' would indicate belief in a personal first principle, whilst 'How did the stars originate?' would suggest a mechanistic view. Ancient myths give us the answers of ancient peoples to the problems of origin and existence, but also show the form in which the questions arose, and thus what the basic attitudes were.

Certain basic questions would occur to early man about the nature of the world he lived in. Was there a world beyond the world he could see and touch? If so, how did it relate to his visible world? And what were the implications for human institutions and for human behaviour? And was there any way in which the human individual, or communities of humans, could affect the divine world for their own advantage?

Intimately linked to the last question was what man felt as his basic needs. Man's first concern has always been, and needs must be, an assured food supply: without it life itself fails. The Lord's Prayer recognizes this basic need, in its petition, 'Give us this day our daily bread'. Many factors could affect early man's food supply. Whilst he still depended upon the hunt, failure of the wild herds to breed could bring disaster. After he had become an agriculturalist, failure of the rains, or of the rising of the river in irrigation regions, could result in famine. Animal epidemics or plant blight equally spelt hunger and death. The factors which controlled the migration of wild animals, and the breeding of herds whether wild or domesticated, and the coming of rain and the rising of the rivers, and the incidence of animal or plant or human disease, were all mysterious. This left man in no doubt that beyond the world he could see and touch there must be a supernatural world which controlled all these things. And so he needed to approach the supernatural world and coerce or persuade it into adjusting events to the benefit of human kind.

Earliest man did not at first see this supernatural force, controlling his world and his life, as God; he saw it in terms of supernatural forces which were mysterious and at first impersonal; technically we call such forces numina (plural of Latin *numen*). Early man felt that storms, rivers, lakes, marshes, mountains, the sun, the wind, fire, were all living beings: although more mysterious, they came into the same category as fish, birds, and animals; sometimes, indeed, there was a direct connection, as of the marshland with its reeds and fish and bird life.

Certain regions of ancient Mesopotamia well illustrate this way of thinking. In the far south lay an area of vast lakes and marshes. In this

269

region was the city of Eridu, probably the oldest Sumerian settlement, and thereby the transmitter of much that was formative in Sumerian religious thinking. The Euphrates brought down silt, which, deposited as sandbanks, became covered with beds of giant reeds. The water was full of life, in the form of fish; and as reed beds sprang up, they would quickly come to swarm with wild pigs and reptiles and birds and other animal life sheltering and breeding there. The Sumerians could thus see the water producing abundant life before their very eyes. Thus in this area a numinous power, the mysterious manifestation of the supernatural, was unmistakably present in the water. Its living force was there to see, in the swaying of the reeds and the rippling of the waters, and the Sumerians could experience its hostile will when it brought floods to destroy fields, settlements and human life. But its will could also be beneficent: when led by irrigation to lifeless arid land, it was creative, and brought life and growth. Also it cleansed. Not only the water, but also the reed beds, the fish, the birds and the animal life associated with it, were all aspects of the same numen.

In the marshy environment of Eridu, the water table was very high, so that wherever one dug one came upon water only a few feet down. And so arose the idea that beneath the earth was a great mass of fresh water, of which the lakes and marshes were the manifestation. In Sumerian this supposed mass of fresh water was known as the *abzu* (Akkadian *apsu*). It was thought of as something with a life and will of its own—a numen. It must be emphasized that the original idea was not that the *abzu* was a supernatural being living in the waters: the *abzu* actually was the waters and all the life in them. And self-evidently, for the earliest Sumerians, the *abzu* had always been there: it was not a created thing and it had no beginning and no end; it just existed.

A corresponding way of thought is evident in other areas of ancient Sumer. In some parts of south Mesopotamia, mainly on the edge of the desert, there were seasonal grasslands, which made possible a way of life based on the herding of cattle, sheep and goats. During the winter the animals would be penned and fed from stored fodder, but in spring came thunderstorms that briefly made the desert lush with herbage and wild flowers, and at that time the herdsmen drove the cattle out to the edge of the desert for pasturage. To bring this sudden transformation of the desert from aridity to lushness, there must, thought early man, be a numinous power within the thunderstorm.

With the lush pastures, the cows and sheep and goats began to breed and to yield milk: here too then, in cattle fertility and in the milk, there must be (so the Sumerians felt) some supernatural force: the breeding animals and their milk were invested with a numinous power. The

Sumerians saw this force visibly present in the milk, but they did not suppose that the milk itself was a god or divine; it was simply the seat of a numinous power. But the desert lushness was of brief duration. The pastures quickly became parched and the milk of the cattle dried up: men felt that as the heat of summer arrived and the vegetation withered into the ground, the numinous power departed.

Another Sumerian region abounded in date-orchards. Here a numinous power was seen in the growth and ripening of the date crop. The crop was stored, but when the store of dates was exhausted, it was felt that the numinous power had departed into the earth. This concept, common to both the cattle-herding and date-growing areas, had important consequences for later mythology.

The will that seemed to manifest itself in some of the numina pointed to a distinction between the manifestation of numinous power and the living being behind it. There was a change of concept: the numen began to be seen not merely as a mysterious force but as a supernatural being controlling a force. Mostly, that supernatural being was initially conceived not in human but in animal (theriomorphic) form. The numinous thunderstorm already mentioned is a good example. The Sumerian term for this power was Imdugud, meaning literally 'heavy cloud', the visible sign of the thunderstorm. Sumerian writing indicated the class to which a thing belonged by signs called determinatives (p. 72), and we find Imdugud written with two determinatives, one denoting that it belonged to the class of the divine, and the other classifying it as a bird. ^{d}Imdugud^{mušen}, as the name was written, thus conveyed the concept 'the supernatural thundercloud in the form of a bird'.

The concept of the *abzu*, the numinous mass of fresh waters, underwent a corresponding development. The idea 'the waters are the *abzu* and they are an elemental power' gave way to 'the waters are the domain in which a supernatural power called Abzu has its abode'. One theriomorphic form in which Abzu came to be seen was that of a great supernatural ibex submerged in the waters, with his antlers showing above as the reeds: out of this concept there eventually developed a god who had a Sumerian name meaning 'the ibex of the *abzu*'.

The development of the separation between the seat of the numinous power and the numinous power itself is seen again in the case of milk. A text explicitly states this distinction. Commenting on the mythic death of the god who later embodied the numinous power, it says: 'You who are not the cream were poured out with the cream: you who are not the milk were drunk with the milk.'

271

The rise of anthropomorphic deities

Soon after 3000 BC major changes came about in the form of society in southern Mesopotamia. As a result of successful irrigation and consequent food surpluses, cities developed, with populations of twenty or thirty thousand or even more. To control the community operations upon which irrigation and fertility depended, there had to be a human leader (not necessarily a king). In a small homogeneous democratic community, although some individuals will command general respect for their service to the community or their personality, feelings of intense reverence towards an individual do not easily arise. But in a large community with a hierarchical structure and inequality of wealth, it is almost inevitable that a feeling of awe will develop towards the great man at the top, who becomes invested with an impressive aspect which we denote by the term 'majesty'. The feelings of awe and power evoked by the community leader in early Sumerian society were analogous to the feelings evoked by numinous powers. The parallel between the two forms of power now led the Sumerians to think of the majesty and power of the waters and the thunderstorm and so on, as belonging to a supernatural ruler in human form associated with those waters and other numinous aspects of nature. By this process of thought, anthropomorphic deities developed. There was a god in human form who had his abode in the *abzu* and controlled it; likewise there was a god in human form who controlled thunderstorms, and so on.

But this left a problem—the relationship of the old theriomorphic numen to the new anthropomorphic god. This was resolved by myths telling of a combat in which the anthropomorphic god vanquished an older non-anthropomorphic numinous being (not quite a god and yet, because it existed before creation, even more than a god). The Babylonian Myth of Creation contains an account of how the god Enki overcame a being called Abzu, who had existed since before creation, and then made his abode inside the *abzu* and took over Abzu's former functions. Another myth relates how the god Ninurta fought and defeated the Anzu bird, which was another form of Imdugud.[1] But the myth reflects the final situation in a development over a long period: we can actually see Imdugud gradually becoming an anthropomorphic god. Gudea, a ruler of Lagash at about 2150 BC, describes his city-god Ningirsu (a form of Ninurta) as he saw him in a dream, and his description includes the words 'As to his head he was a god, as to his wings he was Imdugud'. Clearly Ningirsu (as Gudea saw him) was on the way to becoming anthropomorphic but still retained the wings of the Imdugud bird.

This had further implications for religious development. In the case of the numen of the waters, for example, in the earlier non-anthropomorphic concept, the *abzu* was the source on the one hand of life-giving waters and of cleansing, and on the other of the destructive flood. There was a tension here. With the new religious concepts, this tension was resolved. The hostile aspects of the waters became thought of as belonging to the primeval being Abzu, now evil, whilst the favourable aspects were those of the god. The victory of the god over Abzu (enacted periodically in ritual with accompanying myth) gave an assurance that the Flood would not ultimately triumph. Man gained a sense of permanence and security in his environment.

Even in historical times, there were still relics of theriomorphism, even in Mesopotamia, although less immediately evident than in Egypt. For example, the city-goddess of Isin, in south Mesopotamia, was long envisaged as having a dog's head, and the dog was her emblem. Another goddess is depicted in a form in which she has a fish for her sceptre and fish for her sandals; clearly she was the personification of the numinous power immanent in the shoals of fish racing through the waters. Even the greatest of Mesopotamian deities could be visualized in a non-human form; Ishtar, for example, was said to have four teats:

Her four teats are in your mouth; two you suck and two you milk in front of you.

Clearly, this goes back to the concept of Ishtar as a cow. The god Nergal wore a serpent on his head, implying that once he was a Serpent-god: there was a parallel to this in Egypt, where the pharaoh wore a representation of a serpent on his headdress, probably as a relic of a cult of a Serpent-god in Lower Egypt.

Even in Israelite religion there are traces of earlier theriomorphism. A commandment that runs:

Thou shalt not make . . . any likeness of any thing that is in heaven above, or that is in the earth beneath, or that is in the waters beneath the earth (Deuteronomy 5:8)

only has relevance if the practices prohibited had been current in the past. And we see theriomorphism actually being practised in Aaron's golden calf, and in the calves (or bulls) at Bethel (2 Kings 10:29, etc.).

But the clearest evidence for persisting theriomorphism comes from Egypt. In some prehistoric cemeteries, archaeologists found not only human bodies, but also the bodies of cows, jackals and sheep, wrapped in shrouds just like humans. Obviously, animals buried in that way must have had a special religious significance. Precisely what that significance was is open to discussion, but it is reasonable to link it with the fact that the cow later represented the goddess who was thought of as the Great Mother, and the jackal, as Anubis, was the god of the dead. Probably the most widespread aspect of Egyptian religion (as of others) in the prehistoric period was a fertility cult. In the Egyptian context, with its emphasis in early times upon cattle herding, the obvious symbol of the numen of fertility was the cow, and a Cow-goddess became of considerable importance in Egyptian religion, known principally as Hathor.

We find other gods and goddesses represented in art, or referred to in texts, in the form of a ram, a falcon, a vulture, a lioness, a cat, a cobra, an ibis, a baboon, a crocodile, an unidentified dog-like creature, and other animals. Some of the ancient territorial divisions known as nomes had emblems in animal form, and in some cases a cult of the deity in that form was practised well into historical times. This suggests that some (and possibly all) of these cults were originally localized, with the numen, and later the theriomorphic god, linked to a particular settlement. As some settlements became political and religious centres important far beyond their own locality, their deities acquired a national importance. The most striking instance of this was the prehistoric Falcon-god. Horus, of Hierakonpolis in Upper Egypt. When Upper Egypt conquered Lower Egypt and formed a unified state, the king of Egypt became identified with the falcon Horus as a god. But by this time Horus was more than a falcon: he was also a Sky-god, an easy transition for a bird characteristically seen soaring in the sky with outstretched wings.

But the numinous powers were seen in many other forms than the falcon, and the political supremacy of the Sky-and-Falcon-god Horus may have masked but did not suppress those others. Some other deities were assimilated to Horus, or brought into relationship with him mythologically, and some long continued to be worshipped in their original form in local cults.

The most important syncretism of Horus was with the gods of Heliopolis in Lower Egypt, where, as we have already seen, there was an ancient cult of the Creator-god Atum, who had merged into the Sun-god Re^c. When, after the unification of Egypt, a new capital was built at Memphis, the already important cult of the older centre, Heliopolis, only 25 miles away, made itself felt there. The result was syncretism between Horus and the Sun-god Re^c.

One god developed differently. This was Seth, the final form of a numen represented as an unidentified dog-like animal. In myth he was senior to Horus (whose uncle he was), a rival to him, and associated with the desert. Some egyptologists have interpreted this in terms of two races in competition in prehistoric times, but the data more probably reflect a struggle between an older way of life and the one which was finally dominant. The cults of Horus and his circle were cults of settlements dominated by cattle herding and agriculture. Since Egyptian tradition made Seth not only hostile to Horus, but also of more remote origin and linked to the desert, it is evident that Seth represented religious ideas going back to before the introduction of agriculture and cattle breeding. As embodiment of two basically different ways of life, Seth and Horus could not be assimilated and would remain mythologically in conflict. The unidentified dog-like animal which commonly represents Seth may well have been a hunting dog, of a breed which later became extinct, used by very ancient hunting communities in the more open lands away from the Nile.

Survivals of theriomorphism are equally to be seen in other parts of the ancient world, as for example in the Hittite area, where the Weather-god is frequently represented as standing on a bull.

There was one other Egyptian cult of great significance. This was the cult of Osiris. The myth of Osiris is well known from Greek authors, but we have no continuous account from ancient Egyptian sources, although there are many allusions to it.

The myth has many variants, but baldly the main elements are as follows. There were four characters: Osiris; his brother Seth; Isis, who was both sister and wife of Osiris; and their son Horus. Seth killed Osiris. Isis found the dismembered body, restored Osiris to life long enough to get her with child, and gave birth to Horus, who then fought with Seth. After some hesitation, a divine tribunal finally awarded the rulership to Horus.

Explanations of the myth are many and diverse. Some see an historical basis, with the original Osiris a king who was killed. Others see the myth as an allegory of a struggle between good and evil. To others, it is a myth about the growth of vegetation, with Osiris representing the fertilizing waters.

The essential fact about Osiris is that he is particularly associated with death. Our earliest information about him comes from the Pyramid Texts, dated to the end of the Old Kingdom (c.2350–2155 BC). These, largely magic spells, rituals, incantations and hymns carved on walls inside pyramids, had the object of securing a suitable afterlife for the dead divine king. All the references to Osiris in these texts link him with the resurrection of the king, and all the evidence indicates that the Osiris cult originated in this. Isis may be excluded from consideration, as it is generally recognized that she was in origin the personified throne; moreover, she is absent from the earliest form of this mythology. Also, Osiris is in a different category from Horus and Seth: they are represented in art from prehistoric times, but Osiris does not appear until the historical period. Moreover, whereas theriomorphic representations of Horus and Seth and most other deities are common, there are none of

Osiris. Clearly, unlike most of the other gods, Osiris did not develop out of a prehistoric numen. Rather, he fulfilled a particular human need.

Ancient Egypt was so highly centralized that its wellbeing was felt as intimately linked with its divine king. When the divine king died there was a crisis of confidence. The Egyptians desperately needed reassurance in the face of the fact that their king, a supposed god, was undoubtedly dead. They achieved this reassurance by defiant denial of the fact. This was not an inexplicable oddity of an isolated people of long ago: to deny that death is the end is a widespread human response to a distressing fact. Precisely the same psychology is seen today in the inevitable response of left-wing student groups when the authorities manage to kill a revolutionary leader in one of the world's trouble spots: slogans will appear on public buildings saying 'So-and-so [the dead man's name] lives!'. The cult of Osiris was a way of psychologically negating the fact that the god-king had really died: he had in fact become another god, who, though once dead, rose again. Osiris was always represented as a dead king, wearing the white cloak of the dead and the royal insignia. But on earth the kingship had to continue, and the dead king's son became the living god Horus. Thus in mythology the dead god had to be the father of Horus.

In the myth, Osiris was drowned: this reflects the disappearance of vegetation beneath the waters at the Nile inundation. The rebirth of vegetation after the annual flood was a symbol of resurrection: plants die and sink into the earth, but rise again through their seed. The dead divine king, who had been the power guiding the state, became as Osiris the power within the waters and the earth, and so continued his beneficent function for his people, by safeguarding the inundation and harvest.

Through these concepts, Osiris acquired the aspect of a vegetation god. By the Middle Kingdom the cult of Osiris had become fully assimilated to that of an ancient vegetation god at Abydos, where rites took place to celebrate the inundation and the rebirth of vegetation. Some authorities deduce from this that Osiris was in origin a prehistoric vegetation god, later taken over to represent the resurrection of the dead king. This is impossible. A deity who developed from the numina behind plant life would have left numerous traces from prehistoric times, whereas we do not meet Osiris at all until the beginning of history. Moreover, a god originating from vegetation would from earliest times have been represented with plant symbols, but all early representations of Osiris are in wholly human form; not until well into historical times did plant symbolism become associated with Osiris, so that manifestly this was secondary.

Other elements in the Osiris myth probably grew out of ancient funerary ritual. In the myth, the god's body is dismembered: this probably reflects a memory of an ancient burial custom, no longer practised in the third millennium.

Originally exclusively connected with the dead king, the Osiris cult in time came by extension to offer resurrection to all. So wide was its consequent appeal, that the cult of Osiris and his consort Isis became one of the principal eastern religions introduced into the Graeco-Roman world in the last two pre-Christian centuries; the emperor Commodus was a devotee.[2]

Polytheism in Mesopotamia

We have noted the existence of several ecologically different regions in ancient south Mesopotamia. Although they shared one religion, differences in their circumstances produced different ways of representing the divine powers, and different emphases. Even in adjacent cities, the same supernatural power might be known under different names. Analogy with human society also multiplied deities; just as a human leader exercised authority through junior members of his own family and other subordinates, so the chief god in a local pantheon was imagined as surrounded by members of his family, ministers and servants. Every profession and activity was given its own deity, so that there were, for example, gods of brickmaking and deities of brewing. And so there developed many local pantheons, each with many deities. There came a time when the scribes, who were great fact-grubbers and classifiers, attempted to inter-relate into a systematic scheme all the gods known in Sumerian culture: they put together all deities of all cities in Sumer (and even of such regions as they knew beyond) and produced a most comprehensive pantheon, containing some 3600 names. But this was totally artificial. It represented scribal thoroughness rather than a real religious situation: never at any time was there anyone in Sumer who worshipped 3600 deities. Corresponding situations developed in Egypt and the Hittite area; the Egyptian pantheon was likewise enormous, and Hittite documents sometimes spoke of 'the thousand gods of Hatti'.

Four deities were particularly prominent at all times in Mesopotamia. One was the Mother-goddess under a multitude of forms and names, of which the best known were Inanna in Sumerian and Ishtar in Akkadian; she represented the female principle which dominates all life, and was probably the oldest divine power of all, probably already implicit in prehistoric fertility figurines (see plate 1). Several Sumerian and Akkadian myths show vestiges of a female Creator behind the Creator-deities of what became the standard myths. Ishtar also developed an astral aspect as the planet Venus.

The other principal deities were An (Akkadian Anu), Enlil and Enki (Akkadian Ea). Each of these had in earliest times been head of a local pantheon; the scribal theologians attempted—not wholly successfully—to eliminate the inconsistencies this produced, by regarding these three gods as having particular responsibility respectively for the heavens, the earth and the waters. Despite the formal priority given to An, probably reflecting circumstances of the period and place where the composite pantheon took form, it was effectively Enlil who was chief executive of the gods. Supremacy in world control was known as *enlilutu*, 'Enlil-ship', and even when the city god of Babylon, Marduk, became head of the pantheon, he ruled by virtue of *enlilutu*, which meant in effect that he had assimilated the qualities of Enlil. In Assyria, the national god Ashur was actually known as 'the Assyrian Enlil'.

The name Enki meant 'Lord of the *Ki*', and *Ki* denoted everything from the surface of the earth downwards. When the idea developed that there was a great hollow space, the underworld, beneath the earth, *Ki* came to mean 'underworld', but since Enki had no particular Underworld associations, it is clear that his name went back to a period before that idea developed. His particular connection was with the subterranean waters (the *abzu*), and, because the people of the southern marshlands, where Enki arose, saw all life as derived from the subterranean waters, he became associated with the giving of life and with creativity generally. This came to include human creativity, so that Enki became the god of wisdom and the one who bestowed all human skills. His concern for mankind made him unfailingly benevolent, as against Enlil, who had a notably destructive side, deriving probably from his prehistoric origin as a wind god; Enlil means 'Lord Wind'.

Other gods were too numerous to specify, but amongst the more important of them was the Moon-god Nanna or Sin, the Sun-god Utu or Shamash, the Storm-god under several names, various fertility deities and deities of the underworld, gods of war, plague and death, deities of the scribal craft and other professions, and the great national gods, Marduk of Babylon and Ashur of Assyria.

Egyptian religion

Egyptian religion in its developed form showed marked differences from the religion of Mesopotamia; these differences can be traced back to the effect upon basically similar beginnings of differences in the prehistoric physical and social environment.

The replacement of hunting and food-gathering by food producing as the dominant way of life began later in Egypt than in Mesopotamia. As Malthus pointed out, human populations continually increase until they reach the limits of their food supply. This was as true in prehistory as now. The beginning of agriculture and cattle herding did not result from a deliberate change to secure better nutrition: it was forced upon man by a situation in which hunting and food-gathering no longer met the needs of the increasing population. Man in Egypt was no whit less able than man in Mesopotamia to learn the skills of agriculture and cattle herding, but because of the geographical circumstances of the Nile valley, he remained insulated longer from the pressures compelling him to adopt them. When he did finally adopt them, there seems to have been proportionately less emphasis upon grain production and more upon cattle herding than in Mesopotamia. This meant that, compared with humans in the most advanced parts of western Asia, prehistoric Egyptians were longer intimately concerned with wild animal life, and afterwards had a closer dependence upon domesticated animals. And so, as Egyptian religion took shape, the numina with which the Egyptians peopled the super-natural world behind the world they knew were likely to have a particularly strong link with animals.

After agriculture became fully established, there were again different factors affecting religious forms. In no part of Egypt was rainfall significant for crop production, and so the numen of the thunderstorm never developed as a major factor in Egyptian religion. And the irrigation procedure, although it called for hard work to maximize its benefits, was less complex than in south Mesopotamia. The Nile rose and the land was covered with water; the Nile subsided, and land, manifestly full of abundant life, appeared out of it, ready to be sown, and, under the unfailing sun, quickly to produce ripe crops. The primacy of water was obvious. And so the Egyptians no less than the Mesopotamians accepted the waters as the beginning of everything. As first principles, the waters did not demand explanation, and both cultures were mythologically concerned only with what developed from them. The Egyptians saw that from the waters land arose, and from the land, life. The numinous force which produced new life from the earth as it rose from the waters came to be seen as a Creator-god, called Atum, a name not fully explained by egyptologists but based on a root containing the sense 'completed'; thus Atum implies the idea of bringing fully into existence. A cult based on this concept may well have been widespread but its most prominent prehistoric centre was Heliopolis, near the site of later Cairo. In the historical period a sophisticated mythology developed to explain how Atum came into being.

Another great lifegiving force for the Egyptians was the sun, an equally evident symbol of creation, and so at many places a sun cult also arose. At Heliopolis, the cult of the Sun-god, under the name Re^c, fused with the cult of Atum.

Two other major factors affected the form of Egyptian religion in historical times. The Nile not only engendered life: it also provided excellent communications. This brought political unification between communities much earlier than in Mesopotamia. Still within prehistory, the numerous local settlements along the Nile were fused into two kingdoms, Upper and Lower Egypt; and at the very dawn of history these were united into a single state. For those early Egyptians, the king, with control over the whole of their world and their lives, was invested with an aura of mystery and might like the supernatural powers: as ancient numina developed into gods, the king also became considered divine.

The other major factor developed from the interplay of climate and burial customs. From the Old Stone Age man had in many places buried his dead in a way which indicated belief in continued existence after death. The earliest Egyptians also did this, but their burials were in the desert sand, and the hot dry climate meant that in such circumstances the body did not rot, but desiccated and remained as a withered but still wholly recognizable corpse. In consequence, the Egyptians developed an unparalleled emphasis upon the continued existence of the physical body after death. This put a unique character upon their religion. Early in the First Dynasty (c. 3000 BC), they began to devise artificial means for preserving dead bodies, and from this eventually developed the process known as mummification.

Mummification was a messy and unpleasant process. The details varied from period to period, and even in a single period there were more and less elaborate procedures available. But certain basic elements applied generally. The earliest attempts at preservation were simply a matter of wrapping the dead bodies in linen bandages. But this was insufficient to prevent decomposition, although it concealed it. During the Second and Third Dynasties (down to about 2600 BC), the practice developed of soaking the bandages in resin so that they would set in the form of the body and show the person's features, so giving a convincing representation of the deceased, even though beneath the wrappings the corpse still decomposed to leave little but the skeleton. In the Fourth Dynasty, internal organs began to be removed to facilitate the drying of the inside of the body, which was sometimes packed with linen soaked in resin. The organs themselves were wrapped in linen and stored separately in the tomb, in small containers commonly called Canopic jars. By the Eighteenth Dynasty (c. 1550–1300 BC), much more efficient measures began to be taken to ensure desiccation: now the process began with the body being packed for several days in dry natron, a naturally-occurring form of what we usually call washing soda. It was at this period that the embalmers began the practice of removing the brain, which according to Herodotus was achieved by the unpleasant procedure of breaking into the cranium through the nostrils by means of a chisel, and then extracting the brain material with a probe. The procedures reached their most elaborate form during the Twenty-First Dynasty (from *c.* 1080 BC). Cosmetic simulation of life was all, and from this time the mummy was given a plump lifelike appearance by means of packs of sawdust or other substances bound in linen; originally these were fixed to the outside of the limbs under the bandages, but subsequently they were pushed in under the skin. There was also a change in the treatment of the internal organs, which were no longer stored separately but returned to the body after treatment. Artificial eyes were inserted. Bodies were even improved, as by stitching leather patches over the skin to conceal bedsores. In the late period a substance like bitumen was used in place of resin: the word 'mummy' is derived from the Arabic name for this substance.

Mummification was not restricted to human bodies: specimens of birds, fish and animals were all embalmed, from bulls down to shrews, presumably because of the religious link between fauna and deities.

From death to burial the mortuary procedure took 70 days, although the actual embalming occupied only a part of this time, the remainder being taken up with rituals and transport. It is clear, from examination of actual mummies, that the object of preservation of the body before decay set in was not always achieved. Some corpses had evidently begun to decompose before the embalmers started work on them, and in some cases mummies contain bones from several different individuals, proving that the corpses had begun to disintegrate before wrapping was undertaken. Some of the embalmers were not very scrupulous in their treatment of dead bodies, for, as examples of mummies in museums show, embalmers sometimes made the corpse fit the coffin by breaking its bones or even throwing parts away. Herodotus heard that the embalmers had a bad name for their treatment of the dead, and reports that the bodies of beautiful women were not handed to them until three or four days after death; one embalmer, he says, had actually been caught in the act of necrophilia.

The cultural significance of mummification does not match its curiosity value. It was in no sense important in the general history of human civilization, and it is noteworthy mainly as a major example of perverted human effort sustained over several millennia. One might suppose that it would have brought an intimate knowledge of human anatomy to serve to advance medical science. But the context in which mummification operated nullified any such possibility. The whole operation was based upon the belief that in the religious sphere the image did service for the reality. Egyptian religion offers many examples of this principle. For instance, texts written on the walls of tombs claiming a righteous life for the dead person were mere spells, not ethical codes; they were there to ensure that the deceased gave the correct answers to the afterworld judges about his conduct on earth, and nothing mattered but the correct recitation of the spells; whether or not the answers corresponded to how the deceased person had lived was irrelevant. Paintings in tombs, depicting houses, trees, gardens and pools, magically ensured the presence of such things as real objects in the afterworld. Figurines of servants ensured real servants. In the same way, all that was required for survival after death was the appearance of the body; the state of its organs was irrelevant. Glass eyes were as good for the purpose as real eyes; chaff, sawdust or sand to fill out the abdomen as good as stomach and intestines in undamaged condition. The brain could not be seen in any case and so was destroyed and removed in order to reduce risk of putrefaction of the visible features of the face: provided the skull and a recognizable face remained, the head could still magically operate in the afterworld without a brain. With this attitude, it was impossible that the operations carried out by the embalmers upon the corpse could develop into a scientific study of anatomy or of the nature and functions of the various organs.

Other Religions

Israelite religion is often set aside from all others, as uniquely revealed and true, whilst the rest were evolutionary and false. But acceptance of a revealed element in Israelite religion is not incompatible with seeing in its earliest forms factors common to other religions.

Israelite traditions reflect primitive awareness of numinous forces in the form of sacred stones, sacred trees, sacred springs or wells, and sacred mountains. Beer-sheba had its sacred tree or grove, traditionally linked with Abraham (Genesis 21:33), and there was another given the same connection at Moreh (Genesis 12:6–7), although AV obscures the fact by wrongly translating it as 'plain of Moreh' instead of 'oak (or terebinth) of Moreh'. In Genesis 35:4 Jacob buried a hoard of idols under an oak in Shechem, apparently to put them under the control of a more powerful supernatural force. God's appearance to Moses in the burning bush (Exodus 3:2–5) is an indisputable case of a numen associated with a tree. This is only a brief selection from a large number of Israelite references to trees with numinous associations.

Sacred waters are seen in Numbers 21:17–18, where a direct address to the well—'Spring up, O well!'—shows its numinous power. There is an indisputable instance of a stone with numinous power in the story of Jacob at Bethel (Genesis 28:11–19). Unaware of its numinous connection, Jacob used the stone as a headrest, but when it revealed itself for what it was by giving him a dream, he 'took the stone that he had put for his pillows, and set it up for a pillar, and poured oil upon the top of it, and he called the name of that place Beth-el [meaning "house of a god" or "house of a numen"]'. Sacred mountains in the Israelite tradition were numerous; one need only mention Sinai, Horeb, Carmel, Tabor and Mount Zion itself.

Clearly, underlying Israelite religion in its revealed form, there was, as with other religions, a prehistoric substratum in which humans felt the presence of supernatural powers in nature, not in human or even necessarily in personal form, of the type which we call numina. The unique aspects of developments which occurred in later Israelite religion, claimed (and accepted by me) as carrying divine revelation, are so well known that it is unnecessary to deal with them here.

Hittite religion presents a special problem. The evidence we have comes from a time span which is very brief in terms of ancient religions, and there is much in the religious practices of the Hittite area which is demonstrably of non-Hittite origin. Whereas for Egypt and Mesopotamia we can see continuity and development over upwards of 2500 years, all the data for Hittite religion fall within a time span of at the most eight hundred years (1800–1000 BC), which includes a very shadowy century at the beginning of that period and two centuries of increasing Aramaean influence in the neo-Hittites states which succeeded the Hittite empire after its collapse.

In view of the geography and climate of the Hittite area, it is not surprising that storm-gods and mountain-gods were prominent among many local cults: lists of divine witnesses to treaties include up to eighteen different storm-gods. Such gods developed out of older storm numina and sacred mountains; this is clear from the lists of supernatural forces summoned to witness, which include, after named deities, such still non-anthropomorphic divine powers as 'the mountains, the rivers, the springs, the great sea, heaven and earth, the winds and the clouds'. We also find rites for springs, and sacrifices to mountains and rivers.

The developed pantheon of the Hittites was very mixed. Not surprisingly, in view of the considerable cultural influence of Mesopotamia upon Anatolia, it contained deities of Hurrian and Babylonian origin. The Luwians in southwest Anatolia, an earlier strand of the ethnic group to which the Hittites themselves belonged, provided another group.

Others go back to the ancient population of Anatolia before the Hittite immigration. The West Semitic world supplied at least two deities; one took the form of Elkunirsha, which as *'el qoneh 'eres* would be good Canaanite or Hebrew for 'god, creator of the earth', and the other was Ashertu, which is Asherah of the Old Testament (1 Kings 15:13; 16:33; 18:19, etc., mistranslated 'grove' in AV).

As in Mesopotamia and Egypt, an official state pantheon grew out of the local cults; it was sometimes referred to as 'the thousand gods of Hatti-land'. At its head was the Sun-goddess of Arinnu, 'Queen of Heaven and Earth', 'Lady of the Lands', with her consort the Weather-god of Hatti; both of them were eventually identified with deities in the Hurrian pantheon. There was also a male sun deity, whose origin is obscure, since he was neither another form of the Sun-goddess of Arinna, nor her consort; he may have grown out of an aboriginal Anatolian sun numen.[3] Among the chief deities was Ishtar, of undoubted Meso-potamian origin and retaining her Mesopotamian name and attributes. There were also gods of the Hittite Underworld, the place where ghosts and demons had their home.

Texts show that offerings and festivals took place in Hittite temples in much the same way as in Mesopotamia and Egypt. But probably the most important foci of Hittite religion, and certainly the most prominent extant relics of it, are the many rock monuments throughout the country, presumably going back to forms of cult preceding the building of temples. The most striking of these is a rock sanctuary at Yazilikaya, near Boghazkoi east of Ankara, where there are carvings of two converging processions of deities, with 42 gods coming from one direction and 21 goddesses from the other: not all the deities have been certainly identified, but they are presumably the senior figures in the state pantheon. Some of the deities stand on animals, making clear their theriomorphic origin.

Apart from a few real or supposed god-names on the Linear B tablets, the only direct evidence on pre-Greek Minoan religion is archaeological. This evidence is usually interpreted in the light of later Greek traditions. Such reconstructions have undoubted interest for Minoan survivals in Greek religion, but in some cases they obscure the more primitive stages of the ancient religion of Crete itself.

The archaeological evidence may be divided broadly into two categories: sites and artefacts. As to sites, Crete, unlike Egypt and Mesopotamia, never developed great temples, although there were small chapels in palaces and some of the grander houses. The main sacred sites of the ancient Cretans were of two types: caves, and sanctuaries near the tops of mountains, both identifiable by the remains of animal sacrifices. In some of the caves there were pillars, comparable with the sacred stones of the west Semitic world, well known from the Bible. One of the mountain shrines, Mount Iouktas south of Knossos, provides clear evidence of human sacrifice, and at Knossos itself archaeologists found indications of cannibalism, in the form of children's rib bones from 1450 BC, with cuts on them similar to the cuts a butcher might make on animal bones in the course of stripping off the flesh for food. There is nothing, except doubtful deduction from later Greek religion, by which to make a definite identification of the deities concerned at either the caves or the mountain sanctuaries.

The main artefacts to be taken into account for Minoan religion were cult symbols, frescoes, representations on sarcophagi, scenes carved on seals or other gems, decorations on vessels, and figurines. The most instructive of these are the scenes on seals and gems, typically of quite simple composition. Amongst the most common of these are: a male figure doing reverence to a tree on an altar-like stand; and two animals placed, often symmetrically, on either side of some other symbol, which may be a male figure or a female figure on a mountain or a cult stand bearing vegetation or a pillar. Some of the seals bear a female figure whose relative splendour and prominence suggests that she was a goddess.

The animals, vegetation and pillars, combined with the use of caves and mountains as cult places, suggest survivals of primitive numina in non-anthropomorphic form, comparable with what can be shown for the earliest stages of Mesopotamian and Egyptian religion. The goddess figure on some of the seals points to the stage at which some of the numina were being given anthropomorphic form, with the primary supernatural power thought of as the female principle, as in earliest Mesopotamia. Without relying heavily on reconstruction from later Greek religion, no more specific conclusions can be drawn from this limited evidence.

Two cult symbols were very widespread in Cretan art. These were the double axe, and what is usually designated the horns of consecration, a pair of horns, usually carving upwards and outwards from a horizontal base.

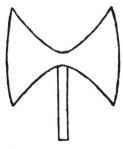

Double Axe Symbol

Horns of Consecration

Although it is evident that the horns of consecration derive from a bull's horns (a few scholars dispute this), we have no knowledge of what either of these symbols indicated in terms of belief, although there are plenty of theories. It seems most likely that the horns linked up with the numinous power evident in the wild bull, and the double axe symbol with the numinous power in the weapon powerful enough to fell a bull.

Many figurines obviously represent goddesses, a further indication of the primacy accorded to the female principle as the powers of the supernatural began to be represented in human form. Sometimes these figures are shown holding snakes or entwined by them. Coiled snakes also occur on some vessels. Since snakes emerge from holes in the ground, they were often in ancient religion (and there are modern survivals, plate 23) given a chthonic (underworld) association, and, because plant life springs from beneath the ground, they became symbols of fertility.

If one uses only the limited archaeological evidence on Minoan religion, without reading back data from later Greek mythology, we have to conclude that Minoan religion remained at a markedly more primitive level than the stages reached in contemporary Egypt or Western Asia.

We know even less about the ancient religion of the Indus valley than about that of ancient Crete. With no texts at all that can be read, we depend for our knowledge wholly upon interpreting archaeological data, which mainly takes the form of buildings and artefacts. The conclusions one reaches from such data depend heavily upon the assumptions one brings to them. Some scholars assume that Harappan culture must have heavily influenced later Hindu religion, and therefore interpret Harappan artefacts in the light of later religion in India. For example, certain stone objects found at Mohenjo-daro have been taken, by analogy with the lingams of Hinduism, as representing phalli or female organs. This has become the basis of an interpretation of the Harappan religion as worship of the Mother-goddess principle. But there is no independent proof that the Harappan stone objects had that kind of significance.[4]

A Finnish scholar published a work in 1985 in which he attempted to give a detailed account of Harappan religion, heavily based on his decipherment (whether supposed or real) of the script. At the time of writing I have not had access to this work.

Human sacrifice and demons

Ancient Crete had no monopoly of human sacrifice in the ancient world; traces of it can be found in almost every civilization. Man values nothing more than human life, and he invests his gods with the same attitude.

Paradoxically this leads to some of his worst excesses, for he has often persuaded himself that to bring pressure or persuasion to bear upon the supernatural powers, the greatest force he can exert is to offer them human lives. The period at which human sacrifice was outlawed is a crude but relevant index to the stage reached in the climb out of the mud of superstition.

In Egypt, traces of human sacrifice, practised in prehistoric times, recognizably survive in the third-millennium Pyramid Texts, but by that time the Egyptians had rid themselves of such excesses in current religion. But practices of that kind long continued in Africa further south, where hundreds of victims were found in royal tombs from the early second millennium BC at Kerma in Sudan. Even as late as the final decades of the pre-Christian era retainers were sacrificed and interred at the funeral of kings in Lower Nubia.[5]

Ancient Mesopotamia also showed some vestiges of the practice; the most dramatic were associated with what are generally called the Royal Tombs of Ur, at about 2700 BC. There were sixteen of these, each in a large pit lined with stone or brick, well over 30 feet deep, approached by two shafts. After the interment of the principal body, there was a ceremonial in which retainers, in one case as many as 74, mainly women, filed into the pit, where they either committed suicide by drinking poison or were killed in some way which produced no disturbance to their headdresses.

A form of human sacrifice continued in Assyria down to the first millennium. When omens showed that a grave danger threatened the king, a substitute king was appointed, to reign for the period of the threat, during which time any evil destined for the king would fall upon the substitute. At the end of the period he and his spouse were ceremonially put to death.

Human sacrifice was also practised by some of the predecessors and neighbours of the Israelites in Palestine, and, according to the biblical record, some Israelites succumbed to that influence. Psalms 106:37–38 explicitly says of earlier Israelites

They sacrificed their sons and their daughters unto devils, and shed innocent blood, even the blood of their sons and of their daughters, whom they sacrificed unto the idols of Canaan,

and Ezekiel 16:20 attributes to God the accusation

Thou has taken thy sons and thy daughters, whom thou hast borne unto me, and these hast thou sacrificed unto them [foreign gods] to be devoured.

Isaiah 57:5 makes a similar charge.

Judges 11:30–39 gives an account of how an Israelite leader sacrificed his daughter as a burnt offering in return for victory over the Ammonites at about 1100 BC, and 2 Kings 3:27 tells of the king of Moab sacrificing his oldest son in the ninth century to secure victory over Israel.

Human sacrifice is well substantiated amongst the Phoenicians, and, as Tertullian and others recorded,[6] in the colonies in north Africa it was practised down to the Roman period.

Not all ancient numinous powers developed into anthropomorphic deities in historical times. Some remained as demons, and these played a considerable part in the beliefs of ordinary people, particularly in Mesopotamia. A mark of demons was their irrationality. Anthropomorphic gods could become enraged at mankind and punish him for particular types of activity, or might take offence at infringement of their rights, but this fell into the pattern of normal human reactions. But demons could show malevolence for no reason at all, other than their very nature. Thus, there was a she-demon, Lamashtu, who delighted in attacking inoffensive nursing mothers and babies: if not warded off by appropriate magic, she would slip in through a door socket to kill a baby.

The Egyptians and the Hittites likewise had their demons. Traces of demons, whose behaviour was characterized by irrational malevolence, are recognizable even in the Bible, despite the spurious orthodoxy in which pious later editors wrapped them. One comes in the story of Jacob crossing the ford of the Jabbok (Genesis 32:22–30). He had sent all his family across and then

> *Jacob was left alone; and there wrestled a man with him until the breaking of the day. And when he saw that he prevailed not against him, he touched the hollow of his thigh; and the hollow of Jacob's thigh was out of joint, as he wrestled with him. And he said, Let me go, for the day breaketh.*

Here we clearly have a troll who will not allow a stranger to cross his river; the demonic nature of Jacob's adversary is emphasized by the fact he only has power at night and must depart before the day breaks. The remainder of the story as told in the Bible is a reinterpretation to bring it superficially within the orbit of Yahwistic religion.

Another instance appears in Exodus 4:24–26 when Moses, having been commissioned by God, was on his way back to Egypt. A demon (who has become Yahweh in the final version of the narrative) suddenly came at Moses at night and for no reason at all tried to kill him, but was foiled by quick thinking on the part of Moses' Midianite wife.

Monotheistic tendencies

We have seen that the huge pantheons of ancient Mesopotamia and Egypt were secondary developments, produced by integrating a number of local pantheons that were originally distinct. Within any region, the original local pantheons had arisen from very similar backgrounds, and therefore in many cases the supernatural powers worshipped (the numen behind the storm, the corn, the sun, etc), differed in little more than name. It was thus easy in later periods to recognize the identity of such deities, and we find, both in Egypt and Mesopotamia, texts which explicitly state that deity A of one city is deity B of another. For example, at the end of the myth describing the defeat of the theriomorphic Anzu by Ninurta (really Anzu's later anthropomorphic form), we read

> *O Ninurta! . . . You have made all enemies submit to the feet of your father Enlil;*
> *You have gained possession of lordship, the totality of the established order. . . .*
> *Shrines with the gods of destinies are bestowed on you. . . .*
> *They gave your name in Elam as 'Hurabtil',*
> *In Susa they call you 'Shushinak'. . . .*
> *They gave your name as 'Pabilsag' in the temple Egalmah. . . .*
> *They gave your name as 'Ninazu' in the temple Ekurmah.*[7]

This tendency to syncretism, operative both in Egypt and Mesopotamia since the third millennium, became very marked in first-millennium Mesopotamia, and was a factor in a movement (never completely realized) in the direction of monotheism. One consequence was a breakdown in the delimitation of functions and personality between deities, so that, for example, Marduk in Babylonia and Ashur in Assyria took over the functions and titles of Enlil. In turn the god Nabu, formally the son of Marduk, came to be addressed with epithets which properly belonged to Marduk himself, so that Nabu, who was not in origin a Creator-god, was now said to create all mankind. An inscription which reads: 'Trust in Nabu, trust not in another god' gives a very clear indication of the crumbling of the old polytheism and a movement in the direction of monolatry. The most explicit evidence of this monotheistic trend in Mesopotamia comes in a first-millennium hymn which specifically states that a number of the great gods are simply hypostases of the god Ninurta:

> *Your two eyes, O Lord, are Enlil and Ninlil;*
> *Your two lips are Anu and Antu;*
> *Your head is Adad, who made heaven and earth, . . .*
> *Your brow is Shala, his beloved spouse, who rejoices the heart;*
> *Your neck is Marduk . . .*

Corresponding syncretistic trends leading in the direction of monotheism can be seen in Egyptian religion, as for example in two hymns to the Creator-god Khnum, dating in their present form to the Roman period but containing older material, which identify Khnum with ten or more other named deities.[8] Such syncretism could extend outside the Egyptian pantheon to the religions of other peoples, so that, for example, in the late second millennium the god Seth was identified with Baal of the West Semitic world (well known from the Bible), and also with Hurrian and Hittite Storm-gods.

Usually these movements towards monotheism within ancient religions were gradual developments. We see this even in Israelite religion, where several distinct patriarchal deities gradually merged into one, a fact usually obscured by the false assumption of the average reader, relying on translations, that such a deity as 'God Most High' (Genesis 14:18) had always been another name for Yahweh. But there are one or two instances of deliberate attempts at reform of the pantheon. The best known is that associated with the Egyptian king Amenophis IV (1365–1349 BC), otherwise known as Akhenaten, who attempted (in the long run unsuccessfully) to introduce a quasi-monotheistic cult of the sun-disk Aten.

Another instance of a deliberate attempt at religious reform came in Mesopotamia at the end of the New Babylonian empire (towards 540 BC), when king Nabonidus introduced certain religious changes, attested both from alterations in temple architecture and from texts. The texts, written to defend the vested interests of the Babylonian establishment, condemned Nabonidus for instituting a heretical cult of the Moon-god Sin, and when his kingdom was attacked by Cyrus the Persian, the opponents of Nabonidus hailed the invader as a deliverer.[9]

Myths

The writings of all the ancient literate civilizations abound in myths. Myth was a way of making the world make sense. The primeval world was a strange, often unpredictable and frightening place: ancient peoples wanted to know where they were, how they came to be there, and why. Above all, they wanted assurance of stability. Myth gave them those answers, and that assurance.

Assurance of a stable world depends first upon the answer to the basic question: how did the world begin? Ancient Egypt had several creation myths; they were basically similar in their psychology, but, because they were associated with different major settlements, they differed in detail. Any account of creation has to start with something pre-existent, if only empty space; the ancient Egyptians started (as did the Mesopotamians) with the waters of chaos; the Egyptians named them Nun. Sometimes the idea of formlessness and non-existence was given a sharper point by the mention, alongside the primeval waters, of boundless space (Huh), darkness (Kuk) and the Hidden (Amun). At a more sophisticated stage, each of the four principles became divided into a male and female aspect.

Out of the waters of chaos arose the primeval hill; this was a reflection in myth of the hillocks which appear each year as the Nile flood subsides. In the commonest form of the story, the Sun-god Atum was sitting on this hill. He then produced other divine beings out of himself, either by spitting or by masturbation. Although from our modern viewpoint, it is more grotesque than edifying to imagine the primeval god sitting all alone on a hill surrounded by water, quietly masturbating, this was not absurd to the earliest Egyptians. Conscious that life could only stem from life, they could envisage no way of passing on the life-force from the first god, except by his semen or his spittle. But before the end of Egyptian civilization, the Egyptians themselves found a better solution.

The better solution comes in a work commonly called the Memphite Theology, inscribed on a stone monument. The Memphite Theology as we have it was written in about 710 BC at the orders of a king of Ethiopian origin named Shabaka, who claimed it was copied from an old worn-out papyrus. Egyptologists long accepted Shabaka's claim, which is credible because the text is written in an archaic form of Egyptian. But now some egyptologists have seen reasons to regard the Memphite Theology as a deliberate forgery, written in archaic language to pass off the fraud.[10]

The Memphite Theology regards not only all other deities, but also men and animals, as owing their continued existence to the creative power of the mind of Ptah, the god of Memphis:

He is in every body and every mouth of all gods, all men, all cattle, all creeping things, and everything that lives.

That is, Ptah is not only a primeval creator-god but is immanent in all life, as the force of continuing creation. This seems to come close to the concept of the Holy Spirit:

O strength and stay, upholding all creation, who ever dost thyself unmoved abide (English Hymnal, 271).

Creation was accomplished by the creative thought and word of Ptah:

The whole divine order came into being through what the heart thought and the tongue commanded.

This is an indisputable foreshadowing of the Logos doctrine of Neo-Platonic Christianity.

The Memphite Theology primarily concerns the relationship between certain deities. If it were a genuine very early work, it could represent an attempt to resolve the theological problem which arose when Memphis, formerly a very minor site, became capital at the beginning of the third millennium, and the major gods and their activity in creation had to be linked with upstart Memphis. The original local creator-god of Memphis bore the name Ta-Tenen, meaning 'the raised land', an obvious reflection of the concept that the world began with a hillock rising from the primeval waters. Ptah was the anthropomorphic form of the god of Memphis, and through his identity with the older Ta-Tenen, Ptah could be seen as himself the primeval waters. This allowed Ptah to be identified with Atum and all the other major divine beings in the Egyptian pantheon.

But this will not serve if the Memphite Theology is a composition not of the third but of the first millennium. At that late date, it could not have marked the origin of new divine relationships; it could only reflect the existence of ancient ones. It could then be a commentary to explain a cult drama, rather like the script of a mediaeval mystery play, in which scenes from ancient myths were enacted. Such a view fits very well with the form of the work, which is certainly not a continuous treatise, but has three main types of material—narrative describing activities in the realm of myth; dialogues; and what one might call rubrics or stage directions. A brief extract will demonstrate this:

[Narrative]. *[The primeval earth-god Geb] gave judgement between Horus and Seth. . . . He appointed Seth king of Upper Egypt in the land of Upper Egypt. . . . And Geb appointed Horus king of Lower Egypt in the land of Lower Egypt, where his father was drowned. . . . Horus stood over one region and Seth over the other. They made peace about the Two Lands.*
[Dialogue]. *Words of Geb to Seth: 'Go to the place where you were born.'*
[Rubric]. *Seth: Upper Egypt.*
[Dialogue]. *Words of Geb to Horus: 'Go to the place where your father was drowned.'*
[Rubric]. *Horus: Lower Egypt.*
[Dialogue]. *Words of Geb to Horus and Seth: 'I have made a decision between you.'*
[Rubric]. *Lower and Upper Egypt.*

The narrative goes on to record that Geb subsequently changed his mind and gave the entire land of Egypt to Horus, and the text then says: 'Reed and papyrus were placed at the great door of the House of Ptah.' Reed and papyrus plants symbolized Upper and Lower Egypt respectively, and so this was a mythological way of expressing two truths: firstly, that Upper and Lower Egypt became united at Memphis, Ptah's town; and secondly, that Ptah subsumed the two gods Seth and Horus.

The Mesopotamians, Hittites and other peoples of the ancient Near East also had their myths of origin. The best known from Mesopotamia, but by no means the oldest, is the so-called Epic of Creation, which was recited at the New Year Festival in Babylon in the first millennium.

At the outset nothing existed, not heaven, not earth, nothing but primordial Apsu, the sweet waters 'their progenitor', and Tiamat the waters of ocean, who bore the epithet 'she who gave birth to them all'. As Apsu and Tiamat mingled their waters life appeared, just as the earliest dwellers of south Mesopotamia saw the teeming reed banks appear where the Euphrates and Tigris empty their waters into the salt sea of the Persian Gulf. A series of life forms ensued, culminating in the pantheon of historical times. These restless new beings disturbed the calm of the ancient ones and conflict arose. The god Ea bound Apsu and made his abode in the sweet waters. There a supergod Marduk was born to him and his spouse. Finally the longsuffering Tiamat herself was roused to act against her tumultuous divine spawn. For battle against these she created a series of monsters. No god but the young Marduk dared face her, and, as his condition for serving as the champion of the gods, he required the older deities to make over to him all their powers.

Marduk defeated Tiamat and from her body created heaven and earth. He set up the constellations and their annual motions, defined the path of Jupiter, set the moon in place with its patterns of waxing and waning and movement in relation to the sun. Then from the blood of the divine being whom Tiamat had made her leader in battle, Marduk, assisted by the creator-god Ea, created man, to perform the service of the gods. In gratitude to Marduk, the gods then built him a city, Babylon, with its towering ziggurat Esagila, 'House of the raised head' (see plate 14B). Finally the epic enumerates the 50 names of Marduk.

This epic subsumed many older myths, and thereby it served to give the Babylonians assurance on many planes. Man has concern for the continued existence of his world, for life itself, for his own place in the scheme of things, for the physical environment, for the seasons, for human institutions, for the political framework of life. The Epic of Creation, which at the New Year Festival each year recounted how the established order arose through Marduk's victory, provided reassurance of the unchanging continuance of the world as the Babylonians knew it. The old primordial forces were still there to maintain the universe, but with their destructive elements bound and their kindly aspect harnessed for man's benefit, Apsu in the form of the benevolent god Ea and Tiamat as Marduk himself. The course of the changing month and year was fixed for ever by the moon and stars. Man's own place was assured, for was he not created for the service of the gods? And Babylon itself and its cults and institutions stood, splendid and eternal, the creation of the gods themselves.

All ancient myths developed to resolve some problem, but it was not always a problem of ultimate origins. A myth might provide reassurance against threatened disaster, or explain some mysterious aspect of life, or resolve tensions in society, or reconcile different levels of religious thought. Often fragments of myths were linked to magical rituals: if one knew through myth the cause of a threat to ordered life, one could use magical rituals to avert it. Thus, it was alarming to see the moon disappearing during an eclipse, and the alarm of the community would manifest itself in rituals to save the moon. But what was really happening? Early man found that these rituals never failed, and he rationalized this by thinking up an explanation which gave him reassurance: in an eclipse the moon was being swallowed by demons, but his magical rituals would always drive the demons away.

The Hittites also had their myths. A number of these were found at Boghazkoi, the site of the old Hittite capital Hattushash over ninety miles east of Ankara. Some go back to the proto-Hattic peoples, and at least one was borrowed from the west Semites, but the major source was the Hurrians, who were also the intermediary for some from Mesopotamia. The Hittite myths of origin contain the same theme of combat with a primordial monster as in Mesopotamia, but the characteristic difference is the prominence given to Storm-gods and mountains, a reflection of the way in which geography shaped the details of mythology. Themes in some of these myths were eventually diffused westwards and entered Greek mythology; a clear example is the theme of a son castrating his father, which occurs in the Hittite Kumarbi myth and again in the Greek myth of Kronos and Ouranos; its ultimate source may be a very obscure Babylonian myth, the *Myth of Harab*, in which a whole series of gods each deposes and kills (but does not castrate) his father, and then incestuously take as wife his own mother.[11]

Ancient religion in practice

Man's interest in the forces and beings of the supernatural world went beyond theological speculation: it had a practical concern. Believing in supernatural forces which acted in a way to affect mankind, man sought ways to make them act to his advantage. The measures he took ranged from coercion—the function of magic—through ingratiation by offerings to humble entreaty in prayer and self-abasement. All these techniques became institutionalized, and everywhere the cult came to include a mixture of magical incantations, offerings, sacrifices and libations, hymns and prayers.

It was the divine powers who maintained the norms upon which all life depended. It was the function of the cult to ensure that man did his part so that the divine powers would continue to do theirs. As anthropomorphic deities developed, they needed provision for their human needs. A dwelling place was essential, in a form appropriate to the nature of the god, and changes in the way of life of the worshippers could alter the god's preferences in this respect. The Israelites, who settled in Palestine after a period of nomadism, provide a good example of this. Yahweh, like his people, had earlier chosen to live in a tent, and when king David proposed to build him a house, he (or conservative elements amongst his worshippers) at first demurred:

> Go and tell my servant David, Thus saith the Lord, Shalt thou build me an house for me to dwell in? Whereas I have not dwelt in any house since the time that I brought up the children of Israel out of Egypt, even to this day, but have walked in a tent and in a tabernacle. . . . Spake I a word with any of the tribes of Israel, . . . saying, Why build ye not me an house of cedar? (2 Samuel 7:5–7).

But the opposition was overcome, and a temple was built for Yahweh at Jerusalem soon after 1000 BC. Mesopotamia and Egypt had had temples for their gods since before history, at first modest little single-roomed shrines, which developed during the third and second millennia into wealthy complexes of great splendour with large staffs.

Anthropomorphic deities required not only houses but also food. We see this again in Israelite religion, where food offerings for Yahweh were decreed at an early period, to be challenged by the prophetic movement in the first millennium. In Mesopotamia and Egypt food offerings to the gods were highly organized, and of such huge quantities that they could become an economic burden upon the community. Food offerings were also a part, but only a part, of the many festivals that had to be celebrated, some monthly, some annually, some at longer intervals.

In all the ancient cultures, the dead became a part of the supernatural world, able to affect their successors for good or ill. They too became the recipients of food offerings from their families, although with considerable differences between the practices of different peoples. Condemnatory allusions by the prophets show that traces of the practice continued in Israel, despite official disfavour, until well into the first millennium, and offerings to the dead were also a part of popular religion in Mesopotamia and amongst the Canaanites. But it was at its most prominent in Egypt, where many tombs were in fact mortuary chapels. Families which could afford to do so would make an endowment for a priest and his descendants in perpetuity to provide tomb-offerings, celebrate festivals and recite the appropriate formulae for the benefit of the dead person. Art in tombs was intended to provide a magical continuation of the life of this world for the benefit of the deceased, and commonly shows all the operations and processes that went on on the dead man's estate (plate 9). This concern for the dead was not mere abstract piety. The dead were believed to have supernatural powers, and letters were often written to the dead. We find a letter of this kind with an appeal to a dead parent for male offspring, and a female figurine in a Middle Kingdom tomb is inscribed in ink with a request that a named daughter of the dead man might bear a child.[12]

Some modern religious sects, particularly within Protestantism, identify themselves with a particular strict moral code, and to offend grossly against such a code puts a person, in the view of some believers, outside the pale of that sect. No ancient religion was identified with a particular ethical system in that sense. Standards of conduct existed, but they were not a manifestation of religious edicts; rather, they arose out of the interaction of humans in society. In time, it became generally assumed (although occasionally questioned) that the standards of conduct accepted by human communities were the standards which the gods approved. Thereby certain aspects of behaviour became thought of as pleasing to the gods, and others as deserving their censure.

It might appear that with such a development a specific ethical code had attached itself to the religion. But the matter is not quite so simple. We do find long lists of sins which might bring affliction upon an offender, but these are not exclusively ethical lists. Commonly one finds ethical offences, ritual offences, and breaches of taboo, even accidental ones, all on the same level. We have, for example, a collection of Babylonian incantations called *Shurpu*, for use in the case of a man who wished to know the reason for which he was troubled by sickness or misfortune.[13] Part of the text goes through a list of possible offences in the form following:

> *So-and-so, son of so-and-so, whose (personal) god is so-and-so, whose (personal) goddess is so-and-so, who is . . . sick, in danger (of death), distraught, troubled,*
> > *who has eaten what is taboo to his god,*
> > *who has eaten what is taboo to his goddess,*
> > *who has said 'no' for 'yes' and 'yes' for 'no', . . .*
> > *who scorned his god, despised his goddess, . . .*
> > *who caused the judge to pronounce false judgement,*
> > *who oppressed the weak woman,*
> > *who estranged son from father, father from son, daughter from mother, mother from daughter, mother-in-law from daughter-in-law, daughter-in-law from mother-in-law, brother from brother, friend from friend, . . .*
> > *who despised his parents, offended his elder sister,*
> > *who gave with small measure and received with big measure, . . .*

who had intercourse with his neighbour's wife,
who shed his neighbour's blood.

Except for the first two lines, all these matters are ethical. But after this we find as further possible causes for the sufferer's troubles, that he may have been one who

went towards a person under a curse, . . .
slept in the bed of a person under a curse,
sat in the chair of a person under a curse, . . .
drank from the cup of a person under a curse.

These final matters are neither ethical nor ritual; they were simply accidental, involuntary and unknowing involvement in someone else's curse.

The manner of dealing with these troubles is significant. Whether it was a deliberate ethical offence like sleeping with one's neighbour's wife, or accidental contamination from contact with a person under a curse, the treatment was never repentance but always magic. After the texts quoted above, the priest-magician used rites introduced by the following rubric:

Take him to the pure ablution house,
Undo his spell, release his spell,
That the disturbing evil of his body—whether a curse of his father, or a curse of his mother, or a curse of his elder brother, . . . by pronouncing the incantation of Ea the spell may be peeled off like this onion, stripped off like these dates, unravelled like this matting. Spell, verily you are adjured by the name of heaven, by the name of earth.

Then follows the incantation:

Like this onion which he peels and casts into the fire, where the flame consumes it utterly, . . . so let oath, spell, . . . sickness, hardship, guilt, transgression, sin, fault . . . be peeled off like this onion, let fire consume it utterly today, may the spell depart so that I may see the light.

Egypt demonstrates a very similar connection between religion and ethics. The Egyptians had collections of spells to be inscribed in tombs and on coffins, intended for the use of the dead man in the afterworld, where he had to make a negative confession before the divine judges. The negative confession was a claim not to have committed various offences. For example:

I have not done evil to men,
I have not mistreated cattle, . . .
I have not blasphemed a god,

I have not despoiled the poor,
I have not broken a god's taboo,
I have not defamed a slave to his master,
I have not caused pain or tears,
I have not killed nor ordered anyone to kill.[14]

But once again, this was not a true incorporation of an ethical system into religion. The tomb ritual, and the recitation of the spells, served by themselves to protect the dead man at the ordeal after death, whether or not he had actually done those things. This is quite clear from the rubric at the head of the chapter, which introduces the negative confession as 'to be uttered . . . in order to purge the man of any sins committed'; it was the spells which were important, not the man's actual conduct.

The ancient civilizations produced texts which show an alternative approach to the problem of the good life; rather than seeking magical absolution of activities possibly offensive to the gods, texts of this class, generally known as Wisdom Literature, at their simplest offered precepts for dealing with the circumstances one may encounter in life, and at their most sophisticated presented a quasi-philosophical treatment of the problem of evil in the manner (although never matching the genius) of the biblical Book of Job.

In Egypt such texts appear as early as the third millennium in the form of Instructions by a prince or vizier to his son, or by a sage to a vizier. The following illustrative extracts come from the *Instruction of Ptahhotep*,[15] probably of Sixth Dynasty date. Ptahhotep, an otherwise unknown vizier, is presented as instructing his son

Do not be arrogant about your learning;
Consult the ignorant as well as the wise.

If you are a man of substance,
And get a son by god's grace,
If he does right and follows you,
And looks after your property aright,
Do eveything good for him. . . .
But if he misbehaves and disregards your command,
And defies everything that is said,
And his mouth utters evil things,
Punish him for all his idle talk.

Beware of the vice of covetousness;
It is a nasty incurable disease. . . .
It separates man and wife;

It is a batch of all kinds of evils,
And a bag of everything discreditable.

The precepts of Ptahhotep amount in total to over 360 lines. They are characterized throughout by a spirit of commonsense and an almost total absence of reference to divine sanctions; although five or six passages speak of prosperity as a gift from god, there is only one which could be taken as a positive statement that the gods punish illdoing. The second-millennium vizier Rekhmire^c (p. 29) gave an account of what he considered decent conduct, with no hint that it was buttressed by fear of divine wrath:

> *I saved the weak man from the strong man; . . . I gave support to the widow; . . . I set up the son and heir in his father's place. I fed the hungry, gave drink to the thirsty. . . . I took no bribes.*

This detachment from the idea of divine sanctions as the ultimate basis of right action is characteristic of Egyptian and Mesopotamian and (with the exception of parts of the Book of Job) Israelite Wisdom Literature. It is true that there are occasional references to the likelihood of a god requiting ill conduct with evil, but these are no more than incidental, no more than lip-service to the conventional view, and not only do these texts not regularly hold up the threat of divine retribution as the basis for right conduct, but they sometimes run against that idea head-on.

A Babylonian collection of precepts, probably of second-millennium origin, demonstrates the ideal of good behaviour as based on humanity and commonsense, largely divorced from threats of the supernatural. For example:

> *Do not do evil to one who has a dispute with you;*
> *Return good to one who does evil to you.*
> *Maintain justice for one who is bad to you;*
> *Be pleasant to your enemy.*

> *Do not utter slander; speak well of people.*
> *Do not say nasty things; speak favourably.*

Two works of religious philosophy are instructive for the Babylonian view of the good life.[16] One, commonly known as *The Poem of the Righteous Sufferer*, explores the same theme as the biblical Book of Job, the problem of the suffering that can hit a person undeservedly. The work, in verse and extending to about 500 lines, probably originated in the late second millennium. It begins with a hymn which, by juxtaposing lines which speak alternatively of the deity's harshness and his clemency, brings out the unpredictable nature of the divine powers. Thus:

> *His lashes are barbed, they tear the body;*
> *His bandaging soothes, it brings life to the doomed.*

In the remainder of the composition a pious Babylonian nobleman tells how the gods and his king deserted him, so that he became an outcast. He goes over his past conduct and finds that it has always been exemplary, and is driven to conclude that it is impossible to know what is pleasing to the gods:

> *O that I knew that these things found favour with the god.*
> *What is good to oneself is an insult to the god;*
> *What is disgusting in a man's own heart is good to the god.*
> *Who knows the will of the gods in the midst of heaven?*

A long description follows of the sufferer's affliction and despair. Finally he was restored to prosperity by the mercy of the god Marduk. The whole tendency of the work is to reject the common view that prosperity and adversity are the automatic divine reward or punishment for good or bad conduct; it is impossible to know the divine will as to right and wrong, and all one can do it to have faith in the divine mercy.

There is a second Babylonian work which examines the connection between conduct and prosperity or adversity; it is generally referred to as *The Babylonian Theodicy*. It takes the form of a dialogue between a sufferer and his friend, with the sufferer giving instances to show that there is no connection between conduct and the lot which befalls a man, and the friend continually restating the conventional view that in the end the gods will reward the pious and punish the wicked. The work is an elegant literary composition, with each speech consisting of 11 lines all beginning with the same syllable, and the succession of syllables yielding a sentence which names the author. In each speech the sufferer or friend gives a courteous acknowledgement of the case the other has just made, and then presents the counter argument. In the following extracts, for reasons of space only the key arguments are quoted:

Friend: *He who is attentive to the god has a guardian angel,*
The reverent man who fears the goddess heaps up abundance.
Sufferer: *[says that his friend's arguments do not cover his case]*
My form is overwhelmed, want overshadows me,
My luck has passed me by, my importance has gone; . . .
The food from my meadows is far from satisfying me,
My wine, the life of mankind, is too little for subsistence.
Friend: *[repeats that piety will bring divine favour]*
Sufferer: *[gives instances of prosperity which was not the fruit of piety and of his own piety not rewarded by divine favour]*

The savage lion who devours the choicest meat,
Did it bring a food offering to appease the wrath of the goddess?
The parvenu whose wealth has multiplied for him,
Did he weigh out precious gold for the goddess Mami?
Have I withheld offerings? I have prayed to the god,
I have dedicated regular offerings to the goddess.
Friend: *[argues that divine retribution will come in time]*
Now consider the lion that you mentioned, the enemy of the cattle;
For the crime which the lion committed the pit-trap awaits him.
The man of position who has piled up treasures,
The ruler will burn him in the fire on a day unforeseen.
Sufferer: *[says this is not his experience]*
They who do not seek the god go the way of prosperity;
They who pray to the goddess, fall into poverty and weakness.
In my tender years I sought the will of the god,
With abasement and prayer I followed my goddess;
It was a profitless task which I bore as a yoke,
For the god set poverty for me instead of riches.
A cripple gets ahead of me, a fool is in front of me;
The rogue is promoted; I am brought low.

And so the discussion continues, with the friend always pressing the conventional view that the key to prosperity is piety, and the sufferer denying the connection, with instances to show the arbitrariness of the incidence of the good and bad things of life.

Indisputably, before the end of the second millennium, there were those in Babylonia whose experience of life made them unable to accept the comfortable old belief that the gods rewarded virtue and punished vice, and led them to begin to seek solutions outside the cultic framework of polytheistic religion. They had begun to ask questions which myth could not answer.

Those who had begun to think over the problems of life in this non-mythological way were of course only a tiny segment of the population. A man like the author of the *Babylonian Theodicy*, who could not only set out a considered criticism of the view on which his civilization was based, but also do it in the form of an elaborate acrostic poem, was an exceptionally endowed man. But the presence of such men in the community, and of those in the scribal schools who read and copied and re-copied such works, was a leaven, which gradually—not in a few years or decades but over centuries—began to erode the old mythological verities, and to prepare the Near Eastern world to receive the new ways of thought about the world and man's place in it, which were to come from Greece.

References

Abbreviations

A.E.L.   M. Lichtheim, *Ancient Egyptian Literature*, 3 vols. (Univ. of California Press, 1975–80)

A.N.E.T.   J. B. Pritchard, (ed.) *Ancient Near Eastern Tests,* (3rd edition, Princeton, 1969)

A.R.   J. H. Breasted, *Ancient Records of Egypt*, 5 vols. (Chicago, 1906–7)

A.R.I.   A. K. Grayson, *Assyrian Royal Inscriptions*, 2 vols. (Wiesbaden, 1972, 1976)

E.A.   J. A. Knudtzon, *Die El-Amarna-Tafeln* (Leipzig, 1915); English edition by S. A. B. Mercer, *The Tell El-Amarna Tablets* (Toronto, 1939)

E.P.   Sir Alan Gardiner, *Egypt of the Pharaohs* (Oxford, 1961)

G.B.   H. W. F. Saggs, *The Greatness that was Babylon* (2nd edition, London, 1988)

J.A.O.S.   *Journal of the American Oriental Society*

J.C.S.   *Journal of Cuneiform Studies*

J.N.E.S.   *Journal of Near Eastern Studies*

M.A.   H. W. F. Saggs, *The Might that was Assyria* (London, 1984)

O.P. II   D. D. Luckenbill, *The Annals of Sennacherib* (= Oriental Institute Publications, vol. II; Chicago, 1924)

P.R.U. III J. Nougayrol, *Le palais royal d'Ugarit* vol. III (Paris, 1955)

P.R.U. IV   J. Nougayrol, *Le palais royal d'Ugarit* vol. IV (Paris, 1956)

1 Pushing back the Frontiers (pages 1–20)

1   *Voyage dans la basse et la haute Égypte*, 2 vols. (Paris, 1802).

2   Later extended to 31; see *E.P.* pp. 46f, 429–53.

3   Egyptian chronology in this book is based on the system in J. von Beckerath, *Abriss der Geschichte des Alten Ägypten* (Munich, 1971).

4   Austen Henry Layard, *Nineveh and its Remains*, 2 vols. (London, 1849); abridged edition edited by H. W. F. Saggs (London, 1970).

5   Standard edition by J. A. Knudtzon, *Die El-Amarna-Tafeln* (Leipzig, 1915). There is an English edition by S. A. B. Mercer, *The Tell El-Amarna Tablets* (Toronto, 1939).

6   Strabo, *Geography*, xv.1.19.
7   For arguments against this identification see D. P. Agrawal, *The Archaeology of India* (Curzon Press, London, 1982), p. 182.
8   *A.R.I.* vol. 2, pp. 137–40.
9   Herodotus, *History*, iii.106–11; Pliny, *Natural History*, xii.63.

2 City-states and Kingdoms (pages 21–46)

1   See K. W. Butzer, 'Perspectives on irrigation civilization in Pharaonic Egypt', pp. 13–18 in D. Schmandt-Besserat (ed.), *Immortal Egypt* (Malibu, 1978), and R. M. Adams, 'Developmental Stages in ancient Mesopotamia', pp. 6–18 in *Irrigation Civilizations: a Comparative Study* (Pan American Union, Washington, D.C., 1955).
2   Herodotus, *History*, ii.99.
3   Klaus Baer, *Rank and Title in the Old Kingdom* (Chicago, 1960). For later research on similar lines see N. Kanawati, *The Egyptian Administration in the Old Kingdom* (1977), N. Kanawati, *Governmental Reforms in Old Kingdom Egypt* (Warminster, 1980), W. A. Ward, *Index of Egyptian Administrative and Religious Titles of the Middle Kingdom* (Beirut, 1982), N. Strudwick, *The Administration of Egypt in the Old Kingdom* (London, 1985).
4   See N. de G. Davies, *The Tomb of Rekh-mi-reᶜ at Thebes* (1943).
5   On this question see *G.B.*, pp. 11ff.
6   See Th. Jacobsen, 'Primitive Democracy in Ancient Mesopotamia', pp. 157–70 in W. L. Moran (ed.), *Towards the Image of Tammuz* (Harvard, 1970).
7   A. Snodgrass, *Archaic Greece* (1980), pp. 31f.
8   *Gilgamesh and Akka* [or *Agga*]. See, for translation, *A.N.E.T.*, pp. 44–7, and for most recent edition, W. H. P. Römer, *Das sumerische Kurzepos «Bilgames und Akka»* (Kevelaer, 1980).
9   *Lamentation over the Destruction of Ur*. For translation and bibliography see *A.N.E.T.*, pp. 455ff.
10   Th. Jacobsen, *The Sumerian King List* (Chicago, 1939).
11   I. M. Diakonoff, *Structure of Society and State in Early Dynastic Sumer* (Los Angeles, 1974), pp. 6f.
12   Barbara Cummings, *Egyptian Historical Records of the later Eighteenth Dynasty*, fasc. 1 (Warminster, 1982), p. 32.

3 Pyramids and Ziggurats (pages 47–61)

1   K. W. Butzer, 'Perspectives on irrigation civilization in Pharaonic Egypt', pp. 13–18 in D. Schmandt-Besserat (ed.), *Immortal Egypt* (Malibu, 1978).
2   K. W. Butzer, op. cit., p. 15.
3   Diodorus Siculus, ii.10; Strabo, *Geography*, xvi.i.5–7.
4   *The Voyages and Travels of Sir John Maundeville, K*ᵗ (Cassell, London, 1909), pp. 38f.
5   For a detailed study of surviving obelisks outside Egypt see E. Iversen, *Obelisks in Exile*, vols. 1 and 2 (Copenhagen, 1968, 1972).

4 Writing (pages 62–97)

1 D. Schmandt-Besserat, *An Archaic Recording System and the Origin of Writing* (Malibu, 1977).

2 The term 'ideogram', meaning 'a sign by which an idea is written', has become generally superseded in assyriological circles by 'logogram' ('a sign by which a word is written') since Adam Falkenstein criticized its use, but its appropriateness for early writing has been defended by I. M. Diakonoff, 'Ancient Writing and Ancient Written Language: Pitfalls and Peculiarities in the Study of Sumerian', pp. 109f. in S. J. Lieberman (ed.), *Sumerological Studies in Honor of Thorkild Jacobsen* (Chicago, 1975).

3 The chronology of the Indus Valley civilization remains in dispute; see D. P. Agrawal, *The Archaeology of India* (Curzon Press, London, 1982), pp. 182–8.

4 See J. T. Hooker, *Linear B: An Introduction* (Bristol, 1980), pp. 19f.

5 G. L. Windfuhr, 'The cuneiform signs of Ugarit', *J.N.E.S.* vol. 29 (1970), pp. 48–51.

6 W. F. Albright, *The Proto-Sinaitic Inscriptions and their Decipherment* (Cambridge, Mass., 1966). A. van den Branden, 'Nouvel essai du déchiffrement des inscriptions sinaïtiques', *Bibbia e Oriente* (Milan) vol. 21 (1979), pp. 155–251.

7 W. F. Albright, op. cit., no. 352.

8 But see the argument on p. 87 about the limited relevance of the direction of writing.

9 Herodotus, *History*, v.58.

10 Diodorus Siculus, III.66.4–67.1.

11 Pliny, *Natural History*, VII.lvi.192–3.

12 W. Johnstone, 'Cursive Phoenician and the Archaic Greek Alphabet', *Kadmos* vol. 17 (1978), pp. 156ff, 162f.

13 F. R. Vellutino, 'Dyslexia', *Scientific American* vol. 256/3 (March 1987), p. 20.

14 R. Mostowfi, 'Proto-Elamite signs on pottery from SE Iran', *Kadmos* vol. 16 (1977), p. 95.

5 Education (Pages 98–113)

1 *A.R.* vol. 1, §§170–5.

2 Diodorus Siculus, 1.81.

3 For translation and commentary see *A.E.L.* vol. 1, pp. 61ff.

4 See R. J. Williams, 'Scribal training in ancient Egypt', *J.A.O.S.* vol. 92 (1972), pp. 214–21.

5 For translation and commentary see *A.E.L.* vol. 1, pp. 184–92.

6 B. Landsberger, 'The third tablet of the series Ea A Nâqu', *J.A.O.S.* vol. 88 (1968), p. 138.

7 See S. N. Kramer, *The Sumerians* (Chicago, 1963), pp. 237ff.

6 Living in Cities (pages 114–127)

1 J. A. Wilson, *The Culture of Ancient Egypt* (Chicago, 1951), p. 34; B. J. Kemp, 'The early development of towns in Egypt', *Antiquity* vol. 51 (1977), p. 192.

2 H. W. Fairman, *Town Planning Review* vol. 20 (1950), p. 35.

3 H. W. Fairman, op. cit., pp. 43f., 46.
4 H. W. Fairman, op. cit., p. 35. But note statement of the most recent excavator, S. Garfi in B. J. Kemp, *Amarna Reports III* (1985), p. 90, that 'the extent of overall town planning at Amarna was very limited'.
5 J. G. Shaffer, p. 46 in G. L. Possehl (ed.), *Harappan Civilization; a contemporary perspective* (Warminster, 1982).
6 *A.E.L.* vol. 1, p. 20.
7 *O.P.* II, pp. 103ff.
8 See J. Johnston Abraham, *Surgeon's Journey* (London, 1957), p. 218).

7 Trade (pages 128–155)

1 See S. N. Kramer, *The Sumerians* (Chicago, 1963), pp. 269ff.
2 For bibliography and full translation see *A.N.E.T.*, pp. 72–99, 503–7.
3 *A.R.* vol. 1, §§ 429–33.
4 E. Porada, 'Remarks on the Tôd Treasure in Egypt', pp. 291, 297 in M. A. Dandamayev *et al.* (eds.), *Studies in Honour of I. M. Diakonoff* (Warminster, 1982).
5 For a good survey of all data and views on Tilmun (Dilmun), see Theresa Howard-Carter, 'Dilmun: at sea or not at sea?', *J.C.S.* vol. 39 (1987), pp. 54–115.
6 Literally: 'If you want to take it, take it! If you don't want to take it, go away!'
7 W. F. Leemans, *Foreign Trade in the Old Babylonian Period* (Leiden, 1960), pp. 39f.
8 *E.A.*, no. 6, lines 8–16.
9 *E.A.*, no. 5, lines 18–27.
10 *E.A.*, no. 7, lines 53–60, 63–72.
11 *E.A.*, no. 14.
12 *P.R.U.* IV, pp. 221f, no. 17.383, lines 1–5, 10–25, 27–30.
13 *P.R.U.* IV, p. 224, no. 17.422, lines 23–7.
14 *E.A.*, no. 27, lines 23–5, 32f.
15 *E.A.*, no. 35, line 14.
16 *E.A.*, no. 39, lines 14–20.
17 On the former wrong translation 'sesame', see page 217.
18 The distinguished Semitist, the late Father M. Dahood, suggested that the etymology of the name Carchemish was 'the trading centre of the god Kamish [biblical Chemosh]', reflecting its importance as a mercantile centre; see G. Pettinato, *The Archives of Ebla*, (1981), p. 307.
19 *P.R.U.* IV, p. 194, no. 17.385.
20 *P.R.U.* IV, pp. 103f, no. 17.130, lines 5–19.
21 *Odyssey*, XIV.280–313.
22 Dated much later by some scholars (see O. Eissfeldt, *The Old Testament* (Oxford, 1965), p. 323), but on the basis of invalid assumptions about Tyre and Sidon just before 700 BC.
23 Some scholars want to make part of this of post-Ezekiel date, but see references in O. Eissfeldt, op. cit., p. 96, no. 7.
24 Herodotus, *History*, IV.42.

8 Law (pages 156–175)

1 For comprehensive commentary and edition see G. R. Driver and J. C. Miles, *The Babylonian Laws*, 2 vols. (Oxford, 1952, 1955). For more recent translation with some improvements see A. Finet, *Le Code de Hammurapi* (2nd edition, Paris, 1983).

2 For bibliography and translation see *A.N.E.T.*, pp. 159–61. For most recent edition see E. Szlechter, *Les lois sumériennes. Le code d'Ur-Nammu; Le code de Lipit-Istar* (Rome, 1983). See also F. R. Kraus, *Königliche Verfügungen in altbabylonsicher Zeit* (Leiden, 1984).

3 For bibliography and translation see *A.N.E.T.*, pp. 523–5. For most recent edition see reference in preceding note.

4 For most recent edition see E. Szlechter, 'Les lois d'Eshnunna', *Revue internationale des droits de l'antiquité* vol. 25 (1978), pp. 109–219.

5 For bibliography and translation see *A.N.E.T.*, pp. 188–96.

6 For standard English edition and translation see G. R. Driver and J. C. Miles, *The Assyrian Laws* (Oxford, 1935; corrected reprint, Aalen, Germany, 1975). See also G. Cardascia, *Les lois Assyriennes* (Paris, 1969).

7 Diodorus Siculus, 1.75f.

8 See, e.g., pp. 5, 17, 53f. in D. Lorton, 'Treatment of Criminals in Ancient Egypt', *Journal of the Economic and Social History of the Orient*, vol. 20 (1977).

9 See *A.N.E.T.*, pp. 214ff.

10 Diodorus Siculus, III.5.

11 *P.R.U.* IV, pp. 126f., no. 17.159.

9 The Brotherhood of Nations (pages 176–194)

1 Ovid, *Metamorphoses, 1.89–100.*

2 J. S. Copper, *The Curse of Agade* (1983), p. 52, lines 45–9 and pp. 56 and 58, lines 155–8.

3 J. Klein, *The Royal Hymns of Shulgi King of Ur* (Philadelphia, 1981), p. 131.

4 For bibliography and translations see *A.N.E.T.*, pp. 199–203.

5 *P.R.U.* IV, p. 188, no. 17.292.

6 E. F. Weidner, *Politische Dokumente aus Kleinasien* (Leipzig, 1923), pp. 92 and 94, no. 7, Vs. 1, lines 41–3.

7 *E.A.*, no. 35, lines 35–42.

8 *P.R.U.* IV, p. 191, no. 17.247.

9 E. F. Weidner, *Politische Dokumente aus Kleinasien* (Leipzig, 1923), p. 108, no. 7, col. 4, lines 32–9.

10 *A.N.E.T.*, pp. 394f.

11 For fuller details see *G.B.*, pp. 125–9.

12 Barbara Cummings, *Egyptian Historical Records of the later Eighteenth Dynasty*, fasc. 1 (Warminster, 1982), p. 32.

13 *A.E.L.* vol. 1, p. 20.

14 *P.R.U.* IV, p. 193, no. 17.423.

15 *P.R.U.* III, p. 142, no. 16.136.

16 *E.A.*, no. 35, lines 30–4.

17 For translations see *A.N.E.T.*, pp. 18–22 and *A.E.L.*, vol. 1, pp. 222–35.

18   For definitive edition see H. Goedicke, *The Report of Wenamun* (Baltimore, 1975).

10 Natural Resources (pages 195–219)

1   Pliny, *Natural History*, VI.35.
2   Robert Graves, *The Greek Myths*, vol. 1 (Harmondsworth, 1955), p. 88.
3   M. McKerrell and R. F. Tylecote, 'The working of Copper-Arsenic Alloys in the Early Bronze Age', *Proceedings of the Prehistoric Society*, new series vol. 38 (1972), p. 212.
4   T. A. Wertime, pp. 1 and 4 in T. A. Wertime and J. D. Muhly (eds.), *The coming of the Age of Iron* (New Haven, 1980).
5   M. Ventris and J. Chadwick, *Documents in Mycenaean Greek* (2nd edition, Cambridge, 1973), pp. 252ff.
6   A. E. Harding, *The Mycenaeans and Europe* (Academic Press, 1984), p. 48.
7   M. Ventris and J. Chadwick, op. cit., p. 257.
8   J. D. Muhly, p. 65, note 135 in T. A. Wertime and J. D. Muhly (eds.), *The coming of the Age of Iron* (New Haven, 1980).
9   H. W. F. Saggs, *Iraq* vol. 30 (1968), p. 154ff.; *A.R.I.*, vol. 1, § 773; *A.R.I.* vol. 2, §§ 13f, 25f, 30, 38, 125, 43.
10 *A.R.I.* vol. 2, §§ 250, 364, 467, 474f.
11 See *G.B.*, p. 36 and pp. 462f., note 5.
12 Pliny, *Natural History*, XVII.9.

11 Mathematics and Astronomy (pages 220–239)

1   Strabo, *Geography*, XVII.806.
2   R. C. Thompson, *The Reports of the magicians and astrologers of Nineveh and Babylon*, 2 vols. [1 = cuneiform texts, 2 = translations] (London, 1900), nos. 273, 274.
3   For fuller details, see *G.B.*, pp. 412f.
4   See O. Neugebauer, *A History of Ancient Mathematical Astronomy*, part 1 (Springer-Verlag, New York, 1975).

12 Medicine (pages 240–260)

1   Herodotus, *History*, II.84 and I.197.
2   *E.A.*, no. 49.
3   The following owes much to P. Ghalioungui, *The Physicians of Pharaonic Egypt* (Cairo, 1983).
4   See E. Tapp, 'Disease and the Manchester Mummies', pp. 78–95 in R. David and E. Tapp (eds.), *Evidence Embalmed. Modern Medicine and the Mummies of Ancient Egypt* (Manchester, 1984), and A. and E. Cockburn (eds.), *Mummies, Disease and Ancient Cultures* (Cambridge, 1980).
5   F. Ll. Griffith, *The Petrie Papyri. Hieratic Papyri from Kahun* (London, 1898), pp. 6f.
6   E. Reiner, 'Babylonian Birth Prognoses', *Zeitschrift für Assyriologie* vol. 72 (1982), pp. 124–38.

7   A. Goetze, 'An Incantation against Diseases', *J.C.S.* vol. 9 (1955), pp. 8–18.

8   But such Babylonian and Assyrian medications were no more primitive and magical than some of the treatments in use by the Romans, as described by Pliny in *Natural History*, XXVIII–XXX.

9   P. Naster and L. Missotten, 'Der Augenarzt in den Gesetzen Hammurapis', *Archiv für Orientforschung*, Beiheft 19 (1982), pp. 317–24.

13 Ancient Religion (pages 267–301)

1   For the most recent edition of the myth see H. W. F. Saggs, 'Additions to Anzu', *Archiv für Orientforschung*, vol. 33 (1987), pp. 1–29.

2   *Scriptores Historiae Augustae*, IX.4–6.

3   On Hittite sun-deities see H. W. Haussig (ed.), *Wörterbuch der Mythologie*, vol. I/I (1965), pp. 196ff.

4   G. F. Dales, 'Sex and Stone at Mohenjo-daro', pp. 109–15 in B. B. Lal and S. P. Gupta (eds.), *Frontiers of the Indus Civilization* (New Delhi, 1984).

5   B. C. Trigger, *Journal of Egyptian Archaeology* vol. 55 (1969), pp. 122f.

6   Tertullian, *Apologeticus*, 9.2.

7   H. W. F. Saggs, *Archiv für Orientforschung* vol. 33 (1987), pp. 23–25.

8   *A.E.L.* vol. 3, pp. 110ff.

9   For fuller details see *G.B.*, pp. 133–39.

10   See *A.E.L.* vol. 3, p. 5.

11   Th. Jacobsen, 'The Harab Myth', *Sources from the Ancient Near East* vol. 2, fasc. 3 (Malibu, 1984), pp. 6–26.

12   E. Baumgartel, 'Tomb and Fertility', *Jahrbuch für kleinasiatische Forschung* vol. 1 (1950), p. 59.

13   For standard edition see E. Reiner, *Šurpu, a collection of Sumerian and Akkadian incantations* (Graz, 1958).

14   *A.E.L.* vol. 2, p. 125.

15   For translation and commentary see *A.E.L.* vol. 1, pp. 61ff.

16   See *G.B.* pp. 392ff., and for full translations W. G. Lambert, *Babylonian Wisdom Literature* (Oxford, 1960), pp. 21–91.

Select Bibliography

Research since the second World War has yielded so much new material, both archaeological and literary, that, although some earlier publications have enduring merits, the reader whose concern is accurate information will in most cases be best served by books of post-1960. Earlier publications are only mentioned if there is no adequate replacement.

The most heavyweight modern English work on the ancient history of Egypt and the Near East comprises the volumes of the revised edition of the *Cambridge Ancient History* (Cambridge University Press, 1970–). Particular periods of particular regions are treated in isolation by specialists, resulting in a great mass of authoritative but ill-integrated detail.

There are several good books covering the civilization of each of the principal areas. For Egypt, one of the best, although with perhaps a little too much emphasis on the political history, is Sir Alan Gardiner, *Egypt of the Pharaohs* (Clarendon Press, 1961). A more recent work, very readable and balanced as well as informative and authoritative, is T. G. H. James, *Pharaoh's People. Scenes from life in Imperial Egypt* (The Bodley Head, 1984). A very important general work, of which the emphasis is indicated by the title, is J. R. Harris (ed.), *The Legacy of Egypt* (2nd edition, Clarendon Press, 1971).

The achievements of the Sumerians of third-millennium Mesopotamia are well covered in S. N. Kramer, *The Sumerians; their History, Culture and Character* (University of Chicago Press, 1963). Amongst books which aim to give a picture of the main features of ancient Mesopotamian society as a whole may be mentioned H. W. F. Saggs, *The Greatness that was Babylon* (Sidgwick & Jackson, 1962, revised edition, 1988), and A. L. Oppenheim, *Ancient Mesopotamia; Portrait of a Dead Civilization* (University of Chicago Press, 1964, revised edition, completed by E. Reiner, 1977); the latter gives particular emphasis to the achievements of the scribal class. For Assyrian history and civilization there is H. W. F. Saggs, *The Might that was Assyria* (Sidgwick & Jackson, 1984).

For the Hittites, the best general work remains O. R. Gurney, *The Hittites* (Penguin, 1952 and subsequent editions); also useful is J. G. McQueen, *The Hittites and their contemporaries in Asia Minor* (revised edition, Thames & Hudson, 1986).

Books on Minoan civilization tend to concentrate on particular aspects (art, writing, chronology, etc.). Three works which gives a balanced overall view are R. W. Hutchinson, *Prehistoric Crete* (Penguin, 1962); Sinclair Hood, *The Minoans; Crete in the Bronze Age* (Thames & Hudson, 1971); and R. F. Willetts, *The Civilization of Ancient Crete* (Batsford, 1977).

In the absence of any generally accepted decipherment of Harappan script, evidence on the Indus Valley civilization is limited to archaeological data and what can be deduced, with varying degrees of credibility, from supposed survivals in later Indian culture, and the available books reflect this situation. Deserving mention is Sir Mortimer Wheeler, *The Indus Civilization* (3rd edition, Thames & Hudson, 1968), but the most balanced account of the present state of knowledge is in pp. 124–197 of D. P. Agrawal's excellent, *The Archaeology of India* (Curzon Press, 1982). G. L. Possehl (ed.), *The Harappan Civilisation* (Aris and Phillips, 1982) is more useful to the professional archaeologist than to the general reader.

W. A. Ward (ed.), *The Role of the Phoenicians* (Beirut, 1968), is a collection of essays of varying usefulness, some of them directly relevant to the general title. S. Moscati, *The World of the Phoenicians* (Weidenfeld & Nicolson, 1968) is a helpful outline. N. K. Sandars, *The Sea Peoples: Warriors of the Ancient Mediterranean* (Thames & Hudson, 1978) gives a useful account of these briefly important groups.

Writing

Some introductions to the beginnings of writing approach the subject historically from the point of view of particular languages, and others use a linguistic approach. D. Diringer, *The Alphabet: a Key to the History of Mankind*, 2 vols. (3rd edition, Hutchinson, 1968) tackles all alphabets; G. R. Driver, *Semitic Writing from Pictograph to Alphabet* (revised edition, Oxford University Press, 1976) is good for the area its title claims to cover. I. J. Gelb, *A Study of Writing* (revised edition, University of Chicago Press, 1963) gives new insights on the problems from the linguistic point of view. In a more specialized area, J. Chadwick, *The Decipherment of Linear B* (Penguin, 1958 and later editions) is basic reading. P. Kyle McCarter, *The Antiquity of the Greek Alphabet and the early Phoenician Scripts* (Scholars Press, Missoula, 1975) is a specialized monograph arguing for an earlier date than that conventionally accepted for the Greek borrowing of the alphabet. More recent material on the Greek borrowing of the Phoenician alphabet and other aspects of the beginnings of writing will be found in specialist journals, particularly *Kadmos* (Berlin).

Translations of ancient texts

The single most useful collection of translations of ancient texts is J. B. Pritchard (ed.), *Ancient Near Eastern Texts relating to the Old Testament* (3rd edition, Princeton University Press, 1969), which goes well outside the biblical limitation implied in its title. W. Beyerlin (ed.), *Near Eastern Religious Texts relating to the Old Testament* (SCM Press, 1978) is briefer and more closely tied to Old Testament parallels, but has some useful material.

For Egypt, the major standard collection of historical texts remains, despite some inadequacies from its age, J. H. Breasted, *Ancient Records of Egypt*, 5 vols. (Chicago University Press, 1906–7). The corresponding corpus of translations of texts from ancient Mesopotamia is D. D. Luckenbill, *Ancient Records of Assyria and Babylonia*, 2 vols. (University of Chicago Press, 1926–7), which despite its title is exclusively concerned with the historical records of Assyria; for material down to 859 BC this has been superseded by A. K. Grayson, *Assyrian Royal Inscriptions*, 2 vols. (Harrassowitz, 1972, 1976). Historical texts of the third and early second millennia from south Mesopotamia are translated in E. Sollberger and J. R. Kupper, *Inscriptions royales sumériennes et akkadiennes* (Cerf, Paris, 1971).

A large selection of translations of Egyptian literary and religious texts is available in M. Lichtheim's excellent *Ancient Egyptian Literature*, 3 vols. (University of California Press, 1975–80). Interesting but rather specialized is R. O. Faulkner, *The ancient Egyptian Pyramid Texts* (Clarendon Press, 1969; revised edition, Aris & Phillips, 1985).

Translations of literary and religious texts from ancient Mesopotamia are scattered. Wisdom Literature is well catered for in W. G. Lambert, *Babylonian Wisdom Literature* (Clarendon Press, 1960). The most productive translator of Sumerian literary texts is S. N. Kramer, in numerous articles in periodicals, monographs, and popular books, including *The Sumerians* listed above. Some important translations of Sumerian literary and religious texts will also be found in two collections of articles by Th. Jacobsen, *Towards the image of Tammuz and other Essays on Mesopotamian History and Culture* (Harvard University Press, 1970), and *The Treasures of Darkness; a History of Mesopotamian Religion* (Yale University Press, 1976).

Technology and Science

Two important works dealing with the raw materials and technologies of the two primary civilizations are A. Lucas, *Ancient Egyptian Materials and Industries* (4th edition, revised and enlarged by J. R. Harris, Edward Arnold, 1962) and (less comprehensive) P. R. S. Moorey, *Materials and Manufacture in ancient Mesopotamia* (Oxford, 1985). Equally important, but limited to metal technology, are J. D. Muhly, *Copper and Tin; The Distribution of Mineral Resources and the Nature of the Metals Trade in the Bronze Age* (Archon Books, Connecticut, 1973) and T. A. Wertime and J. D. Muhly (eds.), *The Coming of the Age of Iron* (Yale University Press, 1980).

The most recent and complete treatment of ancient astronomy is in O. Neugebauer, *A History of Ancient Mathematical Astronomy*, 3 vols. (Springer-Verlag, Berlin and New York, 1975). See also D. G. Kendall *et al.* (eds.), *The Place of Astronomy in the Ancient World. A Joint Symposium of the Royal Society and the British Academy* (Oxford University Press, 1974). For simpler presentations of the material see O. Neugebauer, *The Exact Sciences in Antiquity* (Harper Torchbook, 1962); R. A. Parker, *The Calendars of Ancient Egypt* (Chicago University Press, 1950); B. L. van der Waerden, *Science Awakening, II: The Birth of Astronomy* (Noordhoff, Leiden, 1974); and pp. 13–54 in J. R. Harris (ed.), *The Legacy of Egypt* (2nd edition, Clarendon Press, 1971). These works also cover ancient mathematics.

For some examples of mathematical texts from ancient Mesopotamia see O. Neugebauer and A. Sachs, *Mathematical Cuneiform texts* (American Oriental Society, 1945). Of primary importance for Egyptian mathematics is T. E. Peet (ed.), *The Rhind mathematical Papyrus* (Liverpool University Press, 1923); the Egyptian mathematical procedures are explained in simple form in A. B. Chace, *The Rhind Mathematical Papyrus. Free Translation* (Virginia, 1979).

The best of many books on pyramids is I. E. S. Edwards, *The Pyramids of Egypt* (revised edition, Penguin, 1961 and later reprints); there is no corresponding book, both readable and authoritative, for ziggurats.

Administration, trade and economics

Some works on early Egyptian administration are listed in note 3 to Chapter 2, but the most important contribution to the subject is J. J. Janssen, 'The Early State in Ancient Egypt', pp. 213–34 in H. J. M. Claessen and P. Skalník, *The Early State* (Mouton, The Hague, 1978). Except for specialized research, most of what is published on administration in Mesopotamia is in articles in journals; I. M. Diakonoff (ed.), *Ancient Mesopotamia; Socio-Economic History* (Nauka, Moscow, 1969) contains an important collection of relevant articles by Soviet scholars. F. M. Heichelheim, *An Ancient Economic History*, vol. 1 (Leiden, 1958) was a valiant attempt at covering the whole of ancient trade and economics, but new discoveries have made parts of it out of date. H. Klengel, *Handel und Händler im alten Orient* (Hermann Böhlaus Nachf., Vienna, 1979) gives a good account of trade in the Near East, mainly in the third and second millennia. Amongst composite volumes containing material important for ancient Near Eastern administration and economics may be mentioned J. A. Sabloff and C. C. Lamberg-Karlovsky (eds.), *Ancient Civilization and Trade* (Albuquerque, 1975); J. Harmatta and G. Komoroczy (eds.), *Wirtschaft und Gesellschaft im alten Vorderasien* (Budapest, 1976); and E. Lipinski (ed.), *State and Temple Economy in the Ancient Near East*, 2 vols. (Louvain, 1979).

Laws and Relations between States

The notes to Chapter 8 give reference to the principal editions and translations of laws.

A few Ph.D theses, not easily accessible, treat aspects of ancient international law. G. Kestemont, *Diplomatique et droit international en Asia occidental (1600–1200 av.J.C.)* (Louvain, 1974) is definitive for the limited period with which it deals, but is very specialized. Apart from this, the main source of published information is articles in journals.

Religion

For translations of religious texts, see above.

There is no up-to-date comprehensive treatment of ancient Mesopotamian religion, but a great deal of important relevant material is to be found in the two volumes of papers of Th. Jacobsen listed above. A brief older work, still valuable, is J. Bottéro, *La religion babylonienne* (Paris, 1952). O. R. Gurney, *Some aspects of*

Hittite Religion (British Academy, 1976) contains some interesting material. The best known work on Cretan religion is M. P. Nilsson, *The Minoan-Mycenaean Religion* (Lund, 1950), but not all authorities would accept the author's conclusions. Several scholars have treated the religion of the Canaanite area; the most recent substantial work is A. Caquot and A. Szyncer, *Ugaritic Religion* (Brill, 1980). There are many books on Egyptian religion; two of the more recent ones, both reliable although approaching the data in quite different ways, are S. Morenz, *Egyptian Religion* (London, 1973) and A. R. David, *The Ancient Egyptians; Religious Beliefs and Practices* (Routledge & Kegan Paul, 1982). S. N. Kramer (ed.), *Mythologies of the Ancient World* (Anchor Books, 1961) contains some important material on the relationship of mythology to ancient religion, particularly an essay by R. Anthes on 'Mythology in Ancient Egypt'. H. Franfort *et al.*, *Before Philosophy* (Penguin, 1949), deals in an interesting way with the basic religious concepts of both ancient Egypt and ancient Mesopotamia; its approach is indicated by its sub-titles 'The Intellectual Adventure of Ancient Man; an Essay on Speculative Thought in the Ancient Near East'.

General Index

Index of Biblical references